(Front end paper)

An imaginative artist's version of San Mateo (Fort Caroline), a Spanish fort on the St. Johns River, Florida, in the last half of the 17th century. In 1564, French Huguenots had constructed Fort Caroline. The following year, the Spanish, after founding St. Augustine, captured and renamed it. From the 1671 engraving "Arx Carolina," by an unknown artist. Courtesy, Chicago Historical Society.

EXPLORERS AND SETTLERS

De Soto's discovery of the Mississippi, in 1541, is romantically portrayed in this 19th-century painting by William H. Powell, which hangs in the rotunda of the U.S. Capitol. Though historically inaccurate, it symbolizes the courage and daring of the European explorers, who probed a new continent.

THE NATIONAL SURVEY OF HISTORIC SITES AND BUILDINGS VOLUME V

EXPLORERS AND SETTLERS

Historic Places Commemorating the Early Exploration

and Settlement of the United States

ROBERT G. FERRIS

Series Editor

UNITED STATES DEPARTMENT OF THE INTERIOR

NATIONAL PARK SERVICE  WASHINGTON, D.C. 1968

This volume was prepared by the Division of History Studies, National Park Service, under the general supervision of the Chief, Robert M. Utley. One of a series designed to make available to the public the studies of the National Survey of Historic Sites and Buildings, directed by John O. Littleton, it incorporates survey and evaluation reports prepared by the following National Park Service historians: John Porter Bloom, S. Sydney Bradford, William E. Brown, William C. Everhart, Ray H. Mattison, Frank B. Sarles, Jr., Charles E. Shedd, Jr., Horace J. Sheely, Jr., Charles W. Snell, and Robert M. Utley. These reports were reviewed by the Advisory Board on National Parks, Historic Sites, Buildings, and Monuments and the Consulting Committee for the National Survey of Historic Sites and Buildings. Members of these groups are listed in the Acknowledgments.

The background narrative for this volume is based on a study prepared under contract by Dr. Seymour V. Connor, Texas Technological College. Special contributions to the entire volume were made by Richard E. Morris and John W. Walker, Editorial Assistant and Staff Archeologist respectively, National Survey of Historic Sites and Buildings.

LIBRARY OF CONGRESS CATALOG CARD NUMBER: 66–60013

Contents

Photographs are by the National Park Service except where specified

MAPS

Foreword

The United States today is a mixture of diverse nationalities, cultures, and races. The mixing process began when Europeans first probed the land and has continued into modern times. This volume, which emphasizes significant historic sites and structures, tells the fascinating story of early exploration and settlement and contributes to understanding our past. It commemorates the daring men who conquered a strange, forbidding wilderness and in so doing fostered a heritage of overcoming the unknown — a heritage carried on today in our exploration of space.

We need physical reminders of our past. Otherwise we tend to lose the sense of being part of a continuous process. Visits to historic places provide a refreshing awareness of immediacy and historical reality. They provide an association with our past that is impossible to achieve with the written or spoken word.

This volume has two parts. The first offers a brief, narrative background for the period of early exploration and settlement. The second consists of evaluations and descriptions of historic sites and structures associated with the period.

Historians and archeologists of the National Park Service, United States Department of the Interior, after comprehensive fieldwork, prepared the basic studies from which this publication has been drawn. The studies were reviewed by the Consulting Committee for the National Survey of Historic Sites and Buildings, composed of eminent historians, architects, and archeologists not otherwise connected with the National Park Service; and by the Secretary of the Interior's Advisory Board on

National Parks, Historic Sites, Buildings, and Monuments, which has a similar membership. The findings of the National Survey of Historic Sites and Buildings, achieved through this process, are made available to the public by means of this series of volumes.

The purpose of the Survey is the evaluation of places important in our history and prehistory. Those sites judged to possess exceptional value in illustrating or commemorating the history of the United States are declared eligible for designation as Registered National Historic Landmarks. Upon request, the Secretary of the Interior will provide the owner of a Landmark property with an engraved certificate and a bronze plaque attesting to its value and encouraging its continued preservation. A very few Landmarks may, in addition to possessing national historical significance, meet the standards of suitability and feasibility for park purposes and be considered for addition to the National Park System.

Credit for the preparation of this volume is shared widely by persons both in and out of the National Park Service. In particular, the work of the Service in the general field of historic preservation has benefited inestimably from the assistance provided by the National Trust for Historic Preservation in the United States, cosponsor of the Survey.

We believe that this book will assist students, teachers, travelers, historians, archeologists, preservation groups, and other Americans in understanding and appreciating a period of our history that is both complex and difficult, yet basic to a proper comprehension of American democracy and culture. We earnestly hope that this volume will also focus attention on, and stimulate further activities in, the field of historic preservation. Important as progress is, it should not result in the thoughtless destruction of sites and buildings that commemorate our national heritage.

GEORGE B. HARTZOG, Jr.
Director
National Park Service

EXPLORERS AND SETTLERS

PART I

Explorers and Settlers:

Historical Background

T HE LAND THAT BECAME the United States was in colonial times an extension of the Old World into the New. Through the centuries, the descendants of the original colonists blended their European heritage into the new Nation that evolved. But for the courage and resourcefulness of the Europeans who first explored and settled the unknown wilderness, that evolution would not have been possible.

Our European Heritage

The United States is an amalgam of nationalities, cultures, and races whose basic heritage is European. The amalgam began to take shape long before the Declaration of Independence and is still being formed today. European nations discovered the area of the present United States, explored it, and settled it. For decades after the Nation came into being, they continued to possess or claim substantial territories within its ultimate limits. They also affected the growth and course of the Republic by their alinement in international affairs.

During the first half of the 19th century, the United States trebled in size by acquiring Florida from Spain and the lands west of the Mississippi

[3

River and their historical heritage from France, Mexico, and England. She also benefited during the century from the reinfusion of European influences during the great immigrations, which have carried into the 20th century.

From the beginning, the emergent Nation molded its diverse European heritage with other cultural influences into a new way of life. It modified the English language into a uniquely American form and reshaped the legal and governmental systems of England. It utilized the architectural styles not only of England, but also of France, Spain, Holland, and Sweden. In the trans-Mississippi West, it incorporated Spanish land, mining, and water laws into the legal fabric; and it adapted the ranching terms and methods of Spain to cowboy life. Across the face of the land are registered numerous other European contributions—in language, religion, place names, literature, the arts, music, and social mores.

Thus our Nation has been profoundly enriched by its European heritage. A source of strength, this heritage still lives today—centuries after the initial European exploration and settlement—even though, in the meantime, during prolonged contact with a fresh environment, a distinctive American civilization has been created.

The Old World in the New

In the summer of 1492, a daring Genoese navigator set his sails westward from Palos, Spain, his three tiny ships flying the banners of his royal benefactors, Ferdinand of Aragon and Isabella of Castile. Christopher Columbus was sailing west into the unknown to reach the fabled Cathay of the East. Behind him lay the familiar shores of Europe; ahead stretched two mighty continents whose virgin lands, dense forests, untapped mineral resources, and aborigines were almost completely unknown to him and the civilizations of Europe and Asia. The Old World had earlier made some contacts with the New. Venturesome Norsemen, under Leif Ericson and other leaders, founded Vinland and explored elsewhere along the North Atlantic coast. And fishermen from France may have periodically visited the banks and shoals of Newfoundland. But none of these contacts yielded any permanent fruits.

Such, also, might have been the result of Columbus' heroic voyage but for a variety of factors. In the 15th and 16th centuries, for the first time since the fall of the Roman Empire, Europe was ripe for

"Christopher Columbus at the Court of Isabella." From a mid-19th-century lithograph by V. de Turgin. Courtesy, Chicago Historical Society.

exploitative expansion. It was undergoing cataclysmic changes. The Crusades to save the Holy Lands, in the 11th and 12th centuries, had strengthened and unified the European principalities; the plunder that footmen and knights had hauled back from the opulent East introduced Europeans to new luxuries and stimulated the reopening of trade.

The revival of trade between Western Europe and the East was inevitable, and the commercial revolution that revitalized the stagnate society of the Western World—sparked by the voyages of discovery in the 15th century—was almost as certain. A merchant class arose to serve the demands of commerce, and cities grew up to protect and serve the merchants. An ascendant Western Europe resented the exorbitant prices charged by merchants in the Italian city-states, who dominated trade with the East, and sought to break their monopoly by finding other trade routes.

The intellectual awakening of the Renaissance, which came to full flower in the 15th and 16th centuries, opened new horizons of interest in the sciences and arts. It stimulated learning and the recapture of classical knowledge, and fostered a fresh curiosity and a more pragmatic way of thinking. In the wake of the Renaissance emerged a movement to reform the "universal" church. The Reformation, beginning early in the 16th century, introduced wide-scale religious conflict, ruptured the medieval unity of Christendom, and produced a sectarian fragmentation of the Christian religion. These interrelated changes in European society spelled the doom of the feudal system of the Middle Ages. Feudalism yielded to a stronger political force, the rise of national states.

The four movements—economic, intellectual, religious, and sociopolitical—might have exhausted their strength in Europe had it not been for Spain's accidental discovery of a New World while seeking a better route to the East. This discovery resulted in a major shift in the world trade pattern and gave Europe mastery of the globe for centuries to come.

Who would have believed a few centuries earlier that the "barbarian" heirs of the great Roman Empire in Western Europe would some day dominate the earth, or that their culture would influence all peoples from the Volga to the Yalu and from Lapland to Tasmania, or that London and Paris rather than Mecca and Istanbul would be the cultural and financial centers of civilization? Even more preposterous would have been any idea that some yet unfounded English-speaking nation born on a strange continent would be a world power—that a nation then undreamed of would rise from those distant shores to join the vanguard of civilization.

The New World provided Europe with a vast frontier of expansion and, perhaps even more important as a stimulus, an incredible source of wealth. Within two decades after Columbus' discovery, Spain was importing more than a million dollars a year from the "Indies"; by the end of the first half-century, gold and silver treasures poured into Madrid from the Aztec and Inca fields and increased the expendable wealth of Europe some fifteenfold. Had the rewards not been so immense, the Spaniards might not have been so daring and persistent in their exploration.

From his initial voyage (1492–93), Columbus returned with gold bracelets and ornaments, as well as tales of greater wealth farther west. On this first voyage and three subsequent ones (1493–96, 1498–1500, and 1502–4), he explored extensively throughout the West Indies. Yet he died in 1506, only 2 years after his last voyage, not realizing that he had discovered a continent. But the promise of abundant gold, silver, and other treasure that could be wrenched from the arms of natives enticed adventurous Spanish conquistadors (conquerors), strengthened by long conflict in their homeland with the intrusive Moors, to the New World in search of gold and glory. Missionary padres sought to serve God by converting the native masses.

Conjectural portrait of Ferdinand Magellan, the Portuguese navigator. He died in 1521, during his attempt to circumnavigate the globe. One of his five vessels succeeded. From a late 18th- or early 19th-century painting by an unknown artist. Courtesy, Chicago Historical Society.

Within a few decades, Spanish navigators became familiar with the northern coast of South America, the Isthmus of Panama, the Pacific Ocean, the Gulf of Mexico, the Atlantic shore of North America, and ultimately the general outlines of most of the New World—though for some time enough hiatuses existed in their knowledge so that the dream of a Northwest Passage persisted. The Spanish benefited from the earlier pioneering efforts of the nautical-minded Portuguese, especially those of Prince Henry, "The Navigator," to find a water route to the East. Though King John II of Portugal turned a deaf ear to the pleas of Columbus for sponsorship, between 1429 and 1460 Portuguese seamen had explored 2,000 miles of Africa's northwest coast. In 1498, Vasco da Gama pioneered a route to India around Africa's southern tip. While Portugal directed her energies to the south and east, Spain pursued opportunities to the west, a division of interest formally recognized in 1494 by the Papal Line of Demarcation.

Spain, of all European nations, was particularly qualified to exploit the opportunities. The marriage of Ferdinand and Isabella, in 1469, had united the Houses of Aragon and Castile, and started the country on a spectacular rise to power. The two monarchs finished driving the Moors from the country, consolidated royal power, diminished the pretensions of the lesser nobility, conquered new lands, and advanced homogeneity of religion. Spain became Europe's strongest power. Treasure poured into her coffers as Cortés conquered the Aztec Empire and Pizarro overran the Peruvian Incas. Little wonder, then, that Spain was spurred to ever-quickening exploration or that the other nations of Europe dared to send their own expeditions into the unknown hemisphere—or to plant their flags on soil that Ferdinand and his haughty Hapsburg successors claimed for Spain.

The acquisition of colonies was an integral part of the economic policy of mercantilism, to which many European powers in the course of time adhered. According to mercantilistic theory, gold, silver, and precious gems were the prime measurement of national wealth and power. To obtain these, a nation should export to the maximum extent and restrict imports. The theory further held that colonies, important as sources of raw materials and as captive markets for the mother country's products, should be rigidly controlled.

Because of national pride, too, monarchs vied with one another in subsidizing exploration and colonization. Monarchs and individuals alike sought wealth in precious metals, furs, and other natural resources. Other individual motives were escape from religious, political, and economic oppression and the devastation of the seemingly endless wars in Europe; the desire to convert the pagan Indians to Christianity; land hunger; and the lure of adventure.

During the 16th century, navigators of all nations sought a water passage around or through the American continental block to the fabulous

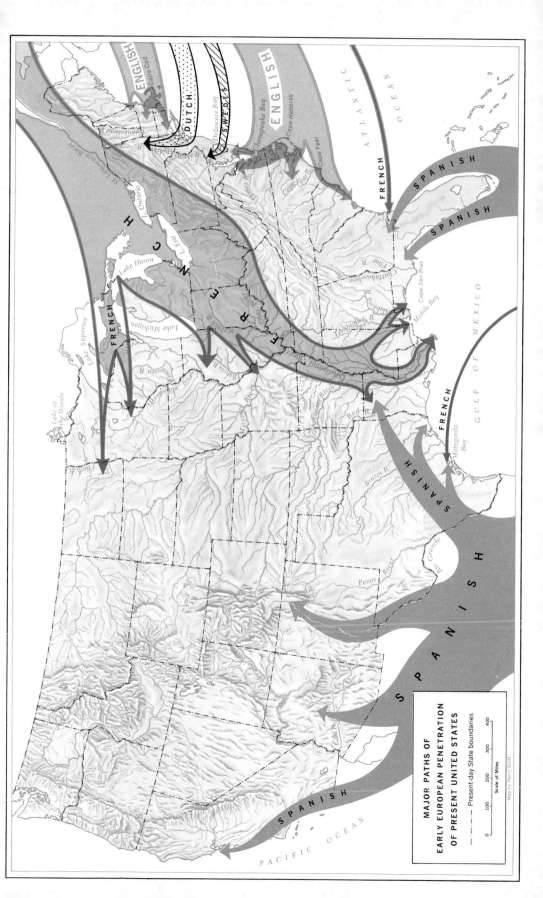

MAJOR PATHS OF
EARLY EUROPEAN PENETRATION
OF PRESENT UNITED STATES

— · — · — Present-day State boundaries

Scale of Miles

0   100   200   300   400

Map by Harry Scott

East while overland expeditions searched North America for the fabled Seven Cities of Gold or other easily conquered and wealthy empires like those of the Aztecs and Incas. Spain, from well established bases in the New World, explored extensively along both coasts of North and South America; and, in addition to exploring much of the Southeastern and Southwestern parts of the present United States, founded at St. Augustine, in 1565, the first permanent settlement by Europeans in what is now the United States.

French explorers claimed the land between the Carolinas and the St. Lawrence, and Huguenots attempted to settle in South Carolina, Florida, and Nova Scotia. Though late in the preceding century John and Sebastian Cabot had provided Henry VII of England with a New World claim, English "sea dogs" preferred to raid Spanish treasure galleons making their cumbersome voyages to Seville's treasury rather than colonize the empty coasts of North America.

Notable exceptions were Sir Humphrey Gilbert and Sir Walter Raleigh, who late in the 16th century threw their fortunes—mostly Spanish gold—into settlement attempts in Newfoundland and "Virginia." Ironically, England's decisive sea victory in 1588 over Philip II's "invincible" armada indirectly caused the doom of Raleigh's colony at Roanoke in "Virginia" by seriously delaying John White's return trip with supplies. But, over the years following the defeat of the armada, the "Spanish Sea" was opened to all comers.

In the next century, imperial rivalry for control of the New World increased in intensity, as other European powers sought to catch up with Spain. The British founded a permanent settlement at Jamestown in 1607; the French at Quebec in 1608; and the Dutch at Nieuw Amsterdam in 1626. During the century, the British spread staunch colonies on the Atlantic coast from South Carolina to Maine. In 1638, the Swedes settled the Delaware Bay region and in 1654 lost possession to Peter Stuyvesant, Director General of New Netherland. Stuyvesant, a decade later, watched in frustrated anger as the English raised their flag over Nieuw Amsterdam and renamed the surrounding area for its new owner, the English Duke of York. Meanwhile, the French pushed up the St. Lawrence and the Great Lakes waterways into the heart of the continent, following such intrepid leaders as Samuel de Champlain to the Great Lakes and La Salle to the mouth of the Mississippi.

The frontiers of three mighty colonial empires now stood in dangerous proximity, and in the 18th century imperial rivalries flared into a vital struggle for control of North America. In a series of four wars, beginning with King William's War (War of the English Succession) in 1689 and ending in the Treaty of Paris of 1763, which ended the French and Indian War (or Seven Years' War), France was forced off the continent. The wars were fought largely in Europe and all except the fourth stemmed from European power struggles, but they resulted in a reshaping of the North American map. England and Spain divided the spoils, the English claiming the eastern third of the present United States and the Spanish the area west of the Mississippi.

Little did the rulers of England and Spain dream that their vast New World empires were to be shattered in paroxysms of revolution or that new nations would arise from the feeble colonial beginnings. But this was to be—and in the course of time the young United States of America grew strong and mature by molding into the vibrant mainstream of her British legacy the diverse heritages of Spain, France, Holland, Sweden, and other European nations.

The Spanish: Conquistadors and Padres

Between 1513, when Ponce de León first set foot in Florida, and 1821, when Mexico gained her independence as well as the Spanish possessions in the present United States, Spain left an indelible influence—especially in the trans-Mississippi West, which the United States began to acquire in 1803. Spain was the leading European power in the early imperial rivalry for control of North America and for centuries dominated the Southeastern and Southwestern parts of what was later the United States—particularly the States of Florida, Texas, New Mexico, Arizona, and California.

Spain held Louisiana territory between 1762 and 1803, and was for the most part content to foster the settlements founded there by France rather than to initiate new ones. She lost Florida temporarily in 1763, but regained it in 1783. Her possessions reached their maximum extent between 1783 and 1803, when they ranged in a crescent from Florida to California.

Except in California, Spain happened to colonize less fruitful regions than did England and France. Yet she tenaciously clung to them long after she had lost her dominance in Europe, some years after the English defeated her armada in 1588. Frustrated in their search for gold and precious metals, the Spaniards were usually forced to try to wrest a living from the barren soil of an inhospitable land by farming and ranching. Finding native labor much scarcer in the present United States than in her possessions to the south, Spain was forced to spread her colonial empire dangerously thin. A small number of soldiers, settlers, and friars controlled the native masses and through their labors obtained what wealth was to be had.

Spain's motives for colonization were threefold: to locate mineral wealth, to convert the Indians to Christianity, and to counter French and English efforts. The Spanish colonization system was highly successful. First, an armed force subdued the natives and established forts, or presidios, for future protection. Then, zealous missionaries moved in to convert the Indians to the religion of Spain and teach them the arts of civilization. Finally, representatives of the King founded civil settlements in conjunction with the presidios and missions. The Crown controlled the highly centralized process through a bureaucracy that burgeoned as the empire expanded. But the story begins in the first years of the 16th century, when Spain first realized that Columbus had discovered, not island outposts of Cathay, but a New World!

SUCCESSES TO THE SOUTH

In the two decades after the first voyage of Columbus, Spanish navigators only began to realize the nature and extent of his remarkable find. The presence of a continental landmass was surmised but not known. Columbus himself had sailed around Puerto Rico; charted most of the remainder of the West Indies; touched on the shores of South America, but without realizing that it was a continent; and mapped the Central American coast from Panama nearly to southern Yucatan. On his first voyage, late in 1492, he had established the colony of Navidad on Hispaniola, but, finding it destroyed on his second voyage, he founded Isabella, in January 1494. Isabella also failed within 2 years, and the colonists established Santo Domingo, the first permanent European settlement in the New World. In 1508–9, while Ponce de León was occupying Puerto Rico and subduing its natives, Vicente Pinzón explored the southern Yucatan coast and Sebastián de Ocampo circumnavigated the island of Cuba. In 1510, the Spaniards occupied Jamaica, and, the following year, Cuba. In 1513, Vasco Núñez de Balboa, who dominated a struggling colony in present Colombia, hacked a trail across the Isthmus of

Panama and discovered the Pacific Ocean. In 1522, one of the five vessels
of the Ferdinand Magellan expedition completed the first circumnavigation of the globe. The lure of adventure and the thrill of discovery whetted
the Spanish desire to explore.

F LORIDA AND THE FOUNTAIN OF YOUTH

Juan Ponce de León was the first Spaniard to touch the shores of the
present United States. As Columbus had not remotely realized the extent
of his momentous discovery, so De León never dreamed that his "island"
of Florida was a peninsular extension of the vast North American Continent. After coming to the New World with Columbus in 1493, he had
led the occupation of Puerto Rico in 1508 and governed it from 1509 to
1512. In 1509, he started a colony at Caparra, later abandoned in
favor of San Juan. He was one of the first of the *adelantados*—men who
"advanced" the Spanish Empire by conquest, subjugation of the Indians,
and establishment of quasi-military government.

In 1513, the aging King Ferdinand awarded De León a patent to
conquer and govern the Bimini Islands, in the Bahamas, of which the
Spaniards had heard but not yet seen. According to a persistent legend,
there De León would find the marvelous spring whose waters would
restore lost youth and vigor. So many wonders had the Spaniards already

The first Spaniard to touch the
shores of the present United
States, Juan Ponce de León. He
discovered, named, and explored
Florida. From an 18th-century
engraving, probably conjectural.

encountered in the Western Hemisphere that only a cynic would have doubted the existence of such a spring.

In March 1513, De León sailed off confidently from Puerto Rico for the Bahamas. Landing briefly at San Salvador, Bahamas, he wound through uncharted islands until he sighted an extensive coastline. He had no reason to suspect that it was anything more than an island, but he followed the coast for a day without rounding its end or finding a suitable landing place. He named the "island" *La Florida,* probably because of the season—*Pascua Florida,* or the Easter festival of flowers. The name came to be applied by the Spanish to the entire present Southeastern United States and beyond.

Then near the 30th parallel, not far from the site of St. Augustine, De León landed at the mouth of the St. Johns River. Determined to be the first to circumnavigate the "island," he turned south, traced the coast around the tip of the peninsula, passed through the treacherous waters of the Florida Keys, and moved up the western coast, perhaps reaching Tampa Bay. After 7 weeks, he gave up hopes of circling the northern tip of his "island"; it was incredibly large—bigger even than Cuba—and he may have suspected that he had discovered the long-sought mainland. If so, it all belonged to his King, for he had earlier planted the Spanish flag and claimed Florida and all lands contiguous to it for Ferdinand.

Of gold and restorative waters, De León had seen nothing; of hostile Indians, predecessors of the Seminoles, he had seen too much. Returning to Puerto Rico in September 1513, he reprovisioned and then spent the next 6 weeks back in the Bahamas fruitlessly searching for the fountain of youth. Before the year was out, he sailed for Spain emptyhanded. Ferdinand rewarded him, however, with new patents to the "islands" of Bimini and Florida, but he was to bear the expense of conquest.

Not until 1521 was De León able to return to take possession of his grant. By that time, his search for the fountain of youth took on a more immediate importance—for he was 61 years of age. At large cost he equipped 2 ships, enlisted 200 men, and set out to found a permanent base from which an exhaustive search could be conducted for the fabled fountain. Not only did he fail to find the fountain, but he also lost his life. Almost as soon as he landed on the western shore of Florida, probably near Tampa Bay, Indians attacked, killed scores of men, and mortally wounded De León himself. The expedition hastily retreated to Cuba, where the "valiant Lion," as his epitaph was to read, died.

EXPLORING THE ATLANTIC AND GULF COASTS

By the time of De León's hapless attempt to exercise his patent rights to the "island" of Florida in 1521, many geographers and navigators realized that Florida was likely the giant arm of a continent. Two expeditions had indicated that this was true, one in 1519 by Alonso de Pineda and another in 1521 by Francisco Gordillo.

The Pineda expedition was the inspiration of Francisco de Garay, Governor of Jamaica. He placed four vessels under the command of Pineda and ordered him to find a water passage around or through the landmass whose existence had been indicated by a series of Spanish explorations during the period 1515–18. Pineda circled west and south around the coast from Florida to Vera Cruz. He named the land off his starboard bow "Amichel"; he called what was probably the Mississippi River "Rio del Espíritu Santo"; and he recommended a settlement at the mouth of the "Rio de las Palmas"—possibly the Rio Grande. Most important of all, he gained a substantial knowledge of the unbroken coastline and revealed that to the west of Spain's island headquarters in the Caribbean lay a huge continental landmass.

Lucas Vásquez de Ayllón, a prominent magistrate in Hispaniola, in 1521 sent out Capt. Francisco Gordillo to sail northward through the Bahamas, strike the shore of the continent, follow part of De León's route, and try to round the "island" of Florida from the east. Up the coast he tacked, extending De León's exploration at least 3° northward, and landing on the shores of present South Carolina. Ignoring orders, he loaded his ship with innocent and friendly natives and put about for Hispaniola. He planned to sell his cargo into slavery to replace the large losses of natives during the first years of the Spanish conquest.

De Ayllón reprimanded him and released the unfortunate captives, but listened greedily to the report of the fair land to the north. Rushing to Spain, he obtained a patent to colonize the region. A reconnaissance expedition in 1525, led by Pedro de Quexos, extended De Ayllón's knowledge of the coast as far as present Virginia. The following year, after extensive preparation, De Ayllón himself set out with 3 vessels, more than 500 colonists, 3 padres, and ample supplies and livestock to establish a lasting settlement on the Atlantic shore. He failed. Attempting to settle first at an unknown site, possibly in present North Carolina, he shifted about 100 miles to the south and founded a crude settlement named San Miguel de Gualdape (Guandape), in South Carolina. He died of a fever before the year was out, and internal dissension rent the settlement into anarchy. Less than a third of the colonists survived to return to Hispaniola.

The previous year, 1525, a Portuguese navigator named Stephen Gómez, also flying the flag of Spain, had completed the exploration of the Atlantic coast by sailing from Newfoundland south to the Florida peninsula in search of the Northwest Passage. Clearly the continental block extended from Newfoundland to Tierra del Fuego. Intrepid Spanish explorers were to be forced off their ships and onto the land if they wished to make additional discoveries, as had Balboa and Cortés before them.

THE FIRST INLAND PENETRATION

Cortés' one-time rival for command, Pánfilo de Narváez, made the first inland exploration in the area of the present United States. In 1526, he obtained title to all lands between the Rio de las Palmas and the Cape of Florida, and the next year left Spain. After stopping at Spanish bases at Santo Domingo and Cuba, in 1528 his expedition of 5 ships and more than 600 colonists, including friars and Negro slaves, landed on the west coast of Florida, probably in the region of Tampa Bay. Narváez split his command and sent his vessels along the shoreline while he led the main body of the expedition by land toward an intended rendezvous point up the coast. The two parties never met. The sea party missed the rendezvous and, after a futile search, returned to its home base.

Harassed by hostile Indians and scourged by privation and disease, the overland group struggled along, the coast. Reaching the vicinity of Apalachicola Bay, the men, greatly reduced in numbers as well as strength, built crude rafts on which they courageously launched themselves westward toward Spanish settlements in Old Mexico. They sailed along the coast to Texas, where storms sank some of the rafts and drove others onto a low-lying, sandy island, probably Galveston Island. Thus began one of the most amazing adventures that has ever befallen any group of men.

The 80 or so survivors were so weak from starvation they could scarcely pull themselves out of the water. They scattered in small groups. Some wandered off and others joined the Indians; many died of hunger and disease. Winter hardships took more lives. The natives, at first friendly, turned belligerent and enslaved the remaining Europeans. Months of miserable captivity stretched out to 5 unbearable years.

Álvar Núñez Cabeza de Vaca, the treasurer and second officer of the Narváez party, obtained a reputation as a medicine man—his knowledge of medicine being a little more advanced than that of the Indians. In 1534, he and three others, including a Negro slave, Estévan, escaped and began an arduous 3-year trek across Texas and into Old Mexico that represented the first exploration by Europeans of any part of the present Southwestern United States. Their reports of great riches were to excite the imagination of men in the Viceroyalty of New Spain and stimulate exploration of the unknown area of New Mexico, to the north.

To the mississippi and beyond

On her fourth expedition to "Florida," Spain scored a major success. Hernando de Soto and Luís de Moscoso, during the years 1539–43, explored extensively throughout the present Southeastern United States and obtained a wealth of information about the lands and peoples of the interior—beyond the Mississippi and as far west as Oklahoma and Texas. De Soto was perhaps the most determined and successful of all Spanish explorers. He had made a fortune as one of Pizarro's lieutenants in the

Hernando de Soto led the fourth Spanish expedition to Florida. He explored much of the present Southeastern United States, and his survivors penetrated Texas. From an 18th-century engraving, probably conjectural.

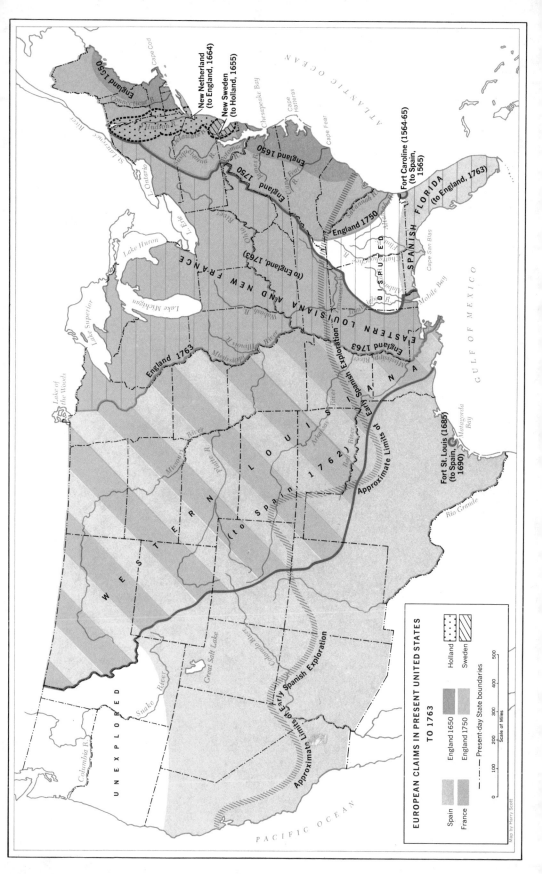

EUROPEAN CLAIMS IN PRESENT UNITED STATES
TO 1763

Map by Harry Scott

| | Spain | England 1650 | Holland | | |
| | France | England 1750 | Sweden | | |

Present-day State boundaries

Scale of Miles
0   100   200   300   400   500

conquest of Peru. As a further reward, Charles V granted him the right to conquer—at his own expense—the land of "Florida," which had not yielded to De León, De Ayllón, and Narváez before him.

Artist's rendition of De Soto at Tampa Bay, Florida, in 1539. From an engraving by James Smillie, after a drawing by Capt. S. Eastman. Courtesy, Library of Congress.

In May 1539, De Soto and more than 600 men landed on the west coast of Florida. Marching north, they spent the winter of 1539–40 in the region of Apalachee, in the Florida Panhandle. In the spring, De Soto led his men northeast through present Georgia to the Savannah River. He then turned northwest, traversed part of South Carolina, fought his way through the mountains, circled back across northern Georgia and central Alabama, and in October reached the head of Mobile Bay.

There a severe battle with the Indians occurred, but the indefatigable De Soto would let nothing deter him. In a remarkable tribute to his leadership, after 18 months of fruitless wandering and the loss of more than 100 men to disease and Indians, De Soto's men continued to follow him when he turned his back on the sea and the outside world and plunged once more into the unknown continent. Moving northwest into present Mississippi, the explorer set up winter quarters.

In March 1541, Indians launched a sudden and catastrophic attack. Although they killed only 11 men, they burned the expedition's clothing and destroyed 50 horses and a large drove of swine. Though many of his followers were clad only in skins, De Soto resumed the march in a north-west direction and on May 8, 1541, discovered the Mississippi River. A month later, he crossed the swollen river on specially constructed barges and set out across present Arkansas. After several months of hard march-ing, the expedition may have penetrated as far as Oklahoma—at the same time as Coronado, who from a base in New Mexico had reached the same general region and was probably only 300 or 400 miles to the west. De Soto then turned back east and set up his third winter quarters, in southwestern Arkansas.

That spring the expedition started down the Mississippi—not to return home, but for the purpose of sending to Cuba for badly needed supplies. De Soto, however, sickened and died on May 21, 1542, and the men sank his body in the middle of the great river he had discovered so that the Indians would not find it and realize that he was mortal. Command devolved upon Luís de Moscoso, who promptly agreed with the men that it was time to abandon the wild venture.

The party decided to strike overland toward Spanish bases to the southwest rather than follow the Mississippi to the coast. Moscoso pene-trated Texas, perhaps as far as the Trinity River, before becoming dis-couraged and returning to the Mississippi. Then, during the fourth winter, 1542–43, the men built small brigantines and prepared for a precarious voyage down the river and out into the gulf. They butchered and dried all the pigs and most of the remaining horses and filled barrels with fresh water. Liberating some 500 Indians whom they had enslaved, they embarked on July 2, 1543. Sixteen days later they floated out into the gulf, and on September 10 landed near Tampico. At the end of the amazing 4-year expedition, only half of the original members were still alive.

THE SETTLEMENT OF FLORIDA

Four times had the Spanish Crown given patents to its bravest *adelan-tados* to conquer and settle Florida—De León, De Ayllón, Narváez, and De Soto. Each had lost his life in the attempt. But the importance of

the Florida peninsula in controlling the Gulf of Mexico could not long
be overlooked. Three more Spaniards were to make futile attempts to
tame the region before a permanent settlement was at last accomplished.

A Florida Indian village. From a 1591 engraving by Theodore de Bry, after
an on-the-scene drawing by Jacques le Moyne de Morgues. Courtesy, Library of Congress.

In 1549, Friar Luís Cancer de Barbastro led a group of missionaries,
supported by a few friendly Indians, from Vera Cruz to the vicinity of
Tampa Bay, where hostile Indians massacred them. Only little more successful was the expedition of Tristán de Luna y Arellano a decade later
from Vera Cruz to the Pensacola Bay area. It consisted of 1,500 colonists,
soldiers, and friars, and 1 year's provisions. A hurricane nearly destroyed
the fleet shortly after it landed; more than half the supplies were ruined;
fever decimated the group; and the Indians, if not openly hostile, were
zealous thieves. But some of the colonists survived. In 1561 Angel de

Villafañe replaced De Luna, who proceeded to Havana. That same year Villafañe, at the direction of the Spanish authorities, set out to found a colony on the Carolina coast. After landing temporarily, probably at Port Royal Sound, in present South Carolina, and later at the mouth of the Santee River, the group sailed for Old Mexico by way of Pensacola Bay.

The prospect of a permanent settlement in "Florida" must then have seemed remote to Spanish officials. But the establishment of French settlements there caused Spain to react with urgency. In 1562, Jean Ribaut and a small party of French Huguenots put ashore at Port Royal Sound to found the religious refuge that the farsighted Adm. Gaspard de Coligny was planning. Before the year ended, Ribaut abandoned the settlement, Charlesfort, but neither he nor Coligny was discouraged. In 1564, a second Huguenot expedition, under René de Laudonnière, landed at the mouth of the St. Johns River and erected a small stockade, Fort Caroline. Discipline soon broke down. Thirteen men stole the only vessel and set out to raid Spanish shipping in the Caribbean. Laudonnière immediately put the remainder of the men to constructing another vessel; when finished, it, too, was stolen by would-be buccaneers.

The French settlement aroused Spanish fury. Philip II, ruler of Spain and Europe's strongest monarch, allotted 600 troops and 3 ships to Pedro Menéndez de Avilés and ordered him to drive the Frenchmen out of his domain. Menéndez furnished a party of colonists and obtained De León's old patent to "Florida." Menéndez and his King were convinced that the Huguenot colony was intended as a base for French piracy. Ten years earlier, French pirates had sacked and burned Havana. Such a New World base as Laudonnière's could not be tolerated—and to add insult to the defenders of the Catholic faith, the Frenchmen were Protestant heretics. Late in August, Ribaut arrived from France with reinforcements.

On September 8, 1565, the Spaniards put ashore and began constructing a fort, around which grew the city of St. Augustine—the oldest permanent European settlement in the United States. Then, Menéndez marched northward and wiped out the settlers at Fort Caroline, which he renamed San Mateo. He next moved southward below St. Augustine, attacked a French party under Ribaut that had set out to fight the Spanish but had been shipwrecked, and put the few survivors to work constructing St. Augustine.

Despite the tireless energy of Menéndez, the Spanish colony in Florida

This fanciful artist's rendition of St. Augustine, pioneer Spanish settlement, is of interest despite its historical inaccuracies. The Castillo de San Marcos at no time resembled the fort as portrayed. The artist probably included the high hills because he mistook the Spanish word for thick forests to mean hills. From the 1671 engraving "Pagus Hispanorum," by an unknown artist, probably prepared in Amsterdam. Courtesy, Chicago Historical Society.

grew slowly. From 1566 to 1571, determined Jesuit missionaries strove to bring Christianity to the reluctant natives in the region. They founded a number of small and temporary missions, but were not too successful in their overall effort. In 1566, they established San Felipe Orista on the Carolina coast, and a few years later may have reached as far north as Chesapeake Bay with other evanescent missions. After 1571, brown-robed Franciscan friars carried the word of God into the marshes and forests of the Florida region. At the height of their success, about 1635, they were ministering to thousands of neophytes at a number of tiny missions, mainly in the provinces of Guale, Timucua, and Apalachee, in northern Florida and coastal Georgia.

None of these missions proved to be permanent, and few of the "converted" Indians could actually be counted as Christians. When, in

1763, Spain surrendered Florida to England, little more than a feeble colony at St. Augustine evidenced two centuries of occupation. Besides the missions, two small outposts in the region called Apalachee, on the northwestern fringe of the peninsula, had been established to help supply St. Augustine: San Marcos de Apalache on the gulf coast, which originated in 1660 but was abandoned and reestablished several times thereafter; and San Luís de Apalache, a few miles north, the center of a temporarily flourishing mission field that was later relinquished during Queen Anne's War.

Over the years, Spanish Florida had suffered countless vicissitudes. In 1586, only 2 years before England ravaged Spain's mighty armada, Sir Francis Drake almost destroyed St. Augustine. Less than a century later, in 1668, another English force again nearly decimated it. Before many more years passed, British settlers from the Carolinas began a series of raids on the Spanish settlements in Florida. During Queen Anne's War, in 1702 the English captured and burned St. Augustine, although they failed to conquer the redoubtable Castillo de San Marcos, constructed in 1672. In 1704, Col. James Moore, attacking from the Carolinas, destroyed five mission-settlements in Apalachee and later that year drove the Spanish out of the province. From then on, Spanish Florida was almost constantly in a state of war with the Carolinas and, after 1733, with Georgia. Attacks on St. Augustine by Gen. James Oglethorpe, the founder of Georgia, resulted in the construction of Fort Matanzas in 1743 as a part of Spain's last desperate effort to hold the region.

Even as British intrusion began to threaten Spanish Florida in the east, the French again encroached on the empire—this time in the west. To meet the threat of France's advance to the mouth of the Mississippi, the Spanish founded an impotent post—Fort San Carlos de Austria— at Pensacola in 1698 and undertook to settle Texas.

New mexico and arizona: outposts of empire

The second major penetration by the Spanish of the present United States was in the Southwest. There, in an arid and inhospitable land, Spanish dreams of gold and precious metals were to become nightmares. But before the reality were the myths. After Cortés' conquest of the rich Aztec Empire and Pizarro's looting of Inca wealth in Peru, should not great or greater riches be found to the north of Old Mexico? Mythmakers and dreamers began to spin wild fabrications. Soon their fantasies were given a touch of reality by the reports of a strange party of three men led by Cabeza de Vaca—survivors of the Narváez expedition to Florida—which arrived in present Mexico after an amazing cross-country trek from the gulf coast of Texas. Thus, interestingly enough, a tenuous thread from Florida stimulated the northward march of New Spain into the unknown lands of New Mexico.

When De Vaca, the other two Spaniards, and the Negro slave Estévan—after 5 years of captivity among the Indians—sought to escape in 1534, they were somewhere inland in Texas, possibly near the site of San Antonio. Traveling sometimes alone, but more often with roving bands of Indians, they wandered south and west. Probably crossing the Rio Grande into present Mexico, they moved westward for several hundred miles, crossed the Rio Grande again in the vicinity of the Big Bend, and then turned to the southwest. In June 1536, they stumbled across a party of Spaniards, who could hardly believe that the starving, nearly naked "savages" who rushed sobbing up to them were really aristocratic hidalgos and their slave.

What a story the men had to tell! The credulous Spaniards, who after the discovery of the riches of the Aztec and Inca Empires might be expected to believe anything of the new continent, were beside themselves with joy. The men's report of the fabled Seven Cities of Gold spread like wildfire, although the narrators made it plain that they had not seen these fabulous cities—only heard of them from the Indians. The Viceroy, Antonio de Mendoza, cautiously decided upon further reconnaissance of the region to the north before sending out the army of conquest for which his eager subordinates clamored.

When De Vaca and his two Spanish companions, not surprisingly, refused to return, Mendoza dispatched Estévan with Fray Marcos de Niza to gain further information. In 1539, the Franciscan friar, accompanied by Estévan and several Indian guides, crossed into the present United States, possibly near the Arizona border community of Lochiel. Nearing the Zuñi pueblos at the Arizona-New Mexico border, he sent Estévan ahead with some of the Indian guides. When the Zuñis killed the Negro, the friar took to his heels. After a hasty trip back, he reported to Mendoza that he had seen a city, one of the Seven Cities of Cíbola, that was more impressive than Montezuma's capital itself. He probably had seen one of the Zuñi pueblos. From a distance, the sun-baked walls may indeed have glittered like gold.

Coronado marches through the Southwestern United States, in 1540–42. Disappointed at not having found the Seven Cities of Gold, he returned to Mexico. From a painting by Frederic Remington. Courtesy, Library of Congress.

Immediately Mendoza began organizing one of the grandest expeditions that Spain ever assembled in the New World. He appointed as commander his young friend Francisco Vásquez de Coronado, Governor of Nueva Galicia, and sent along Fray Marcos. In February 1540, about 250 mounted Spanish troops, nearly 100 footmen, several hundred friendly Indians, 4 priests, remudas of extra horses, and herds of cattle, sheep, and swine left Compostela. At Culiacan the impatient Coronado rushed ahead with 100 mounted men, leaving the slow-moving main body, with the livestock and baggage train, to follow. Crossing into the area of the present United States southwest of Bisbee, Ariz., he struck out toward the northeast until he came upon the Zuñi pueblo of Hawi-kuh—a jolting disappointment. It was not a magnificent city surrounded by gold-crusted walls ornamented with jewels, but a motley rock-and-clay pueblo. Furthermore, its Indian defenders were hostile. Though tired from the rapid march and debilitated by a rationed diet, the Spaniards took the pueblo by storm.

The mounted men with superior arms won the fray. Coronado ensconced himself in the pueblo and sent back one of his lieutenants, Melchior Díaz, to order the main army forward. After doing so, Díaz took a detachment and cut west to the Colorado River, roughly along the southern boundary of Arizona. He failed in his attempt to rendezvous with the expedition's ships—two supply vessels under Hernando de Alarcón—that had sailed the length of the Gulf of California and up the mighty Colorado for a distance of perhaps 50 miles.

The pueblo of Hawikuh was undoubtedly one of the fabled Seven Cities of Cíbola; Fray Marcos shamefacedly returned home, but Coronado determined to pursue the search. During the summer of 1540, another lieutenant, Pedro de Tovar, led a side expedition to Awatovi and the other Hopi villages in northeastern Arizona. López de Cárdenas explored as far west as the awesome walls of the Grand Canyon of the Colorado. He was the first European to view the canyon. Another small expedition under Hernando de Alvarado followed Indian guides northeast to Taos and Pecos Pueblos. Meanwhile, Coronado shifted his headquarters eastward to the pueblo of Tiguex on the Rio Grande, a few miles north of the site of Albuquerque. Heavy fighting ensued with the Indians, who finally surrendered.

From an Indian the Spaniards called the Turk, "because he looked like one," Coronado heard marvelous tales of the rich land of Quivira farther to the east. In the spring of 1541, the entire army, with renewed hope, marched eastward under the Turk's guidance. In truth, the Indian was a native of the Plains country, seeking to escape from captivity among the Pueblo Indians. But he easily duped the Spaniards, who so avidly sought gold and conquest—even though Ysopete, another Plains Indian who accompanied the expedition, denied the Turk's stories. Somewhere along the eastern edge of the Texas high plains, Coronado sent the main army back to Tiguex. With 30 cavalrymen, 6 infantrymen, some servants, and the 2 Plains Indians, he trekked toward the northeast into present Oklahoma and Kansas, which did not yield the riches the Spanish sought. The Turk confessed his duplicity and the Spanish garroted him. At the very time that Coronado was in Kansas, the De Soto expedition—which had originated in Florida—was probably only a few hundred miles to the southeast.

Coronado, frustrated at finding no wealth in Kansas, turned back to Tiguex, where the Spaniards spent a dreary winter before dragging themselves back to their homeland in the south. Not only had their high hopes of riches been dashed, but the inhospitable lands they had traversed were unsuitable for colonization. The discovery by Díaz and Alarcón that Baja (Lower) California was a peninsula and not an island was the only concrete result of the expedition. For about 40 years, New Spain's interest in the north country waned.

New Mexico—which then included present Arizona and the rest of the Southwest—was colonized in 1598 by Juan de Oñate because of the lingering suspicion that the fabled land of Quivira might, in truth, be real, and because of persistent rumors of mineral wealth in the mountains. The Rodríguez and Espejo expeditions of 1581–82 stimulated these rumors. In 1581, Friar Agustín Rodríguez, with two other Franciscans and a small band of soldiers, entered the upper Rio Grande region to convert the Pueblo Indians. The priests remained there without military escort. Fearing that they were lost, the following year Antonio de Espejo went to their rescue. The three friars had been killed; Espejo had little to report, but his return quickened Spanish interest again in the lands to the north. An unlicensed expedition under Castaño de Sosa in 1590 was thwarted when soldiers from Chihuahua overtook it and arrested the leader. About 1590, Indians slaughtered another group, led by Francisco Leyva de Bonilla and Antonio Gutíerrez de Humaña, somewhere in the Plains country.

It was Oñate, sanctioned by the Crown and leading a powerful force, who made the first permanent settlement. Crossing the Rio Grande at present El Paso, he and some 400 followers proceeded up the river to the juncture of the Chama. In that vicinity, in the summer of 1598, they founded the colony of San Juan de los Caballeros in one of two Indian pueblos. Late in the year or early in 1599, they established San Gabriel de Yungue-ouinge at the other pueblo as the capital of New Mexico. From these bases, Franciscan friars scattered to the pueblos and in 1601 Oñate himself rode grandly off with an expedition to find Quivira. He traveled down the Canadian River, across the Texas Panhandle, and probably into the same general region of southern Kansas that Coronado had reached in 1541. On another trip, in 1604–5, he passed though the Gila country of Arizona to the Colorado River, but again found no gold or silver.

The little colony on the Rio Grande grew discontented under Oñate's leadership; he resigned about 1608 and Pedro de Peralta replaced him the following year. Probably in 1610 Peralta moved the capital southward and reestablished it at Santa Fe, which he founded in the foothills of the Sangre de Cristo Mountains. The priests continued to expand their evangelical work among the neighboring pueblos, but otherwise the province grew slowly. In the second decade of the 17th century, perhaps 20 priests were serving some 30,000 converts in more than 40 small churches in the upper Rio Grande area. Military and civilian personnel numbered

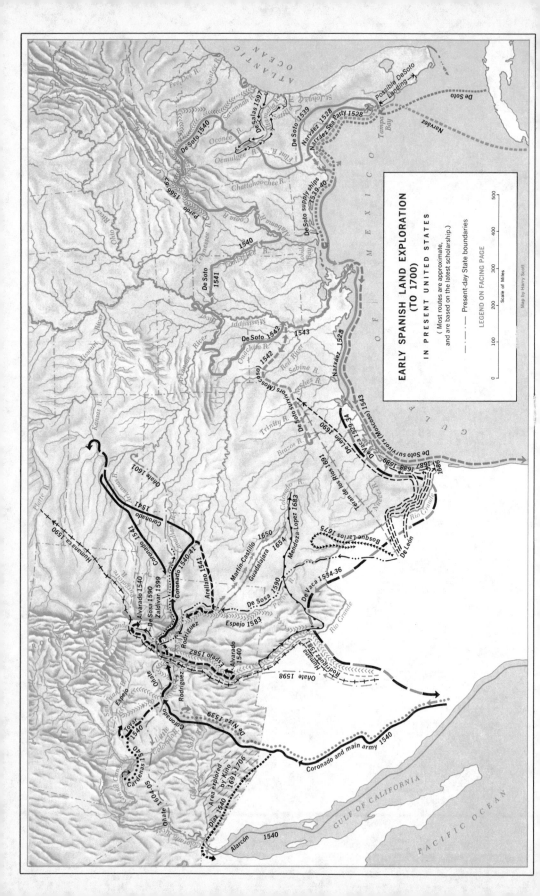

EARLY SPANISH LAND EXPLORATION
(TO 1700)
IN PRESENT UNITED STATES

(Most routes are approximate,
and are based on the latest scholarship.)

LEGEND ON FACING PAGE

— · — · — Present-day State boundaries

Scale of Miles

0   100   200   300   400   500

Map by Harry Scott

ATLANTIC OCEAN

GULF OF MEXICO

GULF OF CALIFORNIA

PACIFIC OCEAN

Possible DeSoto Landing

De Soto

Narváez

Tampa Bay

Narváez 1528

Narváez Sea Party 1528

De Soto supply ships 1539-40

De Soto 1539

De Salas 1597

De Soto 1540

Oconee R.

Oemulgee R.

Pee Dee R.

Saluda R.

Santee R.

Savannah R.

Satilla R.

St. Johns R.

Flint R.

Chattahoochee R.

Coosa R.

Alabama R.

Tombigbee R.

Pardo 1566-67

Ohio River

Tennessee R.

1540

De Soto 1541

De Soto 1542

1543

Ouachita R.

Red River

Sabine R.

Neches R.

Trinity R.

De Soto survivors (Moscoso)

De Soto 1542 (Moso)

Mississippi River

Arkansas River

Canadian R.

Missouri R.

Kansas R.

Platte R.

Humaña ca. 1590

Oñate 1601

Coronado 1541

Coronado 1541

Coronado 1540-41

Arellano 1541

Martin-Castillo 1650

Guadalajara 1654

Mendoza-López 1683

Colorado R.

Brazos R.

De Leon 1690

Terán de los Ríos 1691

De García 1593-94

1687 1688 1689

1690

De Soto survivors (Moscoso) 1543

Narváez 1528

Nueces R.

Rio Grande

De León

Bosque-Larios 1675

De Vaca 1534-36

De Sosa 1590

Espejo 1583

Pecos R.

Rio Grande

Alvarado 1540

De Sosa 1590

Zaldívar 1599

Rodríguez

Espejo 1582

Alvarado 1540

Rodríguez

Oñate

Espejo

Oñate

Tovar 1540

Cárdenas 1540

Little Colorado R.

Grand Canon

Gila R.

Salt R.

Oñate 1604-05

Area explored by Kino 1691-1706

Díaz 1540

Alarcón 1540

De Niza 1539

Coronado

Coronado and main army 1540

Oñate 1598

Humaña 1593

Rodríguez 1581

San Juan R.

Colorado River

Gila R.

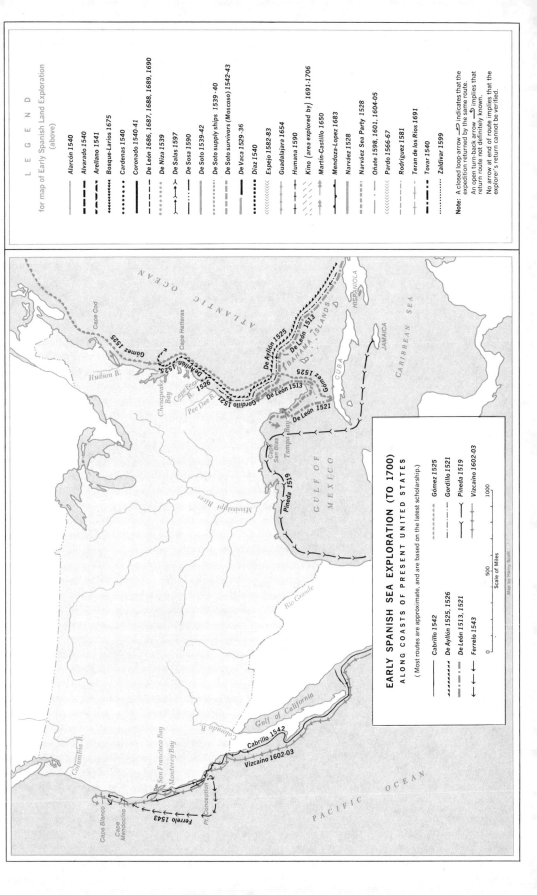

EARLY SPANISH SEA EXPLORATION (TO 1700)
ALONG COASTS OF PRESENT UNITED STATES

(Most routes are approximate, and are based on the latest scholarship.)

—————— Cabrillo 1542	·—··—··— Gómez 1525	
‑‑‑‑‑‑‑ De Ayllón 1525, 1526	—·—·—·— Gordillo 1521	
▪—▪—▪— De León 1513, 1521	⋎⋎⋎ Pineda 1519	
←— Ferrelo 1543	+—+—+ Vizcaíno 1602-03	

Scale of Miles

0   500   1000

Map by Henry Scott

L E G E N D
for map of Early Spanish Land Exploration
(above)

——————	Alarcón 1540
▬▬▬▬	Alvarado 1540
▬ ▬ ▬	Arellano 1541
‹‹‹‹‹‹‹	Bosque-Larios 1675
••••••	Cárdenas 1540
▬▬▬▬▬	Coronado 1540-41
—·—·—·—	De León 1686, 1687, 1688, 1689, 1690
··········	De Niza 1539
↑—↑—↑	De Salas 1597
·—··—··	De Sosa 1590
▬ ▬ ▬	De Soto 1539-42
————	De Soto supply ships 1539-40
▬▬▬▬▬	De Soto survivors (Moscoso) 1542-43
▬▬▬▬	De Vaca 1529-36
▬ ▬ ▬	Díaz 1540
‹‹‹‹‹‹	Espejo 1582-83
+—+—+	Guadalajara 1654
⫽⫽⫽⫽	Humana 1590
⇗	Kino (area explored by) 1691-1706
▬▬▬▬	Martín-Castillo 1650
▬▬·▬▬	Mendoza-López 1683
⋎⋎⋎⋎	Narváez 1528
▬ ▬ ▬	Narváez Sea Party 1528
‹‹‹‹‹‹	Oñate 1598, 1601, 1604-05
—·—·—·	Pardo 1566-67
+—+—+	Rodríguez 1581
+—+—+	Terán de los Ríos 1691
▪—▪—▪	Tovar 1540
··········	Zaldívar 1599

Note: A closed loop-arrow ⟳ indicates that the expedition returned by the same route. An open turn-back arrow ⤸ implies that return route not definitely known. No arrow at end of route implies that the explorer's return cannot be verified.

only a few hundred. Several minor expeditions searched the surrounding mountains and made other tours—as far as west Texas—in the vain pursuit of treasure.

Only the apparent success of the mission effort among the sedentary Pueblo Indians kept the tiny colony in New Mexico alive, for the venture proved unrewarding otherwise. New Mexico settled quickly into an isolation and pastoral lethargy that was to be its chief characteristic for the next two centuries. The small number of Spanish settlers and soldiers—competing with the clergy—exacted burdensome tributes and forced labor from the Indians in an attempt to derive a livelihood. The clergy and civil leaders clashed on many other issues, and civil-military discord seriously weakened the small colony.

Disaster struck in 1680. The padres' success had been more apparent than real, and the Indians proved to be more recalcitrant than they had seemed. Resenting the tributes and the new religion that was forced on them, they rebelled under an unusual leader, Popé. They killed more than 400 Spaniards and drove the rest off their scattered estates and out of Santa Fe. The survivors fled panic-stricken southward into the province of Chihuahua, where the following year they founded El Paso del Norte, now Juarez, Mexico. One small group of friars and loyal Indians continued on and stopped on the north bank of the Rio Grande a few miles southeast of present El Paso. There, also in 1681, they established the mission community of Corpus Christi de Isleta.

That same year, Gov. Antonio de Otermín made an attempt to reconquer New Mexico but failed. A decade elapsed before Diego de Vargas received a commission to reestablish dominion over the province. In 1692, he led a strong force up the Rio Grande. The pueblos submitted with little resistance, and the Spaniards reoccupied Santa Fe. In their absence, the Tano Indians had moved into the town. Friction between them and the newcomers erupted soon into a bloody fight, the Tanos being driven into the mountains. For the next 6 years, like brush fires on the prairie, sporadic rebellions burst out in the pueblos; De Vargas was kept busy chasing from one to another before, finally, he reinstituted complete and lasting Spanish authority.

The history of the province from the time of the reconquest until the newly independent Mexico took it over in 1821 is a record of the ebb and flow of missionary activity in the Indian pueblos; civil-military-religious clashes; the slow spread of ranchos and haciendas into the plateaus away from the rivers; the coming and going of a long line of royal Governors; the building of little villages along the rivers and in the valleys; frequent warfare with the Apaches, Navajos, and Comanches; occasional explorations into the vast, unknown regions surrounding the upper Rio Grande; and, finally, visits by French fur traders from the northeast.

New Mexico was hopelessly separated from the pulse of the Spanish Viceroyalty. It was a distant outpost from which twice a year long caravans made the wearisome trek to Mexico City and back, bringing news, gossip, and supplies. For the most part, the widely scattered towns and ranches were self-sustaining, and even the smallest had some fortifications against Indian attack. The largest town during this period was not the capital of Santa Fe but the village of Santa Cruz, about 20 miles north on the Rio Grande. Twice destroyed by Indian raids late in the 17th century, in 1706 it was reestablished by Gov. Francisco Cuervo y Valdez, who also founded that same year a small post southwest of Santa Fe that he named San Felipe de Alburquerque (later Albuquerque) in honor of the Viceroy. The latter remained a sleepy, pastoral village until after the coming of the Anglo-Americans in the middle of the 19th century.

In the Taos Valley, in northern New Mexico, were three distinct villages: the Indian pueblo; a Spanish villa, Fernando de Taos, a short distance away; and tiny Ranchos de Taos, about 3 miles farther south. The Indians of the Taos Pueblo had been the first to rebel in 1680 and were the last to submit, in 1696, to the reestablishment of Spanish authority. San Gerónimo de Taos, the mission church of the pueblo and one of the earliest in New Mexico, constructed in 1620, was rebuilt in 1706 after being razed during the Pueblo Revolt. In 1723, the Spanish officially established the Taos Fair, whose origins reached far back into prehistoric times. Conducted annually almost every year thereafter for more than a century, it became an important source of contact and commerce with the Plains Indians and French trappers.

From some Plains Indians (Cuartelejo Apaches) the Spaniards learned of a French expedition that had left the Illinois country for the purpose of trading in New Mexico. The Spanish response, as always to French intrusion, was reflexive. In 1720, an expedition under Pedro de Villasur rushed north from Santa Fe. In a fight along the North Platte River with Pawnee Indians, Villasur and his interpreter, Jean l'Archeveque, lost their lives. Months later, 12 survivors of the expedition struggled back to Santa Fe.

In 1727, New Mexicans heard alarming rumors of a French settlement

160 leagues north of Santa Fe, which proved, indeed, to be a French trading post at a Cuartelejo Apache village. Then, in 1739, the Mallet brothers and a party of fur traders appeared in Santa Fe. Spain and France were at peace in Europe, but the Spanish Crown directed the capture of any other Frenchmen who appeared in New Mexico. After 1746, despite the royal injunction, French trappers apparently began to visit the Taos Fair. In the years following 1762, when Spain acquired western Louisiana from France, royal Governors in both New Mexico and Texas made good use of the French traders in dealing with the Indians of the "northern tribes."

In Pimería Alta—the northern region of the province of Sonora, which included present Arizona south of the Gila River—the Spanish were far less active than in neighboring New Mexico. This was especially true in southern Arizona (northern Pimería Alta), where the Spaniards made only a nominal penetration of an area not more than 60 miles square south of Tucson in the Santa Cruz Valley; they had little or no effect on the rest of modern Arizona. Ultimately, in Arizona the Spaniards established three missions, only two of which were active at any one time, and founded a few *visitas* and a small presidio. In southern Pimería Alta, in contrast, Spanish activities were more intensive. There at one time three presidios protected a series of missions and *visitas,* and miners were quite active.

The entradas of De Niza, Coronado, and Oñate, in 1539, 1540, and 1604–5, merely passed through Pimería Alta, but the Jesuit Father Eusebio Francisco Kino thoroughly explored it, beginning in 1687. After founding a group of missions in southern Pimería Alta, in 1691 he entered present Arizona. For the rest of the decade he visited the Indians; stopped at the future sites of the Tumacacori, San Xavier, and Guevavi missions; established Indian rancherías to support envisioned missions; and wandered north to the ruins of Casa Grande on the Gila. In 1700, under his direction, Indians laid the foundations of San Xavier del Bac Mission, ultimately one of the most magnificent in North America, and Kino soon founded San Gabriel de Guevavi Mission. Unable to obtain funds or missionaries from the Spanish Government to operate the missions, however, he returned to his headquarters in southern Pimería Alta, from where he directed activities until his death, in 1711. His successors carried on his efforts there.

In 1732, a new group of Jesuits—mainly Germans—renewed the

apostolic effort in northern Pimería Alta. From Guevavi and San Xavier, despite occasional Apache raids, they continued Kino's work by founding six *visitas* at the rancherías in the Santa Cruz Valley. An uprising of the

This scene illustrates life at San José de Tumacacori Mission, Arizona. The mission Indians engaged in religious, educational, farming, and handicraft activities. From an exhibit at Tumacacori National Monument.

Pima Indians in 1751 jolted the Spanish authorities into a greater awareness of the area, and the following year they founded a presidio at Tubac to protect the small group of settlers in the region; and padres built a mission 3 miles away at the village of San José de Tumacacori. It was from Tubac that Juan Bautista de Anza set out in 1774 to open an overland route to California.

To better cope with Apache depredations, in 1776 the Spanish authorities replaced the presidio at Tubac with one at the site of Tucson. In 1767, the Crown had expelled the Jesuits from all the Spanish colonies, and the Franciscans had moved in. In 1773 they abandoned Guevavi and centered their activities at Tumacacori, and in 1785 began construction of present San Xavier del Bac Mission, which they completed in 1795.

In the 1790's, in addition to the few hundred missionaries and settlers in present Arizona, about 20,000 Hispanic people were living in New Mexico in scores of isolated estates and hamlets scattered along the upper Rio Grande. Their quiet, near-indolent retirement was rudely shattered by the appearance of the Americans on the northern frontier just after the turn of the century. But Spain lacked the power or the energy to push back the tide. After Mexico gained her independence in 1821, together with the Spanish possessions in the present United States, she opened the province to the Yankees, who gained a major inroad into the Southwest via the Santa Fe Trail.

TEXAS—REACTION TO THE FRENCH

Texas was the third major area to be penetrated by the Spanish. Despite sporadic interest by Spanish officials, it received little attention until the founding of San Antonio, in 1718. During the next century, only a few sparse settlements were made, and a handful of missionaries, soldiers, and settlers sought to link the vast province with the rest of New Spain.

As in Florida, Spanish settlement in Texas was in response to a French threat. In 1682, the remarkable French explorer René Robert Cavelier, Sieur de la Salle, floated down to the mouth of the Mississippi, planted the gold and white banner of his country on the riverbank, claimed the entire river system for France, and named it Louisiana in honor of his sovereign, Louis XIV.

La Salle's next venture was an even more serious menace to Spain. Sailing from France and planning to establish a permanent post at the mouth of the Mississippi, in 1685 he landed instead on the Texas coast at the mouth of the Lavaca River. How could such an experienced explorer have missed his destination so far? Was his actual purpose, perhaps with the secret support of his inscrutable King, to move even nearer the Spanish mines of Nueva Viscaya, to the West?

In any event, La Salle erected Fort St. Louis and set out in a *westerly* direction, allegedly to locate the Mississippi's estuary, before turning northeast and headed back to the Illinois country for provisions. Some of his discouraged followers, however, assassinated him somewhere in east Texas. A few survivors made their way back up the Mississippi to Canada; the remainder of the complement at Fort St. Louis succumbed to disease, starvation, and the Indians.

Spanish authorities, learning from coastal Indians of the threat to their northern outposts, began a frantic search by land and water. On his fourth overland expedition, in 1689, Capt. Alonso de León located the French post. Finding it deserted, he burned it to the ground to obliterate any trace of French occupancy on Spanish soil.

In the heat of the alarm over the French, Father Damian Massanet, who had accompanied De León, had little difficulty in obtaining official support for the establishment of a mission among the friendly Tejas Indians, a branch of the Caddo Confederation, in east Texas. Emissaries of the Tejas tribe, whose very name was translatable as friendly, had witlessly invited the Spanish into their midst. In 1690, De León and Massanet founded the San Francisco de los Tejas Mission. The following year they began an offshoot, Santísimo Nombre de María, a few miles away. Domingo Teran de los Rios, appointed "Governor" of the province, crossed Texas bringing additional priests and supplies.

Two years later the disillusioned Indians—among the most civilized in North America—drove the padres out. But a combination of a zealous priest and a forward Frenchman was to bring Spain rushing back into Texas shortly after the turn of the century. Father Francisco Hidalgo, one of the Franciscans who had been at the Tejas mission, feared for the souls of his Indian converts in east Texas. When Spanish authorities failed to support his return, he sent a message to the French, then ensconced at the mouth of the Mississippi, praying that a priest be sent to the Tejas to minister the sacraments to the handful of faithful. Nothing could have delighted the French commander more than this invitation. In 1713, he dispatched a young French woodsman—the clever and charming Louis Juchereau de St. Denis—to the Spanish outpost on the Rio Grande.

Carmel Mission, California, in 1839. Mission activities included farming and stockraising. From a multivolume series, published during the years 1841–54. Courtesy, Bancroft Library, University of California.

St. Denis did not intend to save Indian souls; he sought trade with the northern Spanish settlements. In the next 4 years, he pursued one of the most romantic adventures in the history of the North American frontier. Arriving in July 1714 at San Juan Bautista on the Rio Grande— opposite modern Eagle Pass—he was promptly arrested for trespassing. But his silken tongue and gracious manners won the friendship of the post commandant and he began ardently to court his daughter, or niece. A jealous rival for the girl's hand, however, quickly caused his detention and he was sent to Mexico City.

With facile grace, St. Denis convinced the Viceroy that, although born a Frenchman, he was at heart a Spaniard. The Viceroy not only released him but appointed him cocommander of a Spanish expedition returning to east Texas to set up a presidio and mission field. The sizable expedition of friars, soldiers, and friendly Indians, under the joint command of Domingo Ramón and St. Denis, moved across Texas. During the autumn of 1716, it founded six missions, scattered from the Neches River eastward to present Louisiana, as well as the presidio of Dolores near the midpoint of the chain. No sooner were the Spaniards well established than St. Denis became a Frenchman once again. He hastened to a cache of trade goods that he had left on the Red River, erected a trading post at Natchitoches, and entered into an entirely illegal commerce with his Spanish friends.

In 1718, Martín de Alarcón stopped along the San Antonio River on his way to supply the east Texas outposts. Establishing there a halfway post between the Rio Grande and east Texas, he founded the presidio of Bexar and the mission of San Antonio de Valero, which came to be known much later as the Alamo.

In 1719, the sudden appearance at Los Adaes—the easternmost mission—of a French soldier from Natchitoches caused a wildfire panic. Padres and soldiers alike fled to Bexar seeking safety from what they imagined to be a French attack. Chagrined and embarrassed, Spanish officials appointed the capable Marqués de San Miguel de Aguayo as Governor and captain-general of Texas and sent him into the region with a formidable force of soldiers to reoccupy and strengthen it. In 1720, the beautiful San José y San Miguel de Aguayo Mission was founded in his honor at San Antonio. The Marqués went to east Texas in the summer of 1721. To prevent any further French incursions, he reestablished the six missions and the Dolores presidio and established a presidio at Los Adaes a few miles away from the French settlement of Natchitoches. Then, to extinguish forever any claim France might have to Texas, he marched down the coast and erected a mission and a presidio on the very site of Fort St. Louis, which 30 years earlier De León had burned to the ground.

When Aguayo left Texas in 1722, there were four presidios, nine missions, and small clusters of settlers at San Antonio and at Los Adaes. For the next half-century, Spain's hold on the region was stubborn—if shaky and unsure. In 1731, the Spanish relocated three of the east Texas missions at San Antonio. That same year, a shipload of Canary Islanders, consisting of about 15 families—the first civil colonists in Texas—arrived after a tortuous overland trek from Vera Cruz and settled at San Antonio. For about the next two decades, no major developments occurred. In 1749, the Spanish moved the mission and presidio known as La Bahía del Espíritu Santo back from the mouth of the Lavaca River to the site of Goliad. Six years later, they founded the mission Rosario nearby.

Spanish Franciscans endeavored, without success, to establish missions at the mouth of the Trinity (1756); on the San Gabriel River, in central Texas (1751); on the San Sabá River, 100 miles farther west (1757); and near the headwaters of the Nueces (1762). None of these missions lasted more than a few years, but the one at San Sabá had the most tragic history. Its purpose was to attempt to convert and teach agricultural methods to the terrifying Apaches, who were struggling with the even more frightening Comanches—intruding into west Texas from the north.

In 1758, the year after the founding of the mission, a horde of Comanches swooped down, destroyed it, and massacred the missionaries and their pitiable Tlascalan Indian charges—most of whom had been imported from northern Mexico. Frightened troops in the San Luís presidio across the river were unable—or unwilling—to come to the mission's aid. The next year the Comanches decisively defeated on the Red River a punitive Spanish expedition, consisting of 500 soldiers and Indian allies, which had moved into Comanche country. The reconstructed stone walls of San Sabá stand today as a memorial to the fierce might of the "Lords of the South Plains"—the Comanches. Spain was never able to defeat or contain these Indians, whose raiding range soon extended even farther south and separated San Antonio from the settlements in New Mexico.

By the middle of the 18th century, Spain's occupation of Texas reached its acme. Soon thereafter interest and strength began to wane. In 1762, the year before Florida passed to the English by the Treaty of

Paris, Spain acquired western Louisiana from France. The eastern frontier of New Spain thus moved to the Mississippi and the fear of French encroachment in Texas ended. For this reason, and in the interest of economy, the Spanish authorities completely abandoned the east Texas mission field in 1773. They even ordered the settlers at Los Adaes to move to San Antonio. Before long, some of these settlers insisted on returning to east Texas, even though they had no military protection. In 1779, some of them founded Nacogdoches. By the end of the century, Spanish Texas had shrunk to this feeble village in east Texas, the presidio-settlements in the Goliad vicinity and at San Antonio, and a handful of scattered missions.

During the next two decades, these isolated settlements figured in the movement for independence from Spain. Filibustering expeditions, organized by Mexican patriots, adventurers professing the Mexican cause, or pirates, several times ranged into Texas, captured settlements, and clashed with Spanish forces. When, at last, in 1821, Mexico achieved independence, Texas passed with hardly a tremor from Spanish control; the royal Governor, Antonio Martínez, simply turned his coat about and raised the Mexican tricolor over the 100-year-old plaza of San Antonio. Even before then, however, the preliminary American penetration of Texas that augured independence from Mexico in 1836 had already begun.

California: the last colony

The California coast, endowed with a wonderful climate and peopled by docile Indians, was ideally suited for the pastoral mission system by which New Spain had been slowly extending her northern frontiers. Elsewhere in the present United States the system had either failed or met with only moderate success; in California it thrived and reached perfection. Nevertheless, California was the last area in the United States to be penetrated by Spain—and not until the frontier lay virtually dormant elsewhere. Located as it was so far out on the lifelines of the Spanish Empire in the New World, California was sparsely populated and neglected.

Though the Spanish explored the Pacific coast extensively only a few decades after they began to explore the Atlantic and gulf coasts, they had but meager information about California. At the same time that Moscoso was leading the weary survivors of the De Soto expedition across

Carmel Mission, California, in 1835. From a lithograph by Day & Haghe, published in 1839. Courtesy, Bancroft Library, University of California.

east Texas and Coronado was returning dejectedly homeward from New Mexico, in 1542–43, the Juan Rodríguez Cabrillo expedition of two vessels was cruising northward from Navidad along the Pacific coast of California. After discovering San Diego Bay, Cabrillo moved up the coast to the vicinity of Point Reyes, a storm causing him to miss the Golden Gate. He died shortly thereafter, and Bartolomé Ferrelo assumed command. He reached the vicinity of the Oregon coast—perhaps between the 42d and 44th parallels—before returning to his home port. In 1602–3, Sebastián Vizcaíno also sailed up the coast, into Monterey and Drakes Bay, and explored the coastline of Oregon. Despite this exploration, Spain's chief interest in the area that is now the United States was focused for the next century and a half, not on California and the Pacific coast, but on Florida and the gulf coast region.

In the mid-18th century, Spain was spurred to colonize California by Russian fur-trade and exploratory intrusions on the Pacific coast, from Alaska as far south as Oregon, and the desire to provide supply and watering facilities for her Manila galleons. Colonization began in 1769 with a combined sea and land approach from Baja California. Under the leadership of Gaspar de Portolá and Father Junípero Serra, a Franciscan missionary, the overland expedition reached San Diego Bay in two stages. The sea party, consisting of two vessels of colonists and a supply ship, was less successful. The supply ship was lost at sea; the other two became separated, lost their bearings, and their passengers fell prey to scurvy before they landed. When finally assembled, the little band of California pioneers consisted of 126 persons. On July 16, Father Serra consecrated San Diego de Alcalá Mission.

Two days earlier an overland expedition commanded by Portolá had headed up the coast toward Monterey Bay, which had been discovered by Vizcaíno. Portolá failed to recognize Monterey Bay, but stumbled by accident onto "a very large and fine harbor such that not only all of the navy of our most Catholic Majesty but those of all Europe could take shelter in it." It was, of course, San Francisco Bay. And Portolá had seen only a part of it. After a brief exploration, the party turned south, identified Monterey Bay, and returned to San Diego.

Presidio of Monterey, in 1791. During the Spanish and Mexican periods Monterey was the hub of social, military, economic, and political activities in California. From a drawing by José Cardero. Courtesy, Bancroft Library, University of California.

There the men found a critical situation. Fifty men had died, the natives had become unruly, and the little colony was on the point of starvation. Most wanted to abandon the enterprise and return home, but

Father Serra vowed that he would never leave. Just when things looked the blackest, the sails of a supply ship were sighted, and the venture was saved. Quickly Portolá and Serra organized another expedition to Monterey Bay. In June 1770, to secure Spain's hold on the California coast, the Spanish founded the presidio of Monterey and the mission San Carlos de Borroméo.

During the next 2 years, as additional Franciscans and colonists arrived in California, Father Serra busied himself with establishing new missions between San Diego and Monterey. In 1771, he relocated the San Carlos mission a few miles away from the presidio at Monterey along the Carmel River, from which it took its permanent name. Traveling down the coast, in July 1771 he founded San Antonio de Padua Mission; and, in September, the mission San Gabriel Arcangel, about 9 miles east of the site of Los Angeles. A year later, he dedicated another mission, San Luis Obispo, between San Antonio and San Gabriel. In 1774, he moved the San Diego mission to a new site 6 miles away from its original location.

Two major problems yet faced the California venture: the opening of a land supply route from Spanish bases in Old Mexico and the occupation of the San Francisco Bay region. Many more colonies were needed, as well as livestock for a stable economy. The presidio and missions, remote from Spanish New World bases, were entirely dependent upon the uncertain arrival of supply ships. Father Serra returned to Mexico City, obtained the enthusiastic support of the new Viceroy, and helped plan a remarkable expedition from Sonora that was to culminate in the founding of San Francisco.

Meanwhile, Juan Bautista de Anza, the captain of the presidio at Tubac, had written the Viceroy of his proposed route to California.

The Spanish explorer Juan Bautista de Anza. In 1774, he founded an overland route from Tubac, Arizona, to San Gabriel Mission, California. Subsequently he explored the San Francisco area and in 1777–78 served as Governor of New Mexico. From a conjectural painting, by an unknown artist, at Tumacacori National Monument, Arizona.

"The Mission of San Francisco, Upper California," probably San Francisco de Solano (Sonoma) Mission, in 1835. From a lithograph by Day & Haghe, published in 1839. Courtesy, Bancroft Library, University of California.

Appointed to lead the expedition being planned by Father Serra, Anza in 1774 opened the route from Tubac to Los Angeles. He traveled down the Gila to the Colorado, into the deserts and sand dunes of the California border—where his party almost lost its way—up San Felipe Creek into the Sierra Nevada, through San Carlos Pass, and then down into the valley of Los Angeles.

Returning to Tubac after a visit to Monterey Bay, Anza organized a colonizing expedition that departed in November 1775 for San Francisco Bay. With about 225 settlers, he reached Monterey in January 1776. Not Anza but his second in command actually founded a colony at the Golden Gate, in the autumn of 1776. The settlers built a presidio overlooking the harbor, and some distance from the bay, on a stream named Dolores, Father Serra erected a little mission. Anza himself left to become Governor of New Mexico and never returned to California, but his route was used to help colonize and supply the Pacific coast from Sonora. In 1776, Fathers Francisco Atanasio Domínguez and Silvestre Escalante failed in an attempt to develop an overland route from Santa Fe, New Mexico, to California.

The settlements in California grew and prospered. Monterey became the capital; in 1777, one of Anza's lieutenants established the village of San José; in 1781, the Spanish founded the pueblo of Los Angeles; and the following year, Santa Barbara Presidio. The last of the pueblos established was Villa de Branciforte (Santa Cruz), in 1797. The mission system expanded even more rapidly than the civil settlements—despite occasional Indian resistance and the martyrdom of some Franciscans. The padres founded San Juan Capistrano the same year as San Francisco Asís, 1776; Santa Clara, 1777; San Buenaventura, 1782; Santa Barbara, 1786; Purísima Concepción, 1787; Santa Cruz and Soledad, 1791; San José, San Miguel, San Fernando, and San Juan Bautista, 1797; and San Luis Rey, 1798. Three small missions were added to the chain early in the 19th century: Santa Inez, 1804; San Rafael, 1817; and San Francisco Solano, 1823.

In all, the Franciscans founded 21 missions in California—the last one, in 1823, during the Mexican administration—and small settlements grew up around most of them. The economy of Spanish California was agrarian, as in most other Spanish colonies, the missions being its chief element and forced Indian labor its main support. This economy continued for the first 12 years of the Mexican regime. In 1833, however, Mexico began secularizing the missions, despite the strenuous opposition of the padres, who had successfully forestalled similar Spanish decrees. These decrees called for the freedom of the Indians from missionary control, the granting to them of citizenship and lands, and the conversion of the missions into pueblos under civil jurisdiction.

Juan Bautista de Anza's second expedition to California, in 1775–76. Anza led about 225 colonists from Tubac to Monterey. They later settled at the site of San Francisco. From a painting, by Cal Peters, at Tumacacori National Monument.

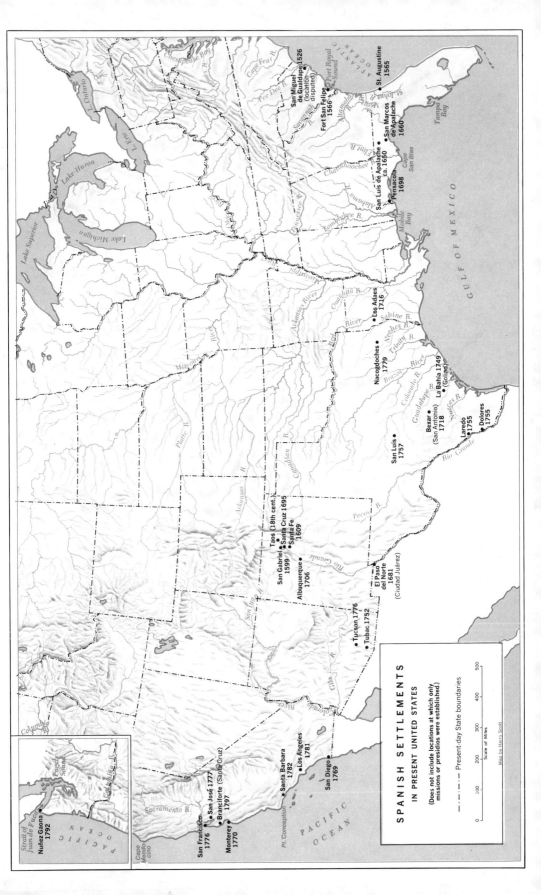

SPANISH SETTLEMENTS
IN PRESENT UNITED STATES

(Does not include locations at which only
missions or presidios were established.)

— · — · — Present-day State boundaries

Scale of Miles

0   100   200   300   400   500

Map by Harry Scott

Inset (upper left):

Strait of Juan de Fuca

Nuñez Gaona
1792

Puget Sound

Columbia R.

PACIFIC
OCEAN

Cape
Mendocino

West Coast labels:

San Francisco 1776
San José 1777
Branciforte (Santa Cruz) 1797
Monterey 1770
Sacramento R.
Pt. Conception
Santa Barbara 1782
Los Angeles 1781
San Diego 1769

Southwest labels:

Taos (18th cent.)
Santa Cruz 1695
Santa Fe 1609
San Gabriel 1599
Albuquerque 1706
El Paso del Norte 1681 (Ciudad Juárez)
Tucson 1776
Tubac 1752

Gila R.
Colorado R.
San Juan R.
Rio Grande
Pecos R.
Canadian R.
Arkansas R.
Platte R.
Missouri R.

Texas / Gulf labels:

Los Adaes 1716
Nacogdoches 1779
San Luis 1757
Bexar (San Antonio) 1718
La Bahía 1749 (Goliad)
Laredo 1755
Dolores 1755
Sabine R.
Neches R.
Trinity R.
Brazos R.
Colorado R.
Guadalupe R.
Nueces R.
Rio Grande

Southeast labels:

San Miguel de Gualdape 1526 (location disputed)
Fort San Felipe 1566
Port Royal Sound
St. Augustine 1565
San Marcos de Apalache 1660
San Luis de Apalache ca. 1650
Pensacola 1698
Chattahoochee R.
Flint R.
Alabama R.
Tombigbee R.
Mobile Bay
Cape San Blas
Tampa Bay
St. Johns R.
Savannah R.
Cape Fear R.
Tee Dee R.
Chesapeake Bay

GULF OF MEXICO

ATLANTIC OCEAN

PACIFIC OCEAN

L. Ontario
L. Erie
Lake Huron
Lake Michigan
Lake Superior

Ohio R.
Mississippi R.
Tennessee R.
Ouachita R.
Red River

The Franciscans, maintaining that the Indians were not ready for freedom and not wishing to give up their temporal powers, vehemently opposed secularization. Friction and hostility with Mexican officials ensued. The Indians poorly comprehended the new measures, designed for their progress, and the missionaries influenced them against the Mexican Government. Destroying livestock and mission property, many of them fled into the wilderness. Vandals raided deserted missions and confiscated property and lands. The Mexican Government, realizing its failure, in 1845 issued a proclamation providing for the rental or sale of the missions. The result of a decade's confusion was, besides the tragic scattering of the neophytes, the destruction of most of the mission buildings.

San Luis Rey de Francia Mission, California, in 1829. From a lithograph by G. & W. Endicott, published in 1846. Courtesy, Bancroft Library, University of California.

The fortunate combination of mild climate, fertile soil, and Indian labor provided Spanish settlers in colonial California a life of leisure, ease, and even indolence. Some Spaniards and a larger number of Creoles, who had come from impoverished circumstances in Old Mexico, formed the upper layer of the socioeconomic structure and participated in the bounteous prosperity and life of idyllic graciousness. Thus California remained loyal to Spain during the first years of the independence movement in Mexico, which came to fruition in 1821, and only with some reluctance joined the Mexican Republic. Political unrest and turmoil in the 1830's and early 1840's presaged the official acquisition of California by the United States in 1848, at the end of the Mexican War.

IMPERIAL CONFLICT ON THE PACIFIC COAST

During the final decades of her tenure in North America, Spain became alarmed because of English and Russian expansion on the Pacific coast, between California and Alaska, and sought to assert her own claims in the region. Deciding to explore the area further and determine her ability to maintain her interests, she sent out a series of exploring expeditions, which also acquired much data on geology and natural history.

In 1774, Juan Peréz sailed almost to the tip of southern Alaska to observe Russian activity, but he learned nothing. The following year the Spanish dispatched Bruno Heceta and Juan Francisco de la Bodega y Quadra on a similar mission. Heceta mapped the estuary of the Columbia River and was the first European to land in the present State of Washington, at Point Grenville, where he proclaimed Spanish possession of the Pacific Northwest. He then returned to his home base. Bodega continued northward alone, landed at several points along the coast, and reached as far as Bristol Bay, in southwestern Alaska.

In 1778, Capt. James Cook of the British Navy explored the northwestern coast of the present United States in a search for the Northwest Passage. In 1789, as the Spanish set out with a similar aim, as well as to establish sovereignty over the Pacific Northwest, they were alarmed to find both British and American ships at Nootka, on the west coast of Vancouver Island, where in 1788 Capt. John Meares, an Englishman, had erected a fort. The Spanish seized the British ships, and built new fortifications. As a result, England and Spain were on the verge of war. In 1790, unable to obtain allies, Spain signed in Madrid the Nootka Sound Convention, which granted the British the right to explore, settle, and trade in the region north of San Francisco. Spain, however, did not agree to abandon her existing settlements there.

England immediately dispatched Capt. George Vancouver to reconnoiter the region. En route, in 1792, he visited Monterey, San Francisco, and various other Spanish settlements along the California coast, causing

Capt. George Vancouver's *Discovery* on the rocks, in Queen Charlotte Sound, Canada, in 1794. Its sister ship stands by. Vancouver explored the west coast of North America during the years 1791–95. From an engraving by B. T. Pouncy, after an on-the-scene drawing by Z. Mudge. Courtesy, Bancroft Library, University of California.

the Spanish to strengthen their defenses. Passing the Columbia River, he moved on to the Strait of Juan de Fuca and Puget Sound, where the Spanish expedition of Alejandro Malaspina was still exploring after its return from Lituya Bay, Alaska.

The Spanish, who had just founded a small settlement called Nuñez Gaona at Neah Bay, in the present State of Washington, moved it to Nootka. While Vancouver was probing northern Washington, Capt.

Fort Ross, California, in 1828. In 1812, the Russians founded the fort as a fur trading post and agricultural center to supply their colonies in Alaska. In 1841, they sold it to John A. Sutter. From a sketch by an unknown artist, published in 1834–35. Courtesy, Bancroft Library, University of California.

Russian house at Fort Ross, California, in 1841. From a sketch by an unknown artist, published in the year 1844. Courtesy, Bancroft Library, University of California.

Robert Gray, an American, arrived in the Pacific Northwest to search for sea-otter and other skins. In 1792, he sailed a few miles up the Columbia River, the first white man to do so, and laid the basis for later claims by the United States. The Lewis and Clark Expedition (1804–6) reinforced these claims.

In 1812, about a decade before Spain lost California and the rest of her territory in North America, the Russian-American Fur Company established Fort Ross, about 60 miles north of San Francisco, as a fur trading post and agricultural center for supplying her settlements in Alaska. The Spanish were somewhat alarmed by this new incursion of a foreign power. In only a few years, however, they lost all their possessions in North America to the United States and the newly independent Mexico.

DOWNFALL AND DEMISE

Although indeed continuous on the maps, the Spanish provinces were in no sense unified; each was a separate entity, having little political or economic connection with the others. Spanish claims in the present United States reached their maximum extent in the years between 1783 and 1803—when Spain's dominion stretched from Florida to California in one vast empire. In 1763, by the Treaty of Paris, Spain had lost Florida but 1 year earlier she had gained western Louisiana. In 1783, the treaty ending the American War for Independence restored Florida to her domain.

Surprisingly, Spain's empire in the New World reached its acme long after Spain had begun to lose her dominance in Europe—a process set in motion by the defeat of her armada by the English in 1588. By international politics, not active colonization, she obtained Louisiana and regained Florida, then but a remnant of a once lively colony. In the vast territory of Louisiana, Spanish control rested lightly on already existing French institutions. Not until more than 3 years after Spain acquired the territory did she form even a superficial government, at New Orleans. By 1800, the settlements in Texas had dwindled to a few thousand persons. The little colony along the upper Rio Grande, in New Mexico, was as dormant as ever. Southern Arizona showed even fewer signs of life, and in California the last burst of Spanish energy quickly spent itself.

Wife of a Monterey soldier. From a drawing, in 1791, by José Cardero, a member of the Malaspina expedition. Courtesy, Bancroft Library, University of California.

A Monterey soldier. From a drawing, in 1791, by José Cardero, one of several artists on the Malaspina expedition. Courtesy, Bancroft Library, University of California.

In the 19th century, disintegration and dismemberment of the empire were rapid. In 1803, France regained Louisiana and immediately sold it to the United States. In 1810 and 1812, settlers in West Florida—a few French and Spanish but mostly newcomers from the United States—revolted and sought annexation by the United States. In 1818, Gen. Andrew Jackson, directly asserting U.S. interest in Florida, marched into West Florida and captured Pensacola. Because of these troubles and her inability to control the Florida Indians, Spain, in the Adams-Onís Treaty (1819), ceded Florida to the United States and obtained a delineation of the disputed Texas boundary.

At about the same time, came the greatest blow. Imbued with the ideas of the French Revolution—liberty, equality, and fraternity—and inspired by the example of U.S. independence to the north, Spain's own colonies in North and South America began breaking away early in the 19th century. When Mexico gained independence in 1821, she acquired the Spanish possessions of Texas, New Mexico (including most of present Arizona), and California. These areas grew as restive a few years later under the despotism that evolved in Mexico, as Old Mexico had grown under Spanish rule. Texas, colonized by many Anglo-Americans, gained independence in 1836, and 9 years later the United States annexed the Republic of Texas. New Mexico lay supine under the iron control of Manuel Armijo, a minion of the Mexican centralists, but California trembled for 15 years on the verge of open rebellion. When war broke out between the United States and Mexico in 1846, many residents of the Southwest welcomed the American troops as liberators. In 1848, by the Treaty of Guadalupe Hidalgo, the bulk of the old Spanish border-lands passed to the United States. Then the Gadsden Purchase, in 1853, added a strip of land to southern Arizona and New Mexico.

OUR SPANISH HERITAGE

Although the one-time Spanish territory gained by the United States in the trans-Mississippi West from Mexico was enormous and the gold soon discovered in California vitally affected Western development, perhaps the most rewarding and durable value of the Spanish borderlands was the heritage that lay in the land—from the Pacific to the Atlantic roughly south of the 40th parallel.

This heritage is most clearly evidenced by Spanish place names—from

Castillo de San Marcos, in Florida, to San Juan Capistrano Mission, on the Pacific coast. Florida, Colorado, Nevada, and California are Spanish names, and New Mexico is only slightly anglicized. The nomenclature of scores of cities, counties, rivers, and mountains also reveals that the Spaniards were the first Europeans to trod the land.

The language of Castile lingers not only in place names in the old Spanish borderlands, but more vividly on the tongues of men. Hundreds of words of Spanish derivation also enrich the modern English vocabulary; a few examples are lasso, calaboose, rodeo, sombrero, mesquite, and arroyo. From Florida to California, the Roman Catholic Church has thousands of adherents, and other aspects of Spanish culture are present. Architecture has the flavor of Madrid and Granada; ornamentation, of Oaxaca and Saltillo; art, of Mexico City and Guadalajara.

The origins of the cattle industry that has become the backbone of the Western economy are Spanish. The practice of working cattle from horseback, branding, trail driving, roundups, and even the cattle themselves and other livestock are all of Spanish origin. Less obvious, but

California *vaqueros* ply their trade. San José Mission is in the background. From a lithograph by L. M. Lefevre, published in 1839, after a drawing by Captain Smyth. Courtesy, Bancroft Library, University of California.

equally important, elements of the Spanish heritage are various modifications of statutory and common law that are attributable directly to the
regulamientos of Spain. Among these are property, mining, and range
laws. Also, the arid Western States have adopted the Spanish concept of
prior usage rights to water in streams and rivers instead of the age-old
English doctrine of riparian rights.

In all these ways, and in numerous others, Spanish conquistadors,
padres, and settlers have left their mark on the American image.

The French: Trappers and Traders

Not long after the Spanish conquistadors began to move into the present
Southeastern United States, the French did so in the north. The French
penetration—which ultimately extended from the Great Lakes to the Gulf
of Mexico—was of an entirely different nature than that of the Spanish.
Generally characterized by commercial exploitation of a fruitful but
cold land, except in the warmer climes of Louisiana, rather than permanent settlement of a sunny and arid one, it was a veneer over the native
life, not a lasting and deep-rooted influence. The tiny, scattered, and
heterogeneous French settlements also contrasted sharply with the well-
ordered English, Dutch, and Swedish towns on the Atlantic coast.

Adventuresome and individualistic *coureurs de bois* and voyageurs
gradually penetrated the winding waterways and the deep forests. Ultimately exploring almost two-thirds of the continent, they founded
small missions and temporary posts deep in the river-threaded heartland
rather than great religious edifices and cities that could be easily supplied
by sea. Lonely trappers and traders, living with Indian women, used their
isolated huts as bases of operations. The amenities of civilization were rare
in the far reaches of New France.

The soil of the Mississippi Valley was fertile, but the restless commercial activities of the French did not encourage stable agrarian development, and they did not recognize the immense agricultural potential of
the rich soil that stretched away from the rivers of the heartland. Claiming a much larger territory than her major rivals—England and Spain—
and beset with European wars, France never could enforce total sovereignty over the vast wilderness. For all these reasons, she was the first of
the three major European powers to be driven out of the present United
States—in 1763—and few physical remains of her occupation exist today

except in Louisiana, where settlement was more intensive than elsewhere.

Like the other European powers, France was impelled by a desire to spread Christianity, to find wealth, and to counter the efforts of other nations; and her New World colonies were also closely tied to her under the mercantilistic system. She, too, hoped to find a new water route to the East through the North American Continent. Her exploring expeditions naturally probed the present Northeast United States, whose shores were already known to her fishermen and were conveniently accessible from northern Europe. French explorers sailed down the St. Lawrence, across the waterways of Canada, through the Great Lakes, and finally to the Mississippi River and its vast drainage system. Instead of discovering a water passage through the continent, they found endless forests filled with fur-bearing animals and Indians eager to trade pelts for trinkets, muskets, and brandy.

The French Empire in North America thus came to be based on the trade in furs, originally controlled from permanent settlements in Canada. Intrepid frontiersmen plunged into the wilderness to barter and bargain, while the mother country tried to control the lucrative business by granting monopolies, forming companies, and utilizing other administrative devices. During the 17th century, most of the furs were brought into Montreal to a great annual fair. But both licensed traders and free-lancers operated with increasing freedom as the French Empire spilled thinly into the heart of the continent. Frenchmen also did some mining for copper and lead in the upper Mississippi country, but transportation, manpower, and other problems hampered their efforts.

Side by side with the voyageurs, friars brought Christianity to the Indians. Most of them were strong-willed Jesuits, although Recollect Friars of the Franciscan Order accompanied Champlain and La Salle. French missionaries were far more mobile and had a less lasting influence on the native population than their Spanish counterparts. They founded no major missions, such as San José in Texas, San Xavier in Arizona, or San Luis Rey in California. Instead, scores of temporary mission stations, where priests read masses and performed the sacraments, dotted the forests of the northland. Nor did the French missionaries ordinarily attempt, as did the Spanish, to teach the arts of civilization to the Indians. The Spanish attitude toward the natives was paternalistic; the French, fraternalistic. The French adapted to the ways of the Indian; the Spanish "civilized" him.

With a few exceptions, mainly in Louisiana, the French settlements consisted of a few families of *habitants*, who farmed the river lands in the vicinity of the forts, trading posts, missions, and Indian villages that were the centers of frontier life. Added to this small and more or less stable population were scores of restless traders, soldiers, and missionaries, continually on the move into the wilderness.

PRELUDE: COASTAL EXPLORATION

The first Frenchmen in the New World were "summer people"—fishermen who, perhaps even before Columbus' voyage, plied from the shores of Normandy to the shoals of Newfoundland to harvest the teeming codbanks of the North Atlantic. They fished, they did some trading with the natives, and they returned to France; they maintained no log-books of their voyages, and they were secretive about their quiet invasion of Spain's "exclusive" rights in the New World.

Francis I, however, who ascended the ancient throne of Charlemagne in 1515, was determined to challenge the ripening domination of Spain and her new Hapsburg monarch, Charles V. He contested, unsuccessfully, the election of Charles as Holy Roman Emperor; he sent troops to conquer some of Charles' territories in the north of Italy; and he brought the immortal Leonardo da Vinci to entertain his court in France.

But perhaps of the most lasting significance—determined that France would not be left behind in the race for empire—Francis sent an Italian navigator, Giovanni da Verrazano, across the seas in 1523–24 to establish a French claim to North America and find a passage to the East. After making a landfall, apparently somewhere along the Carolina coast, Verrazano turned north, hugged the coast around Cape Hatteras, sailed beyond the Chesapeake and Delaware Bays into New York Harbor and Narragansett Bay, around Cape Cod to Cape Breton Island, and finally back to France. He missed the great Gulf of the St. Lawrence and failed to find a water route to the East, but he provided France with a claim in the New World and announced her King's intentions.

OPENING THE ST. LAWRENCE

A decade later Francis turned to a hardy sailor of Brittany, Jacques Cartier, to renew his overseas ambitions. Scion of several generations of mariners, Cartier had earlier sailed to Portuguese Brazil and probably to the fishing banks off Newfoundland. In 1534, he set off in two small

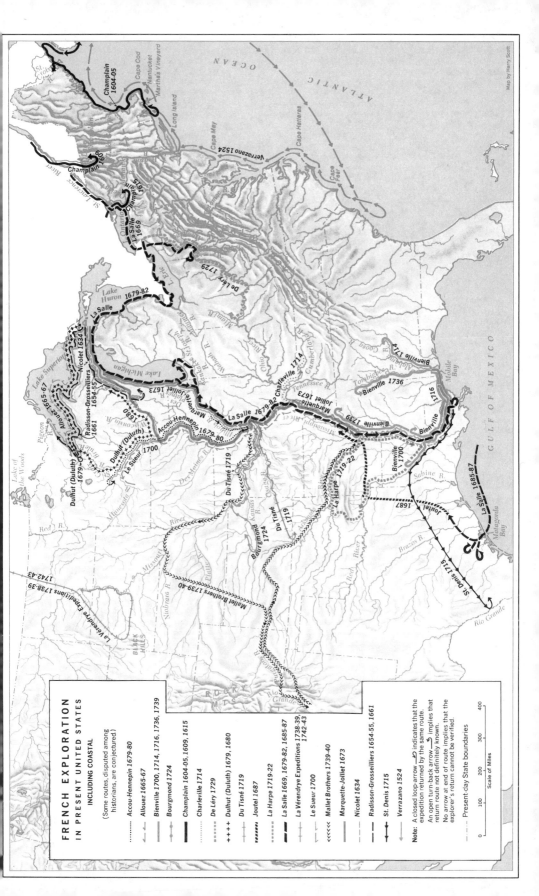

FRENCH EXPLORATION
IN PRESENT UNITED STATES
INCLUDING COASTAL

(Some routes, disputed among
historians, are conjectural.)

Accou-Hennepin 1679-80
Allouez 1665-67
Bienville 1700, 1714, 1716, 1736, 1739
Bourgmond 1724
Champlain 1604-05, 1609, 1615
Charleville 1714
De Léry 1729
Duthut (Duluth) 1679, 1680
Du Tisné 1719
Joutel 1687
La Harpe 1719-22
La Salle 1669, 1679-82, 1685-87
La Vérendrye Expeditions 1738-39, 1742-43
Mallet Brothers 1739-40
Marquette-Jolliet 1673
Nicolet 1634
Radisson-Grosseilliers 1654-55, 1661
St. Denis 1715
Verrazano 1524

Note: A closed loop-arrow ↺ indicates that the
expedition returned by the same route.
An open turn-back arrow ↰ implies that the
return route not definitely known.
No arrow at end of route implies that the
explorer's return cannot be verified.

–––––––– Present-day State boundaries

Scale of Miles

0   100   200   300   400

Map by Harry Scott

vessels with a royal commission to find a water route to the East—and it seemed at first as if he might have done so, for he discovered the broad waters of the St. Lawrence. After landing and planting a large cross to claim the land for his sovereign, he sailed around the perimeter of the Gulf of St. Lawrence and returned home.

Support for another voyage to the promising western waters was prompt and generous. Cartier sailed in May 1535, with three ships and a crew of more than 100, and moved across the Atlantic and up the St. Lawrence. As the river narrowed and the current to the sea flowed stronger, his earlier suspicion that he had not found a route around the continent was confirmed. Putting ashore in September at Stadacona, an Indian village (the site of Quebec), Cartier decided to spend the winter there. During the last days of autumn, however, he struck inland with his smallest vessel and reached the falls of the St. Lawrence, near the site of Montreal. From the Indians, with whom he exchanged presents, he heard tales of vast waterways to the west—the Great Lakes—and returned to Stadacona with reborn hope.

But this was the first of many harsh and trying winters that French pioneers were to spend in the ice and snow of Canada. By spring, a third of the expedition had died, and the emaciated survivors had no heart for further exploration. Abandoning one ship for want of a full crew, they headed back for France, where they arrived in July 1536. The King and many Frenchmen found Cartier's report interesting, but not sufficiently encouraging to finance another voyage. Not until 1541 could Cartier find another backer, the Sieur de Roberval, a nobleman of Picardy.

Roberval obtained from the Crown a license to explore and colonize the St. Lawrence at his own expense. He outfitted Cartier with three ships and himself with a like number. But from the beginning the expedition was plagued with bad luck, indecision, and dissension. In the spring of 1541, Cartier impatiently sailed from France ahead of his patron and pushed on to Stadacona. There he spent the winter of 1541–42, and in June 1542 joined Roberval in St. John's Harbor, Newfoundland. Roberval, whose departure had been delayed 1 year, was anxious to continue the explorations. Cartier was not, and slipped away to France. Roberval proceeded to Stadacona, where he encamped for the winter. Perhaps it was an unduly harsh season, or the newcomers were unprepared; when spring at last arrived, the survivors could hardly wait to return home.

HUGUENOT SETTLEMENT ATTEMPTS

France's next efforts at conquering the New World—two decades later—were motivated less by dreams of wealth and glory than by the desire of some Frenchmen to escape religious persecution. After Francis I died, civil and religious wars broke out in France that ultimately led to the downfall and expulsion of the Huguenots (Protestants). Fearing further punishment and reprisals, some Huguenots immediately emigrated elsewhere in Europe and others sought a refuge in the New World.

To establish such a refuge, the Huguenot leader, Adm. Gaspard de Coligny, in 1562 sent out Jean Ribaut, who landed at Port Royal Sound, in present South Carolina, and founded a tiny post, Charlesfort. When he returned to France, he left 30 volunteers behind to hold the post, but they bickered, abandoned the settlement, and sailed for France in a hastily constructed vessel. A passing English ship miraculously rescued the starving band, half-crazed from drinking salt water and reduced to cannibalism.

Yet the Huguenots were not disheartened. Under the leadership of

In 1564, René de Laudonnière landed with a group of Huguenot settlers along the St. Johns River, in Florida, where he built Fort Caroline. He found that the Florida Indians were worshipping a column erected 2 years earlier by Jean Ribaut during an unsuccessful colonizing attempt. From a 1591 engraving by Theodore de Bry, after an on-the-scene drawing by Jacques le Moyne de Morgues. Courtesy, Library of Congress.

René de Laudonnière, who had returned to France with Ribaut, in 1564 they made another attempt at settlement—Fort Caroline—at the mouth of the St. Johns River in Florida. This aroused the anger of Spain's Philip II. The following year, Pedro Menéndez de Avilés established St. Augustine and massacred the Huguenots, including Jean Ribaut. Thus Spain prevented French occupation of the southern Atlantic coast.

But France was not to be deterred for long from reentering the contest for empire. Early in the 17th century, two enterprising leaders took over the direction of French efforts in the New World: Pierre du Guast, Sieur de Monts, a Huguenot leader; and Samuel de Champlain, a young geographer who came to be called the "Father of New France." In 1604, De Monts received an exclusive monopoly of the fur trade, and he enlisted Champlain's aid in founding a permanent settlement in New France to serve as a trading post and a religious haven for Huguenots. Choosing an unfavorable site on St. Croix Island, near the northern boundary of Maine, Champlain's group spent a miserable winter, during which nearly half died of scurvy. When spring came, the survivors moved across the Bay of Fundy to a more suitable site at Port Royal, Nova Scotia, which they called Acadia and where they resided until returning to France in 1608. Meanwhile, in 1604–5, Champlain had explored the New England coastline as far south as Narragansett Bay and as far north as Nova Scotia.

INLAND PENETRATION

In 1608, Champlain planted a permanent settlement, called Quebec, adjacent to the Indian village of Stadacona, as a base for his explorations. The colonists survived the rigors of the winter only because of his grim determination. During the period 1609–15, Champlain struck boldly into the wilderness; he penetrated as far to the south as the southern tip of the lake that bears his name, up the Ottawa River into Canada, along the shores of Georgian Bay to Lake Huron, and back to the eastern end of Lake Ontario. Sometimes with him, and always with his encouragement and support, Jesuit fathers and some Franciscans carried the cross up the rivers and into the forests. Some successes, many disappointments, and a few failures attended their efforts.

To insure Indian acquiescence in his designs for colonization and development of the fur trade, Champlain early cultivated an alliance with the tribes that formed an unwilling buffer between French Canada and

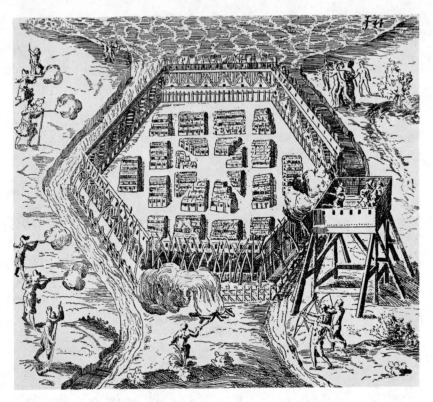

The palisaded Onondaga (Iroquois) fort, in present New York, attacked in 1615 by Samuel de Champlain and his Huron allies. From Champlain's own sketch, published in 1619. Courtesy, Smithsonian Institution.

the powerful Iroquois. In 1609, he had been persuaded by his Huron Indian friends to join them in an attack on the Iroquois near Lake Champlain—and again, in 1615, on the Oneida village south of Oneida Lake. Thus the French incurred the undying hatred of the five-nation Iroquois Confederacy, of which the Oneida were members, and this had repercussions for nearly a century. When the Iroquois finally overcame the Hurons, bands of the Confederacy—armed by Dutch traders in the Hudson Valley—spread out across southern Canada threatening to leave no Frenchman alive. In the Iroquois War (1642–53), the Indians twice nearly captured the newly founded Montreal and killed hundreds of Frenchmen, including several priests.

Indian attacks were not the only problems for the French. Several times Champlain was forced to return to France to obtain additional backing. In 1627, Cardinal Richelieu organized the Company of One Hundred Associates and took over the control of New France. When dissension rent this group, affairs in New France suffered from poor administration, as well as from Indian attacks. Following Champlain's death, in 1635, New France declined for more than two decades. In 1663, however, King Louis XIV took control away from the quibbling Associates and reorga-

Pierre Radisson and Sieur de Grosseilliers, fur traders and explorers, with Indian guides. They were among the first white men to explore and trade in the Lake Superior region. From a painting by Frederic Remington, published in 1906.

nized it under the jurisdiction of a civil administrator.

The year before Champlain's death, his lieutenant, Jean Nicolet, had traversed Lake Huron and the northern tip of Lake Michigan, and initiated trading compacts with the Indians in the Wisconsin area. In 1654 and 1655, the Sieur de Grosseilliers and his brother-in-law Pierre Radisson traced his route and established a lucrative trading post on the Wisconsin shore of Lake Michigan. Subsequently they explored Lake Superior, and in 1661 founded a post called Fort Radisson on its western shore.

"The Building of the *Griffon*." Built above Niagara Falls in 1679 by La Salle, the vessel was lost a few months later while returning, loaded with furs, from Green Bay. From an engraving in a book by Père Louis Hennepin, published late in the 17th century. Courtesy, Chicago Historical Society.

QUASHING THE INDIAN THREAT

The demise of the Associates and the arrival in New France of such powerful leaders as Jean Talon, Count Frontenac, and René Robert Cavelier, Sieur de la Salle, stimulated expansion. Under Talon, a French army of more than 1,000 troops arrived in Canada; in 1666, it defeated the aggressive Iroquois and their allies and achieved relative peace for two decades. The same year, to prevent future Indian depredations, as well as to check the incursions of English trappers, the French built Fort La Motte at the upper end of Lake Champlain; 1 year earlier, Fort Chambly had been constructed on the Richelieu River, north of the lake. Their position strengthened, Frenchmen plunged again into the forests and soon pushed the frontiers of New France all the way to the Gulf of Mexico.

TO THE MISSISSIPPI

Père Claude Jean Allouez explored Lake Superior from 1665 to 1667. At his little mission station near the western end of the lake, he heard from the Indians of a great river to the west. Père Jacques Marquette determined to investigate. In 1673, accompanied by Louis Jolliet and five others, he left St. Ignace Mission and ascended the Fox River, which flows into Green Bay, crossed over to the Wisconsin River, and followed it to the upper Mississippi. The party then descended the Mississippi to the mouth of the Arkansas. These Frenchmen were not the first Europeans to sight or travel the Mississippi; De Soto and Moscoso had done so a century and a half before.

The report of the exploration was rushed back to Quebec, where, in 1672, Count Frontenac had arrived as Governor of the province. He and his friend, the remarkable La Salle—who earlier may have penetrated the Ohio River Valley—listened with deep interest. Prior to that time, the two men had been involved in projects to open the western lake country to French trade.

PROBING THE ILLINOIS COUNTRY

In 1673, La Salle established Fort Frontenac on Lake Ontario to defend against the intrusion of English traders from the east. On two trips back to France, he obtained a title of *seignior* in the new Canadian nobility, a right to trade in furs, and authorization to erect additional posts and seek a water passage to the Gulf of Mexico. In 1678, he and his lieutenant, Henry de Tonty, and a party of Franciscans arrived at Niagara Falls. There, in 1679, above the falls they built a blockhouse fort, Fort Niagara, to guard Lake Ontario and the approaches to the west, and constructed a special boat to transport them through the Great Lakes.

Overcoming one obstacle after another, La Salle led his party to the site of Green Bay to trade, from where he sent the boat, loaded with furs, back to Fort Niagara for supplies. He then traveled by canoe down Lake Michigan and around its southern tip to the mouth of the St. Joseph River, where he built the semipermanent Fort Miami. After waiting in vain about 3 months for the supply boat to arrive, he ascended the St. Joseph to the site of South Bend, crossed to the Kankakee River, and descended it to the Illinois, which he followed to Lake Peoria. In 1680, at this lake he built Fort Crèvecoeur. After sending Michel Accou and Père Louis Hennepin to explore the upper Mississippi, he set out to return to his base at Fort Frontenac for supplies, and left Henry de Tonty in charge of Fort Crèvecoeur. Subsequently, by messenger La Salle directed Tonty to move to Starved Rock.

Disaster struck. The Sioux captured Accou and Hennepin, who had

René Robert Cavelier, Sieur de la Salle, envisioned a French empire in North America. He did much to achieve his dream by exploring and founding posts in the vast Illinois country. From an 1882 conjectural painting by G. P. A. Healy. Courtesy, Chicago Historical Society.

followed the Illinois and Mississippi up to the Wisconsin. The Frenchmen stationed at Fort Crèvecoeur pillaged and deserted it. Iroquois and Illinois hostilities in the Starved Rock area forced Tonty to withdraw to Green Bay, from where he moved to Mackinac. La Salle himself was met at Montreal by creditors, political enemies, and the news that the boatful of furs he had dispatched from Green Bay the previous year had never been heard from. Again his indomitable will prevailed. He obtained renewed backing, and in the summer of 1680 set out once more for the Illinois country, where he found that Fort Crèvecoeur had been destroyed and that Tonty had left Starved Rock. After spending the winter at Fort Miami, he returned to Mackinac and rejoined Tonty.

DESCENT OF THE MISSISSIPPI

Meanwhile, Accou and Hennepin, after wandering about Minnesota and falling captive to Indians, were rescued by another explorer, Daniel Greysolon, Sieur Dulhut (Duluth), Tonty's cousin. Dulhut traversed both the Fox-Wisconsin and St. Croix portages and renewed the fur trade with the Indians west of Lake Superior. Hennepin later made the absurd claim that he had traveled to the mouth of the Mississippi. This feat was accomplished by La Salle and Tonty and recorded by Père

Zenobius Membré, who accompanied them. The party entered the Mississippi from the Illinois River in February 1682. In April they reached the
mouth of the Mississippi, where La Salle ceremoniously planted the
French flag and claimed the entire drainage system for Louis XIV.

"Daniel Greysolon, Sieur Dulhut (Duluth), at the Head of the Lakes, in
1679." Dulhut, a fur trader, explored the lands west of Lake Superior.
From a painting by F. L. Jaques. Courtesy, Minnesota Historical Society.

LA SALLE'S TEXAS VENTURE

La Salle returned to France to report his magnificent addition to the
empire and to answer those who attempted to discredit him. In 1682–83,
Tonty constructed Fort St. Louis at Starved Rock and reoccupied Fort

Indians plundering Père Hennepin's party, in 1681. From an engraving in a book by Hennepin, published in 1704. Courtesy, Library of Congress.

Miami. With renewed support from the Crown and intending to establish a colony at the mouth of the Mississippi, La Salle gathered an expedition of 4 ships and nearly 400 colonists. He sailed from France in July 1684, little realizing the disaster that lay ahead. He fell sick and almost died; the Spaniards captured one of his ships; he quarreled with his principal mariner, Captain Beaujeau; and his men almost mutinied. The three ships passed the mouth of the Mississippi, and early in 1685 sailed into Matagorda Bay, on the Texas coast. One ship foundered in the bay and was lost. Then Beaujeau treacherously sailed away in another ship, loaded with men and supplies. The remaining ship landed near the mouth of the Lavaca River, and the colonists hastily erected Fort St. Louis. A month later, they moved to a new location 5 miles away. Meanwhile, the debilitated La Salle undertook to lead overland reconnaissances to locate the Mississippi. Strangely enough, he apparently traveled westward. Was the great explorer lost? Or was he, in reality, more interested in locating Spanish mines for some secret purpose of his sovereign?

In any event, circumstances soon forced La Salle to abandon his reconnaissances. Supplies at Fort St. Louis dwindled, and he lost his last ship in eastern Matagorda Bay. Unerringly now, he set out northeast— toward the Mississippi—to return to the Illinois country for provisions.

The strength of the post had been reduced to less than 100; La Salle took 17 men with him and left the remainder behind. On this, his last trek, mutineers assassinated him, in 1687, somewhere in east Texas. They

La Salle lands in Matagorda Bay, Texas, 1685. From an engraving in a book by Père Louis Hennepin, published in 1704. Courtesy, Library of Congress.

stripped his body and left it to the wolves, divided the meager spoils, and forced the innocent members of the party to accompany them. But soon the murderers quarreled among themselves, and La Salle's friends, including Henry Joutel, escaped.

All the mutineers except the enigmatic Jean l'Archeveque, who turned up in Santa Fe years later, were lost or killed by the Indians. Ascending the Mississippi, Joutel and his party met at the mouth of the Arkansas none other than Henry de Tonty, who had floated down from Starved

Rock with a party looking for La Salle. Leaving some of his men to establish what came to be known as Arkansas Post, Tonty returned to Canada with Joutel. Arkansas Post was of intermittent value to France in the years that followed.

Back at Fort St. Louis, in Texas, after months of waiting for La Salle's return, the starving remnant of his colony despaired. Some died; the rest deserted the fort and went to live with the Indians. Fear of French encroachment in Texas stimulated Spanish efforts there. In 1689, the Spanish expedition of Capt. Alonso de León burned the French fort to the ground. La Salle was dead and his most ambitious venture a failure. But scores of intrepid trappers, traders, and missionaries followed him into the heartland of North America.

Extension of french influence

In the mid-17th century, the French possessions lay on a chain of waterways extending from the great river system of the St. Lawrence, through the Great Lakes, and down the Mississippi Valley to the Gulf of Mexico. French claims to this vast region were announced by explorations such as La Salle's; and they were affirmed by the establishment of forts and small settlements, the extension of the fur trade and missionary efforts, and the spread of influence over the Indians. After 1670, condi-

"Shooting the Rapids." Voyageurs used the Montreal canoe, illustrated here, which was larger than the North canoe, on the Great Lakes. From a painting by Mrs. Edward Hopkins. Courtesy, Public Archives of Canada.

tions were especially favorable for the development of the frontier. The French had quelled the Iroquois in 1666. To check further Indian depredations and the incursions of English trappers, they then founded a series of forts.

Jesuits and trappers spread out into the western country. In 1668, at a well known and strategic location on the straits between Lake Superior and Lake Huron, Père Marquette had established a mission to the Chippewas. There, in 1671, the French held a grand council with the Indians of the region, and over the years a village called Sault Ste. Marie arose. An equally strategic point was the Mackinac Straits, a few miles to the south of Sault Ste. Marie, between Lakes Michigan and Huron. In 1670–71, missionaries founded St. Ignace Mission on Mackinac Island, and 2 years later relocated it at the tip of the peninsula on the north side of the straits, where soldiers built a small fort to protect the missionaries. Later, during the period 1715–20, the French erected Fort Michilimackinac on the southern shores of the straits. The straits area and Sault Ste. Marie were centers of missionary, as well as fur-trading, activity. From these and other bases, French missionaries penetrated the hinterland and carried the word of God to the Sioux, Chippewas, Illinois, Fox, and other tribes. The missionaries established small outlying stations, impermanently occupied for visitations.

Meanwhile, the fur trade expanded into the western country. Along the upper Mississippi, traders founded a number of posts, some of them temporary. Among the most prominent were Fort St. Croix (1680), near the portage to western Lake Superior; La Baye (1684), at the southern tip of Green Bay; Fort St. Antoine (1685), on the Mississippi between the St. Croix and Wisconsin Rivers; and Fort St. Nicolas (ca. 1685), at the mouth of the Wisconsin River, around which arose the settlement of Prairie du Chien. Troops occasionally occupied these posts, but they were primarily used as bases by the *coureurs de bois*—dare-devil Frenchmen who took to the forest to trade with the Indians.

The passage between Lakes Huron and Erie was the last of the connecting links in the chain of the Great Lakes that the French fortified. In 1686, they erected a small post, Fort St. Joseph, north of Lake St. Clair near the entrance to Lake Huron. Then, in 1701, Antoine de la Mothe Cadillac built Fort Pontchartrain at the southern entrance to Lake St. Clair. This fort proved to be the most important and durable of those along the Great Lakes, and around it grew up the village of Detroit. The two forts protected the water route through Lakes Ontario and Erie.

"The Buffalo." From an engraving in a book by Père Louis Hennepin, published late in the 17th century. Courtesy, Chicago Historical Society.

Previously, most of the traffic from Montreal had passed up the Ottawa River, over the portage at Nipissing, into Georgian Bay, on the northeast of Lake Huron, and then through Lake Huron to Sault Ste. Marie and Lake Superior or to the Mackinac Straits and Lake Michigan.

The growing popularity of the route through Lake Erie resulted in the opening of the Wabash portage late in the 17th century to facilitate travel to the Illinois country. To protect the route, about 1704 the French founded Fort Miami at the western end of the Maumee River; in 1719, Fort Ouiatenon, on the Wabash; and, in 1735, Fort Vincennes, also on the Wabash. Besides the Wabash River route, two other earlier portage routes, which had been used by La Salle, led into the Illinois country from southern Lake Michigan. One of these was by way of the St. Joseph River, which flows into eastern Lake Michigan, to the Kankakee River, in present Indiana; the other was via the Chicago portage to the Des Plaines and Illinois Rivers. Forts Miami, St. Joseph, and St. Louis protected these two routes.

From construction in 1683 to abandonment in 1691, Fort St. Louis was an important center of French influence in the Illinois country. Subsequent posts in the region were Cahokia, near present East St. Louis, founded in 1698; at Kaskaskia, a few miles down the Mississippi, in 1703; and at St. Denis, just above the Mississippi-Ohio juncture, in 1702. These villages, conveniently situated in a fertile area between the Great Lakes and the Mississippi Delta, were a source of agricultural produce for other settlements.

DEVELOPMENT OF LOUISIANA

Not long after La Salle's initial penetration of the lower Mississippi region in 1682 and his aborted Texas venture in 1685, the French took steps to found permanent settlements along the lower Mississippi. In 1698, the Le Moyne brothers, the Sieur d'Iberville and the Sieur de Bienville, sons of a prominent Quebec official, obtained a patent from Louis XIV to colonize the mouth of the Mississippi. Early the next year, the expedition of 4 vessels and about 200 colonists and soldiers temporarily landed at Dauphin Island, in Mobile Bay. It then moved westward in the gulf to Ship Island, just offshore from present Biloxi, Miss. Leaving the fleet and colonists at the island, Bienville and Iberville explored the lower Mississippi in small boats. Though they separated at one time,

A dance of the Natchez Indians. From an on-the-scene drawing by Antoine du Pratz, published in 1758. Courtesy, Smithsonian Institution.

they finally reunited at the island. After Iberville sailed away to Canada, the colonists and soldiers settled on the mainland at Old Biloxi, near present Ocean Springs, and constructed Fort Maurepas. Bienville continued his exploration of the region. When Iberville returned, the brothers built Fort de la Boulaye about 40 miles below the site of New Orleans and garrisoned it between 1700 and 1707.

Because of adverse conditions at Fort Maurepas, including disease, a shortage of food, and poor morale, Iberville decided to relocate most of the colonists on the Mobile River, about 30 miles above its entrance into Mobile Bay. There he built Fort Louis de la Mobile, and set up a post on Dauphin Island as port of entry to the colony. In 1710–11, after Iberville's death, Bienville moved the colony to the site of Mobile, and built a new Fort Louis, renamed Fort Condé in 1720. The Mobile settlement, despite the protests of the Spanish commander at nearby Pensacola, grew steadily and soon numbered more than 1,000. Other settlers founded New Biloxi, which became the seat of government for Louisiana, and some soon moved up the rivers and streams into present Alabama, Arkansas, Mississippi, Tennessee, and beyond. As early as 1700, Pierre Charles le Sueur had led an expedition of 20 men northward against the treacherous current of the Mississippi as far as the Minnesota River, where he set up a temporary base called Fort L'Huillier. Iberville had visited Arkansas Post, and Bienville had explored along the lower Red River.

In 1712, Louis XIV, anxious to develop Louisiana but having an empty treasury, turned to a commercial venture. He granted Sieur Antoine Crozat a trading monopoly and other rights in the province, whose boundaries were set to take in the settlements in the Illinois country, including St. Denis, Kaskaskia, Cahokia, and Starved Rock, but not those in the Wisconsin region. Crozat sent Antoine de la Mothe Cadillac to replace Bienville as Governor. Cadillac immediately invoked the enmity of the settlers by imposing a series of severe restrictions on them, paying trappers low prices for skins, and charging exorbitant prices for supplies. He also failed to maintain the good relations with the Indians that Bienville had inaugurated. In 1715, stirred by rumors of mineral wealth in Missouri, Cadillac investigated the area but found nothing. When he returned, he found that the Indians had risen against the settlers. In 1717, the disillusioned Crozat recalled him to France.

That same year, Crozat turned his patent over to one of the most amazing promotional enterprises in Western European history—the Company of the West, a stock concern headed by John Law, a glamorous

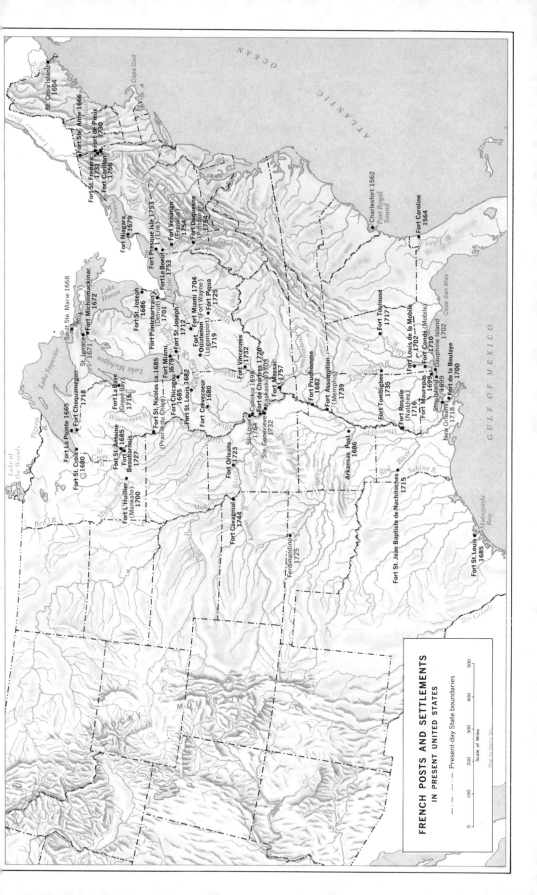

FRENCH POSTS AND SETTLEMENTS
IN PRESENT UNITED STATES

— · — · — Present-day State boundaries

0   100   200   300   400   500
Scale of Miles

Map by Harry Sco...

St. Croix Island 1604
Fort Ste. Anne 1666
Fort de Pieux 1730
Fort St. Frederic 1731
Fort Carillon 1756
Fort Niagara 1679
Fort Presque Isle 1753 (Erie)
Fort Venango (Franklin) 1754
Fort Duquesne (Pittsburgh) 1754
Fort Le Boeuf 1753
Charlesfort 1562
Fort Caroline 1564
Sault Ste. Marie 1668
St. Ignace 1671
Fort Michilimackinac 1672
Fort St. Joseph 1686
Fort Pontchartrain (Detroit) 1701
Fort St. Joseph 1712
Fort Miami 1685
Fort Miami 1704 (Fort Wayne)
Ouiatenon (Logansport) 1719
Fort Piqua 1725
Fort Toulouse 1717
Fort Louis de la Mobile
Fort Conde (Mobile) 1710
Dauphine Island 1702
Fort de la Boulaye 1700
Fort La Pointe 1665
Fort Chequamegon 1718
Fort La Baye (Green Bay) 1716
Fort St. Nicolas ca. 1685 (Prairie du Chien)
Fort Chicagou 1685
Fort St. Louis 1682
Fort Crèvecoeur 1680
Fort Vincennes 1732
Fort de Chartres 1720
Cahokia 1699
Kaskaskia 1703
Fort Massac 1757
Fort Prudhomme 1682
Fort Assumption (Memphis) 1739
Fort Tombigbee 1735
Fort Rosalie (Natchez) 1716
Fort Maurepas 1699
Ship Island 1716
New Orleans 1718
Fort St. Croix 1680
Fort St. Antoine 1685
Fort Beauharnois 1727
Fort L'Huillier (Mankato) 1700
St. Louis 1764
Ste. Genevieve 1732
Arkansas Post 1686
Fort Orleans 1723
Fort Cavagnial 1744
Ferdinandino 1725
Fort St. Jean Baptiste de Nachitoches 1715
Fort St. Louis 1685

ATLANTIC OCEAN
GULF OF MEXICO
Cape Cod
Port Royal Sound
Cape San Blas
Matagorda Bay
Rio Grande
ROCKY MOUNTAINS
Lake Superior
Lake Michigan
Lake Huron
L. Ontario
L. Erie
Lake of the Woods
Pigeon R.
Red R.
St. Laurent River
Wisconsin R.
Mississippi R.
Missouri R.
Des Moines R.
Kansas R.
Osage R.
Arkansas R.
Red River
Sabine R.
Ohio R.
Wabash R.
Cumberland R.
Tennessee R.
Tombigbee R.
Alabama R.
Coosa R.
St. Johns R.
St. Croix R.
Minnesota R.

Scotsman. After failing in his attempt to found a Government-sponsored national bank in his mother country, in 1716 Law had persuaded the French Crown to endorse his scheme to exploit the resources of Louisiana. The following year he formed his company, which absorbed Crozat's patent. Then, in 1718, as the speculative shares in Law's ventures soared in price, the Crown agreed to back his banknotes. Shortly thereafter, the King authorized one of Law's companies, in return for a guarantee to pay a specified portion of the national debt, to manage the mint, issue coinage, and collect all national taxes.

Based largely on rumors of wealth in the lower Mississippi region, speculation in Law's stock reached proportions unparalleled in Europe at the time. Law proposed, among other things, to settle 6,000 whites and

The Natchez Indians hunt buffalo. From an on-the-scene drawing by Antoine du Pratz, published in 1758. Courtesy, Smithsonian Institution.

3,000 Negro slaves in Louisiana. He actually settled 700 German colonists near Arkansas Post. In 1720, the "Mississippi Bubble" burst, the complex structure of Law's corporate system collapsed, and the colony near Arkansas Post was abandoned, the settlers moving to a site near New Orleans. Thousands of people who invested in Law's scheme lost money, but Louisiana enjoyed a sudden spurt of growth and publicity.

Under the impetus first of Crozat's company and then of the boom generated by John Law, the French expanded all their frontiers in Louisiana. In 1714, Bienville occupied a site just north of present Montgomery, Ala., which he fortified in 1717 and named Fort Toulouse. Only intermittently garrisoned, it served as a spearhead for French efforts to gain Indian allies in the imperial contest with the English and Spanish, as well as a defensive outpost for the protection of the settlements at Mobile Bay. In 1716, Bienville established a fort and trading post at the Natchez Indian village up the Mississippi from the site of New Orleans. Named Fort Rosalie, the post became the center of a significant settlement and was a key French post between 1716 and 1763. It was of such strategic value that over the course of time it quartered Spanish, British, and United States troops. The village on its flank became the city of Natchez, Miss.

While Bienville was thus engaged with Forts Toulouse and Rosalie, one of his young proteges, Louis Juchereau de St. Denis, had contacted the Spanish on the Rio Grande and persuaded them to reopen their mission field in east Texas. In 1717, St. Denis built a trading post at Natchitoches on the Red River in Louisiana. From this key post, the French not only smuggled goods for several decades into the Spanish Empire, but they also controlled the "northern tribes," which lived in the region of the Red and Canadian Rivers, especially the important Taovayas. In a few years, St. Denis' post grew into a prosperous village.

In 1718, Bienville at last set out to found a city on the site he had chosen almost two decades earlier. He laid out New Orleans and 4 years later moved there the seat of government for Louisiana from New Biloxi. Almost overnight, New Orleans began to rival Quebec and Montreal as the metropolis of New France. Despite a flood in 1719, it grew rapidly. In 1722, the King gave the Capuchins ecclesiastical jurisdiction over Louisiana, and 5 years later the Jesuits and the Ursuline Sisters arrived in strength. To promote the growth of New Orleans, Bienville imported from France a shipload of marriageable girls, who were chaperoned by the nuns until satisfactory mates could be found. The voyageurs and *coureurs de bois* flocked down the river to vie for their hands. Bienville also settled a small group of Germans in one section of the town, and welcomed immigrants from all nations. Into New

"The French Voyageur." From a painting by Mrs. Samuel B. Abbe. Courtesy, Minnesota Historical Society.

Orleans began to flow virtually all the commerce of the Mississippi Valley, from the Illinois country and even farther north. By 1762—when France transferred western Louisiana, including New Orleans, to Spain—the city was one of the six largest in North America.

In 1720, the French had erected Fort de Chartres, a temporary base, in the Illinois country. The fort and the nearby village of Prairie du Rocher bloomed for a brief time. The settlement, however, was never as important as its neighbors, Kaskaskia, where the Jesuits established an academy, and Cahokia, where the Sulpicians maintained an Indian school. Across the Mississippi from Kaskaskia a fourth settlement—Ste. Genevieve—joined the little cluster of Illinois villages. Originally a fur depot, by 1740 it had developed into a town. Because of its location on the west bank of the river and its ready availability to the trappers and

"French Habitation in the Country of the Illinois." From an engraving by an unknown artist, published in 1826. Courtesy, Chicago Historical Society.

traders who were penetrating deeply into the Missouri country, it soon equaled if not surpassed the other Illinois towns. Another factor promoting growth was the opening of small lead mines in the Missouri Ozarks, which also utilized it as a port.

In 1731, the 20-year monopoly granted to Crozat—transferred to Law, and thereafter owned by the bankrupt Company of the Indies—was abandoned, 1 year before it expired. Louisiana once again became a royal province. Despite the confusion of the era of commercial control, it had brought expansion and prosperity. It had also linked the Illinois country to Louisiana—a natural occurrence because of the Mississippi River connection—and fostered the growth of both areas. Because of Indian trouble and natural hazards, the northern portage route from the Illinois country to the Great Lakes was almost abandoned in favor of the river route south. Thus, most of the French communities lost their connections with the northern settlements and became identified with New Orleans and Louisiana. And it was largely from the Louisiana settlements that the great fur trade of the trans-Mississippi West developed.

THE WESTERN FUR TRADE

St. Denis' post at Natchitoches was one of the first centers of the western fur trade. From there, in 1719, Bernard de la Harpe explored the Red River and crossed the prairies to the Arkansas River just above its junction with the Canadian River. Three years later he returned to the same region and made commercial alliances with the Plains Indians that resulted in a thriving trade in buffalo robes. Thereafter, French traders followed both the Red and the Arkansas into the Plains country with increasing frequency.

Meantime, the traders Étienne Veniard de Bourgmond, during the period 1712–17, and Claude Charles du Tisné, in 1719, explored the Missouri country and traded with the Pawnee, Osage, and Arapaho tribes. In 1723, Bourgmond erected and garrisoned Fort Orleans, on the Missouri River, in present Carroll County, Mo., to exploit the trade of the region and serve as a French outpost. He maintained the fort until 1728, when he abandoned it. In 1724, illness forced him to turn back from an attempt to reach Santa Fe. Bourgmond and Du Tisné probably probed westward individually as far as the North Platte River.

It was from one of the posts in the Illinois country that a remarkable French exploration departed. In 1739, Pierre and Paul Mallet led a small trading expedition across the prairies and plains into Spanish

New Mexico. They probably followed the general route of the Santa Fe Trail of a century later, and entered Taos by way of Raton Pass. Their arrival at Santa Fe caused consternation among the Spanish officials. Already rumors of French activities had reached the Spanish through the Apache Indians; now there could be no question. Because the two nations were not at war, however, in 1740 the officials allowed the Mallets to return peaceably to New Orleans.

The aged Bienville—still the leading spirit in Louisiana—was delighted with the exploits of the Mallet brothers. Trade with the Spanish, even though illegal, was far more promising than trade with the Indians. New Mexico was an inviting prospect for French commerce. In subsequent years, Frenchmen trickled across the plains and over the mountains by various routes into New Mexico. Forbidden entry by royal decree, they nevertheless slipped surreptitiously into Taos until about 1762, when Spain assumed control of western Louisiana.

Among the last of the great French explorations were those of the Vérendryes. Though they had little bearing on the history or settlement of our Nation and the routes are disputed among historians, they have

"The Brothers La Vérendrye in Sight of the Western Mountains, New Year's Day, 1743." From a drawing by C. W. Jefferys. Courtesy, Imperial Oil Collection.

provoked the imaginations of men for more than two centuries. Pierre Gaultier de Varennes, Sieur de la Vérendrye, was commander of Fort Nipigon, on the northern shore of Lake Superior, when he obtained a monopoly of the northwestern fur trade to finance his search for the Northwest Passage. The French authorities were alarmed not only by the activities of the English Hudson's Bay Company in Canada, but also by those of the Spanish to the south. La Vérendrye established a line of posts in present Canada and Minnesota, notably Fort St. Charles on Lake of the Woods in the Northwest Angle of Minnesota, and Fort La Reine on the Assiniboine River in Manitoba.

Using Fort La Reine as a base of operations, in 1738–39 La Vérendrye and two of his sons, Louis-Joseph and Francois, penetrated the upper Missouri at a point probably near the site of Bismarck, N. Dak., where they wintered with the Mandan Indians and then returned to Fort La Reine. In 1742, the two sons and two companions traveled to the Bismarck vicinity, then set out in a southwesterly direction. On New Year's Day 1743, they sighted what were probably the Black Hills. Turning eastward, they trekked to the Missouri River, where they apparently buried a lead plate, found in 1913 near Fort Pierre, S. Dak. From this point, they likely ascended the Missouri to Apple Creek and crossed overland on their return trip to Fort La Reine.

Twilight of empire

French energies in North America were soon diverted from exploration and settlement to defense against the expanding English. As early as 1613, England had reacted to the French threat in North America by sending an expedition from Virginia under Capt. Samuel Argall to wipe out the feeble French colony at Port Royal, which had been reestablished in 1610 following the failure and abandonment of the first colony there 2 years earlier. In 1629, the English occupied Quebec itself for a short time.

When the French quelled the Iroquois in 1666, they may have had a moment of opportunity to dominate the English by moving into the Hudson Valley and New England. But they vacillated too long. England seized the initiative by capturing the Dutch settlements on the Hudson River and taking over the Iroquois fur trade, which the Dutch had found so profitable.

Three European wars between England and France were reflected in

Fort Beauharnois, a French post and site of a Jesuit mission, erected in 1727 on the west bank of the Mississippi River, in present Minnesota. From a charcoal drawing by Fletcher Sultzer. Courtesy, Goodhue County Historical Society, Minnesota.

minor struggles between their colonies: King William's War (1689–97); Queen Anne's War (1702–13); and King George's War (1745–48). Because in all of these wars French colonists suffered losses to their British counterparts, in the period of peace after 1748 France determined to so strengthen her hold on the Mississippi Valley that England could not shake it. In 1749, she dispatched Celoron de Blainville from Montreal into the Ohio Valley, occupied by Indians and English traders, to affirm French claims to the region. The principal result of his trip was increased hostility on the part of the pro-English Indians.

In the period 1750 to 1755, the French augmented the fortifications at old Fort Niagara as well as those at Fort St. Frederic, which in 1731 had been built on Lake Champlain. Also, in 1753, they rebuilt Fort de Chartres. New posts included Fort St. John (1748), on the Richelieu River north of Lake Champlain; Fort de la Presentation (1749), northeast of Lake Ontario; Fort Rouille (1749), on the western shore of Lake Ontario; Fort Presque Isle (1753), east of Lake Erie in present western Pennsylvania; Fort Le Boeuf (1753), also in western Pennsylvania; and, of primary importance, Fort Duquesne (1754), at the Forks of the Ohio.

Thus by the mid-18th century the final conflict, long deferred by the unwillingness of either side to make an all-out effort, was at hand. Englishmen were spilling over the Appalachians into the Ohio Valley, erecting trading posts and blazing trails into the heartland claimed by France.

It was the construction of Forts Le Boeuf and Duquesne that provoked the French and Indian War and brought disaster to the French in North America. Shortly after they built Le Boeuf, a small contingent of troops from its garrison seized and occupied Venango, an English trading post. Maj. George Washington, only 21 years of age, was dispatched from Virginia in the winter of 1753–54 to protest the action. His remonstrations were in vain, both at Venango and Le Boeuf, although he was courteously treated despite his youth.

To counter the rebuff, English officials in Virginia decided to drive the French out. In March 1754, Washington and 300 Virginia militia set out across the mountains to construct a defensive post at the strategically located Forks of the Ohio. A month earlier Capt. William Trent

Artist's rendition of the Battle of Monongahela, in 1755, one of the bloodiest in the French and Indian War and a major French victory. A group of Frenchmen and their Indian allies are shown here ambushing Gen. Edward Braddock's troops. From a wood engraving by John Andrew, after Billings, published in 1858. Courtesy, Library of Congress.

Louisbourg, on Cape Breton Island, Canada, in 1758, besieged by British Gen. James Wolfe. It was a major French base during the French and Indian War. From an engraving by P. Canot, after an on-the-scene drawing by Captain Ince of the 35th Regiment. Courtesy, Library of Congress.

and about 30 men had proceeded to the site. Unknown to Washington, they had been captured by an overwhelming force of French and Indian allies, who constructed Fort Duquesne as their own defensive outpost against the English. While Washington advanced steadily but slowly through the mountains, French scouts carefully watched his progress. On May 28, the first skirmish occurred.

Learning from prisoners of the strong force ensconced at Fort Duquesne, Washington attempted to provide a defense for his troops from the certain French attack. At Great Meadows he and his men hastily threw up a log palisade they called "Fort Necessity." On July 3, 1754, more than 600 French and Indians, skilled at forest combat and attacking from natural forest cover, invested the little fort. After 9 hours of heavy fighting, Washington surrendered, but he was allowed to march from the post with the "honors of war," on a date that was to prove portentous—July 4.

The martial conflagration thus ignited soon spread to most of the nations of Europe and about 100 colonial posts around the globe. The next year, the French troops successfully defended Fort Niagara and routed the proud British force under Gen. Edward Braddock that attempted to conquer Fort Duquesne. In 1756, the war, so far confined to the New World, broadened to Europe. The following year, when the British were still off balance, the French brought in fresh European troops and captured post after post along the English frontier. But in 1758 the tide of fortune turned. When Quebec fell to the British in September 1759,

"A View of the Taking of Quebeck by the English Forces Commanded by Gen. Wolfe," in 1759. Soon after Quebec capitulated, the French and Indian War ended and Canada came under British rule. From an engraving by an unknown artist, published in 1760. Courtesy, Library of Congress.

the war in America was over to all intents and purposes—even though hositilities continued for another year. In the spring of 1760, the French besieged Quebec; and, late in the summer, the British surrounded Montreal. Finally, in September, the Governor of Canada surrendered the whole of Canada to England.

As the defeat of France elsewhere in the world became assured, in 1762 she hastily consigned western Louisiana to her ally Spain by the secret Treaty of Fontainebleau. Then, in the Treaty of Paris the following year, she surrendered the rest of her North American possessions to Great Britain. Spain had to relinquish Florida in return for the restoration of her key posts of Havana and Manila, which had fallen to the British Navy. The French Empire in the New World was no more—although for a few weeks in 1803 France repossessed Louisiana from Spain, but almost immediately transferred it to the United States.

OUR FRENCH HERITAGE

Our heritage is richer because of the men of France who came to this continent and explored and settled the wilderness. The breadth of their achievements and the depth of the heritage they bequeathed to the United States transcends their small numbers. A substantial part of this heritage was mixed into the mainstream of America through 6,000 unhappy Acadians, who were expelled in 1755 from Acadia (Nova Scotia) by the British, its new rulers under the terms of the Treaty of Utrecht. The Acadians at first scattered throughout the British colonies, from Maine to Georgia, but most of them finally settled in Louisiana. Henry Wadsworth Longfellow's poem *Evangeline*, an epic about the Acadian odyssey, is the most widely known tribute to the French heritage in the United States.

Other persecuted Huguenots, also seeking refuge and religious freedom, contributed another equally important segment of our French heritage. They settled in clusters from Rhode Island to South Carolina, especially in Charleston, and enriched the cultural patterns evolving in the colonies. Therefore, much of the flavor of France in the United States today stems not from areas that once were French colonies but from French settlers in the British colonies.

In the final analysis, the city of New Orleans is the heart of French influence. The Illinois settlements quickly lost their French characteristics, but southern Louisiana clung to French customs and traditions. Today, more than a century and a half after the Louisiana Purchase, French is still spoken in New Orleans and many parts of Louisiana. Roman Catholicism remains the principal religion. Even the political subdivisions of the State are called parishes, not counties. Much of the

New Orleans, in 1803, viewed from the Plantation of Marigny. From a painting by Boqueto de Woieseri. Courtesy, Chicago Historical Society.

legal code is rooted in the Roman law of France rather than the common law of England, which prevails elsewhere in the United States. Proud Creoles have cherished their traditions, and through them a happy combination of graciousness and gaiety has filtrated into American life. Mardi Gras, first celebrated by Bienville's colonists in 1702, has been a regular part of Louisiana life ever since and has been enjoyed by many Americans.

French place names, scattered from the Rockies to the Alleghenies, are a constant reminder of the golden era of the voyageurs and *coureurs de bois,* whose songs are still sung. Evidences of French colonial architecture still remain in Louisiana and other places in the Mississippi Valley.

The Dutch and the Swedes: Patroons and Plowmen

Another European nation, newly risen to power, was not to be denied a share of the New World wealth. Holland, or the Netherlands, was almost as quick as Britain and France to seize the opportunities in North America. Dutchmen as well as Englishmen, however, clashed before long with the newly arrived Swedes, whom they felt were encroaching on their territory. New Netherland soon conquered New Sweden, only to fall itself to Britain, whose settlers surrounded it on all sides. Though the Dutch and Swedish phases of colonial history were short-lived—from about 1614 until 1664—the settlers of the two nations contributed substantially to our national heritage.

DUTCH EXPLORATION

The various provinces that comprised the Netherlands passed from the estates of the Dukes of Burgundy to the Hapsburg family in the late Middle Ages. Philip II, Hapsburg heir in the mid-16th century to most of Europe as well as Spain, ruled the Low Countries through a despotic overlord who precipitated a revolt that culminated in 1581 in the independence of Holland. The meteoric rise of the little Dutch Republic to a powerful position among the nations of Europe is one of the most dramatic in history—as well as a tribute to its form of government.

The enterprising burghers of Amsterdam soon began to seek a share in the trade of both the East Indies and the New World. In 1602, the States General (the parliament) chartered the Dutch East India Company and boldly authorized it to capture what it could of the Eastern trade from

Henry Hudson meeting with the Indians along the Hudson River. An Englishman, he probed the North American Continent for the Dutch East India Company. After exploring the coast from Newfoundland to Virginia, he sailed into New York Harbor and up the Hudson River to the site of Albany. From a painting by J. L. G. Ferris. Courtesy, William E. Ryder and the Smithsonian Institution.

other nations.   In 1609, the company employed Henry Hudson, an English navigator who twice had unsuccessfully sought the Northwest Passage in northern waters for the Muscovy Company, to probe the North American Continent.   On the *Half Moon,* he struck the coast of Newfoundland, turned south as far as Virginia, and then returned up the coast to Delaware Bay. He continued northward and entered New York Harbor. When he first sighted the "Great River of the Mountains," or the "Great North River," later named for him, he excited hope among the crew that the passage to the East had been found. The *Half Moon* moved upstream for 11 days, to the site of Albany, before Hudson, observing the narrow channel and shallow water, decided that he had not found the passage to the East and returned to Holland. The next year, no longer employed by the Dutch, but sponsored by a group of English adventurers, he still pursued the passage. But his crew mutinied and set him adrift to perish on the cold waters of the great northern bay that now bears his name.

ESTABLISHMENT OF NEW NETHERLAND

Although the Dutch East India Company was disappointed that Hudson had not found a passage to the East, other Dutchmen grasped the opportunities presented by the discovery of the Hudson River. The Dutch Republic now had a New World claim. The year after Hudson's voyage, in 1610, Dutch traders began flocking to the Hudson Valley. They did not come to stay, but to trade with the Indians, who usually welcomed them and exchanged furs for trinkets, kettles, knives, hatchets, and guns. In repeated visits between 1610 and 1613 the traders familiarized themselves with the Hudson Valley from its mouth to the juncture of the Mohawk River. A few then apparently pushed westward to the Delaware River.

In 1613, Adriaen Block discovered Hell Gate, explored Long Island Sound and the Connecticut River, gave his name to Block Island, rounded Cape Cod, and traveled along the Massachusetts coast past the site of Boston. The same year, Cornelius May circled the southern shore of Long Island and explored Delaware Bay and the Delaware River as far as the mouth of the Schuylkill River. The next year, 1614, the merchants who had financed these explorations organized the New Netherland Company and obtained from the States General a monopoly on the fur trade in the region between the 40th and 45th parallels. Having determined that the heart of the fur trade was at the head of navigation on the Hudson, the company immediately erected Fort Nassau on Castle Island, just below the site of Albany. It never garrisoned the fort, however, which served simply as a trading post. Relations with the Iroquois bands who came to the post to trade were quite friendly. In 1614, a Dutchman erected a small trading post on the island at the mouth of the Hudson River that was inhabited by the Manhattan Indians. In 1617, a spring flood destroyed Fort Nassau.

In 1618, the States General did not renew the charter of the New Netherland Company. The last significant act of the company, that same year, was the cementing of friendship with the Iroquois by a formal treaty, which insured their continued hostility toward the French and provided a buffer for the Dutch colonists. In all likelihood, the friendship between the Dutch and Iroquois prevented the French from occupying the Mohawk and Hudson Valleys and confined them to the lake region to the west. For several years after the expiration of the New

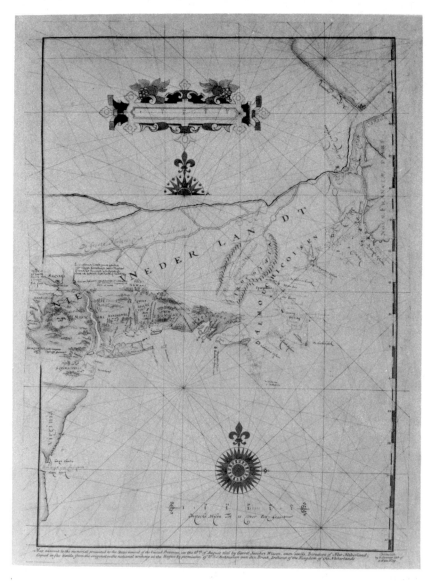

Adriaen Block's map of New Netherland, 1614. From a facsimile of the
original, in the national archives of the Netherlands. Courtesy, Museum of
the City of New York.

Netherland Company charter, the area was open to free traders, who
apparently took advantage of the opportunity.

The success of these independent traders alone did not provoke the
organization of the company that was to guide the future destinies of
New Netherland. The lucrative possibility of harrying the commerce

of Spain—a nation that all Dutchmen hated—was the basic reason for the charter issued by the States General in 1621 that authorized formation of the Dutch West India Company, a vast and wealthy corporation which was given a monopolistic control over New Netherland. The company's fleet consisted of more than 30 warships, 20 armed sloops, and a large fleet of merchant ships.

Although not at first intending to colonize, in the spring of 1624 the company sent out 30 families, mostly Protestant Walloons fleeing persecution in Belgium, under the leadership of Cornelius May. He located most of the settlers around Fort Orange, which was erected on the site of old Fort Nassau, and some on the Delaware River across from the mouth of the Schuylkill, where they built a new Fort Nassau. Still others he distributed around the post on Manhattan Island and on Staten Island. The handful of religious refugees was at first thinly scattered in the new land; not more than a few families were settled at any one location. When May returned to Holland in 1625, he left William Verhulst in charge.

The company organized the New Netherland government on the basis of the authority contained in its charter. It vested control in the board of directors in Holland, who represented the shareholders. The board chose a Director General to govern the colony. Given full executive and judicial authority, he was assisted by a local council that was also selected by the board of directors in Holland. At critical times, he called quasi-representative assemblies into being, but they were in no sense legislative bodies. The government was, therefore, virtually an autocracy under the Director General.

Peter Minuit was the first of these. He actually landed on Manhattan Island in May 1625, prior to his official appointment, bringing more settlers. His instructions from the company included this important injunction: "In case there should be any Indians living on the aforesaid island . . . or claiming any title to it . . . they must not be expelled with violence or threats but be persuaded with kind words . . . or should be given something . . . and a contract should be made . . . to be signed by them." For 60 guilders worth of trinkets—the traditional $24—Minuit concluded a bargain with the principal sachem of the Manhattans that permitted the Dutch to settle among them. Therewith, at the lower end of the island, in 1626, he established the village of Nieuw (New) Amsterdam, which consisted of a small fort and a cluster of homes. The company transferred the settlers at Fort Nassau and most of

New Amsterdam, in the 1650's. From a watercolor by an unknown artist, in the national archives of the Netherlands. Courtesy, Museum of the City of New York.

those from Fort Orange back to reinforce the new village, and shipped in a boatful of Negro slaves to meet the growing demand for labor.

In the colonization plan of 1624, the company created two classes of colonists: freemen, whose transportation and upkeep for 2 years the company financed, and who were eventually permitted to own homes and farms; and indentured servants, who worked on the company's farms. Colonists were not authorized to engage in the fur trade, which was reserved for licensed traders. The farms were called *bouweries*. Those owned and operated by the company were adjacent to Nieuw Amsterdam in lower Manhattan—the origin of today's "Bowery." But few Dutchmen came to live or work on the company *bouweries*, conditions at home being too peaceful and prosperous.

Most of the immigrants so far had been Walloon families. To induce further settlement, in 1629 the company devised a new scheme. In the "Charter of Privileges to Patroons," it authorized princely grants of land—16 miles along one bank or 8 miles along opposite banks of any navigable river—to "patroons," who would bear the costs of settling 50 adults on these manors within 4 years. The patroons were to enjoy the rights of feudal lords; the occupants of their land would be tenants-at-will, pay crop rents, and look to the patroon for the administration of justice.

The company directors rushed to avail themselves of this opportunity. Would-be patroons—most of whom stayed at home and managed affairs through an agent—shortly claimed some of the best lands in the Hudson Valley. One director held title to all of Staten Island, but most of the patroonships were located up the river. The most successful of these was Rensselaerswyck, near the site of Albany. Kiliaen Van Rensselaer, an Amsterdam pearl merchant, enlarged his grant by purchasing more land from the Indians, and acquired the greater part of two present counties.

Most of the patroonships were failures, primarily because of the restrictions on tenants. A short distance away, the English colonies had begun to thrive, and, as one Englishman wrote: "What man will be such a fool as to become a bare tenant . . . when for crossing Hudson's River that man can for a song purchase a good freehold." In 1640, the company modified the patroon system and 6 years later abandoned it entirely. By the end of the Dutch period, all but two of the patroonships had reverted to company ownership.

Perhaps the most significant failure among the patroonships was that of a company director named De Vries, near Cape Henlopen, at the entrance to Delaware Bay. He settled some 30 families in 1631 at the site of Lewes, Del., under the leadership of Capt. Pieter Heyes, and named the settlement Zwaanendael, or Swaanendael, meaning "Valley of the Swans." The colonists planted crops and built a palisade of upright logs to protect their huts before Heyes returned to Holland for supplies. In his absence, the colonists aroused the antagonism of the Indians in the area; a surprise attack in 1632 wiped out all the Dutchmen but one.

The same year that De Vries planted the settlement at Zwaanendael, the company recalled Minuit and discharged him as Director General. In 1633, it replaced an acting director with Wouter Van Twiller, the second Dutch Governor, an incompetent and indecisive man. Though he was a nephew of Kiliaen Van Rensselaer, the company dismissed him in 1637 and he retired to Rensselaerswyck. Van Twiller's successor was William Kieft, who was even less popular. Kieft served as Director General from 1637 to 1646. His regime is distinguished by a war with the Indians, a quarrel with the English then in Connecticut, and a clash with the citizens of New Netherland that led to his dismissal.

The Dutch only temporarily occupied the British-claimed Connecticut River Valley for trading purposes until 1633, when they bought lands—

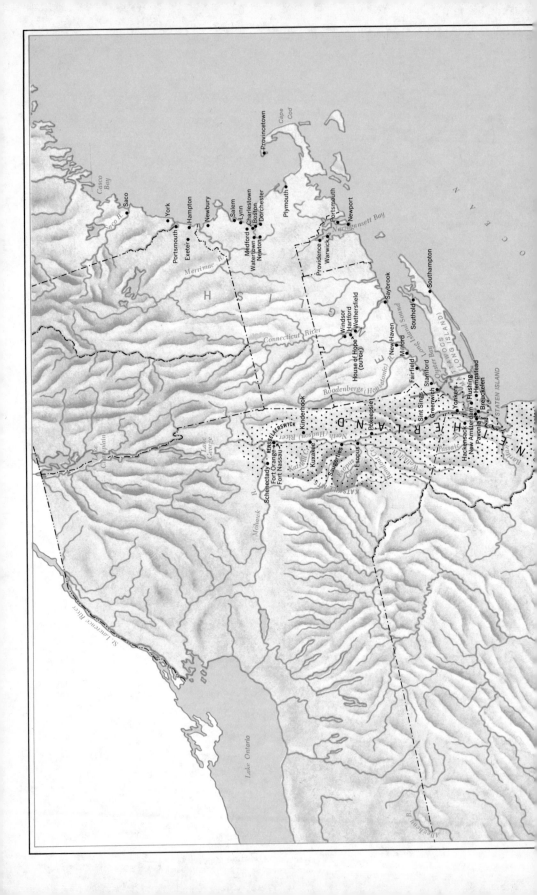

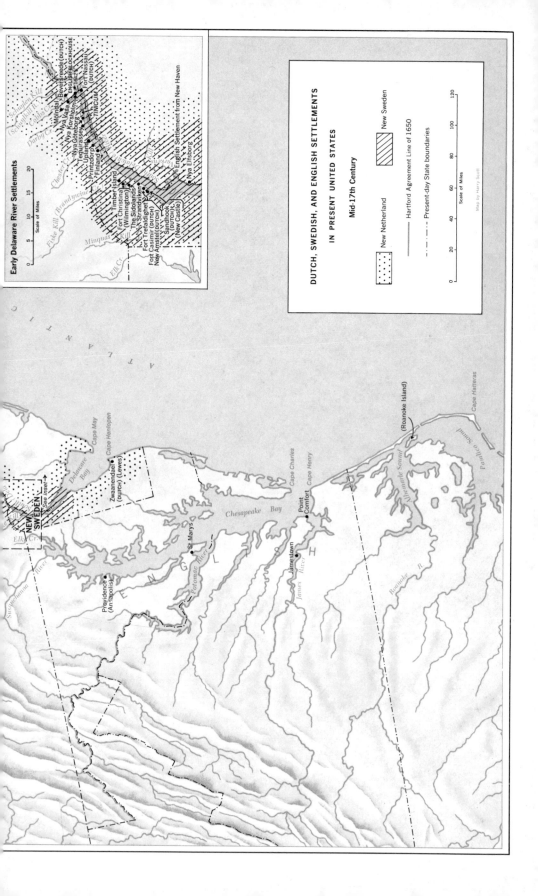

Early Delaware River Settlements

Scale of Miles
0   5   10   15   20

(Schuylkill Kill)
Schuylkill
Mouat Bever-reede (dutch)
1642
AUSTEL'S BLOCKHOUSE
Cobbs Creek
Fort Nassau (dutch)
Darby Cr.
Nya Vasa
Nya Korsholm
Chester Cr.
Nya Göteborg
Tequirassey
TINICUM
Fiske Kill
Brandywine
Uplandt
Printzdorp
Finland
Minqua
Elk Cr.
Timber Island
Fort Christina (Wilmington)
St. Jöransholm
Strandviken
The Sidelands
Fort Casimir (dutch)
Fort Trefaldighet
Sandhoek (New Castle)
New Amstel (dutch)
English Settlement from New Haven
Nya Elfsborg

DUTCH, SWEDISH, AND ENGLISH SETTLEMENTS
IN PRESENT UNITED STATES
Mid-17th Century

New Netherland   New Sweden

————— Hartford Agreement Line of 1650
—··—··— Present-day State boundaries

Scale of Miles
0   20   40   60   80   100   120

Map by Harry Scott

A T L A N T I C

ATLANTIC

Cape May
Cape Henlopen
Delaware Bay
Zwaanendael (dutch) (Lewes)
NEW SWEDEN
See inset →
Elk Cr.
Susquehanna River

Cape Charles
Cape Henry
Point Comfort
Chesapeake Bay
St. Marys
Potomac River
Providence (Annapolis)

E N G L I S H

Jamestown
James River

Roanoke R.

(Roanoke Island)
Albemarle Sound
Pamlico Sound
Cape Hatteras

as was their regular custom—from the Pequot Indians and began a permanent settlement on the site of Hartford. They named it Fort Good Hope (House of Good Hope). Gov. John Winthrop of Massachusetts promptly notified Director General Van Twiller that the Dutch were trespassing. Van Twiller was his indecisive self, and neither Governor took further action. But a small party of Englishmen from Plymouth ignored the Dutch, sailed 10 miles up the Connecticut River, and established the town of Windsor. In 1635, three entire towns moved from Massachusetts to the Connecticut Valley, one group settling around Fort Good Hope. Kieft's querulous attempts to oust the English caused only friction.

Perhaps the Director General would have taken stronger measures in Connecticut if he had not been so involved at home with Indian troubles. Kieft tried to collect a tribute from the Indians living in the vicinity of Manhattan. His inept handling of their refusal provoked the series of attacks from 1641 to 1645 known as the Indian War, during which the natives laid waste to many of the outlying settlements of New Netherland. During the war, in 1642, Kieft called a special council of the heads of families on Manhattan Island. This meeting elected a board, called the Twelve Men, to advise the Governor. A despot errs in bringing a representative assembly into being; the Twelve Men demanded reform and a popularly elected council. Kieft angrily dismissed them, but renewed Indian attacks forced him in 1643 to call another general assembly, and he formed a council of Eight Men. Resenting Kieft's haughty arrogance and taxation measures, this council also demanded reform and appealed to the States General in Holland.

The company discharged Kieft, but the people of New Netherland found little comfort in his successor. Peg-legged Peter Stuyvesant, who had lost a leg in defense of the company's interests in the West Indies, was as autocratic as Kieft and even more hot-tempered. Royally announcing on his arrival in 1647 that he would govern the colonists "as a father his children," Stuyvesant banished Kieft's accusers and threatened to hang them if they appealed to the States General. In answer to a demand for representation, Stuyvesant replied: "We derive our authority from God and the Company, not from a few ignorant subjects. If the nomination and the election of magistrates were to be left to the populace . . . then each would vote for one of his own stamp—the thief for a thief; the rogue, the tippler, the smuggler for a brother in equity."

"King Peter's" reign was not a happy one, but he was an industrious and competent executive. The Indian troubles at an end, in 1650 he turned to settle the problem with the English. With surprising tact he

Peter Stuyvesant, last Governor of New Netherland. In spite of his unpopularity, he was a competent and industrious executive. From a painting, probably conjectural, by an unknown artist. Courtesy, New-York Historical Society.

negotiated a treaty with the New England Confederation—never ratified by either national government—to establish a boundary between New Netherland and New England. This line split Long Island in half and extended north about 20 miles east of the Hudson and parallel to it; it is approximately today's eastern boundary of New York State.

The next year, 1651, Stuyvesant turned his attention southward to face a menace to the company's domain. In 1638, Swedish settlers and traders had moved into the Delaware region. The Director General armed a fleet of 11 vessels and swept into the bay with much "drumming and cannonading" to announce the Dutch claim to the feeble Swedish settlements, whose population probably never exceeded 400. Landing near the mouth of the Delaware, he built Fort Casimir. All vessels entering or leaving New Sweden would have to pass under the Dutch guns.

FOUNDING OF NEW SWEDEN

Sweden's great King, Gustavus Adolphus, who raised his nation to a powerful position in Europe, was interested in the potential of the American fur trade. After he died, his daughter's regent continued this interest, spurred undoubtedly by William Usselinx, a merchant prince of Amsterdam who had been one of the original promoters of the Dutch West India Company. In 1637, the Swedish Government chartered the New Sweden Company, one of the directors of which was none other than Peter Minuit, late Governor of New Netherland. After being recalled to Holland from New Netherland, he had offered his services to Sweden, whose enthusiasm for New World colonization he undoubtedly stimulated.

In December 1637, Minuit sailed out of Gothenburg in 2 vessels, loaded with about 50 emigrants, bound for Delaware Bay to found New Sweden. He proceeded up the Delaware River to the site of Wilmington, where he landed in the spring of 1638. After bartering with the Indians for the land, he erected Fort Christina, which he named for the youthful Queen of Sweden.

Minuit perished at sea the following year, but his leaderless colonists fared quite well. The Indians at the head of the bay were friendly and anxious to trade. Though of motley origin, the colonists proved more than equal to subduing the wilderness. Many were petty convicts, released from Swedish prisons to serve out their terms in the New World; others were recruits from Finland; and some were Dutch who for one reason or another joined the Swedes. In 1640, Peter Ridder replaced Minuit as Governor. The following year, uninvited but not entirely unwelcome, a group of disaffected Puritans from New Haven settled among them.

Two years later, a new Governor arrived: Johan Printz. He founded about a dozen new posts and settlements along the Delaware River in a 15- to 20-mile radius around Fort Christina, and moved the capital from the fort to one of the islands at the mouth of the Schuylkill River, Tinicum Island, near the site of Philadelphia. Under his able, if autocratic, leadership, New Sweden became nearly self-sufficient. Occasionally in lean times it had to purchase supplies from New England at an exorbitant price, but on the whole it fared well during the decade of Printz's administration.

Ascendancy of the dutch

The most serious problem of New Sweden was that both the English and Dutch looked upon it as an intrusion on land that each of them claimed. Perhaps because of the alliance of the three nations in the Thirty Years' War against their common enemy, Spain, the Swedes were not molested until after the war ended, in 1648. William Kieft, of New Netherland, had earlier sent a formal protest about the Swedish intrusion to Governor Printz. Stuyvesant acted. After he had negotiated the boundary agreement with the stronger English, on his north, in 1651 he brought a small fleet into Delaware Bay and with much fanfare erected Fort Casimir.

Printz protested in vain that Sweden had purchased the land from the Indians. Such agreements with the natives were nominal at best. The Indians had no concept of land ownership and willingly "sold" the same land again and again—to Swedes, to Dutchmen, and to Englishmen. Often not even the same Indian band was involved in these duplicate transactions. But, even if the "deeds" were valid, it would have mattered little, for European rivalry in North America intensified.

Not receiving provisions and additional colonists he had requested from the company, Printz resigned in 1653 and sailed for home, leaving New Sweden leaderless and restive. His successor, Johan Rising, who arrived the following year, could do little to curb the inevitable trend. How much longer New Sweden would have had a nominal existence if Rising had not asserted her position will never be known. But his first action brought doom to the colony.

Finding Fort Casimir inadequately garrisoned, in 1654 Rising attacked and forced its surrender. Retaliation came 15 months later, when Stuyvesant appeared in Delaware Bay with three ships and a sizable army. Again with cannon shot, drum roll, and trumpet blast he proclaimed Dutch sovereignty. The Swedes, who had occupied Fort Casimir, hastily capitulated. One Swedish soldier, who had deserted before the surrender, was shot—the only casualty of the *opera bouffe*. Fort Christina and the other posts soon joined in the surrender, and New Sweden became a part of New Netherland.

FALL OF NEW NETHERLAND

Many of the Swedish and Finnish colonists from New Sweden, including Governor Rising himself, returned to Nieuw Amsterdam with the victorious Stuyvesant. There they joined the already heterogeneous population of the infant metropolis, which included some Negro slaves. As early

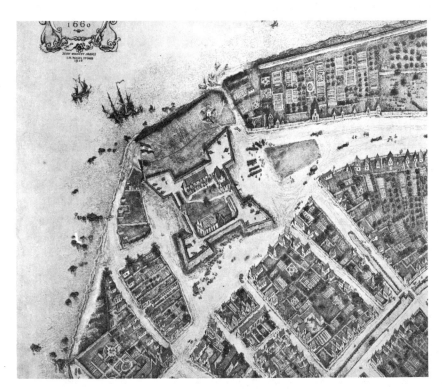

New Amsterdam, including Fort Amsterdam, in 1660. From a detail of I. N. Phelps Stokes' redraft of the Costello plan. Courtesy, Museum of the City of New York.

as 1640, the Dutch West India Company had opened New Netherland to all the peoples of Europe. A number of Europeans emigrated, many of whom sought freedom from religious persecution at home. Stuyvesant, a staunch member of the Dutch Reformed Church, insisted on religious conformity. Soon after his arrival, he initiated rigid and intolerant policies of religious enforcement that were contrary to those of the Dutch Church, though the ministers in Nieuw Amsterdam supported them. The Governor forbade Lutherans to engage in public worship, fined and banished the Baptists, and cruelly punished Quakers. Even the company's directors were embarrassed by this misplaced zeal and ordered him to permit in New Netherland the freedom of conscience that existed in Holland.

Added to this source of resentment was Stuyvesant's refusal to consider any reforms or to allow popular assemblies. Protests availed the growing population nothing. Furthermore, Stuyvesant introduced measures to curb smuggling; to regulate the fur trade; to prohibit the sale of guns, ammunition, or intoxicants to the Indians; and to collect high tariff duties. All of these, of course, were to the benefit of the company and its profit balance, but most of the settlers felt that they were detrimental and dictatorial.

In another field, Stuyvesant incurred even greater unpopularity. Intemperance was widespread in Nieuw Amsterdam; one-fourth of all the buildings were "brandy shops, tobacco or beer houses." While not at-

"The Fall of New Amsterdam, 1664." When Col. Richard Nicolls sailed into New York Harbor with four English vessels, Gov. Peter Stuyvesant prepared to fight. The citizens of New Amsterdam persuaded him to surrender. From a painting by J. L. G. Ferris. Courtesy, William E. Ryder and the Smithsonian Institution.

tempting to prohibit alcoholic beverages, Stuyvesant did restrict their sale for certain hours on Sundays. It was a decree hopeless to enforce despite its timidity. In the long run, whether Stuyvesant deserved it or not, New Netherlanders blamed him for all the dissatisfactions that they felt. When the final crisis came, they refused to support him.

Haunting all the Dutch administrators was the fact that the small colony sat in the midst of vigorous British settlements, which had a far greater population. Secondly, Dutch merchant ships had begun to carry cargoes, especially the profitable tobacco, in the New World trade—in direct violation of Britain's Navigation Acts. After the Peace of Westphalia, in 1648, Britain turned her attention to the Dutch, with whom she clashed indecisively in the first Anglo-Dutch War, 1652–54. As long as Nieuw Amsterdam was open to Dutch ships, the Navigation Acts could not be enforced. Even Massachusetts, Connecticut, and Rhode Island had rejected the mercantile theory to the point of opening their harbors to Dutch vessels.

In March 1664, the restored King Charles II acted. He granted all the region embraced by New Netherland to his brother, James, Duke of York. Parliamentary leaders assenting to an armed conquest, Charles appointed Col. Richard Nicolls as Lieutenant Governor of the province and ordered him to prepare an invasion. In August 1664, he led an English fleet of four vessels and several hundred fighting men into New York Harbor. He offered liberal terms of surrender to the inhabitants, who were given 18 months to decide whether they wanted to remain or not and were guaranteed all the rights of English citizens, including liberty of conscience and trading privileges. Furthermore, they were permitted to continue any Dutch customs not contrary to the laws of England. Impotently Stuyvesant blustered and raged. He would be "carried out dead" before he permitted surrender. But his "children" rebelled and refused to support him. With hardly a shot, on August 26, 1664, Nieuw Amsterdam capitulated and welcomed the English. Soon thereafter, the rest of New Netherland capitulated. The Treaty of Breda (1667), which ended the second Anglo-Dutch War, confirmed the loss of the colony.

OUR DUTCH AND SWEDISH HERITAGE

Ironically, it was the magnetic influence of English liberty on the Dutch and Swedes that caused the ignominious downfall of the peg-legged tyrant of New Netherland. The New Netherlanders eagerly embraced the British heritage, and New Amsterdam, already a polyglot of races and customs, quickly took on a decided English atmosphere. The Dutch, basically so much like their English cousins, became absorbed in the new way of life and did not cling tenaciously to their traditions.

Nevertheless, the influence of Holland was stamped on the province, and the language, customs, and architecture of Dutch America helped shape the city, as well as the State of New York that was later to emerge. The striking cleanliness of the Dutch villages, the style of their buildings, and their close-knit design lingered for centuries. And, as did the English, French, and Spanish in other areas, the Dutch and Swedes enriched the map with place names. Most important, the solid Dutch families who settled in Manhattan and the Hudson Valley produced an unusual number of prominent citizens and national leaders: the Rensselaers, the Cortlandts, the Schuylers, the Van Burens, and the Roosevelts, among others.

Fewer in number than the Dutch, the Swedish colonists contributed less to the developing American culture. One specific contribution of much importance attributed to them is the introduction of the art of log construction. Whether a Swede or a Finn in New Sweden built the first true log house in America may never be known. But so suitable was it to the environment that the technique spread throughout the colonies. None of the other national groups that came to the New World were familiar with log construction in their native land. Whether known later as a "cabin" or a "dog run," this style and method of construction seems clearly to have originated in New Sweden.

The British: Colonials and Progenitors

Of all the European influences on the United States, those of the English were the most substantial and enduring. British colonials were the basic progenitors of the new Nation. Many of them were escaping from the religious persecution that convulsed England in the 17th century. Indeed, the desire for religious freedom was a major factor in colonization. However, proprietors or companies, whose motives included the desire for profit, founded many of the colonies. At the same time, they also provided the outlet that many believed England needed for her surplus population.

Despite the claim in the New World provided by John Cabot's voyage in 1497, the British were the last of the three major European powers to attempt to settle. Yet, by 1700, they had established substantial colonies all along the Atlantic coast. [Development of the British colonies during the period 1700–1783 is treated in *Colonials and Patriots,* Volume VI in this series.] Though by that time the colonies had some degree of unity because of the common language and overall English control, they had made little progress toward unification. Their efforts were hampered because of the separate founding of the colonies and the lack of roads and communications. Despite the need for defense against the Indians, French, Spanish, and Dutch, six plans for union in the 17th century failed; some of these involved only two or three colonies, and the British Government sponsored some of them.

Yet colonial Englishmen, influenced by the freedom and opportunities in the New World, gradually evolved into "Americans." Their outlook and ideas began to differ from those of their compatriots in the British Isles, though they maintained strong loyalties toward their native land. The English colonies lacked the gold and silver of New Spain and the wealth in furs of New France. But, based on trade, agriculture, and fisheries, colonial wealth steadily increased. New settlers arrived to take advantage of the opportunities, and the population soon surpassed that of the French and Spanish colonies.

Establishing a claim

England became unified late in the 15th century. On Bosworth Field, in 1485, Henry Tudor put an end to the civil strife of the Wars of the Roses and crowned himself Henry VII. Forcefully bringing recalcitrant

John Cabot, the English explorer, a conjectural portrait. His voyages in 1497 and 1498 laid the foundations of England's claim to North America. From a late 18th- or early 19th-century painting by an unknown artist. Courtesy, Chicago Historical Society.

nobles to heel, he strengthened his authority. For the first time in nearly a century, the country had stability in government and a considerable degree of peace and prosperity. Henry, therefore, could devote his attention to the promotion of commerce. He encouraged English merchants to enter foreign trade, supported the formation of trading companies, and restricted the activities of the foreign merchants in London and Bristol, who had monopolized trade. Columbus even sent his brother to England when he failed to obtain support from the Portuguese or Spanish Kings for his proposal that Cathay could be reached by sailing west across the Atlantic. Henry VII agreed to finance the voyage and urged Columbus to come at once to England. But, before the latter left Spain, the Spanish monarchs experienced a change of heart and supported the voyage that was to give Spain an empire.

Meanwhile, Henry VII never gave up his hope of obtaining for England a share of the rich Eastern trade. British merchants established a trade link with Iceland about 1490. And, encouraged by news of Columbus' voyage, on March 5, 1496, Henry VII granted letters-patent to the "well-beloved John Cabot" and his three sons to sail across the Atlantic to Asia. An Italian-born navigator, Cabot had lived in England since 1484. As a youth, he had visited the East, and when he arrived in London he had already decided that an all-water route could be found

John and Sebastian Cabot, English explorers, land in North America, in 1497. From a wood engraving by an unknown artist, published in 1855. Courtesy, Library of Congress.

to the trading centers there. He may have made a few trips to Iceland before the King commissioned his trans-Atlantic voyage.

In May of 1497, Cabot left Bristol with a crew of 18 and, after a voyage of 52 days across the North Atlantic, landed on Cape Breton Island and took possession of the land for Henry VII. From there, he explored several islands in the Gulf of St. Lawrence and in August returned to England and the praise of Henry VII, who granted him new letters-patent. When Cabot sailed again, in 1498, he had perhaps 5 or 6 ships, whose crews totaled some 300 men. The King personally financed a substantial portion of the expedition's cost. On his second voyage, Cabot probably explored the North American coast from Newfoundland south to the Delaware or Chesapeake Bays.

Having failed to find the shores of Cathay (China) or Cipango (Japan), the English turned in the opposite direction. Henry VII's son, Henry VIII—better known for his marital involvements and his break with the Pope—enthusiastically began to build "a fleet the like of which the world has never seen." John Cabot's son, Sebastian, became a renowned navigator. After serving Spain for a number of years, he returned to England and opened the northern sea-land route to Moscow. He also helped found the company of Merchant-Adventurers, predecessor of the Muscovy Company, and became its president for life.

Thus, for nearly a century, England's interest was diverted from the New World, and her energies were concentrated on the development of a commercial empire and a merchant fleet that became second to none in Europe. But John Cabot had given England a claim to the northern shores of the New World, and in the course of time the "sea dogs" and other English mariners were to breathe new life into it.

HARASSING THE SPANISH

When Henry VIII died, in 1547, he left his throne to his sickly son, Edward. After Edward died, in 1553, while yet a minor, the scepter passed to Mary. "Bloody" Queen Mary, half-Spanish daughter of Henry's first marriage, to Catherine of Aragon, tried with fire and sword to return England to the papal fold and against all counsel wedded her ambitious cousin Philip II of Spain. Her death, in 1558, spared the English a questionable future as Hapsburg vassals. But under Mary's half-sister, Elizabeth, the third of Henry VIII's children to ascend the Tudor throne, England entered a golden age of exploration and expansion. The Queen promptly restored the Church of England as the state religion

Queen Elizabeth was the first English monarch to encourage colonization of the New World. During her reign, England entered a golden age of exploration and expansion. From a 1596 engraving by an unknown artist.

and embarked upon a policy of ecclesiastical compromise and domestic tranquillity. Abroad, she coyly flirted with her former brother-in-law, Philip II of Spain, while secretly encouraging her admiring liegemen to enrich themselves—and her—by raiding and harassing Spanish commerce. It was a delightful game.

Shortly after Elizabeth's ascension to the throne, John Hawkins began illicitly smuggling slaves into Hispaniola. He then shifted to the plundering of Spanish treasure galleons, and ultimately to the raiding of coastal towns in Spain's colonial empire. By about 1570, usually with royal connivance, English sea rovers were regularly attacking the Spanish treasure fleets. The Queen knighted both Hawkins and Francis Drake, whose exploits are better known. Drake not only pillaged towns and ships in the Caribbean. In 1577, he also passed through the Strait of Magellan and, in a series of surprise attacks, looted Spanish settlements on the Pacific coast. While on this incredible escapade, in 1579 he landed on the California coast. Then, laden as he was with plunder that he feared Spanish men-of-war might wrest from him if he returned through the strait, he boldly struck out across the Pacific. He completed his circumnavigation of the globe in 1580, when he arrived back in England. His hold bore treasure that repaid his financial backers some 5,000 percent on their investment and added more than a quarter of a million pounds to the Queen's coffers.

Seeking the northwest passage

About this same time, during the period 1576–78, Martin Frobisher made three voyages to the northernmost part of the New World, exciting short-lived rumors that he had discovered gold west of Frobisher's Bay and, at long last, the Northwest Passage to the Orient. After his first exploring expedition, he and his associates organized the Company of Cathay, which went bankrupt after the failure of two subsequent expeditions. A few years later, John Davis revived his project of seeking a Northwest Passage. He, too, made three voyages into the icy waters beyond the Hudson Strait, between 1585 and 1587, the results of which were as disappointing as Frobisher's.

First settlement attempts

An ardent advocate of the existence of a Northwest Passage and a shareholder in Frobisher's Company of Cathay, Sir Humphrey Gilbert turned the Queen's attention to colonization projects. In 1578, a royal grant in hand, he set out from Plymouth to found an English colony in some part of the new lands "not actually possessed by any Christian prince." Storms and misadventures drove him back to England, but he was undaunted. Using funds that he had solicited from his countrymen, in 1583 he left England again, with 5 ships and more than 250 colonists. But the colony that he established in Newfoundland also ended disastrously, and on the return trip he was lost at sea.

The first Englishmen arrive in "Virginia." Roanoke Island is shown in the bay. From an engraving by Theodore de Bry, after John White's on-the-scene drawing.

The following year, Elizabeth renewed Gilbert's grant in the name of his half-brother, Sir Walter Raleigh—poet, soldier, historian, and adventurer—who had invested heavily in Gilbert's second effort. Plans were again laid for an English colony in the New World. Raleigh first sent out an expedition, led by Philip Amandas and Arthur Barlowe, to make a reconnaissance of the North American coast. In 1584, sailing by way of the Canaries and the West Indies, it traveled up the coast to present North Carolina, explored the region, and returned to recommend it enthusiastically for a colony. Raleigh christened the new land "Virginia"—for the "Virgin Queen"—and appointed Sir Richard Grenville to establish a settlement. Grenville, a renowned sea rover, left in 1585 with 7 vessels and about 100 colonists. After brief exploration, the group settled on Roanoke Island. Grenville placed Ralph Lane in temporary charge and sailed away, promising to return the next year with supplies.

Obsessed with the dream that they might discover gold in the New World as the Spanish had done, the colonists were little inclined to labor at clearing fields and planting crops. By summer of the following year, they were constantly quarreling and warring with the Indians, from whom they had first obtained supplies, and were nearly out of provisions. In June a fleet approached—not Grenville but Drake, returning from a triumphant raid in the West Indies. Discouraged, Lane and his men returned to England with Drake. They had missed Grenville and the supply expedition by only a few weeks. After a brief and futile search, being "unwilling to loose possession of the country which Englishmen had so long held," Grenville stationed 15 of his men at the post on Roanoke Island and hastened southward to cruise for Spanish prizes. The 15 were never heard from again.

But Raleigh persisted. In 1587, he dispatched another and larger group of colonists to Roanoke under the leadership of John White. The group landed and refurbished the fort built by Lane. Among the 150 colonists were 17 women, one of whom was White's daughter, the wife of Ananias Dare. At this tiny outpost of England, she gave birth to the first English child born in America, Virginia Dare.

Late in 1587, White returned to England for supplies, and Raleigh patiently equipped another fleet to supply his colony. But destiny interfered. Philip of Spain had finally tired of Elizabeth's sport and had launched a mighty armada to destroy English seapower once and for all— even perhaps to invade England itself. During defense preparations, the Queen requisitioned Raleigh's entire supply fleet into the royal service.

Southern Algonquian Indians fishing along the coast of present North Carolina. From an on-the-scene watercolor by John White, 1585. Courtesy, Smithsonian Institution.

England's momentous victory in 1588 over the Spanish Armada in the English Channel was a major turning point in history, for Spanish seapower, as well as Spanish dominance in Europe, was dealt a severe blow. Elizabeth's grand triumph, however, meant Roanoke's demise. By the time White was able to return to the colony, in 1590, it had disappeared. The mystery of its fate has never been solved. The bare letters C-R-O-A-T-O-A-N—the name of an Indian tribe and island south of Cape Hatteras—carved in the bark of a tree were the only clue.

JAMESTOWN AND THE FOUNDING OF VIRGINIA

The defeat of the Spanish Armada made the New World safer for the English. Though the Raleigh ventures failed, they excited interest in colonization. Between 1602 and 1605, a few expeditions, including those led by Bartholomew Gosnold and Capt. George Weymouth, unsuccessfully attempted to settle groups of colonists at various points along the Atlantic coast. The next British attempts were to be made by joint-stock companies, which had emerged in the 16th century. Early successes of the Muscovy and Levant companies in Europe had led to the organization of the highly profitable East India Company, and a number of others. Chartered and loosely supervised by the Crown, these companies began to lead in the expansion of the British Empire.

In 1606, a group of merchant investors founded the joint-stock Virginia Company and obtained a charter from James I that authorized colonization of the lands claimed for England by John Cabot. From the first, the company consisted of two groups: The London Company, whose domain was the southern coast; and the Plymouth Company, the northern. The latter made the first attempt at colonization, but it was unsuccessful; in August 1606, the Spanish captured a shipload of about 30 colonists in the West Indies. Another expedition of the company, commanded by George Popham, left England in May 1607 and landed in August on the New England coast near the mouth of the Kennebec River, in present Maine. There the colonists built Fort St. George, a church, and 15 small huts. Late the following year, a shortage of supplies, the severity of the winter, and dissension and idleness brought about the end of the colony, and the survivors returned to England.

Meantime, in 1607, the London Company had established a successful settlement in Virginia. In December 1606, the company had dispatched a full-scale colonization expedition from London that consisted of 3

Capt. John Smith's map of Virginia, published in London, in 1612. Courtesy, Smithsonian Institution.

small ships—the *Susan Constant, Godspeed,* and *Discovery*—that carried about 140 men. Christopher Newport, an experienced navigator, was in command until the group landed. In a sealed box in his cabin were the names of the Governor and council of the colony.

After entering Chesapeake Bay and landing temporarily on April 26, 1607, at Cape Henry, where they stayed for 4 days, the colonists moved up the James River to find a more defensible location. On May 13, the colonists selected a site and named it James-Forte, or Jamestowne. A swampy, wooded peninsula about 30 miles from the sea, it provided good docking facilities and satisfactory defense against the Indians. But malaria-bearing mosquitoes swarmed about, fresh-water springs were insufficient, and the profuse trees were not only an obstacle to clearing the land, but also provided natural cover for the Indians.

When Newport opened the sealed instructions, the names of the seven councilors were revealed. Among them were Edward M. Wingfield, who was selected as Governor; Bartholomew Gosnold, a navigator; and Capt. John Smith, whom Newport had placed in irons during the voyage for his fractious behavior. Yet, in the long run, it was Smith who was to save the colony. From the outset, troubles and dissension plagued the governing council. Wingfield served as Governor only a few months; he was removed from the council in September and replaced as Governor by John Ratcliffe. Capt. George Kendall, another council member, was executed for treason, and Gosnold died of malaria.

Newport, who had returned to England for supplies and more settlers in June of 1607, arrived back in Jamestown in January the following year to find that only 38 of the original settlers had survived disease and Indian ambuscade. Because the colony continued to dwindle alarmingly, in April 1608 Newport set out on his second trip to England; he returned in October with supplies and about 70 settlers, including the first 2 women. The previous month, Smith, who had gained the ascendancy in the council, had succeeded Ratcliffe as Governor. Initiating rigid discipline, he directed the erection of a blockhouse fort, a score of cabins, and a well. He also forced the colonists, who traded with the Indians to obtain corn, to raise livestock and chickens, as well as to plant crops.

The plight of the colony caused so much alarm in England that in May 1609 the King issued a new charter to the London Company which placed responsibility for government of the colony solely in the hands of the directors. Confidence reinspired, shareholders raised additional funds, and in June 1609 a well equipped relief expedition of 9 ships and 500 settlers left England. Lord Delaware (de la Warr) was appointed as Governor, but delayed his departure. Sir George Somers, Sir Thomas Gates, and Christopher Newport led the expedition. Caught in a hurricane, one of the vessels foundered and another bearing Gates and Somers was wrecked in the Bermudas. In August, the remaining seven, carrying about 300 settlers, including women and children, limped into Jamestown.

Smith was in charge of the colony, but the newcomers refused to recognize his authority. Once more quarrels broke out among the colonists. Smith, badly burned by a gunpowder explosion and discouraged by the turn of events, returned to England and left Jamestown leaderless. The winter of 1609–10 was devastating. Food became so scarce that the colonists first ate their horses and dogs, then tried to catch rats and snakes. During this "starving time," the population slumped from about 500 to 60.

Meanwhile, Gates and Somers had constructed two small ships and in May 1610 reached Jamestown. Overcome by what they saw, they loaded the nearly demented survivors and turned down the James River for home. Only by coincidence was the colony saved from abandonment. Lord Delaware, aboard one of three ships commanded by Capt. Samuel Argall, put into the river's mouth just as Gates and Somers were about to sail out into the sea. The fortuitous meeting would not have occurred had young Argall not determined to "trace the ready way" straight across the mid-Atlantic, rather than sailing by way of the Canaries, the West Indies, and the Florida coast. The year before, when bringing supplies to Jamestown, he had proved the feasibility of the new route, his use of which now saved the colony.

Delaware ordered the outward-bound ship to put about and took charge of the overwhelming task of rebuilding not only the colony but also the colonists' morale. Progress was soon apparent under his wise leadership, but in the spring of 1611 he became ill and returned to England. Thereafter, he governed the colony through deputies. The first of these was Sir Thomas Dale, a strict disciplinarian but a competent leader. "Dale's Laws," as his regulations were called, were necessarily severe. However, his leadership was constructive and the colony survived. The colonists erected buildings, planted crops, established outposts, and made peace with the Indians.

Peace with the Indians was the result of the enterprise of Argall, who in 1613 met Pocahontas, the youthful daughter of the Indian chief Powhatan, along the shores of the Potomac. She was married to a neighboring chief, but Argall resolved to "possesse myself of her by any Stratagem that I could use, for ransoming of so many Englishmen as were Prisoners with Powhatan . . . as also to get such Armes and Tooles as he and other Indians had got." He had only to trade the chief a copper kettle for the girl, who was delighted to accompany the Englishman back to Jamestown. There John Rolfe became attracted to her and married her. As a result, until Powhatan died, relative peace prevailed with the Indians. Rolfe took his bride to visit London. There she gave birth to a son, but she died soon afterward.

In 1617, Rolfe returned to Virginia as secretary to Argall, who had just been appointed as Deputy Governor. Under Dale (1611, 1613–16), Gates (1611–13), and Argall (1617–19)—however strict the martial rule—the colony began to prosper. A new charter in 1612 encouraged emigration from England; the introduction that same year by Rolfe of West Indian tobacco provided Virginia with an economic base; the colonists founded a dozen or so inland settlements; and the population reached more than 1,000.

In 1618, the company decreed the end of martial rule in Virginia and

The first women arrive at Jamestown, Virginia, in 1619. Recruited by the Virginia Company to help stabilize the colony, the women became wives of the settlers. From a sketch by an unknown artist, published in 1876. Courtesy, Library of Congress.

instructed Lord Delaware to institute a popular assembly. He died en route to the colony, however, and his successor, George Yeardley, in 1619 brought into existence the first representative assembly in America, the Virginia House of Burgesses. In the same year, the first Negroes landed—apparently as indentured servants rather than slaves. And, the following year, to supplement the small group of women who had come in 1609, a group of marriageable maidens arrived.

Yet, in the years immediately following, the colony barely survived. In 1622, the Indians laid waste to the outlying settlements and killed about 350 colonists. Even more serious were the chronic problems of disease and lack of food and other necessities; many deaths resulted and numerous colonists returned to England. Between 1619 and 1624, more than 4,000 colonists joined the few hundred already in Virginia, but by the end of the period the population was only 1,275. Because of adverse conditions in the colony and political trends in England, in 1624 James I annulled the charter of the Virginia Company and made Virginia a royal colony directly under his control.

Despite all the early trials, over the years a plantation-small farm system began to extend along the coasts and rivers of Tidewater Virginia. As the colonists grew stronger, they began to assert their rights. In 1635, they temporarily deposed the royal Governor; and, in 1676, a century before the Declaration of Independence, some of them rose in open rebellion against the administration of Sir William Berkeley. Nathaniel Bacon and his followers drove Berkeley from Jamestown, which they put to the torch and almost completely destroyed because they considered it to be a "stronghold of oppression." Bacon died, Berkeley was replaced, and the rebellious spirit cooled, but Jamestown never fully recovered. In 1699, the year after the statehouse accidentally burned, the General Assembly moved the seat of government to Williamsburg. Within a few years, Jamestown was practically abandoned. About the time of the War for Independence, the isthmus connecting it with the mainland was washed out and an island created. The town ceased to exist.

THE MASSACHUSETTS SETTLEMENTS

Not long after the founding of Virginia, other Englishmen established another colony to the north. In 1620, a shipload of religious dissenters, later known as Pilgrims, debarked from the *Mayflower* on the western shore of Cape Cod Bay, on the coast of Massachusetts. The nucleus of the group were Puritan separatists, part of a congregation of nonconformists of Scrooby parish in Nottinghamshire, England. Because of the strict enforcement of the religious laws by James I, in 1608–9 the entire congregation of about 100 had moved to Holland seeking toleration. In 1620, they received permission from the Crown and financial backing from the London Company to migrate to Virginia. About 35 members of the congregation chose to do so; they first traveled to England, where they joined another group of dissenters. The *Mayflower* carried 101 passengers and a crew of 48. They were the first Englishmen—but by no means the last—to escape Stuart persecution in the New World.

The religious situation in England had grown complicated since Henry VIII separated the established church from Rome and placed himself at its head. In the last years of his reign, pressure from Protestant reformers forced him to modify much of the ecclesiastical code. After his death, the regents of his young son stimulated the Protestant movement. Mary then had attempted to reverse the tide, but Elizabeth wisely chose a middle course. She instituted moderate reforms in the Church of Eng-

A romanticized rendition of the Pilgrims signing the Mayflower Compact, in 1620, on board the *Mayflower*. The compact is a landmark in U.S. constitutional development. From an engraving by Gauthier, after T. H. Matteson. Courtesy, Library of Congress.

land and, though not disposed to tolerance of Protestants, did not rigorously enforce the regulations that restricted them.

A large group arose that wanted to continue the process of reform. Gradually they came to be called Puritans. Those Anglicans who would "purify" the church from within were known as conforming Puritans; those favoring stronger measures, as nonconformists, dissenters, or separatists. Religious disputation was the rage of the day, when translations of the Bible were first beginning to reach the hands of the people, who were also stimulated by the controversies that the Reformation had fostered. Interestingly enough, the version on which the Scrooby Pilgrims based their dissent was probably the Bishops' Bible, not the King James translation used today by most Protestant sects.

By authorizing this magnificent translation, James I undoubtedly hoped to put an end to dissent; instead, he only quickened it. His other religious policies, which grew harsher toward the end of his reign, were also designed to stamp out the heresy that was budding all over England. The King increased the pressure on nonconformists and separatists, and churchmen grew more and more intolerant, even of the conforming

Puritans. But the more vigorous the pruning, the healthier the plant became. After James died, in 1625, his son Charles I (1625–49) proved to be even less tolerant. A bloody revolution cost Charles his throne and his life, and the Puritan colonies in New England grew rapidly.

The Pilgrims, authorized to settle in Virginia, for some reason deviated from their planned course—perhaps more by design than accident—and founded a colony on land belonging to the Plymouth Company in an area that Capt. John Smith had visited in 1614, during an exploring expedition from Jamestown, and named "Plimouth." Realiz-

Pilgrims going to church. The lives of the Massachusetts colonists centered around church activities. From a painting by George H. Boughton (1833–1905). Courtesy, Library of Congress.

ing that they were outside the jurisdiction of the London Company and seeking to control some turbulent members, before landing the leaders drew up the Mayflower Compact. Assented to by most of the freemen in the group, it created a sort of government by social compact. Its signers swore to "convenant and combine ourselves together into a civill body politick." This idea of voluntary obedience to lawful majority rule was unique in the 17th century and is a landmark in U.S. constitutional development.

The Plymouth colony was successful mainly because of the grim determination and industry of its inhabitants. The location was one of the most unfavorable for colonization on the Atlantic coast, combining as it did bitter climate and rocky, infertile soil. Furthermore, the Pilgrims arrived at the onset of winter, in November, and construction began in late December. The colonists continued to live on the ship while a meetinghouse and homes were built. The first winter was especially severe, a famine being averted only because friendly Indians supplied corn.

The stamina and fortitude of the colonists was augmented by excellent leadership: John Carver, the first Governor, who died in 1621; Miles Standish; William Brewster; and William Bradford, who had been a young boy at the time of the emigration to Holland, and who was elected Governor by popular vote in 1621 and served most of the time until 1657. In 1621 and 1630 Bradford obtained patents from the Council for New England (successor of the Plymouth Company) that permitted the Pilgrims to remain on the land that they had occupied. As the years passed, they were able to pay not only for the land but also for the costs of their migration. But at first life was a constant struggle. By 1630, the population of the Plymouth colony was only 300. Within a decade, however, because of a great migration of Puritans from England who were escaping the persecution of Charles I, it leaped to about 3,000.

In 1629, the Massachusetts Bay Company organized on a joint-stock basis and obtained from the King a charter authorizing it to establish a colony in New England and to govern it in much the same way as the Virginia Company governed Jamestown. The new company was the successor of the New England Company (1628–29), which had purchased land in the area of Massachusetts from the Council for New England (1620–35), which succeeded the Plymouth Company. In 1628–29, the New England Company had begun a settlement at present Salem. This settlement incorporated small groups of colonists from Dorchester, England, already at the site, who had moved there in 1626 from Gloucester, which they had settled in 1623.

The Massachusetts Bay Company was chartered as a commercial rather than a religious enterprise. But most of the stockholders were

Puritans. In August 1629, a significant event in U.S. constitutional development occurred: the signing of the Cambridge Agreement. This agreement marked the acceptance of the offer of John Winthrop and 11 other prominent nonconformists to migrate to America as members of the board of directors if the headquarters of the company were transferred to the New World. All company officers not willing to migrate resigned, and Massachusetts was designated as company headquarters.

The agreement had far-reaching significance because the company was authorized to govern the colony; when its headquarters, officers, directors, and principal stockholders moved to the colony itself, Massachusetts became completely self-governing and legitimately authorized by the Crown. Furthermore, the charter became the basis of the government—in essence a written constitution superior to the officers of the company themselves.

The great Puritan migration began. Winthrop was elected Governor. Carrying the charter with him, in 1630 he headed the first contingent of colonists. Before the end of the year, approximately 2,000 persons had migrated to Massachusetts. In the ensuing decade, more than 200

"The First Thanksgiving, 1621." From a painting by J. L. G. Ferris. Courtesy, William E. Ryder and the Smithsonian Institution.

ships transported about 20,000 Puritans to Massachusetts, which thrived almost from the beginning. In rapid succession, the towns of Boston, Cambridge, Watertown, Charlestown, and 18 others were founded. Other Puritans went to the West Indies in this, the largest mass exodus of Englishmen in history.

The evolution of representative self-government based on a written document is undoubtedly the most lasting contribution of the Bay Colony to American life. Initially, Winthrop and a handful of company directors attempted to keep control of the colony in their own hands, and Winthrop kept the charter locked in his trunk. Eventually, however, the free-holders demanded that the charter be produced. In time, the Puritan leaders broadened suffrage, created a representative assembly, and evolved a bicameral legislature. Yet, for the most part, the original, tightly knit, Puritan oligarchy retained close control of the government. Church and state were interwoven; personal behavior and religious practices were closely related and supervised.

For this very reason and because of the fact that the Puritans would not tolerate divergent religious views, dissenters founded other colonies in New England. Winthrop and his assistants, seeking to protect their "holy experiment," were probably more intolerant of diversity in religion than Charles I. They drove hundreds of "otherwise thinking" people out of Massachusetts—to the lasting benefit of the Nation that later emerged on the Atlantic coast.

RHODE ISLAND AND RELIGIOUS EXILES

The first serious conflict produced the colony of Rhode Island—founded by Roger Williams, champion of religious liberty and humanitarianism. Williams was a nonconforming Welsh minister who in 1631 migrated to Massachusetts. Almost immediately, he fell into disagreement with the authorities. He preached such heretical ideas as freedom of conscience in religious matters, a complete separation of civil and church laws, and Indian land ownership. He contended that the government should not compel any man to attend church services nor dictate the nature of these services, that church tithes and civil taxes were two entirely different matters, and that the King and the colonists would not have title to the land until they purchased it from the Indians.

Because of Williams' popularity, the Puritan oligarchy at first tried to quiet him by argument and reason, but finally decreed his banishment from the colony. To escape being sent back to England, in the winter

Fortifications at Oswego, New York, in 1767. In the 18th century, Oswego was of strategic importance in controlling Lake Ontario. In 1756, during the French and Indian War, the French destroyed the British fort on the site, but after the war the British rebuilt it. From an engraving by Gavit & Duthie, published in 1767. Courtesy, Chicago Historical Society.

of 1635 he fled to Narragansett Bay, where Indians befriended him. He purchased land from them and established the village of Providence as a haven for other dissenters from the Boston orthodoxy, some of whom arrived the following spring.

Subsequently, as religious unrest continued, many other dissenters emigrated from the Massachusetts Bay Colony. Anne Hutchinson, wife of a wealthy Boston Puritan, voiced religious opinions disturbingly different than those emanating from most of the pulpits. A warm personality and an excellent conversationalist, she held weekly meetings in her home to discuss the sermons and the preachers. Advocating as she did the necessity of faith alone for salvation rather than moral behavior and "good works," she minimized the role of the clergy. Her views were heretical to Winthrop and the church elders, who were committed to the Bible, as interpreted by the clergy, as the sole source of religious inspiration. But many approved of her views, and she gained a substantial following. She finally clashed with the Puritan authorities, especially Winthrop, in a power struggle to control the General Court, but they emerged victorious. They convicted her of heresy and treason, imprisoned her for a short time, and finally excommunicated and banished her.

Anne Hutchinson and her family and a large number of followers moved to an island in Narragansett Bay, where in 1638 they established the town of Portsmouth. A year later one of her followers, William Coddington, founded Newport on the southern side of Aquidneck Island, or Rhode Island, as it was later renamed. In 1638, Samuel Gorton, who had been cast out of Massachusetts and Plymouth for blasphemous opinions, was likewise rejected by the Hutchinsonians at Portsmouth. He moved to the mainland below Providence, where he started the settlement of Warwick.

Fearing persecution from Massachusetts, Williams united the towns of Providence, Portsmouth, and Newport, and in 1643 carried their petition for a separate government to England. There the outcome of the civil war between the Roundheads and the Crown was yet undecided. In 1644, Williams received from the Roundhead Parliament—what was left of it—a charter uniting the three towns into the colony of Rhode Island and authorizing self-government. Three years later, Warwick joined the union. After Charles II was restored to the throne, he issued, in 1663, a royal charter, based on the parliamentary grant. Until 1842, this document served as Rhode Island's constitution.

The government of Rhode Island was patterned after that of Massachusetts with two major exceptions: church and state were completely separated, and religious toleration was guaranteed. Rhode Island became, therefore, a haven for religious minorities and dissenters, including Jews and Quakers, although toleration of the latter strained even Roger Williams' beliefs.

CONNECTICUT AND ECONOMIC OPPORTUNITY

The movement into the fertile Connecticut River Valley was motivated less by a desire to seek religious freedom than to escape the tyranny of unproductive and rocky farmlands. It began in 1633, when a small group from Plymouth moved west into Dutch territory and settled at Windsor, some 10 miles above Fort Good Hope, a Dutch post. In 1634, a number of farmers from Massachusetts founded Wethersfield. The following year, some 60 families moved from Newtown (Cambridge) and established Hartford adjacent to Fort Good Hope. Then, in 1636, virtually the entire Massachusetts villages of Dorchester, Watertown, and Newton made a mass exodus to the new locations in Connecticut.

Thomas Hooker, pastor of the Newtown congregation, did not disagree with Winthrop in theological matters, but he did object to the oligarchical government of Massachusetts. Insisting that "the foundation of authority is laide in the consent of the governed," he opposed the re-

The British 60th Foot (Royal-American) Regiment, some of whose members are pictured here, was a regular British regiment consisting of about 4,000 men. Most of the personnel consisted of American colonists. From a drawing by Frederick E. Ray, Jr. Courtesy, the artist, the Company of Military Historians, and the Chicago Historical Society.

stricted suffrage in Massachusetts. Under his leadership, a movement to unify the Connecticut towns resulted in the Fundamental Orders of Connecticut, devised and adopted in 1639 by representatives of the towns. This document, which has been called the first written constitution in the New World, set up a government similar to that in Massachusetts except that church membership was not required for voting and the franchise was much broader. With minor modifications, until 1818 it served as Connecticut's constitution. In 1662, Connecticut received a royal charter.

THE NEW HAVEN THEOCRACY

Theophilus Eaton, a wealthy merchant of London, and John Davenport, a radical nonconforming minister, in 1637 brought a shipload of Puritans to Massachusetts. There they found the controversy between Winthrop and the Hutchinsonians at its height. Feeling that the Massachusetts authorities had not been sufficiently strict, they moved on to Long Island Sound, west of the Connecticut River, where in 1638 they founded a Bible commonwealth, New Haven. The following year its residents established a theocracy even more autocratic than that in Massachusetts.

Within a few years, emigrants from the Massachusetts Bay Colony and England founded more than a dozen settlements in the vicinity, and by 1644 these had all federated with the town of New Haven to form a colony contiguous to Connecticut. New Haven was probably the most radical of the Puritan commonwealths. It had no charter from either Parliament or the Crown, and it was accused of harboring the men responsible for the beheading of Charles I. In 1662, the royal charter of Connecticut officially joined it to Connecticut. Only with much reluctance did New Haven acknowledge this union 2 years later.

MAINE AND NEW HAMPSHIRE

The first attempts at colonizing Maine began with two ill-fated ventures, the French settlement at St. Croix Island in 1604–5 and the English Popham settlement on the Kennebec in 1607–8. Between 1622 and 1624, English colonists made permanent settlements at Monhegan, Saco, and York. During the large Puritan migration of the next decade, the Englishman Sir Ferdinando Gorges promoted colonization expeditions to Maine, and established several small, isolated farming and fishing communities along the southern coast. The English settlements were restricted primarily to the southern coastal area of Maine because of the French trading posts along the St. Croix River.

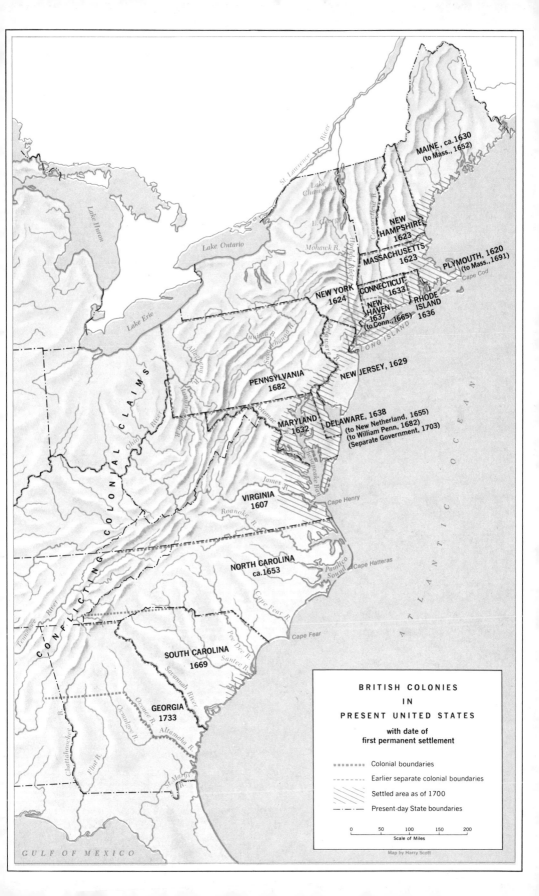

MAINE, ca. 1630
(to Mass., 1652)

NEW
HAMPSHIRE
1623

MASSACHUSETTS
1623

PLYMOUTH, 1620
(to Mass., 1691)
Cape Cod

CONNECTICUT
1633

NEW YORK
1624

NEW
HAVEN
1637
(to Conn., 1665)

RHODE
ISLAND
1636

LONG ISLAND

NEW JERSEY, 1629

PENNSYLVANIA
1682

MARYLAND
1632

DELAWARE, 1638
(to New Netherland, 1655)
(to William Penn, 1682)
(Separate Government, 1703)

C O N F L I C T I N G   C O L O N I A L   C L A I M S

VIRGINIA
1607

Cape Henry

James R.

Roanoke R.

NORTH CAROLINA
ca. 1653

Pamlico
Sound   Cape Hatteras

Cape Fear R.

A T L A N T I C   O C E A N

Cape Fear

SOUTH CAROLINA
1669

Pee Dee R.

Santee R.

Savannah River

GEORGIA
1733

Ocmulgee R.

Oconee R.

Altamaha R.

St. Marys R.

Chattahoochee R.

Flint R.

Tennessee River

Lake Huron

Lake Ontario

Lake Erie

Lake Champlain

L. George

St. Lawrence River

Mohawk R.

Connecticut R.

Hudson River

Delaware R.

Juniata R.

Susquehanna R.

Allegheny River

Potomac R.

Ohio River

Chesapeake Bay

GULF OF MEXICO

BRITISH COLONIES
IN
PRESENT UNITED STATES

with date of
first permanent settlement

▪▪▪▪▪▪▪ Colonial boundaries

‒ ‒ ‒ ‒ Earlier separate colonial boundaries

////// Settled area as of 1700

‒ ·‒ ·‒ Present-day State boundaries

0   50   100   150   200
Scale of Miles

Map by Harry Scott

In New Hampshire, as early as 1623, a group of colonists from England had settled at Odiorne's Point, near present Portsmouth. At about the same time, another group founded Dover. New Hampshire's largest early settlement, Exeter, was established as an unorthodox Puritan settlement in 1639 by John Wheelwright, the nonconformist brother-in-law of Anne Hutchinson, who had been banished from the Massachusetts Bay Colony. Shortly thereafter, however, orthodox Puritans from the Bay Colony settled at nearby Hampton. Perhaps because of the lack of religious unanimity, but more likely because of quarrels and litigation over land ownership, the settlements in New Hampshire and Maine never formed any sort of political union as had those in Massachusetts, Connecticut, Rhode Island, and New Haven.

The Maine-New Hampshire region had been granted in 1622 to Gorges and John Mason jointly by the Council for New England. In 1629, they agreed to split their grant, Mason taking the area of present New Hampshire; and Gorges, Maine. However, the charter of the Massachusetts Bay Colony, issued the same year, included these areas. In 1641, the Bay Colony arbitrarily extended jurisdiction over the settlements in New Hampshire and Maine. The heirs of Mason and Gorges protested. After considerable legal maneuvering and delay, in 1677 the matter was finally decided against Massachusetts, which then bought Maine from the Gorges heirs. Two years later, in 1679, New Hampshire became a royal colony.

BEGINNING OF NEW ENGLAND UNITY

The need of the New England colonies for a common defense against the Indians resulted in the beginning of unity there. Throughout most of the colonial period, New England faced danger from hostile Indians. The first real trouble began in 1633, when settlers moved into Pequot country in Connecticut and alienated the Indians. Sporadic attacks occurred until 1637, when the Pequot War began with an attack on Wethersfield. Wreaking a terrible vengeance, Massachusetts and Connecticut militia burned the Pequot fort at Mystic and killed most of the 600 or so inhabitants. The militia pursued them, killed many, and captured others and made them slaves of the colonials or sold them into slavery in the West Indies. Others who later surrendered were distributed among the Mohegan, the Narragansett, and the Niantic—English allies. Thus the Pequots lost their identity as a separate tribe.

Representative uniforms and equipment of the New England Independent
Companies. For several decades, the English colonists were responsible
for their own protection. Around 1675, because of increasing Indian hostility and Anglo-Dutch rivalry, England began sending Independent Companies, the first British regulars in America. From a drawing by Eric I.
Manders. Courtesy, the artist, the Company of Military Historians, and
the Chicago Historical Society.

Fear of additional Indian attacks led in 1643 to the formation of the
New England Confederation—the first attempt at intercolonial cooperation—consisting of Massachusetts, New Haven, Plymouth, and Connecticut. Each of the four had an equal voice in the council, although Massachusetts outnumbered the others three to one in population and furnished
most of the funds. Nevertheless, the confederation was fairly active for
about two decades, though theoretically it existed until 1684.

In 1645, the confederation conducted a victorious campaign against
the Narragansett Indians; in 1650, negotiated the Hartford Treaty with

Peter Stuyvesant of New Netherland; established a system of criminal extradition; insisted that member colonies regulate church membership and exclude Quakers from their jurisdictions; and, finally, led a stumbling but ultimately victorious defense in King Philip's War (1675–76). One of the bloodiest Indian uprisings in colonial history, this war was caused by the increasing encroachment of the Puritans on Indian lands. King Philip (Metacomet), chief of the Wampanoag tribe and son of Massasoit, who originally befriended the Pilgrims, led his allies in a series of raids on New England towns and settlements. They won numerous victories and destroyed 12 towns, but confederation-sponsored troops finally defeated them.

About this time, a movement developed among the disenfranchised in Massachusetts to convert it to a royal colony. This movement coincided with growing distrust in England over the virtual independence of Massachusetts and with hostility toward her disregard of the Navigation Acts. In 1677, Massachusetts lost her claim to Maine and bought it from the heirs of Gorges; in 1679, a royal commission separated New Hampshire from Massachusetts. In 1682, Edward Randolph, who had been appointed by the Crown as surveyor and collector of customs in New England, dispatched to authorities in England a series of reports hostile to Massachusetts. Consequently, the Lords of Trade filed a suit in chancery to cancel the charter of the Massachusetts Bay Company. The charter was canceled in 1684, and Massachusetts became a royal colony.

Because of the fragmentation of New England into so many small colonies and the recalcitrant independence of the Puritans, in 1686 the Crown organized the Dominion of New England to centralize royal control over the northern colonies. The King appointed Sir Edmund Andros as Governor-General and established the capital at Boston. Within a couple of years, Andros was able to bring into the Dominion the colonies of Maine, New Hampshire, Massachusetts, Plymouth, Connecticut (already united with New Haven), Rhode Island, New York, and East and West New Jersey. His task of controlling them was an impossible one, however, and he incurred the animosity of all classes. The year after the Glorious Revolution unseated James II in 1688, because of his Catholic leanings, insurgents in Boston, declaring for the newly crowned William and Mary, imprisoned Andros and the Dominion came to an end. A similar uprising in New York squelched Andros' deputy there.

In 1691, Massachusetts was granted a new charter, as a royal colony, and to it was attached not only Maine, as formerly, but also Plymouth. The charters of Rhode Island and Connecticut were restored, and separate royal governments were reestablished in New York and New Hampshire.

THE PROPRIETARY COLONIES

After the founding of Virginia, the British Crown established all the other middle and southern colonies under the proprietary system, which it had previously used to settle Maine and New Hampshire. Under this system, which succeeded the joint-stock company as a device to build England's colonial empire, the King granted large areas and the sovereign right to rule them to proprietors, his favorites or those to whom he was indebted. The proprietors were, in essence, feudal lords, though they were sometimes required to yield to the people certain political privileges and powers. The proprietors granted land to settlers on their own terms, could mortgage their grants, or could make subgrants.

MARYLAND: ANOTHER RELIGIOUS REFUGE

Sir George Calvert was a close friend and supporter of James I. For his services, in 1617, James rewarded him with a knighthood; in 1619, named him secretary of state; in 1620, gave him a substantial annuity; in 1623, granted him lands in Newfoundland; and, in 1625, named him Baron of Baltimore and deeded him a large estate in Ireland. In 1624, Baltimore had announced his adherence to Roman Catholicism and resigned as secretary of state because of his unwillingness to take the Oath of Supremacy. In 1627, he attempted to settle the Newfoundland grant, which he called Avalon, but abandoned it because of the severity of the weather. The following year, he visited Virginia, where he found the climate favorable.

Denied permission to live in Virginia because of his religion, Lord Baltimore returned home and appealed to the King for help. Charles I, who may have had secret inclinations toward Catholicism, granted him a tract of land north of Virginia, but before the grant was consummated Lord Baltimore died, in 1632. The grant passed to his son Cecilius Calvert, second Lord Baltimore, who named the region of the grant "Maryland" and proceeded to establish a haven for English Catholics.

"*Ark* and *Dove*." These ships brought the first colonists to Maryland. From a modern watercolor by John Moll. Courtesy, Maryland Historical Society.

The grant conveyed almost absolute powers to the Baltimores. They could not only own and dispose of the land, but they could govern it with few restrictions. Their laws and decrees, however, had to be in harmony with those of England and had to be made "with the advice, assent, and approbation of the freemen or the greater part of them or their representatives."

The young Baltimore soon organized a colonizing expedition and appointed his brother, Leonard Calvert, to lead it. In 1634, more than 200 settlers, in 2 ships, landed in Maryland and established the town of St. Marys. Twenty men in the group were "gentlemen" and received feudal grants from Baltimore; the remainder were laborers and workmen. About half were Catholic, two of whom were Jesuit priests. From the beginning, the colony fared far better than any previous English settlement in the New World. The location was favorable, the Indians were friendly, and Governor Calvert made certain to profit from the mistakes that had been made in settling Virginia. Moreover, he could obtain emergency supplies from Virginia or New England instead of making a long voyage to England.

Despite the colony's prosperity, its growth was slow because, strangely enough, few English Catholics cared to migrate; and because Baltimore insisted on an obsolescent plan of land tenure, which involved the renewal

"Founding of Maryland." From a painting by Emmanuel Leutze. Courtesy, Maryland Historical Society.

of long-outmoded feudal concepts. Under this plan, in the first years some 60 manors of 1,000 acres or more were established. Yeomen farmers, however, formed the backbone of the venture.

Partially to encourage the migration of Protestant workingmen to populate his grant and partially in the spirit of religious freedom, in 1649 Baltimore—with the approval of his assembly—officially proclaimed the religious toleration that he had practiced from the beginning. He was also probably motivated by the ascendancy of the Puritans in England at the time and the threat that they posed to the continuation of his grant. The Maryland Toleration Act promised freedom of worship and assembly to all who would profess belief in the Holy Trinity.

Many Puritans had immigrated into Maryland in 1648, including a substantial group from Virginia. Within a short time, the Puritans wielded more power than the Catholics. In 1654, they gained control of the assembly; deposed Baltimore's Governor, William Stone, himself a Puritan; and amended the Toleration Act to exclude all but Puritans. Meanwhile, Lord Baltimore had been deprived by the Puritan Parliament of his rights to govern the colony. He appealed to Oliver Cromwell, who ultimately sided with him against the Puritan rebels in Maryland. In 1657, his rights were restored and the bigotry of the amended Toleration Act corrected.

In the wake of the anti-Catholicism of the Glorious Revolution in England, in 1691 the third Lord Baltimore lost his governmental privileges, and Maryland became a royal colony. His conversion to the Anglican faith in 1713, however, prompted the return of the proprietorship 2 years later, the Baltimores retaining control until the War for Independence. But intolerance of Catholicism, which had begun after 1691, continued to plague Maryland. The fear of Catholicism was not restricted to Puritans; it was present in all other Protestant groups. In England, French Catholic support for the deposed Stuart pretenders to the throne was a constant menace to the stability of the government.

The Carolinas — Proprietors and the Crown

In the 16th century, the three major European powers all unsuccessfully tried to found permanent settlements in the Carolinas. These attempts included those of the Spaniard De Ayllón, in 1526, at two unknown sites; the Frenchman Jean Ribaut's Charlesfort, in 1562, at Parris Island; a Spanish settlement, in 1566, also at Parris Island; and Raleigh's two English settlements, between 1585 and 1590, at Roanoke Island. As elsewhere in the New World, England was later in settling than the other European powers, but more persevering. It was she who made the first permanent settlements in the Carolinas.

All of present North Carolina and approximately the northern half of

Consisting of about 600 frontiersmen, R o g e r ' s Rangers was a British-American corps that served in the French and Indian War. The rangers acted as advance scouts for the armies of British Generals Abercromby and Amherst. Shown here are an officer and two rangers. From a drawing by Frederick T. Chapman. Courtesy, the artist, the Company of Military Historians, and the Chicago Historical Society.

South Carolina were included in "Virginia" as granted by James I in 1606 to the London and Plymouth Companies. In 1624, however, when "Virginia" became a royal colony, the lands that had not been settled reverted to the King, including all the above portions of the Carolinas. Five years later, shortly after bold Virginia hunters and traders had begun probing southward into the Carolinas, Charles I granted the "Province of Carolana" to Sir Robert Heath, his Attorney General. The boundaries were defined as 31° and 36° north latitude, which extended English claims down through present Georgia, even farther into Spanish-claimed territory. The plans of Heath and his colleagues for settlement of the Carolinas came to naught.

When Charles II regained his throne in 1660, he reclaimed the Carolina grant and 3 years later reissued it to eight men who had aided in the Restoration. The charter gave them the powers of government, specified guarantees for the political rights of the settlers, and authorized the granting of toleration to religious dissenters.

Despite the powers granted the proprietors, they profited little from the Carolinas and did not contribute much to their growth. Their administration was in general marked by poor management, neglect, impractical political experimentation, a low rate of settlement, and recurrent clashes between the Governors and the settlers. The low rate of settlement was attributable in part to circumstances beyond the control of the pro-

The Southern Algonquian Indian village of Secota, situated on the north bank of the Pamlico River, in present Beaufort County, North Carolina. The letters identify parts of the town. From an engraving by Theodore de Bry, after an on-the-scene water-color by John White, 1585. Courtesy, Smithsonian Institution.

prietors. Few settlers could be induced to emigrate from England during the period of comparative religious peace that followed the great migration of Puritans to Massachusetts, in the 1630's. As a result, many of the settlers in the Carolinas came from the British West Indies, especially overcrowded Barbados. Therefore, more than any other British colonies, the Carolinas were influenced by the economic and social attitudes of West Indian planters, as manifested particularly in the adoption of a strict slave code.

The proprietors were unsuccessful in instituting workable local governments, and their theoretical ideas of government were quite impractical. For example, in 1669, they called upon John Locke, a political philosopher whose writings were markedly to influence colonial patriots a century later, to draft the "Fundamental Constitutions of Carolina." This document presented an impractical feudal scheme of polity and land tenure as the basis for proprietary government. It created a petty nobility, with such fanciful titles as landgrave, cacique, and palatine, which was to control two-thirds of the land. The lower classes were slaves, serfs, and freemen. Other provisions pertained to a popular assembly, natural rights, and religious toleration. The proprietors attempted to persuade the colonial legislatures to approve the Fundamental Constitutions, but they were never successful.

One of the first steps of the proprietors was to designate three "counties": Albemarle, north of the Chowan River, in present northeastern North Carolina; Clarendon, south of Albemarle in the Cape Fear region; and Craven, south of Cape Romain, in South Carolina. The latter county, which received the greatest attention from the proprietors, was the most successful. Albemarle progressed slowly, but Clarendon had only a short-lived existence.

A few settlers from Virginia, lured by the prospect of cheaper and better lands, began crossing over the present North Carolina boundary into the Albemarle area at least a decade prior to the charter of 1663. Even though the proprietors offered tax exemptions and generously granted lands to newcomers, the county grew slowly and proved unprofitable for the proprietors, partly because they invested little in it, in money, supplies, or direction. They also failed to institute a stable government. The agitated settlers deposed Governor after Governor.

Problems in Albemarle were soon aggravated unknowingly by the proprietors themselves. In 1665, they obtained a new charter that extended the boundaries of the Carolinas one-half degree to the north and 2 degrees to the south. The latter placed the boundary south of St. Augustine, the major settlement in Spanish Florida, and the former took still more of the lands that had originally been included in Virginia. This action, plus competition in tobacco production, created resentment on the part of Virginians toward Albemarle. Because Albemarle lacked good harbors and navigable rivers, communication with the outside world was mainly limited to land, especially with Virginia. Virginia's hostility, plus the uncertainty of land titles, high quitrents, bad government, apathy of the proprietors, and difficulties in marketing tobacco, the chief money crop, resulted in unrest, confusion, slow growth, and even armed rebellion in Albemarle. However, over the course of time the settlement expanded, particularly after the first town, Bath, was incorporated, in 1705.

Prior to the designation of Clarendon "county," some New Englanders and a group of Barbadians settled near the mouth of the Cape Fear River. Later, in 1665, another party of Barbadians made an attempt to settle in the region, but the colony failed within 2 years because of friction with the earlier settlers and Indian hostility.

Glowing reports of the Port Royal region, coupled with the abandonment of Clarendon in 1667, caused the proprietors to shift their interest to Craven "county," to which they gave their major attention and expenditures. After making plans to bring settlers from England, Ireland, Barbados, and the Bahamas, the proprietors purchased three ships, which sailed from London in August 1669. Storms wrecked two of them after they had left Barbados, and only the *Carolina* reached its destination, the following March, after being repaired at Bermuda. Instead of remaining at Port Royal as instructed, the colonists settled on Albemarle Point (Old Charles Town), at the mouth of the Ashley River. The site was low, open to attack, and infested with malaria. In 1680, the main body of settlers moved to the junction of the Ashley and Cooper Rivers, the site of Charleston.

During its first decade, the colony proved a disappointment to the proprietors. It failed to grow in population as expected, it did not return the anticipated profit, and it refused to put most of the provisions of Locke's "Fundamental Constitutions" into effect as the proprietors had directed. In 1682, the proprietors launched two campaigns, one aimed at recruiting immigrants and the other at reforming the government.

The former was very successful. To attract settlers, the proprietors revised the "Fundamental Constitutions" to allow even greater religious freedom by denying the Anglican Church the right to tax non-Anglicans and by giving each congregation, regardless of sect, the right to tax its own members. This action enticed about 500 English Presbyterians and Baptists to the colony between 1682 and 1685. Immigrants came from Scotland and France as well; in 1684, a group of Presbyterian Scots founded a colony at Stuart's Town, near Port Royal, and before 1690 at least 600 French Huguenots had settled in South Carolina. In 1686, the Spaniards destroyed Stuart's Town, and the Scots fled to Charleston.

To the settlers, the most important of the proprietors' directives for reforming the government were aimed at gaining control over the Indian trade, stopping the traffic in Indian slaves, and preventing the use of the colony as a pirate haven. To put these reforms into effect, the proprietors had to replace the Barbadians who were in control of the government, for they were involved in both the Indian and pirate trades. As a result, a decade of political chaos occurred, and the colony floundered aimlessly without effective direction. The colony's leadership divided into two bitterly opposed factions: the proprietary group, composed mainly of new immigrants; and the antiproprietary group, made up primarily of old settlers. The controversy reached a climax when the parliament demanded a government based on the charter of 1663. The proprietors ordered the parliament dissolved and all laws rescinded. By 1690, not one statute was in force. The Governor, after attempting to rule by executive decree, finally placed the colony under martial law. A revolt occurred in 1690, and one of the proprietors, a former Governor of Albemarle who had been banished in 1689, became Governor. He immediately summoned parliament and won the support of the popular party. Within a short time, however, he began disobeying instructions of the proprietary board and was recalled to England.

His banishment from Albemarle in 1689 had been followed by the appointment of a Governor of "that part of Carolina that lyes North and East of Cape Feare." This action marked the practical end of Albemarle "county" as a unit of government and the real beginning of North Carolina as a separate colony. Two years later, a "Governor of Carolina," who resided in Charleston, received a commission and authority to appoint a deputy for North Carolina. In 1694, he was empowered to appoint deputies "both in South and North Carolina." The two regions were then governed separately, but in 1712 a Governor of North Carolina was named "independent of the Governour of Carolina."

In 1729, because of the repeated failures of the proprietors and their continuing disputes with the populace, the Crown once again took over the Carolinas as royal colonies. At that time, the only major settlements were those at Albemarle and Charleston. During the century, however, settlers began to move inland into the piedmont and the mountains and help create the modern States of North and South Carolina.

THE DUKE OF YORK'S GRANT

Only a few months before the English conquered New Netherland in 1664, Charles II granted the territory as a proprietorship to his brother, James, Duke of York, to hold with all customary proprietary rights. James, keeping for himself the Hudson Valley and the islands in the harbor, renamed the province, as well as the town on Manhattan Island, New York. He conveyed the southern part of his grant, between the Hudson and the Delaware Rivers, to two loyal Stuart supporters, Lord John Berkeley and Sir George Carteret, who named it New Jersey. New York was quickly amalgamated into the English colonial system and enjoyed a continuing prosperity. When James assumed the throne, the province automatically became a royal colony. It was attached briefly to the Dominion of New England, but regained separate status after the Glorious Revolution (1688).

New Jersey had few settlements when it passed into the possession of the new proprietors. A scattering of Swedes, Dutch, and Finns had filtered into the area from New York. Almost as soon as English control was asserted, New England Puritans moved into the area. They were welcomed by the proprietors' representative, who in 1665 founded the village of Elizabethtown. Because immigration into New Jersey was encouraged by promises of religious toleration, representative government, and moderately priced land, the colony was populated rather quickly.

In 1674, Lord Berkeley sold his interest in New Jersey to two English Quakers. From them, it passed into the hands of three others, one of whom was William Penn. In 1676, Carteret agreed with them to split the colony into East and West Jersey and ceded the latter to them. In 1688, James II reasserted his governing right and brought the Jerseys into the Dominion of New England. After the collapse of the Dominion, in 1689, East and West Jersey reverted to full proprietary control. In 1702, however, the proprietors surrendered their governing power to the Crown, but retained their land titles. In 1738, New Jersey was reestablished as a separate royal colony.

In 1682, to obtain access to the seacoast, William Penn acquired Delaware from the Duke of York, who between 1664 and 1680 had taken over the area on the assumption that it was part of his grant and had divided it into three counties, or "Territories." After Penn's purchase, these counties were at first governed as part of Pennsylvania and basked in the same prosperity. In 1701, however, they were authorized to form a separate assembly, which occurred in 1704, and the colony of Delaware was born. But it remained under the jurisdiction of the Penn family until the War for Independence.

PENNSYLVANIA: A QUAKER PROPRIETORSHIP

Pennsylvania was the most successful of the proprietary colonies. Adm. Sir William Penn was a wealthy and respected friend of Charles II. His son, William, was an associate of George Fox, founder of the Society of Friends—a despised Quaker. When the senior Penn died, in 1670, his Quaker son inherited not only the friendship of the Crown but also an outstanding unpaid debt of some magnitude owed to his father by the King. In settlement, in 1681 he received a grant of land in America, called "Pennsylvania," which he decided to use as a refuge for his perse-

"The Landing of William Penn, 1682." From a painting by J. L. G. Ferris. Courtesy, William E. Ryder and the Smithsonian Institution.

cuted coreligionists. It was a princely domain, extending along the Delaware River from the 40th to the 43d parallel. As proprietor, Penn was both ruler and landlord. The restrictions on the grant were essentially the same as those imposed on the second Lord Baltimore: colonial laws had to be in harmony with those of England and had to be assented to by a representative assembly.

Penn lost little time in advertising his grant and the terms on which he offered settlement. He promised religious freedom and virtually total self-government. More than 1,000 colonists arrived the first year, most of whom were Mennonites and Quakers. Penn himself arrived in 1682 at New Castle and spent the winter at Upland, a Swedish settlement on the Delaware that the English had taken over; he renamed it Chester. He founded a capital city a few miles upstream and named it Philadelphia—the City of Brotherly Love. Well situated and well planned, it grew rapidly. Within 2 years, it had more than 600 houses, many of them handsome brick residences surrounded by lawns and gardens.

Shiploads of Quakers poured into the colony. By the summer of 1683, more than 3,000 settlers had arrived. Welsh, Germans, Scotch-Irish, Mennonites, Quakers, Jews, and Baptists mingled in a New World utopia. Not even the great Puritan migration had populated a colony so fast. Pennsylvania soon rivaled Massachusetts, New York, and Virginia. In part its prosperity is attributable to its splendid location and fertile

A group of Cherokee Indians brought to London in 1730 by Sir Alexander Cuming. From an engraving by Isaac Basire, after a painting by Markham, in the British Museum. Courtesy, Smithsonian Institution.

Symbolic scene representing the various treaties William Penn negotiated with the Indians in Pennsylvania. The Indians admired Penn because he dealt fairly with them in land transactions and protected them. From an engraving by John Hall, 1775, after a painting by Benjamin West. Courtesy, Library of Congress.

soils, but even more to the proprietor's felicitous administration. In a series of laws—the Great Law and the First and Second Frames of Government—Penn created one of the most humane and progressive governments then in existence. It was characterized by broad principles of religious toleration, a well-organized bicameral legislature, and a forward-looking penal code.

Another reason for the colony's growth was that, unlike the other colonies, it was not troubled by the Indians. Penn had bought their lands and made a series of peace treaties that were scrupulously fair and rigidly adhered to. For more than half a century, Indians and whites lived in Pennsylvania in peace. Quaker farmers, who were never armed, could leave their children with neighboring "savages" when they went into town for a visit.

By any measure, Penn's "Holy Experiment" was a magnificent success. Penn proved that a state could function smoothly on Quaker principles, without oaths, arms, or priests, and that these principles encouraged in-

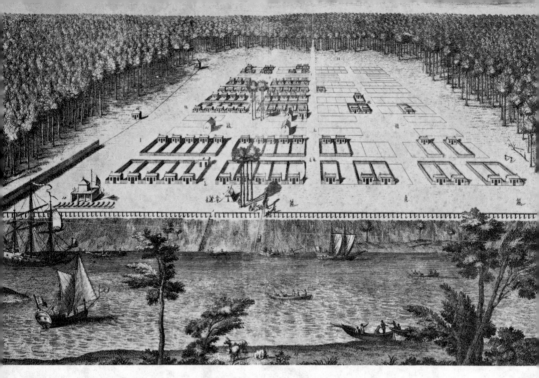

Savannah, in 1734, the year after James Oglethorpe founded the city and colony of Georgia. From an engraving by P. Fourdrinier, after an on-the-scene drawing by Peter Gordon. Courtesy, Library of Congress.

James Oglethorpe, founder of the colony of Georgia, presents Tomochichi, chief of the Yamacraws, to the Lord Trustees of the colony, in England. Oglethorpe, wearing a black suit, stands in the center. From a painting by William Verelst, 1734. Courtesy, Smithsonian Institution.

dividual morality and freedom of conscience. Furthermore, ever a good businessman, he made a personal fortune while treating his subjects with unbending fairness and honesty.

GEORGIA—EARLY PENETRATION

By 1700, the last of the British colonies in the present United States, Georgia, had not yet been founded. Not until 1733 did the philanthropist Gen. James Oglethorpe begin to settle the colony, which he had conceived as a refuge for oppressed debtors in English prisons [*Colonials and Patriots,* Vol. VI in this series, pp. 19–20]. As the 17th century neared an end, however, the British were beginning to penetrate the area. English traders set up posts on the Savannah, Oconee, and Ocmulgee Rivers and were active along the Chattahoochee and as far west as the Mississippi. Winning the friendship of two powerful Indian tribes, the Creek and the Chickasaw, they created the antagonism with the Spanish and the French that resulted in the international clashes of the early 1700's.

SOCIAL AND CULTURAL LIFE

Life in early colonial times was harsh, and the refinements of the mother country were ordinarily lacking. The colonists, however, soon began to mold their English culture into the fresh environment of a new land. The influence of religion permeated the entire way of life. In most southern colonies, the Anglican Church was the legally established church. In New England, the Puritans were dominant; and, in Pennsylvania, the Quakers. Especially in the New England colonies, the local or village church was the hub of community life; the authorities strictly enforced the Sabbath and sometimes banished nonbelievers and dissenters.

Unfortunately, the same sort of religious intolerance, bigotry, and superstition associated with the age of the Reformation in Europe also prevailed in some of the colonies, though on a lesser scale. In the last half of the 17th century, during sporadic outbreaks of religious fanaticism and hysteria, Massachusetts and Connecticut authorities tried and hanged a few women as "witches." Early in the 18th century, some other witchcraft persecution occurred, in Virginia, North Carolina, and Rhode Island. As the decades passed, however, religious toleration developed in the colonies.

Because of the strong religious influence in the colonies, especially in New England, religious instruction and Bible reading played an important part in education. In Massachusetts, for example, a law of 1647 required each town to maintain a grammar school for the purpose of providing religious, as well as general, instruction. In the southern colonies, only a few privately endowed free schools existed. Private tutors instructed the sons of well-to-do planters, who completed their educations in English universities. Young males in poor families throughout the colonies were ordinarily apprenticed for vocational education.

By 1700, two colleges had been founded: Harvard, established by the Massachusetts Legislature in 1636; and William and Mary, in Virginia, which originated in 1693 under a royal charter. Other cultural activities before 1700 were limited. The few literary products of the colonists, mostly historical narratives, journals, sermons, and some poetry, were printed in England. The *Bay Psalm Book* (1640) was the first book printed in the colonies. Artists and composers were few, and their output was of a relatively simple character.

OUR BASIC ENGLISH HERITAGE

Our American heritage is basically English, as infused through the British colonies that ultimately revolted and formed a new nation. Of all the English colonial roots of the American way of life, those concerned with government and democracy are the most basic. The distance from the mother country, the cheapness of land, and the scarcity of labor created a social and political atmosphere that was quite liberal for the times. In strong contrast to the royal autocracy that prevailed in the French and Spanish colonies, a considerable degree of self-government flourished. Social distinctions were less important than in England. Suffrage, though restricted by property and church membership qualifications, was broadened as time went on.

Arbitrary rule in the English settlements was short lived. The traditions of Parliament, trade guilds, and merchant associations encouraged the King to permit the formation of local representative assemblies, even in the proprietary colonies; the first meeting of such an assembly was the Virginia House of Burgesses, in 1619. In New England, the Congregational religious background influenced the growth of democracy, as did also the conduct of town meetings. The governments of most of the colonies were based on some form of written document, which stemmed from the issuance of charters and grants by the Crown to joint-stock companies and proprietors, and were potentially democratic in form. Conflicts between the royal Governors and the lawmaking colonial assemblies occurred early. By obtaining control of the revenue and refusing assent to unwanted taxes, the assemblies gained a measure of control over the Governors, of whose powers they were always suspicious.

Associated with our English heritage of democratic institutions and constitutional government is the emphasis placed on individual rights. Wherever the British colonists settled, they carried with them the fundamental belief that they were entitled to all the rights and freedoms of Englishmen. Not the least of these rights was that of having some representation in the branch of government that levied taxes on them. Over the breach of these rights, the colonists finally fought the War for Independence, which separated them from the British Empire. As time went on, they blended into the concept of individual rights the freedom of conscience and religious belief.

Outstanding among our other rich English legacies are those in language, literature, architecture, and common law.

Epilogue—The United States: An Amalgam

During the colonial period of U.S. history, most of the nations of Western Europe planted their seeds in the fresh soil that was to nourish the growth of the United States of America. Spain spread her blood, language, and traditions from Florida to California. France sowed a rich heritage throughout the length of the Mississippi Valley. Holland and Sweden transplanted roots to the banks of the Hudson and the Delaware. In the course of time, the offshoots of all these plantings were grafted onto the oak-solid trunks of the British colonies on the Atlantic shore. From the beginning, the hybrid was nurtured by immigrants of various races and religions from scores of other lands.

The amalgamation of such rich and diverse national, cultural, and racial elements into a free and democratic society has created the United States of America—a harmonious blending of cultures, languages, and traditions that mirrors the hopes and aspirations of all mankind.

PART II

Explorers and Settlers:

Survey of Historic

Sites and Buildings

A FULL APPRECIATION of our national historical heritage can never be gained by the reading of historical narrative or formal study alone—interesting and important though such study is. Visits to historic sites and buildings rekindle, stimulate, and broaden historical interest and knowledge; they add new dimensions to the past. The numerous sites and buildings that are described below illustrate an intriguing and vital epoch in our history: early exploration and settlement. They reveal the widespread activities of the various European nations, the clashes of imperial rivalry, and the beginnings of the amalgam of nationalities, cultures, and races that became the United States.

Sites and buildings associated with the epoch are scattered throughout the United States. They include: Missions, pueblos, presidios, houses, memorial parks, ruins, and lost sites. Spanish sites, which indicate the broad geographical extent of Spanish exploration and settlement, range from the lower Atlantic seaboard across the Southeast and the gulf coast to the Southwest and the Pacific coast. The remains or ruins of various forts, missions, and trading posts in the Great Lakes region, the

[135

Mississippi Valley, and the Southeast are remnants of the French Empire in the New World. Dutch and Swedish sites are in New York, Pennsylvania, Delaware, and New Jersey. Because sites pertaining to the later English colonial period, after 1700, are described in a separate volume of this series, *Colonials and Patriots*, those treated in this volume are proportionately fewer than those for Spain, France, Holland, and Sweden. Indian archeological sites have been included that reveal European contact and extent of exploration.

The identification, maintenance, preservation, and reconstruction of historic sites and buildings associated with the period of early exploration and settlement present some unique problems because of the passage of so much time and the paucity and obscurity of the early historical records. More sites have been "lost" than in later periods of history; some sites were definitively located only after exhaustive historical and archeological research. Also, as would be expected, more of these historic buildings are in ruins or partial ruins than are those of later times. All these problems have been encountered by the various governmental and private groups and individuals on the National, State, county, and local levels that maintain historic sites and buildings representing the period.

Some of the fruits of the National Survey of Historic Sites and Buildings program are presented in this volume, which also includes sites in the National Park System that illustrate early exploration and settlement. State universities, park departments, and historical societies throughout the Nation have done important work in this period of history, as have also many county and municipal governments. Private organizations, too, have made substantial contributions. These include, for example, on the National level, the National Trust for Historic Preservation; on the State level, in California, the Daughters of the American Revolution, the Native Daughters of the Golden West, and the Native Sons of the Golden West; on the city level, in New Mexico, the Historic Santa Fe Foundation and the Old Santa Fe Association. Examples in the East include Sleepy Hollow Restorations, Inc., in New York; the Society for the Preservation of Virginia Antiquities; the Association for the Preservation of New England Antiquities; the Antiquarian and Landmarks Society of Connecticut; the Plymouth Antiquarian Society, in Massachusetts; and the St. Augustine Historical Society, in Florida. Private local associations of historians and archeologists have also done much valuable work.

The efforts of all these organizations, as well as those of numerous others and scores of private owners, have fostered our national heritage

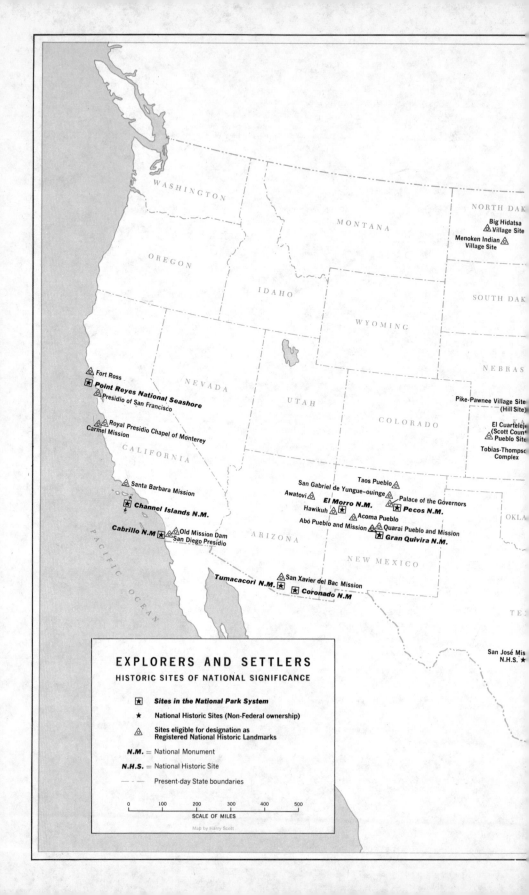

WASHINGTON

OREGON

IDAHO

MONTANA

WYOMING

NEVADA

UTAH

COLORADO

CALIFORNIA

NORTH DAK

SOUTH DAK

NEBRAS

OKLA

TE

NEW MEXICO

ARIZONA

PACIFIC OCEAN

Big Hidatsa
△ Village Site

Menoken Indian
Village Site △

Pike-Pawnee Village Site
(Hill Site)

El Cuarteleje
(Scott Coun
△ Pueblo Site

Tobias-Thompso
Complex

△ Fort Ross
★ **Point Reyes National Seashore**
△ Presidio of San Francisco

△△ Royal Presidio Chapel of Monterey
Carmel Mission

△ Santa Barbara Mission

★ **Channel Islands N.M.**

Cabrillo N.M. ★ △△ Old Mission Dam
San Diego Presidio

Taos Pueblo △

San Gabriel de Yungue–ouinge △
Awatovi △ **El Morro N.M.**
Hawikuh △ ★ **Pecos N.M.**
△ Acoma Pueblo
Abó Pueblo and Mission △ Quarai Pueblo and Mission
★ **Gran Quivira N.M.**

Palace of the Governors

Tumacacori N.M. △ San Xavier del Bac Mission
★ △ **Coronado N.M**

San José Mis
N.H.S. ★

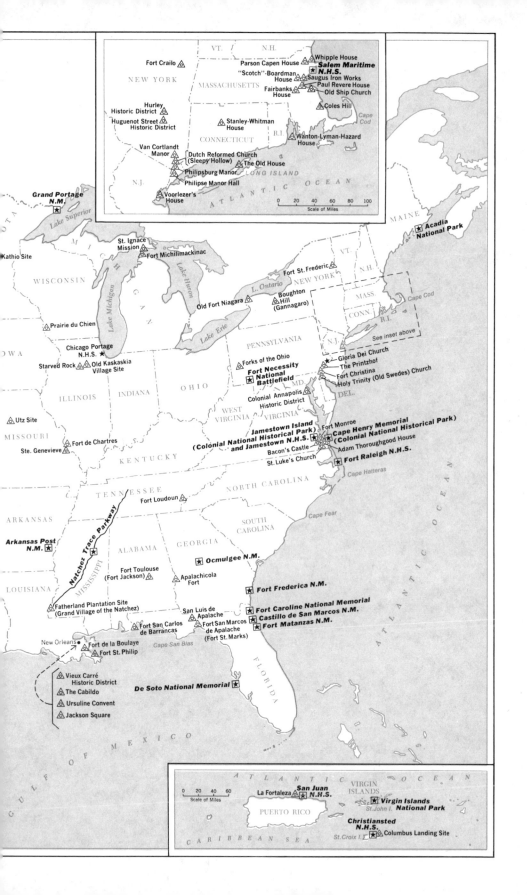

Inset (upper):

VT. / N.H.

Fort Crailo △

Parson Capen House △

Whipple House △
★ **Salem Maritime N.H.S.**

NEW YORK

MASSACHUSETTS

"Scotch"-Boardman House △△
Fairbanks House △
Saugus Iron Works △
Paul Revere House △
Old Ship Church △

Hurley Historic District △

Huguenot Street Historic District △

R.I.

Coles Hill △

Cape Cod

△ Stanley-Whitman House

CONNECTICUT

Wanton-Lyman-Hazard House △

Van Cortlandt Manor △△

Dutch Reformed Church (Sleepy Hollow) △
△ The Old House

Philipsburg Manor △

Philipse Manor Hall △

N.J.

LONG ISLAND

ATLANTIC OCEAN

Voorlezer's House △

Scale of Miles
0 20 40 60 80 100

Main map:

Grand Portage N.M. ★

Lake Superior

Kathio Site △

St. Ignace Mission △

Fort Michilimackinan △

MICHIGAN

WISCONSIN

Lake Huron

Lake Michigan

Prairie du Chien △

Chicago Portage N.H.S. △

Starved Rock △△ Old Kaskaskia Village Site △

IOWA

ILLINOIS

INDIANA

OHIO

Utz Site △

MISSOURI

Fort de Chartres △

Ste. Genevieve △

KENTUCKY

TENNESSEE

Fort Loudoun △

Natchez Trace Parkway

MISSISSIPPI

Fatherland Plantation Site (Grand Village of the Natchez) △

Arkansas Post N.M. ★

ARKANSAS

LOUISIANA

New Orleans ●

Fort de la Boulaye △

Fort St. Philip △

Vieux Carré Historic District △

The Cabildo △

Ursuline Convent △

Jackson Square △

ALABAMA

GEORGIA

Fort Toulouse (Fort Jackson) △

Apalachicola Fort △

San Luis de Apalache △

Fort San Carlos de Barrancas △

Fort San Marcos de Apalache (Fort St. Marks) △

★ Ocmulgee N.M.

★ Fort Frederica N.M.

★ Fort Caroline National Memorial
Castillo de San Marcos N.M. ★
★ Fort Matanzas N.M.

De Soto National Memorial ★

FLORIDA

Cape San Blas

GULF OF MEXICO

Fort St. Frederic △

L. Ontario

NEW YORK

Boughton Hill (Gannagaro) △

Old Fort Niagara △

Lake Erie

PENNSYLVANIA

Forks of the Ohio △
Fort Necessity National Battlefield ★

WEST VIRGINIA

MD.

VIRGINIA

Colonial Annapolis Historic District △

VT.

N.H.

MASS.

CONN.

R.I.

Cape Cod

See inset above

N.J.

DEL.

★ Gloria Dei Church
The Printzhof
Fort Christina
Holy Trinity (Old Swedes) Church

Fort Monroe
Jamestown Island (Colonial National Historical Park) and Jamestown N.H.S. △
Cape Henry Memorial (Colonial National Historical Park)
Adam Thoroughgood House
★ **Fort Raleigh N.H.S.**

Bacon's Castle △

St. Luke's Church △

Cape Hatteras

NORTH CAROLINA

Cape Fear

SOUTH CAROLINA

ATLANTIC OCEAN

Inset (lower):

ATLANTIC OCEAN

VIRGIN ISLANDS

La Fortaleza △ *San Juan N.H.S.* ★

St. John I. ★ **Virgin Islands National Park**

PUERTO RICO

Christiansted N.H.S. ★

Columbus Landing Site △
St. Croix I.

CARIBBEAN SEA

Scale of Miles
0 20 40 60

by making it possible for Americans to visit and enjoy many of the historic sites and buildings illustrating early exploration and settlement that are described below. The sites and buildings are arranged alphabetically by State and Territory within the following five categories: Units of the National Park System; National Historic Sites in non-Federal ownership; sites eligible for the Registry of National Historic Landmarks; Historic Districts eligible for the Registry; and sites of sufficient importance to merit attention but which are not considered to be nationally significant when measured and evaluated by the special Landmark criteria (pp. 421–422).

A. Sites in the National Park System

The principal aim of the National Survey of Historic Sites and Buildings is to identify nationally important historic sites that are not units of the National Park System, but no such survey would be complete without mention of sites in the system. The sites described below are those administered by the National Park Service that have primary or secondary associations with the phases of history treated in this volume. Further information about a particular site may be obtained by writing directly to the superintendent at the address indicated.

1. Natchez Trace Parkway, Alabama-Mississippi-Tennessee

Location: Traverses the States of Mississippi, Alabama, and Tennessee, from Natchez to Nashville; address, P.O. Box 948, Tupelo, Miss. 38801.

Early inland explorers and settlers in the Southeastern part of the present United States discovered a network of animal trails and Indian paths that formed a wilderness road between present Natchez and Nashville. During the 18th century, Frenchmen, Englishmen, Spaniards, and Americans used the road. French explorers, missionaries, soldiers, and traders called it a "trace," a French word for "trail." Shortly after arriving at the gulf coast in 1699, the French first explored the trace area; in 1716, they established Fort Rosalie at the site of Natchez. In 1763, the French ceded the region to the English, who occupied it until 1779. The English, who used the trace mainly for the purpose of trading with the Natchez, Choctaw, and Chickasaw tribes, called it the "Path to the Choctaw Nation."

Scenic Natchez Trace Parkway generally follows the route of the old Natchez Trace. Indians, Spaniards, Frenchmen, Englishmen, and Americans used the trace. For several centuries, it was an important trade route and emigrant road in the old Southwest.

At the end of the War for Independence, in 1783, Spain claimed the territory between the Mississippi and Chattahoochee Rivers, as far north as Memphis, as a reward for her wartime aid to the colonies. This territory included Natchez, at the southern end of the trace, which remained under Spanish control until it passed to the United States in 1798, though in the interim the population had remained predominantly English-speaking. The United States immediately organized the Mississippi Territory. At the northern end of the trace, beginning about 1780, American settlers were populating Nashville. Kentucky traders and other frontiersmen rafted their goods downriver to Natchez or New Orleans, but used the trace—which they sometimes called the Chickasaw Trace—returning home. Frequently, they brought back Spanish silver. By 1800, about 1,000 made the trip each year, and mail service was initiated along the trace.

From 1800 to 1820, the trace was the most traveled road in the old Southwest. Over it passed a variety of colorful frontier characters: Missionaries, boatmen, Indian hunting parties, mounted postmen, and U.S. soldiers. A vital economic and social artery, it bound the old Southwest to the rest of the Nation. It was used for frontier defense in the "cold war" with Spain, until she abandoned all claims to Florida in 1819, and became a valuable military and post road. At the beginning of the War of 1812, between the United States and England, Andrew Jackson and his Tennessee Militia used it to travel to Natchez and after the war returned over it in triumph.

By 1820, the trace was no longer needed for frontier defense. Rivalries with Spain and England had ended, and the Indians were being forced westward. The new steamboat traffic robbed the trace of its trade. As Alabama, Mississippi, and Tennessee became more populous, sections were abandoned and others incorporated into local road systems. The trace lost its frontier character.

The Natchez Trace Parkway is still under construction and follows roughly—crossing, recrossing, and at times paralleling—the route of the old Natchez Trace. When completed, it will make possible a leisurely 450-mile drive through a protected zone of forest, meadow, and field that is rich in prehistoric and historic associations. Evidences of the aboriginal Indian inhabitants abound along the trace. Markers indicate historic sites, and interpretive exhibits point out their significance. The main visitor center is at Tupelo, Miss.

Conjectural likeness of Francisco Vásquez de Coronado, based on contemporary descriptions. From a charcoal portrait by Peter Hurd. Courtesy, the artist and Roswell Museum and Art Center, Roswell, New Mexico.

2. Coronado National Memorial, Arizona

Location: Cochise County, on Montezuma Canyon Road, about 30 miles west of Bisbee; address, Star Route, Hereford, Ariz. 85615.

This memorial is located along the United States-Mexico border near the point where the great Spanish expedition under Francisco Vásquez de Coronado entered the present United States in 1540. It commemorates the first major European exploration of the U.S. Southwest—only one-half century after Columbus' discovery of America and more than one-half century before the first permanent English settlement, at Jamestown. Coronado Peak affords a sweeping view of the country through which the expedition marched. Exhibits along the footpath to the peak provide information on the expedition and the natural features of the region. The memorial was established by Presidential proclamation in November 1952.

3. Tumacacori National Monument, Arizona

Location: Santa Cruz County, on U.S. 89, about 48 miles south of Tucson; address, P.O. Box 67, Tumacacori, Ariz. 85640.

This monument features a typical old mission church that illustrates Spanish colonial endeavor and commemorates the introduction of Christianity into what is now southern Arizona. The mission of San José de Tumacacori was a northern outpost of a mission chain constructed by Franciscan priests in the 1700's on sites established by the Jesuits in what was then the State of Sonora, New Spain.

The great Jesuit missionary-explorer Father Eusebio Francisco Kino first came into the Tumacacori region in 1691 when he visited the small Sobaipuri Indian village of San Cayetano de Tumacacori, thought to have been situated within a few miles of the present mission. By 1698, Tumacacori had an "earth-roofed house of adobe," fields of wheat, and herds of cattle, sheep, and goats. When a missionary was assigned to Guevavi, to the southeast, Tumacacori became a *visita* of that mission.

The year after the Pima Rebellion of 1751, Spanish authorities moved the village of San Cayetano de Tumacacori to the place where the mission now stands and renamed it San José de Tumacacori. They erected a small mission at the site and founded a presidio at Tubac, 3 miles to the north. In 1773, Apache raids forced the closing of Guevavi, and San José de Tumacacori Mission—then under the Franciscans—became district headquarters. Construction of the present building started around 1800, apparently, and it was in use by 1822, when the Mexican period began.

Under Mexican administration, the power of the Roman Catholic Church weakened. Missions were required to become parish churches, and the Government supplied no funds to support mission activity. As late as 1841, a priest is known to have been at Tumacacori, but in 1844 Mexico sold the mission lands to a private citizen. Four years later, when the last devout Indians left Tumacacori, they took with them to San Xavier del Bac Mission, near Tucson, certain church furnishings, including statues that are still used there. The Tumacacori church fell into ruins, but its massiveness preserved it from complete destruction.

Tumacacori National Monument, totaling 10 acres, was established in 1908. Administered by the National Park Service, it is no longer associated with any religious order. Some repair work was done to the old buildings in 1921, including a new roof over the long nave. Repair work since then has been limited entirely to preserving existing original construction. A reminder that Spain was active on the frontier in the

Modern view of San José de Tumacacori Mission, Arizona. Built by Franciscan priests on the site of an earlier mission, San José served as the northern outpost of a Sonoran mission chain.

Southwest long before the United States became a nation, this typical old mission church remains today an inspiring symbol of the faith, courage, and vigor of the early missionary priests, as well as of the great loyalty and devotion of the Indian converts.

4. Arkansas Post National Memorial, Arkansas

Location: Arkansas County, on Ark. 1 and 169, about 8 miles northeast of Gillett; address, Superintendent, Hot Springs National Park, P.O. Box 1219, Hot Springs National Park, Ark. 71902.

Arkansas Post, founded near the mouth of the Arkansas River, was the first European settlement in the lower Mississippi Valley and the territory of the later Louisiana Purchase. Established in 1686 among the friendly Quapaw Indians by Henry de Tonty, lieutenant of the famed explorer René Robert Cavelier, Sieur de la Salle, the first post was small, may not have been utilized continuously, and was probably abandoned during the period 1700–1720. As French activities increased along the lower Mississippi, especially in the decade following the establishment of John Law's colony about 1720, Arkansas Post thrived. In the last half of the century, the Spaniards and Americans took over the post. It flourished under the Americans. After the War of 1812, American settlers rapidly populated the area, and the post became the capital of Arkansas Territory. Although the capital was later moved to Little Rock, the post became a key point in steamboat traffic and a strategic Civil War military site.

Because of subsequent changes in location of Tonty's early post and the vagaries of the Arkansas River, the precise location of the site cannot be determined. Formerly a State park, the National Memorial was authorized by an act of Congress on July 6, 1960. On June 23, 1964, it was accepted by the National Park Service, which made plans to enhance the interpretive program.

5. Cabrillo National Monument, California

Location: San Diego County, on Point Loma, 10 miles southwest of downtown San Diego, via Pacific Boulevard (U.S. 101) and Rosecrans Street; address, P.O. Box 6175, San Diego, Calif. 92106.

Cabrillo National Monument commemorates the discovery of the coast of Alta California in 1542 by Juan Rodríguez Cabrillo, a Portuguese navigator in the service of Spain. Cabrillo's landing at San Diego Bay, which he called San Miguel Bay, marks the first contact of Europeans with that part of the New World. The expedition, consisting of two small vessels, the *San Salvador and Victoria,* originated at Navidad, on the west coast of present Mexico. It was the first Spanish expedition to pass beyond Cabo del Engaño (Cape Deceit).

At San Diego Bay, the ships anchored behind the high land of Point Loma. On going ashore, apparently at Ballast Point, a group of men were attacked by a small party of Indians, but land parties briefly explored the region. Cabrillo sailed northward along the California coast, and sighted or landed at many places. Unfortunately, he died, at San Miguel Island, in January 1543. His grave, the location of which is unknown and unmarked, is probably near Cuyler Harbor. Bartolomé Ferrelo, the chief pilot, who succeeded to command, again turned northward and reached the northernmost point of the expedition, probably the general area of the Rogue River in present southern Oregon.

From Cabrillo National Monument one of the outstanding seascapes of the world can be viewed: an inspiring scene comprising the ocean, bays, islands, mountains, foothills, valleys, and plains that surround the city of San Diego. Also visible are the following sites located on Ballast

Point in the Fort Rosecrans Military Reservation on Point Loma: the probable landing place of Cabrillo, September 28, 1542; the landing place of Sebastián Vizcaíno, who named the bay San Diego, in November 1602; and the former site of the Spanish coastal battery, Fort Guijarros, built in 1797.

The 81-acre National Monument, established in 1913, contains one of the first lighthouses on the Pacific coast, the San Diego Lighthouse, put into operation in 1855. A visitor center is planned that will contain exhibits relating to Spanish exploration and settlement.

6. Channel Islands National Monument, California

Location: Anacapa Island, 10 miles from the mainland, southwest of Port Hueneme; Santa Barbara Island, 38 miles from the mainland, southwest of Los Angeles; address, P.O. Box 6175, San Diego, Calif. 92106.

The eight Channel Islands, from south to north, are San Clemente, Santa Catalina, San Nicolas, Santa Barbara, Anacapa, Santa Cruz, Santa Rosa, and San Miguel. Channel Islands National Monument includes the centrally located pair, Santa Barbara (650 acres) and Anacapa (700 acres). The prime aim of the National Park Service in these islands is to preserve and protect biological and geological phenomena for the benefit of the public. The islands, however, were among the first places visited and identified by the early Spanish explorers of the California coast. Juan Rodríguez Cabrillo, California's discoverer, died in 1543 on the island farthest northwest, San Miguel.

Santa Barbara and Anacapa Islands are undeveloped, having no permanent structures or accommodations of any kind. During summer months and on weekends throughout the year, boat service is available to Anacapa from Port Hueneme, Calif. A ranger is stationed on Anacapa during the summer. Boat service is not available to Santa Barbara, which has no ranger assigned. Both islands retain their pristine appearance, looking now just as they did when first seen by the Spanish more than 400 years ago.

7. Point Reyes National Seashore, California

Location: Marin County, on Calif. 1, about 35 miles northwest of San Francisco; address, Point Reyes, Calif. 94956.

Point Reyes and Drakes Bay are mainly associated with the great Spanish

Drakes Bay, California, well known to Spanish explorers of the 16th and 17th centuries, may have been a landing place of the Englishman Sir Francis Drake in 1579 during his circumnavigation of the globe. It is now a part of Point Reyes National Seashore.

explorers of the Pacific coast during the 16th and 17th centuries, though Miwok Indians had lived for centuries before on the peninsula where Point Reyes is situated. Drakes Bay was then, as now, a harbor sheltered by Point Reyes from northerly winds but exposed to southern storms. Juan Rodríguez Cabrillo probably sighted the bay and the point in November of 1542. After attacking Spanish ships, Sir Francis Drake may have beached and repaired his vessel, the *Golden Hind,* at Point Reyes in 1579 before starting across the Pacific to complete the first English circumnavigation of the globe. On Point Reyes he may also have erected a temporary stone fort and taken possession of "Nova Albion" for Queen Elizabeth.

At Drakes Bay, in 1595, the Spanish explorer Sebastián Rodríguez Cermeño suffered the first recorded shipwreck in California waters when his Manila galleon, the *San Agustín,* was blown ashore near the mouth of Drakes Estero, which adjoins Drakes Bay. Archeologists have recovered from Indian mounds on the shores of the estero quantities of porcelain and iron spikes that almost surely came from the galleon. After 1 month's stay at Drakes Bay, which Cermeño called the Bay of San Francisco, he set out on a thorough exploration of the California coast.

In 1603, the Spanish explorer Sebastián Vizcaíno, coming north from Monterey, sailed into Drakes Bay, but did not land because of strong winds. He named the headland "Punta de los Reyes," or Point Reyes. The Spanish attempt to reach Monterey and Drakes Bay (at first called the Bay of San Francisco) by land led to the discovery of one of the best natural ports in the world. The Portolá expedition, traveling up the coast from San Diego in 1769, was actually seeking the ports of Monterey and the "Bay of San Francisco" (Drakes Bay) when it accidentally sighted for the first time the harbor that is now called San Francisco Bay.

Point Reyes National Seashore, authorized in 1962, will ultimately include Point Reyes and the 28 miles of beaches on Drakes Bay. These seashore areas are little changed since they were first sighted by the Spanish in 1542.

McClures Beach, Point Reyes National Seashore, California. Such seashore areas have changed little since first sighted by Spanish explorers in the 16th century.

Constructed in St. Augustine late in the 17th century by the Spanish, Castillo de San Marcos figured prominently in the Anglo-Spanish rivalry for control of the present Southeastern United States.

8. Castillo de San Marcos National Monument, Florida

Location: St. Johns County, St. Augustine; address, 1 Castillo Drive, St. Augustine, Fla. 32084.

This well-preserved fort figured prominently in the Spanish-English struggle for the present Southeastern United States during the 17th and 18th centuries. The Spanish began to construct it because of the English threat to Florida posed by the founding of Charleston, S.C., in 1670, only 2 years after the sack of St. Augustine by English pirates. As early as 1586, when Sir Francis Drake had raided St. Augustine, the English had shown their determination to destroy the Spanish monopoly in the New World.

Construction of the castillo began in 1672 and required almost 25 years. Spanish artisans and drafted Indian labor built substantial walls, 30 feet high and up to 12 feet thick, of the native shellstone called coquina, with mortar made from shell lime. The walls were built in a symmetrical design, in the style developed by Italian and Spanish engineers.

The castillo was well armed and manned, for the region was in turmoil. Spanish forays against the Carolinas and Georgia (1686, 1706, 1742) emanated from the castillo, which between 1683 and 1743 was also the target of six raids and sieges by pirates, Indians, and Englishmen. Though

England gained possession of Florida, including the castillo, at the end of the French and Indian War, in 1763, Spain regained control of Florida at the end of the War for American Independence and held it until the United States acquired it early in the 19th century. The U.S. Army renamed the castillo Fort Marion, and used it as a prison, Seminole and Southwestern Indians, among others, being imprisoned there.

During the Civil War, Confederate forces occupied the fort briefly before Federal troops assumed control in 1862. Ironically, its last military use—as a prison during the Spanish-American War (1898)—was against the nation that built it. Established in 1924 as a National Monument by Presidential proclamation, the fort was placed under the jurisdiction of the War Department, which in 1933 transferred it to the National Park Service. The original name was restored 9 years later.

9. De Soto National Memorial, Florida

Location: Manatee County, on Tampa Bay, 5 miles west of Bradenton; address, P.O. Box 1377, Bradenton, Fla. 33506.

This memorial commemorates De Soto's landing with a 600-man army in Florida on May 30, 1539. The exact site of the landing is not known, but it was probably between Tampa Bay and Estero Bay (Fort Myers). De Soto was the third Spaniard to lead an expedition into Florida. Ponce de León, as early as 1513, had accomplished some initial land and sea exploration. In 1528, Pánfilo de Narváez and 400 colonists had landed at Tampa Bay and marched overland to the vicinity of Apalachicola Bay, where they built small boats and sailed westward in the gulf.

De Soto's expedition is especially significant because—more than 60 years before the first permanent English settlement, at Jamestown—during the period 1539–43 it explored 4,000 miles of wilderness throughout the present Southeastern United States. Penetrating as far as Oklahoma and east Texas, it gained for Spain a broad and valuable knowledge of the interior lands and peoples. When De Soto died near the Mississippi River, his lieutenant, Luís de Moscoso, completed the exploration.

De Soto National Memorial was established in 1949. To commemorate the 400th anniversary of De Soto's landing, in 1939 the National Society of Colonial Dames of America erected the De Soto trail marker, located at Shaw's Point, which overlooks the mouth of the Manatee River.

10. Fort Caroline National Memorial, Florida

Location: Duval County, 10 miles east of Jacksonville, 5 miles north of Fla. 10; address, 1 Castillo Drive, St. Augustine, Fla. 32084.

This memorial commemorates a French attempt in 1564–65 to establish a colony in the present Southeastern United States, at a time when no other European colony existed in the present United States. By planting this colony, France hoped for a share of the New World, claimed by Spain. This French move forced Spain to act—by founding St. Augustine—and brought on the first decisive conflict between European powers within the area of the present United States. At Fort Caroline, the battle between France and Spain for supremacy in North America was joined.

The patron of the French colony was Adm. Gaspard de Coligny, a Huguenot who planned the colony at Fort Caroline as a haven for his persecuted coreligionists and as the basis for a French claim to counter that of Spain in the New World. In 1561, the Spanish King had forbade any further attempts by his subjects to colonize Florida because of the previous failures there and his lack of interest in the area. Thus, the time seemed ripe for the French. Following the failure of an earlier attempt at settlement, under Jean Ribaut in 1562 at Port Royal Sound, S.C., in June 1564 three vessels under the command of René de Laudonnière brought some 300 colonists, mostly Huguenots, from Havre de Grace to the St. Johns River. The colonists settled about 5 miles from the mouth of the river on a broad, flat knoll on the river shore in the midst of Timucua Indian country. With Indian help, they built a triangular fort of earth and logs that enclosed several palm-thatched buildings and named it Caroline in honor of King Charles IX. They built other houses in the meadow outside the fort. Vainly searching for gold and silver, they clashed with the Indians, upon whom they were dependent for food, and some even mutinied.

The French fort was a threat to Spanish commerce, for the Spanish treasure fleets had to sail past it on their return to Spain. It was also a potential base for attacks upon the Indies. The French asserted that it was their territory; the Spanish, that it was a pirates' nest on their land. In August 1565, Jean Ribaut brought reinforcements. Shortly thereafter, the Spaniard Pedro Menéndez de Avilés founded St. Augustine, captured and occupied Fort Caroline, killed almost all the Frenchmen, and renamed it San Mateo. In 1568, vengeful Frenchmen, who sailed from Bordeaux, with Indian allies they obtained in Florida, attacked and slaughtered most of the garrison.

The deepening of the St. Johns River in 1880 inundated the site of Fort Caroline. However, the carefully constructed replica of Fort Caroline at the National Memorial illustrates French defiance of a powerful enemy by establishing a colony on the edge of an unknown world.

11. Fort Matanzas National Monument, Florida

Location: St. Johns County, on Anastasia and Rattlesnake Islands, 14 miles south of St. Augustine on Fla. A1A (Ocean Shore Boulevard); accessible also by Intracoastal Waterway; address, 1 Castillo Drive, St. Augustine, Fla. 32084.

The deciding scenes in the Spanish-French struggle for Florida, in 1565, occurred in the vicinity of Fort Matanzas National Monument, where Spain achieved potential control of the entire continent of North America and actual domination of the present Southeastern United States for nearly 200 years. During most of that period, Matanzas was a typical Florida military outpost, strategically important as a defense to the south entrance of St. Augustine, the capital of Spanish Florida.

The year after the French established Fort Caroline, in 1564, Pedro Menéndez de Avilés arrived under orders from the Spanish Crown to

Matanzas Tower, constructed by the Spanish in the years 1740–42 on the site of earlier fortifications, was a key defense of St. Augustine, capital of Spanish Florida.

drive the intruders out of Florida. He founded St. Augustine as his base of operations and seized Fort Caroline when the French commander, Jean Ribaut, and a party of some 558 who had set out from the fort to attack the Spanish were shipwrecked far south of St. Augustine. The party marched up the coast in two groups. Menéndez and about 40 men met the first group of about 208 when they were halted by their inability to cross the inlet south of Anastasia Island. Deploying his small force so that it appeared much larger, Menéndez persuaded the Frenchmen to surrender and put all but eight of them to the knife.

A week later the second group, numbering about 350, under Ribaut himself, arrived at the same place and were also met by Menéndez. Seeing evidence of the previous incident, about 200 Frenchmen fled south, but the Spanish finally captured most of them. Ribaut and the remainder surrendered, and all but 16 were promptly killed. Thus, the location was named *Matanzas,* meaning "slaughters."

Matanzas came to occupy a key position in the defenses of St. Augustine. By 1569, a blockhouse for 50 soldiers had been built. Later, a "sentinel house" was located at Matanzas, one of a system along the coast. A sentinel house consisted of a thatched palmetto hut, equipped with wooden watchtowers, which accommodated about six soldiers. When the soldiers at Matanzas sighted a ship, a runner carried the news to St. Augustine.

The present structure, called Matanzas Tower by the Spanish, was built after the English siege of Castillo de San Marcos in 1740 by Gen. James Oglethorpe, founder of Georgia. Construction on marshy little Rattlesnake Island, near the mouth of the Matanzas River, was difficult, but the tower was completed before the end of 1742 in spite of lack of royal support. The English garrisoned it during the period they held Florida, 1763–83, after which the Spanish reoccupied it. Spain, however, had little concern for her crumbling New World empire in the early 19th century, and the interior of the tower was already in ruins when Florida passed to the United States, in 1821.

Mantanzas Tower is still impressive although partially destroyed. It was designated as Fort Matanzas National Monument in 1924 by Presidential proclamation; and in 1933 transferred from the War Department to the National Park Service. A visitor center lies almost directly across from it on Anastasia Island. The monument area includes property on both sides of the inlet.

12. Fort Frederica National Monument, Georgia

> *Location: Glynn County, on St. Simons Island, via Brunswick-St.*
> *Simons Highway or inland waterway, 12 miles north of Brunswick;*
> *address, P.O. Box 816, St. Simons Island, Ga. 31522.*

Fort Frederica was headquarters for Gen. James Oglethorpe's military operations against the Spanish in Florida during the War of Jenkins' Ear (1739–42), a part of the Anglo-Spanish struggle for control of the Southeastern part of the present United States. An old British fortification on St. Simons Island dating from the early days of Georgia history, the fort illustrates Britain's determination to hold this area of the coast—an area claimed by the Spanish, who were well entrenched at St. Augustine. Built in 1736 by a group of colonists led by Oglethorpe—who had first arrived in Georgia with a group of settlers in 1733 and founded Savannah—it was surrounded by a typical English village, the southernmost British settlement at the time. Two years later, troops from England and Gibraltar arrived.

The year after the founding of Fort Frederica, soldiers stationed at Fort Frederick, near present Port Royal, S.C., had been transferred to St. Simons Island, where they built an additional fortification, Fort St. Simons, or Delegal's Fort. The British built a series of other fortifications in the region, including Fort St. George, on Fort George Island, and Fort St. Andrew, on Cumberland Island. Fort Frederica was the headquarters and became the springboard for attack and base for defense against Spanish Florida.

Within a decade after the end of the War of Jenkins' Ear—during which Spain had futilely attacked Fort Frederica in a last attempt to gain the Georgia territory she had claimed for two-and-a-half centuries—the fort was practically abandoned. By 1756, the English had withdrawn the few soldiers stationed at the fort, removed many of the cannon and used them to fortify other parts of Georgia, and the town had fallen into ruins. Under the terms of the Treaty of Paris in 1763, which ended the French and Indian War, Britain acquired Florida and British-Spanish tensions eased in the region.

Archeological excavations at Fort Frederica National Monument have unearthed the long-buried foundations of many dwellings. Within the fort area, various buildings have been excavated, including the bastion towers and the barracks building as well as the town gate and the moat. Markers explain the excavations.

13. Ocmulgee National Monument, Georgia

> *Location: Bibb County, on U.S. 80 and 129, adjoining Macon; address, P.O. Box 4186, Macon, Ga. 31208.*

Though this National Monument is noted chiefly for its prehistoric Indian remains, it also has close associations with the phases of history treated in this volume. An English trading post was established at this site about 1690. Soon thereafter a number of the important Creek Indian towns on the Chattahoochee River, no longer free to trade with the English because of Spanish interference, moved into the general vicinity of the English post. The people of one of these towns, Ocmulgee, settled adjacent to the post.

Archeological excavation has shown that the post consisted of several log buildings surrounded by a stockade of upright logs. The stockade had five sides. Access through the longest of these, 140 feet in length, was provided by two gates. Two of the other sides were 100 feet in length; and two, 50 feet.

The remains of a wide trail have also been found. This trail, which ran parallel to the longest wall of the stockade and extended some distance on either side of the post, was a section of the Lower Creek trading path. Crossing the present State of Georgia, the path ran along the fall line from Augusta to Columbus and was the main route followed by the English traders. It likely was used by Henry Woodward, who in 1685 opened the trade with the Creeks on the Chattahoochee, and by a Colonel Welch, who in 1698 initiated trade with the Chickasaw of northern Mississippi.

Both the trading path and the post at Ocmulgee played an important part in the expansion of English trade and in the struggle between the Spanish and the English for control of the Southeast. The combined English and Creek force that in 1702 destroyed Santa Fé, a Spanish mission in north-central Florida, probably set out from Ocmulgee, as did possibly the English and Creek war party that later in the year defeated the Spanish and Apalachee force on the Flint River.

Col. James Moore's army of 50 Carolinians and 1,000 Creeks, which in 1704 destroyed 5 of the Spanish missions in the province of Apalachee and captured more than 1,000 Apalachee Indians, formed at Ocmulgee.

The Creek war parties that destroyed two more Apalachee missions in June of that year were also likely from Ocmulgee. These campaigns forced the Spanish to abandon the province, which had supplied foodstuffs for both St. Augustine and Havana and served as a base for Spanish efforts to win over the Creeks.

The Ocmulgee trading post continued in existence until the Yamassee War (1715–17), when the Creeks, under "Emperor" Brim, killed off the traders scattered throughout their territory and attacked outlying settlements. They undoubtedly murdered the traders at Ocmulgee and destroyed the trading post. At the end of the war, the Creeks, fearing reprisal by the Carolinians, moved their towns back to the Chattahoochee River.

Ocmulgee National Monument preserves the remains of an unusual concentration of Indian villages. Excavation has indicated that the site was occupied by six successive Indian cultures, beginning about 8,000 B.C. and ending with the Creeks in A.D. 1717. Artifacts representative of all these cultures are displayed in the park's visitor center, which houses the largest archeological museum in the South. One earth lodge has been restored to appear as it did a thousand years ago, when the Indians used it and the seven mounds at the park for religious ceremonies. The outline of the trading post stockade is marked by horizontal logs.

14. Acadia National Park, Maine

Location: Hancock County; park headquarters at Bar Harbor, Mount Desert Island; address, P.O. Box 338, Bar Harbor, Maine 04609.

La Cadie (Acadia) is a name derived from an Indian word meaning "the place," and was originally applied by the French to the North American coast from present Nova Scotia to New Jersey. In 1604, Pierre du Guast, Sieur de Monts, a Huguenot gentleman and soldier, undertook to establish Acadia as a New World dominion of France. Assisted by Samuel de Champlain, he founded a colony on an island in the St. Croix River; the settlers later relocated at Port Royal. Champlain then embarked upon further explorations and discovered Mount Desert Island, now in Acadia National Park. In 1613, this island became the site of the first French Jesuit mission in America, Saint Sauveur, on Fernald Point in Somes Sound. At this mission began the epic of French-English rivalry

In 1604, Samuel de Champlain, the famous French explorer, discovered and named Mount Desert Island, pictured here. In 1613, the island was the site of a Jesuit mission, but permanent occupation did not occur until just after the French and Indian War, when some New England colonists settled there.

in North America; a few weeks after its founding, Capt. Samuel Argall sailed up from Virginia and destroyed it.

For the next 150 years, the present Maine coast was a sort of no man's land. Sieur de la Mothe Cadillac, later founder of Detroit and Governor of Louisiana, owned Mount Desert Island in the late 1600's and may have resided for a time on its east shore. No permanent settlement was made there, however, until after the British victory over the French in 1763. At that time, groups from other parts of New England founded settlements. The island passed through the hands of many owners during the ensuing years: the Province of Massachusetts; Sir Francis Bernard, English Governor of the Province; Sir Francis' son; and Cadillac's granddaughter. Eventually, it was subdivided among the sturdy New Englanders who had earlier settled there and engaged in farming, lumbering, shipbuilding, and fishing.

The advent of steampower in the later 1800's resulted in drastic changes as steamboats began to bring in large numbers of summer visitors. Bar Harbor subsequently became synonymous with summertime among America's wealthier citizens. In 1916, a Presidential proclamation recognized the special scenic beauties of the area by creating Sieur de Monts National Monument; it was later called Lafayette National Park, the first National Park east of the Mississippi River. In 1929, the name was changed to Acadia. Primarily of interest for its marine scenery and its natural features, it is also historically noteworthy.

15. Salem Maritime National Historic Site, Massachusetts

Location: Essex County, Derby Street, Salem; address, Custom House, Derby Street, Salem, Mass. 01970.

Although Salem's maritime supremacy was of greater significance in later periods of history, particularly during the War for Independence, Salem has some important associations with the phases of history treated in this volume. Until the West was opened and began to yield to the pioneers after the War for Independence, most Americans lived within reach of the sea and naturally turned to it for adventure, a livelihood, and even riches. Indeed, the sea was the first frontier as well as the first highway. From the beginning, the colonists depended upon it for communication with the homeland and with other colonies.

Salem and other New England ports figured prominently in the colonial and early republican economy. Beginning soon in the 17th century, sailing vessels based at Salem plied the sealanes of the world, as they built the commerce upon which Yankee strength came to rest. Founded in 1626 by Roger Conant as the plantation of Naumkeag and established 2 years later as the first town in the Colony of Massachusetts Bay, Salem owed its prosperity to a seaboard location. From the very beginning, her colonists engaged in maritime pursuits; fishing and shipping were soon the leading industries. As early as 1643, fish, lumber, and provisions were being sent to the West Indies in exchange for sugar and molasses, staples that were brought home and made into rum. Gradually the orbit of trade was extended to Europe, for the most part to Portugal and Spain, which offered a ready market for dried fish and supplied salt, wine, fruit, iron, and Spanish dollars in return.

This trade and that with the West Indies—which after 1700 developed into the "triangular trade" between New England, the West Indies, and Africa—thrived until 1763, when the long struggle between France and England for the mastery of the American Continent finally came to an end and the English Government began to enact and enforce measures that stringently limited the commerce of the American colonies. Under these conditions, the economic life of Salem, like that of all ports along the Atlantic seaboard, came to a standstill and a discontent engendered that grew into resistance and eventually resulted in rebellion.

Designated a National Historic Site in 1938, Salem Maritime occupies an area of about 9 acres bordering on Salem Harbor. It preserves a group of structures and wharves that have survived from the period of the town's maritime greatness.

16. Grand Portage National Monument, Minnesota

Location: Cook County, on U.S. 61, about 38 miles northeast of Grand Marais and 49 miles southwest of the Canadian cities of Fort William and Port Arthur, Ontario; address, P.O. Box 666, Grand Marais, Minn. 55604.

This 9-mile portage route, connecting the Great Lakes with the interior network of waterways, was probably used by the Indians before the arrival of Europeans. The first recorded visit of a European was that of La Vérendrye, in 1731, who called it the Grand Portage and inferred that it was already well known by that name. From then until the French and Indian War, French traders pushed farther and farther into the Canadian Northwest, and practically all of the traffic passed over the Grand Portage. Voyageurs landed trade goods from large lake canoes at a post on the shore of Lake Superior and prepared them for portage to Pigeon River and conveyance into the interior in smaller canoes.

The period of most active use of Grand Portage was after 1783, when the famous North West Company was formed and some 20 years after the British had taken over Canada. The log stockade at Grand Portage was especially busy every July and August, when the brigades bringing goods from Montreal met the trappers and traders coming in from their posts scattered throughout the region. Employees received—and largely spent—their annual wages, and the company held its annual meeting.

The North West Company established Fort Charlotte where the portage came into Pigeon River, as well as a stockaded lake post that served as a central depot at Lake Superior. Other firms maintained rival posts in the vicinity, but their history is obscure. After 1803, when the North West Company established Fort William on the Kaministiquia, Grand Portage rapidly declined in importance. John Jacob Astor's American Fur Company built a post there after the War of 1812, which for a while was a central station in the Lake Superior fishing industry. Eventually proving unprofitable, it was abandoned, apparently in the 1840's.

In 1922, historians explored and mapped the portage route and discovered the remains of the principal posts. In 1936–37, the Minnesota Historical Society directed archeological work at Grand Portage, and the following year the stockaded lake post was reconstructed under the auspices of the Bureau of Indian Affairs, U.S. Department of the Interior. The National Monument was established in 1960 following conferences with the Minnesota Chippewa Tribal Council and the Grand Portage Band of the Chippewa Tribe, through whose reservation the route passes. Additional archeological investigation and restoration work was begun in 1962.

17. El Morro National Monument, New Mexico

Location: Valencia County, 42 miles west of Grants near N. Mex. 53; address, Ramah, N. Mex. 87321.

El Morro, the best-known inscription rock in the Southwest, is a massive, 200-foot-high pointed mesa of soft sandstone which, for more than three-and-a-half centuries, Spanish, Mexican, and American travelers used to record their visits. The ancient route that connected Acoma and the Rio Grande pueblos on the east with the Zuñi and Hopi pueblos on the west passed by. On the very top of the rock are ruins of Zuñi Indian pueblos that were abandoned long before the coming of the Spaniards. The rock was not only a conspicuous landmark, but its environs also provided a favorable camping and watering place in a dry region. Rain and melted snow from El Morro, which drained into a large natural basin below, provided a year-round supply of good water.

Fifteen years before the Pilgrims landed in Massachusetts, Don Juan de Oñate in 1605 etched the first identifiable Spanish inscription on El Morro. He was returning from his claimed discovery of the *mar del sur* (South Sea)—actually the Gulf of California. Coronado and other earlier Spanish explorers had almost certainly passed by El Morro, and in the 17th and 18th centuries many other important figures in the history of the Southwest inscribed their names. A number of these inscriptions can still be seen, notably that of Don Diego de Vargas, reconqueror of New Mexico. El Morro was also inscribed by the U.S. soldiers who occupied New Mexico in 1846; several years later by gold seekers and overland emigrants bound for California; and, in 1857, by members of Lt. Edward F. Beale's camel caravan.

This massive 200-foot-high mesa, El Morro, in New Mexico, is of archeological and historical interest. On its top, lie ruins of prehistoric Indian
pueblos. The rock is covered with inscriptions, many of them carved by
Western explorers and emigrants.

Established by Presidential proclamation in 1906, El Morro National Monument is about 2 square miles in area and lies at an elevation of more than 7,000 feet. Besides the inscriptions, Indian petroglyphs and partially excavated mesa-top Indian ruins are of interest.

18. Gran Quivira National Monument, New Mexico

Location: Torrance and Socorro Counties, off U.S. 60, on N. Mex. 10, about 26 miles south of Mountainair; address, Route 1, Mountainair, N. Mex. 87036.

The Mogollon Indian *Pueblo de las Humanas* (Gran Quivira) and two associated Spanish missions, all in ruins, are preserved in this National Monument, which commemorates 17th-century Spanish missionary activities among the Salinas pueblos of central New Mexico. Don Juan de Oñate, in 1598, was the first European known to have visited this pueblo, records of whose history are far from complete. About 1627 a missionary built a small church dedicated to San Isidro at the site, apparently a subsidiary to the mission of San Gregorio de Abó, 20 miles to the northwest.

Thirty years later another missionary enlarged the church facilities and rededicated them to San Buenaventura. His conversion efforts, however, did not flourish because the Indians, threatened by Apache raids, drought, famine, and pestilence, abandoned the pueblo sometime between 1672 and 1675. The survivors, and those from other villages of the area, moved to the Rio Grande Valley near Socorro to join their kinsmen or went down the valley to the El Paso area.

Ruins of San Buenaventura Mission, at Gran Quivira National Monument, New Mexico. These and other ruins at the site commemorate 17th-century Spanish missionary activities among the Salinas pueblos of central New Mexico.

Gran Quivira National Monument, embracing 611 acres, was established in 1909. The visitor center contains archeological and historical exhibits. From the center, a self-guided tour passes through the ruins of the old mission churches and the pueblo. Some of the ruins are completely excavated and some only partially. The tour demonstrates the evolution of pueblo life throughout many centuries, both before and after the coming of the Europeans.

19. Fort Raleigh National Historic Site, North Carolina

Location: Dare County, on N.C. 345, about 3 miles north of Manteo, on Roanoke Island; address, P.O. Box 457, Manteo, N.C. 27954.

Fort Raleigh National Historic Site, on Roanoke Island, is the scene of the earliest English colonizing attempts within the limits of the present United States and the birthplace of the first English child born in the New World, Virginia Dare, on August 18, 1587. Two attempts by Sir Walter Raleigh at settlement, in 1585–86 and 1587, failed because of supply problems and Indian attacks.

The first colony, originally consisting of 108 persons, was founded by Raleigh's cousin, Sir Richard Grenville. Settling on the north end of Roanoke Island in 1585, the colonists constructed dwellings and a fort and began to plant crops and explore the area, while Grenville returned to England for supplies. He left Ralph Lane in charge. The colony fared badly. Sir Francis Drake visited it in 1586 and took the survivors back to England. Soon afterward, Grenville returned and found the colony deserted. After searching along the coast, he left 15 men to hold the island for Queen Elizabeth and returned to England.

Restored earthen fort at Fort Raleigh National Historic Site, North Carolina. Late in the 16th century, in 1585–86 and 1587, Sir Walter Raleigh made two attempts to found a colony on Roanoke Island—the first English colonizing efforts within the present United States.

The second colony consisted of 150 settlers, who arrived at Roanoke Island in 1587, under the leadership of John White. Finding only desolation and the bones of one of Grenville's men, they began to rebuild the settlement. White returned to England for supplies, but found it in danger of an invasion by Spain. The Queen, refusing to spare a large ship, dispatched two small pinnaces to the colony, but they never reached it. When White returned to the colony in August of 1590, he found that the colonists had disappeared.

Fort Raleigh, designated a National Historic Site in 1941, consists of 144 acres. The fort, probably built by Lane, was investigated by archeologists in 1947–48 and restored in 1950. The village site, presumably close by, has not yet been located. At the Waterside Theater, the Roanoke Island Historical Association presents a noted pageant-drama, *Lost Colony* by the playwright Paul Green, during the summer months.

20. Fort Necessity National Battlefield, Pennsylvania

> *Location: Fayette County, on U.S. 40, about 11 miles east of Uniontown; address, Route 1, Box 311, Farmington, Pa. 15437.*

At this battlefield, on July 3, 1754, occurred the opening engagement in the French and Indian War, a 7-year struggle between the French and English for control of the North American Continent. It was also George Washington's first major battle. French-English rivalry in the trans-

Reconstructed stockade at Fort Necessity National Battlefield, Pennsylvania. In 1754, at this battlefield French and English troops clashed in the first major battle of the French and Indian War, a long struggle for control of the North American Continent.

"Braddock's Retreat, July 9, 1755." Early in the French and Indian War, Gen. Edward Braddock sought to capture Fort Duquesne from the French. Wounded in the attempt, he died during his retreat. From a painting, in 1865, by Alonzo Chappel. Courtesy, Chicago Historical Society.

Allegheny territory approached a climax in the 1750's. In the spring of 1754, the British sent Lt. Col. George Washington and a small force from Virginia to contest French possession of the Forks of the Ohio, where the French had erected Fort Duquesne. After defeating a French scouting party at Great Meadows, Washington built a temporary fort there which he called "Fort Necessity." A battle ensued, after which the British were forced to surrender and then allowed to return to Virginia. The French destroyed Fort Necessity and returned to Fort Duquesne. By greater exertions later, however, the British won the war.

Fort Necessity National Battlefield became a part of the National Park System in 1933, and Fort Necessity State Park was transferred to it in 1962. The latter transfer added to the site sections of Great Meadows, where the 1754 battle was fought and part of which George Washington later owned. A stockade, storehouse, and entrenchments have been reconstructed on the exact site of the original structures. The site of Washington's skirmish with the French scouting party and the grave of Gen. Edward Braddock, commander in chief of the British forces in the Battle of Monongahela (1755), also may be seen.

21. Cape Henry Memorial (Colonial National Historical Park), Virginia

Location: Princess Anne County, on U.S. 60, about 10 miles east of Norfolk; address, Superintendent, Colonial National Historical Park, P.O. Box 210, Yorktown, Va. 23490.

Sea-weary English colonists, who were soon to found the first permanent English settlement in the New World, caught sight of Cape Henry, at the entrance to Chesapeake Bay, on April 26, 1607—their first view of Virginia. Having spent almost 5 months crammed aboard three tiny craft, they stopped off at Cape Henry for 4 days before proceeding up the James River to Jamestown, where they settled permanently.

The Cape Henry Memorial comprises a quarter acre, on which stands a memorial cross erected in 1935 by the National Society, Daughters of American Colonists, to mark the approximate site of the landing. It is completely surrounded by the Fort Story Military Reservation, of which it was formerly a part. The War Department transferred the memorial area to the Department of the Interior in 1939. The memorial is administered as part of Colonial National Historical Park, which also includes Jamestown, Yorktown Battlefield, and the Colonial Parkway.

No facilities or special services are available. Visitor passes are issued by military personnel at the entrance to the Fort Story Military Reservation. Religious and patriotic observances are held annually at the memorial, usually on the Sunday closest to April 26. These are sponsored by the Order of Cape Henry, 1607.

Nearby, and of special interest although not under National Park Service jurisdiction, is the old Cape Henry Light (1791), the first lighthouse erected by the Federal Government.

22. Jamestown Island (Colonial National Historical Park) and Jamestown National Historic Site (Non-Federal Ownership), Virginia

Location: James City County, 10 miles southwest of Williamsburg on the Colonial Parkway; address, Superintendent, Colonial National Historical Park, P.O. Box 210, Yorktown, Va. 23490.

At Jamestown Island, originally a peninsula, is commemorated the first permanent English settlement in America, in 1607. The first years at

Old Tower, in the foreground, believed to have been a part of a brick church begun in 1639, is the only standing ruin of 17th-century Jamestown, Virginia. Today it adjoins a memorial church, in the right rear background, erected in 1907 by the Colonial Dames of America on the foundations of the original church.

Jamestown were difficult for the settlers, who struggled constantly against sickness, starvation, and hostile Indians, and nine-tenths of them died. After 1699, when the seat of government was moved to Williamsburg, the settlement was virtually abandoned. About the time of the War for Independence, the isthmus connecting Jamestown with the mainland was washed out and the town ceased to exist.

In 1893, the Association for the Preservation of Virginia Antiquities acquired title to 22½ acres on Jamestown Island. In 1940, the Secretary of the Interior designated this acreage as Jamestown National Historic Site, under an agreement between the association and the Department of the Interior to provide for unified development of the whole island. Except for the association tract—now reduced to 20 acres because of donations to the park—the remainder of Jamestown Island is in Federal ownership. Visitors may take a walking tour and 3- and 5-mile driving tours of the island.

From a parking area, near the original townsite of Jamestown Island, a footbridge leads to the visitor center. From there, a walking tour extends over the townsite along the old streets and paths to the church, the statehouse sites, and the ruins of early houses, taverns, and shops. The visitor is guided along the way by various markers and recorded messages. In nearby Festival Park, the Commonwealth of Virginia maintains exhibits relating to the history of Jamestown.

23. San Juan National Historic Site, Puerto Rico

Location: City of San Juan; address, P.O. Box 712, San Juan, P.R. 00902.

The major Spanish defenses of Puerto Rico comprise the San Juan National Historic Site: the forts of El Morro, El Cañuelo, and San Cristóbal; La Casa Blanca (The White House); and the old city walls. They demonstrate Spanish power in the New World. Spain began constructing some of them in the 16th century; thus they are the oldest fortifications of European origin in present U.S. territory. Puerto Rico did not yield the gold the Spanish sought, but it served as an effective base for exploration and defense. Ponce de León established the first colony there, at Caparra, in 1509, and used it as a base from which he sailed to Florida. In 1521, the Spaniards founded San Juan, their first permanent colony in the present territory of the United States, and constructed mighty fortifications to protect their treasure fleets and new base.

La Casa Blanca was built in 1525 as a home for the Ponce de León family. Until 1779, the heirs owned it. In the early years, it was the only stronghold for protection of the townspeople against marauding Carib Indians and pirates. Located on the harbor side of San Juan Island, near historic San Juan Gate, it was the formal entrance to the city through the surrounding defensive wall, where Spanish colonial officials were ceremoniously greeted as they stepped ashore. Now occupied by the Commanding General of the Antilles Command, U.S. Army, it is not open to the public.

Castillo de San Felipe del Morro (Castle of St. Philip on the Headland) rises 140 feet above the sea at the west end of the island. Begun about 1539, it was the first authorized defensive work, but did not assume

Battery of El Morro, one of several forts preserved at San Juan National Historic Site, Puerto Rico. The Spanish constructed El Morro between 1539 and the late 1700's.

its present proportions until the late 1700's. On the landward side, beyond the moat, is a broad grassy slope. Behind the walls are storerooms, gunrooms, quarters, chapel, and prison. Huge cisterns lie beneath the spacious courtyard, from which ramps, tunnels, and stairways lead to the various parts of the complex. The windswept limestone ramparts that crown the headland were a familiar sight to seafaring men for centuries.

El Cañuelo, or San Juan de la Cruz (St. John of the Cross), is a 50-foot-square fort across the harbor entrance from El Morro. Its walls are about 15 feet high, and the flat roof provides a platform for cannon. The Spanish began construction about 1610, when 200 slaves were brought to San Juan and artisans arrived from Spain to work on the defenses.

Castillo de San Cristóbal looms grimly above the city of San Juan. Its construction began about 1633, and by 1678 it resembled its present aspect. As at El Morro, a courtyard, or *plaza de armas,* is surrounded by gunrooms and barracks. Tunnels lead up to a main gundeck. Highest of all is the Caballero de San Miguel, a massive, two-tiered gun platform 150 feet above the sea at the east end of the island.

The city wall still stands around much of the old town, including the harbor front between El Morro and La Fortaleza. Other impressive remains extend from El Morro to San Cristóbal, on the ocean front. Construction of the walls began in the 1630's and continued intermittently for more than 150 years. On the landward side, much of the wall was razed during the 1800's as the city expanded.

The fortifications of San Juan have a colorful history. In 1595, Sir Francis Drake was lured to San Juan to capture 35 tons of precious metal, awaiting shipment to Spain. His 23 ships and army of 3,000 men faced 1,500 Spaniards with 100 cannon behind the partially developed defenses. Beaten off, Drake sailed for Panama and soon died of fever. Three years later George Clifford, Earl of Cumberland, succeeded with a land attack. After a 2-week siege, Cumberland's standard rose over El Morro on June 21, 1598. Dysentery then accomplished what the Spaniards could not. Though forced to leave, the invaders tore down the land wall of El Morro and carried off 80 Spanish cannon.

In 1625, a Dutch fleet under Gen. Bowdoin Hendrick suffered little damage from El Morro's guns. After seizing the other fortifications, the Dutch threw a blockade around El Morro and began an artillery duel. But 38 days after they entered the harbor they were driven away. In 1797, the strengthened defenses of San Juan were again successful, against a much greater threat, when a British fleet of 60 vessels, bearing an army of 7,000 men, launched an attack. Gen. Ramón de Castro's defense of the eastern part of the city held firm; the Spaniards won the ensuing artillery duel and successfully counterattacked.

Adm. William Sampson, U.S. Navy, engaged the modernized batteries of San Juan with his flotilla for 2½ hours on May 12, 1898, during the Spanish-American War, but neither side suffered much damage. U.S. forces landed on the southern side of Puerto Rico, but before they reached San Juan an armistice had been signed. Spain's long rule over the island, including the fortifications that now comprise San Juan National Historic Site, came to an end in 1898, when the United States acquired it.

The National Historic Site was established in 1949, but the U.S. Army uses the forts under a cooperative agreement between the Department of the Interior and the Department of the Army. Regulated public access is permitted, under the supervision of the National Park Service.

24. Christiansted National Historic Site, Virgin Islands

*Location: City of Christiansted, St. Croix Island, Virgin Islands;
address, Superintendent, Virgin Islands National Park, P.O. Box
1707, Charlotte Amalie, St. Thomas, V.I. 00802.*

This site includes approximately three city blocks, comprising 7½ acres,
on the Christiansted waterfront, including Fort Christiansvaern, the Old
Danish Post Office, Old Danish Customhouse, Steeple Building, and Government House. It commemorates the discovery of America, the European struggle for colonial empire, and especially the development of
the Virgin Islands under the Danes. Seven flags have flown over
Christiansted, the capital of the Danish West Indies when "sugar was
king."

St. Croix Island is the first territory now under the flag of the United
States to have been discovered by Columbus—on November 14, 1493,
during his second voyage to the New World. Columbus named the island
Santa Cruz (Holy Cross), which was inhabited by fierce Indians and un-
attractive to colonists during the 16th and early 17th centuries. During
the period 1625–50, French freebooters and Dutch and English settlers
apparently lived on the island at various times. In 1650, however, a
Spanish expedition from Puerto Rico drove out all Europeans, only to be
expelled itself several months later by a French force from St. Kitts Island.

Harbor and wharf of Christiansted, on St. Croix Island, Virgin Islands, probably in the first half of the 19th century. From a lithograph by an unknown
artist.

The French, who called the island St. Croix, sold it in 1651 to the Knights of Malta, a private religious-military order. They later regained possession of it as a crown colony, but about 1696 the King transferred the French population, which consisted of 147 white settlers and 623 slaves, to Haiti. The island remained largely uninhabited until 1733, when the Danish West India and Guinea Company, which for some years had held neighboring St. Thomas and St. John Islands, purchased it.

Although earlier efforts had been made by other European nations to colonize St. Croix, under the Danes St. Croix boomed. It became a major sugar producer, bound to both Europe and America by close commercial, social, and cultural ties. By 1755, the population had reached 10,200, including 9,000 slaves. Some cotton was grown, but sugar was the principal crop. Despite the prosperity of the colonists, the company was almost bankrupt by 1755, and gladly sold out to the Danish King, under whose rule the three islands remained until the United States purchased them for $25 million in 1917.

Sugar production increased from 1½ million pounds in 1755 to 46 million pounds in 1812, during a period when the Danish West Indies were near the economic center of gravity of the New World, among the "Fabulous Sugar Islands," as the Lesser Antilles were known. Their importance during the latter 18th century is difficult to conceive today. In such a stimulating environment, Alexander Hamilton, one of the Founding Fathers of the United States, lived during his youthful years. He worked for a Christiansted merchant during the period 1766–72.

Fort Christiansvaern, the first public building in Danish Christiansted, was originally the residence of the Governor. Little is known of the history of the Old Danish Customhouse, apparently erected between 1779 and 1815, and the Old Danish Post Office. The Steeple Building was the first church to be erected by the Danes, who started construction in 1750 and 3 years later first put the building to use. A conspicuous feature of Christiansted harbor today, it is an unusual representative of Danish colonial architecture. Built of rubble-masonry, it is one story high, and the four-tiered steeple is 77 feet high. John Wilhelm Schopen, a merchant and official of the Danish West India and Guinea Company, built the present Government House as his home. It has been renovated and enlarged over the years since then, and now consists of three floors, which total about 37,200 square feet. On the second floor is a ballroom about 98 by 22 feet. Most of the period furnishings in the building are the gift of the Danish Government.

Christiansted National Historic Site is administered by the National Park Service in cooperation with the Government of the Virgin Islands.

25. Virgin Islands National Park, Virgin Islands

Location: St. John Island, Virgin Islands; address, P.O. Box 1707, Charlotte Amalie, St. Thomas, V.I. 00802.

This park consists of about two-thirds of St. John Island, the most beautiful and least disturbed of the three major American Virgin Islands. A veritable island paradise, St. John is of interest chiefly because of its unique natural wonders. However, its history, as well as that of the islands, is also absorbing. Columbus discovered the islands in 1493, on his second voyage to the New World, and named them in honor of Saint Ursula and her 11,000 virgins. In the years that followed, Dutch, English, Spanish, French, and Danish adventurers came to the islands. The Danes first arrived in the 1670's, but did not found a permanent colony on St. John until 1717. Before long, the settlers took over all the land on the island that could support the cultivation of sugar and cotton, and imported slaves. Slave unrest often disturbed the peace, however, until the King of

St. John Island, about two-thirds of which comprises Virgin Islands National Park, has unique natural beauty. Although discovered by Columbus in 1493, it was not colonized until the first part of the 18th century.

Denmark abolished slavery in 1848, a move that helped bring about the end of the plantations, many of whose ruins may still be seen in the park.

The United States acquired St. John, along with the other Danish Virgin Islands, from Denmark in 1917. In 1956, Congress authorized the establishment of the park, which was dedicated on December 1, 1956, when Jackson Hole Preserve, Inc., of which Laurance Rockefeller is president, presented more than 5,000 acres of the original parkland to the people of the United States. The population of less than 1,000 that remains on the island is concentrated in the Cruz Bay and Coral Bay areas outside the park. Scheduled boat service is available at Red Hook Landing, St. Thomas Island, for the 30-minute passage to the park entrance at Cruz Bay, St. John Island.

B. National Historic Sites in Non-Federal Ownership

A few National Historic Sites in non-Federal ownership are located throughout the United States. These are not units of the National Park System but, as authorized by the Historic Sites Act of 1935, are administered under the provisions of cooperative agreements by the owners with the Department of the Interior. The owners agree to maintain the property in a manner consistent with good preservation practices, for which purpose they may receive assistance from the National Park Service as provided in the agreements. The Park Service provides bronze plaques for the sites. The following sites illustrate the phases of history treated in this volume.

1. Chicago Portage National Historic Site, Illinois

Location: Cook County, Old Chicago Portage Forest Preserve, junction of Portage Creek with Des Plaines River, just west of Harlem Avenue on the line of 47th Street.

Chicago owes its very existence to its strategic location on the Chicago-Illinois River route, one of the natural arteries leading from the St. Lawrence River system to the Mississippi. The portage at Chicago was discovered in September 1673 by Père Jacques Marquette and Louis Jolliet as they returned from their voyage of exploration down the Mississippi River. Marquette, in failing health, spent the winter of 1674–75 near the portage, and passed over it on other trips, as did also René

[174

Site of Chicago, in 1820. The second Fort Dearborn, built in 1816, is situated to the left of the main river channel. From a lithograph by J. Gemmel, published by D. Fabronius, probably in 1857. Courtesy, Chicago Historical Society.

Robert Cavelier, Sieur de la Salle, Henry de Tonty, and many other Frenchmen until about 1700, when Indian hostility kept Europeans out of the area. The Indians continued to use the portage extensively.

During the French and Indian War and the War for Independence, the portage resumed its important position in non-Indian travel and commerce. In the Treaty of Greenville (1795), the Indians ceded to the United States "a piece of Land Six Miles Square, at the mouth of Chickago River, emptying into the southwest end of Lake Michigan, where a fort formerly stood." In 1803, U.S. soldiers erected the first Fort Dearborn at the river's mouth, and trade continued to be extensive until the beginning of the War of 1812, when the residents of the fort abandoned it. They began the trip to Fort Wayne, but before they had gone 2 miles Potawatomi Indians murdered most of them and then set fire to the fort.

In 1816, soldiers constructed the second Fort Dearborn, and trade again resumed over the portage. It diminished in importance, however, as the Illinois fur trade declined, though it continued to have commercial value into the 1830's. Work began in 1836 on the Illinois and Michigan Canal—finished in 1848—which followed the water-and-portage route, as does the present Sanitary and Ship Canal.

The western end of the Chicago portage route, where Marquette and Jolliet landed, is located in the Old Chicago Portage Forest Preserve, which is managed by the Forest Preserve District of Cook County, Ill. At the eastern end of the portage route, on the north end of Grant Park, are the sites of the two Fort Dearborns. In 1952, a cooperative agreement between the Cook County Forest Preserve District and the Department of the Interior authorized the designation of Chicago Portage as a National Historic Site.

2. Gloria Dei (Old Swedes') Church National Historic Site, Pennsylvania

> *Location: Philadelphia County, Delaware Avenue near Christian Street, South Philadelphia.*

Only 8 years after the Swedes established the first European settlements along the banks of the Delaware River, a group of colonists at Wicaco, now South Philadelphia, began to use a small log blockhouse, originally utilized for defense against the Indians, as a mission of the state church of Sweden. In 1700, they built the present Gloria Dei, or Old Swedes', Church, on the same site.

Gloria Dei (Old Swedes') Church, constructed in 1700 by Swedish settlers, is the oldest church in Philadelphia. It is still an active church.

One of the finest public buildings and the oldest church in Philadelphia, it is an ivy-covered, red-brick building in Flemish and common bond and has glazed headers. The only touches of Swedish architecture are a steep-peaked gable over the main entrance, a square belfry, and a small spire. Some of the interior embellishments were brought from Sweden by the settlers. These include a stone baptismal font near the pulpit and a cherubim figurehead, once a decoration on the prow of a Swedish ship, which hangs below the organ loft. The church also contains many relics and documents pertaining to the English colonial and War for Independence periods.

In 1789, the church separated from the mother church in Sweden, and in 1845 was admitted into the Convention of the Protestant Episcopal Church of the Diocese of Pennsylvania. Still an active religious center, as well as an important historic site, in 1942 it was declared a National Historic Site.

3. San José Mission National Historic Site, Texas

> *Location: Bexar County, on U.S. 281, about 4 miles south of San Antonio.*

One of the finest surviving Spanish missions in North America, San José was one of a series of frontier missions that stretched across the Southwestern part of the present United States in the 17th and 18th centuries. It was named San José y San Miguel de Aguayo Mission when it was founded in 1720, at the instigation of the Franciscan Fray Antonio Margíl de Jesus, one of the greatest of the Spanish missionaries on the northern frontier of New Spain. Margíl was responsible for establishing the earlier east Texas missions of Dolores, Guadalupe, and San Miguel— all of which Spanish officials closed in 1720 because of fear of French aggression from Louisiana.

San José Mission grew rapidly and steadily, the first temporary adobe structures being replaced by stone buildings. By the middle of the 18th century, it was one of the most flourishing on the northern frontier. More than 200 Indian convert residents cared for 2,000 head of cattle and 1,000 sheep and produced 3,000 bushels of corn annually. When the Franciscans departed from the mission, after the civil authorities secularized it in 1794, diocesan priests (the secular clergy) presided until the Franciscans returned again, in 1931. The dome and roof of the central

Main entrance to San José Mission, Texas. Founded in 1720 by Fray Antonio Margíl de Jesus, the mission is a fine example of an 18th-century Spanish mission in the Southwestern United States.

Cloisters of San José Mission, Texas.

building had meanwhile caved in, and vandalism and neglect resulted in other damage. In 1912, the Catholic Church initiated a restoration program, to which the people of San Antonio contributed generously.

Grinding room in the old grist mill overlooking San José Mission, Texas.

During the period 1934–37, the program was intensified and the church was restored and rededicated to religious uses. In 1930, the San Antonio Conservation Society had bought the ruins of the granary from the descendants of Pedro Huizar, the artist responsible for the famous rose window and facade.

The entire San José Mission property was designated a National Historic Site in 1941, under an agreement with the Texas State Parks Board and the Archbishop of San Antonio, who administer the property in cooperation with the National Park Service. A special advisory board for the site provides advice on matters of preservation, development, and general administration. It is composed of representatives from the U.S. Department of the Interior, the Texas State Parks Board, the Archbishopric of San Antonio, the County of Bexar, and the San Antonio Conservation Society.

C. Sites Eligible for the Registry of National Historic Landmarks

Most of the historic sites in this group have been judged by the Advisory Board on National Parks, Historic Sites, Buildings, and Monuments to meet the criteria of "exceptional value" for commemorating or illustrating the phases of U.S. history treated in this volume. A few, however, which have primary associations with other phases of history, have been included in this section and the "Other Sites Considered" section because of their secondary or peripheral associations with the period treated in this volume. As historic sites of national importance, all of them have been declared by the Secretary of the Interior to be eligible for inclusion in the Registry of National Historic Landmarks. Some have already been designated Registered National Historic Landmarks, and others will receive the designation upon application of the owners. A few have been proposed for addition to the National Park System.

1. Apalachicola Fort, Alabama

Location. Russell County, on the west bank of the Chattahoochee River, near Holy Trinity.

Ownership and Administration. Privately owned.

Significance. The northernmost Spanish outpost on the Chattahoochee River, this fort was built by the Spanish about 1689 in an attempt to prevent the English from gaining a foothold among the Lower Creek Indians. It was a key Spanish outpost in the imperial struggle to control the Indians in the present Southeastern United States.

Beginning in 1675, Spanish missionaries attempted to convert the

Lower Creeks along the Chattahoochee, but they were unsuccessful. When the Indians came under the influence of English traders 10 years later, the Spanish retaliated with punitive raids. Despite the burning of several Lower Creek towns and the construction of Apalachicola Fort in the heart of the Indian territory, the Spaniards failed to gain control over the tribe.

The Lower Creeks moved many of their towns to the Ocmulgee and Oconee Rivers in present Georgia to be nearer the English. Aided and led by the English, the Creeks destroyed many of the Spanish missions among the Timucua Indians and seriously threatened even St. Augustine. The Spanish abandoned and destroyed Apalachicola Fort in 1691 because of the English threat.

The palisade of the fort was rectangular, roughly 61 by 53 feet, and had corner bastions. It was constructed of wattle and daub and reinforced by an exterior half-wall of clay. A moat surrounded the palisade. Limited archeological excavations at the site, conducted by the Smithsonian Institution and the University of Alabama, have uncovered evidence of the fort which agrees with the historical records. Majolica sherds and olive jar fragments, of Spanish origin and correct time period, were found.

Present Appearance. The site, on the margin of the Walter F. George Reservoir, is well preserved; the line of the moat is clearly visible. The land is now utilized for pasture.[1]

2. Fort Toulouse (Fort Jackson), Alabama

Location. Elmore County, at the junction of the Coosa and Tallapoosa Rivers, on a gravel road, 4 miles southwest of Wetumpka.

Ownership and Administration. State of Alabama; Department of Conservation.

Significance. From its construction in 1717 until the end of the French and Indian War, in 1763, this fort was the offensive-defensive eastern outpost of French Louisiana. Situated just below the southern tip of the Appalachian Highland, at the junction of the two main tributaries of the Alabama River, it protected the French settlements from Mobile Bay westward to New Orleans. It was also the spearhead of the French drive to wrest control of the present Southeastern United States from the Spanish and English. In 1814, after defeating the Creek Indians at Horseshoe

Bend, Andrew Jackson occupied the abandoned site. He constructed a new fort at the location of the old one and named it Fort Jackson, in August 1814 the scene of the treaty that officially ended the Creek War.

Present Appearance. The Coosa and Tallapoosa Rivers follow nearly parallel courses for some distance above their junction, and form a narrow peninsula a mile long and only a few hundred yards wide. A privately owned tract that extends upstream from the junction includes the site of an ancient Indian village, where one large mound is discernible and the ground is liberally sprinkled with sherds. East of this tract is the 6-acre Fort Toulouse tract, owned by the State.

Adjoining the tract on the south and east is private property containing the Isaac Ross Cemetery, which dates from at least the War of 1812. In 1897, about 200 bodies were removed from this cemetery to the national cemetery in Mobile. Most of them were the remains of men who had been assigned to Andrew Jackson's army, but some of them may have been Frenchmen. Amateur archeologists have carried on excavations at the Indian village site, but not at the State-owned Fort Toulouse tract. The fort area includes two monuments and the remains of what appears to have been a powder magazine.[2]

3. Awatovi, Arizona

Location. Navajo County, on the southern tip of Antelope Mesa, about 8 miles south of Keams Canyon.

Ownership and Administration. Hopi Indians.

Significance. Awatovi was the first of the Hopi villages to be visited by the Spanish and the first to capitulate. Then one of the largest and most important of the villages, it had been in existence for about 450 years. The first European visitor, in 1540, was Pedro de Tovar, whom Coronado dispatched to the Hopi villages a week after the capture of Hawikuh. A skirmish occurred when Tovar arrived, but the inhabitants quickly sued for peace and offered presents of cloth, skins, turquoise, and maize. The five remaining pueblos then offered fealty to the King of Spain. Tovar returned to Hawikuh and reported to Coronado what the Hopis had told him of a great river to the west where giants lived. Coronado immediately sent out a party under García López de Cárdenas, whom the Hopis provided with supplies and guides. The party visited the Colorado River, but found no giants.

The Spanish did not visit Tusayan (Hopiland) again until 1583, when the Antonio de Espejo expedition spent several days at the Hopi villages before turning southwest to the Verde Valley. Don Juan de Oñate, in

1598, found the Hopis ready to capitulate formally to the King of Spain. Oñate visited the pueblos again in 1605, and Capt. Gerónimo Márquez in 1614, but not until 1629 did the Spanish make any substantial missionary effort among the Hopis.

From then until the Pueblo rebellion of 1680, during which time Awatovi was under Franciscan tutelage, it had little contact with the Spanish military and no direct contact with Spanish settlements. The Hopis expected reprisals for participating in the 1680 rebellion, but none came. When Diego de Vargas, the reconqueror, arrived in 1692, the Hopis reswore their allegiance to Spain, and he departed without incident.

In 1699, the Christian faction among the Hopis, probably residents of Awatovi, sent a delegation to Santa Fe to ask for missionaries. They offered to rebuild their mission. Three Spanish priests then made a brief visit to Awatovi. They reported that most of the Hopis were hostile and would not listen to them, and they also recommended that a garrison be posted at Awatovi to protect the Christian Indians from the other Hopis. Soon thereafter, Fray Juan de Garaycoechéa was well received at Awatovi and baptized 73 children. He was induced not to try to visit the other villages, however, and Awatovi's reception of him marked its doom. Near the end of 1700, the other Hopis sacked and destroyed the pueblo, killed all the men, and redistributed the women and children among the other villages. The site was never reoccupied.

Present Appearance. Little remains today of the three church structures except parts of the friary associated with the second church, built of sandstone, which are visible, as are parts of the sandstone masonry pueblo. Dr. J. O. Brew, of the Peabody Museum, Harvard University, excavated the site between 1935 and 1939. He uncovered a large amount of aboriginal material—such as pottery and stone and bone artifacts—but only a few fragments of porcelain, metal, or other Spanish materials. The fields and gardens near Awatovi are cultivated today by the descendants of the women and children who survived the destruction of the village in 1700. They live at the First and Second Mesa pueblos.[3]

4. San Xavier del Bac Mission, Arizona

Location. Pima County, 2 miles west of U.S. 89, about 9 miles south of Tucson.

Ownership and Administration. Roman Catholic Church.

Significance. This is one of the finest surviving examples of Spanish mission architecture. The farthest north of the 24 Spanish missions of

San Xavier del Bac Mission, near Tucson, Arizona. Padre Francisco Kino founded the mission in 1700, but Apaches later destroyed it. In 1797, Franciscans erected the present structure, an excellent example of Spanish Renaissance architecture.

Pimería Alta, it commemorates the missionary activities of the famous Jesuit padre, Eusebio Francisco Kino, its founder. In 1700, Kino established the mission, for the Papago Indians, on a site about 2 miles from the present structure. After his death, in 1711, missionary work in most of Pimería Alta was sporadic because of a shortage of priests, but the Jesuits continued their work until the Pima Rebellion of 1751. After the Spanish Government founded the presidio at Tubac in 1752, the missionaries returned. In 1762, a number of Sobaipuri Indians, who had abandoned the San Pedro Valley to the Apaches, came to San Xavier for refuge.

In 1767, the Spanish Crown expelled all Jesuits from the missionary field. Franciscans then carried on the mission work in Pimería Alta, but soon after they occupied San Xavier the Apaches destroyed it. The Franciscans promptly began rebuilding the mission in its present location and consecrated it in 1797. In 1813, the Spanish secularized it. A decade later, when the Mexican regime took over, the few remaining padres abandoned it. In 1857, the Franciscans reoccupied it, after the lands south of the Gila River had passed to the United States under the terms of the Gadsden Purchase (1853). Early in the present century, the Catholic Church began restoration and followed the old plans to a large extent, except in the atrium and dormitories. San Xavier is still an active parish church, attended mainly by Papago Indians.

Present Appearance. San Xavier is distinguished architecturally and artistically. The well-preserved buildings are constructed of burned adobe brick and lime plaster, in Spanish Renaissance architectural style. This style is typified by the lavish baroque churches of Mexico, of which San Xavier is the only example within the United States.[4]

5. Carmel Mission, California

Location. Monterey County, Rio Road, Carmel.

Ownership and Administration. Roman Catholic Church.

Significance. Mission San Carlos de Borroméo, or Carmel Mission, was the most important of the California missions from an ecclesiastical standpoint. It was the headquarters of the two great Franciscan padres, Junípero Serra and Fermín Francisco de Lasuén, under whose guidance

Mission San Carlos de Borroméo (Carmel Mission), in 1791, before construction of the present church. This mission served as headquarters of Fathers Serra and Lasuén, who founded 18 of the 21 California missions. From a drawing by José Cardero. Courtesy, Bancroft Library.

and inspiration 18 of the 21 California missions were established. Records for the missions and a library of 2,500 volumes were housed at Carmel, which served as a personnel and supply center for the founding of new missions and the strengthening of old ones. Both Serra and Lasuén are buried at the mission.

Father Serra founded Carmel Mission on June 3, 1770, at the Presidio of Monterey, as the second mission in California. In December 1771, he relocated it at the present site, 3 miles south of Monterey, to remove his Indian neophytes from the corrupting influence of the presidial garrison. Serra and his devoted companion, Father Crespi, who were based at the mission for the remainder of their lives, served not only the local area but also the other California missions. As father-president, Serra was responsible for establishing nine missions, all of which he visited frequently to provide encouragement and counsel. Ascetic, humble, and meek, yet a vigorous fighter in defense of the religious as against the political order, he rightfully earned the title of spiritual father of California.

When Serra died, in 1784, Father Lasuén succeeded him and ably continued his work. Lasuén was not only tactful in dealing with political and military authorities, but he was also a builder of architecturally sound missions. Before he died, in 1803, he founded nine missions in California. In 1793, he laid the foundations of the present Carmel Mission church, which was built of sandstone from the slopes of Carmel

Modern view of Carmel Mission, built between 1793 and 1797. A feature of its ornate facade is the star-shaped Moorish window.

Valley and lime manufactured from abalone shells. The finished church was dedicated in 1797, when the mission had a record number of Indian neophytes, 927. A decline followed, marked in part by the transfer of California mission headquarters to Santa Barbara after Lasuén's death. The number of neophytes was down to 381 in 1820 and 150 by 1834, when the Mexican Government secularized the mission.   By 1846, when Governor Pico offered the church for sale, it was almost totally destroyed, and the other buildings were also in ruins. In 1852, the church roof collapsed, and the tiles were carried off to be used in other structures.

Present Appearance. In 1859, the United States, which had acquired the mission as part of the Gadsden Purchase (1853), returned it to the Catholic Church. A new roof was built over what remained of the 1797 church, and in 1884 the structure was rededicated as a church. Full restoration of the mission, which began in the 1920's, was at first pursued with more zeal than historical precision. Since 1933, however, the work has continued on the basis of more careful research and the use of native building materials.

The facade and portions of the stone walls of the church are original. The remainder of the structure and all the other buildings are reconstructions. The most distinctive design feature is the ornate facade, which has a slightly irregular and star-shaped window of Moorish design. The church is furnished with the ancient stone font, where the Indians were baptized, as well as original paintings and statues that were returned to the building as part of the reconstruction program. Before the altar are situated the graves of Fathers Serra, Crespi, and Lasuén.[5]

6. Fort Ross, California

Location. Sonoma County, near the town of Fort Ross.

Ownership and Administration. State of California; Division of Beaches and Parks.

Significance. Fort Ross was established by the Russian-American Fur Company in 1812 for the threefold purpose of exploiting the rich fur hunting grounds of the California coast, opening trade with Spanish California, and providing an agricultural depot to supply Russian settlements in Alaska. Ivan Kuskoff, who began the construction, arrived in the spring of 1812 with 95 Russians and about 80 Aleuts. By

Commandant's House, at Fort Ross, California. Established in 1812 by the Russian-American Fur Company, Fort Ross supplied Russia's settlements in Alaska with farm produce and was a center for Russian-Spanish trade.

fall, enough progress had been made so that the fort was officially dedicated, although it was not completed until 1814.

The fort was built near the ocean on a plateau, about 1 square mile in extent, which terminates at the ocean in a precipice about 70 feet high. Redwood was used for all construction, including the stockaded walls, which measured 12 feet high. The quadrangular enclosure measured about 276 by 312 feet. Two hexagonal-shaped, two-story blockhouses at diagonally opposite corners of the stockade defended the walls. Eight cannons were mounted in 1812, and the number increased to about 50 by 1841, when more than 50 structures had been built.

Inside the walls were the commandant's house, officers' quarters, barracks for the Russian employees, a chapel, and 3 storehouses and offices; outside the wall were 37 redwood huts for the Aleuts, a windmill, farm buildings, granaries, cattle yards, a tannery, and workshops for blacksmiths, coopers, bakers, and carpenters. The population of the post, including Russians, Aleuts, and California Indians, never exceeded 400.

Fort Ross was not successful as an agricultural colony. Level land in the immediate neighborhood was scarce and not particularly fertile.

Also, the prevalent coastal fog caused the grain to rust, and rodents caused much crop damage. Farming was carried on rather ineffectively both by private individuals and by the fur company. Not until 1826 were any considerable shipments of grain made to Sitka, only 216,000 pounds being forwarded during the period 1826–33.

In 1833 the company opened a new farming center, Slavianka, near the mouth of the Russian River, midway between Fort Ross and the Russian port at Bodega Bay. The new establishment had uneven success— good at first, but disappointing between 1835 and 1840. The Russians obtained animals from the Spanish for stockraising, in which they had some success. At first, because of the scarcity of pasturage around Fort Ross, the cattle strayed over the forested mountain ranges half of the year, where many fell prey to bears and Indians.

To improve livestock management, in 1833 the company established two small ranches south of Fort Ross. The first, called the Kostromitinof Ranch, was located just south of the mouth of the Russian River and consisted of about 100 acres; the second, the Tschernick, or Gorgy's, Ranch, was about 5 miles north of Bodega Bay, at Russian Gulch. The latter also included a vineyard and some fruit trees. In the last 15 years of the fort's existence under Russian management, the managers exported some 216,000 pounds of salt beef and 18,000 pounds of butter to Sitka, as well as considerable quantities of excellent tanned leather.

As time went on, the Russian company decided to abandon its operation. In 1839, because of the great excess of costs over revenue in maintaining the fort, the company leased the southern coastal strip of southeastern Alaska to the Hudson's Bay Company, which agreed to

Russian Greek Orthodox Chapel, built about 1828, is one of several restored buildings at Fort Ross, California.

furnish the Russian Alaskan settlements with agricultural commodities produced on its Columbia River farms. In 1841, John A. Sutter purchased Fort Ross for $30,000 in cash and a specified amount of agricultural products over the succeeding 4 years. The last Russians withdrew in January 1842.

In addition to illustrating Russian activities in North America, Fort Ross exemplifies the threat of foreign intrusions into America that produced the Monroe Doctrine (1823) and heightened colonial activity on the part of certain European powers, notably the British.

Present Appearance. In 1906, the California Landmarks League donated 3.01 acres of the fort site and the Russian Chapel to the State. In 1928, Fort Ross was assigned to the Division of Beaches and Parks as a State Historical Monument, and since then has been gradually restored. The chapel, commandant's house, and part of one blockhouse—all of which were still standing in 1906—have been carefully restored, and a second blockhouse and the stockade reconstructed.[6]

7. Old Mission Dam (Padre Dam), California

Location. San Diego County, in Mission Gorge, just north of U.S. 80, 13 miles northeast of Old Town, San Diego.

Ownership and Administration. City of San Diego.

Significance. Old Mission Dam, whose associated aqueduct and flume extended about 5 miles to the Mission of San Diego de Alcalá, was one of the first major irrigation engineering projects on the Pacific coast of the United States. It impounded water from the San Diego River, and for much of the year provided an assured supply, which was released as needed for agricultural and domestic purposes.

San Diego de Alcalá Mission, founded by Father Junípero Serra July 16, 1769, on Presidio Hill, was the first of the 21 California missions. In 1774, Serra moved the mission 6 miles to its present location, both to free his Indian neophytes from the adverse influences of the presidial garrison and to obtain a location affording more water. Despite a native rebellion in 1775, the mission became one of the wealthiest and most populous in California.

New structures were erected during the period 1776–80, and by 1800 more than 1,500 Indian neophytes were attached to the mission. Earthquake damage in 1803 led to further rebuilding and enlargement. By

Old Mission Dam, a major irrigation project of the early 19th century, supplied water to the Mission of San Diego de Alcalá. A flume carried water about 5 miles from the dam to the mission grounds.

1813, the mission had assumed its present form. In 1824, the maximum population of 1,829 Indians was attained, but in 1835 they dispersed when the Mexican Government secularized the mission, after which the buildings were neglected and deteriorated rapidly.

The precise dates of construction of Old Mission Dam, as well as the aqueduct and flume, cannot be ascertained. Not likely begun before 1800, the dam was probably started in 1803, following a 2-year drought. By 1817, it had certainly assumed its final form. Of solid masonry, it was about 220 feet wide, 13 feet thick at the bottom, and 12 feet or more high. Native stone and locally produced cement were used to construct the dam, aqueduct, and flume. The flume, 2 feet wide and 1 foot deep, conducted water to the mission gardens and vineyards some 5 miles distant.

Present Appearance. By 1867, the dam and the aqueduct-flume system were reportedly in ruins. About 7 years later, they were repaired and again put to use. The remains of the dam, still impressive today, impound a small amount of water. The dam will be included in San Diego's proposed Fortuna Mountain-Mission Gorge Metropolitan Park. No substantial remains of the aqueduct or flume are visible. San Diego Mission has been largely reconstructed since 1931.[7]

8. Presidio of San Francisco, California

Location. San Francisco County, south side of Golden Gate, San Francisco.

Ownership and Administration. U.S. Government; Department of Defense.

Significance. This presidio, which guarded the finest harbor on the Pacific coast, figured prominently in the extension of Spanish settlement into northern California and was the northernmost bastion of the Spanish New World Empire and the chief barrier against British, Russian, and American expansion in California. Under its aegis, between 1776 and 1821, the Spaniards established four missions, two pueblos, a royal rancho, and an *asistencia.* In 1817 and 1821, Spanish exploring expeditions that penetrated the interior and the area above San Francisco Bay also used the presidio as a base. Between 1821 and 1836, under Mexican rule, the presidio continued to be the main military base in northern California.

In 1776, 7 years after the discovery of San Francisco Bay, Lt. Col. Juan Bautista de Anza, from Tubac, selected the site for the presidio.

Commandant's House, erected in the period 1776–78 at the presidio of San Francisco, now serves as an officers' club. It has been considerably altered throughout the years, but its front facade incorporates a large part of the original adobe walls.

Lt. José Joaquín Moraga supervised construction, which he initiated on a temporary basis. The buildings were primitive structures—palisaded walls and flat roofs covered with sod or tules. The military reservation of the presidio consisted of 1,564 acres. Construction was slow, however. In 1792, or 16 years after the establishment of the post, only three of the four exterior walls had been completed. Year after year, from 1776 to 1835, under both Spanish and Mexican administrations, adobe buildings that had replaced the original log buildings were constructed or repaired in the dry season, only to be damaged during the rainy season. A church, commandant's house, guardhouse, barracks, and warehouses were constructed over the years. Whether because of lack of suitable alternative building materials, lack of familiarity with other methods, binding instructions from officials in distant places—or a combination of all these reasons—presidial commanders continued to use building methods not suited to the climate. Earthquakes also caused damage.

Capt. George Vancouver, who visited San Francisco Bay in 1792, observed that the presidio—equipped as it was with only two cannons, one mounted on a carriage and the other on a log—was practically defenseless. His visit and other developments in the Pacific area led the Spanish to strengthen San Francisco's defenses by bringing in additional troops and weapons.

In 1793, the Spanish began to construct a new fort, Castillo de San Joaquín, located about $1\frac{1}{3}$ miles northwest of the presidio on Punta del Cantíl (now called Fort Point). They completed the castillo in 1794, but its exact shape and dimensions are not known because it was apparently modified appreciably during later repairs and alterations. Upon its 10-foot-thick walls were mounted 12 cannons. In the center was a one-story barracks, built of adobe and roofed with tules, which contained two rooms. In 1796, about 225 persons, including families of soldiers, were reportedly living at the presidio.

In 1797, the troops erected the battery at Yerba Buena, located at Point San José (later called Black Point and then Fort Mason), to protect the anchorage at Yerba Buena Cove. Hastily thrown together of brushwood, fascines, and earthworks, it had eight embrasures and mounted five cannon. A sentinel daily visited the battery, which was not permanently garrisoned. When the battery was completed, the third fortification on the bay, San Francisco was the strongest military post in Spanish California. From an original population of 63, by 1820 the San Francisco District had grown to 670 Spaniards and 5,400 mission

Indians. At the close of the Spanish period, the next year, 134 soldiers and 20 guns defended the presidio. Its strength declined during the Mexican period. In 1836, the year after the government transferred the military headquarters of northern California to Sonoma, it withdrew all the soldiers from the presidio. Most of the remaining buildings disintegrated rapidly; only one has survived, and that only partially.

Yerba Buena Pueblo, which grew into the modern city of San Francisco, was established in 1835, not far from the presidio, by the Mexican Government.

Present Appearance. The site of the 1776 Presidio of San Francisco forms the southern portion of the present U.S. Presidio parade ground, and is situated on Moraga Avenue, between Graham and Mesa Streets. Except for the commandant's house, no surface remains are extant. The site is open and free of intrusions. Four Spanish cannon are on the parade ground, and two more are at Fort Mason. The presidio still

Aerial view of San Francisco. The Spanish presidio was located in the left foreground. Between the years 1776 and 1822, it served as a base for Spanish exploration and settlement of northern California. Courtesy, U.S. Army.

includes about 1,460 acres of the original Spanish reservation.

Though the commandant's house survives, it has been extensively altered since the original construction during the period 1776–78. This one-story adobe structure, on the south side of Moraga Avenue opposite the intersection with Graham Street, is now used as an officers' club. Its front section still incorporates about 75 percent of the original adobe walls.

Castillo de San Joaquín was located at the site now occupied by Fort Point. All traces of the castillo were destroyed in 1853, when the cliff on which it stood was lowered by some 90 feet and Fort Point erected. The present Fort Mason includes the site of the former battery at Yerba Buena. Nothing remains of the battery, but its site is identified by a historical marker in the small park north of the loop on the north end of Sheridan Road.[8]

9. Royal Presidio Chapel, California

Location. Monterey County, 550 Church Street, Monterey.

Ownership and Administration. Roman Catholic Church.

Significance. Monterey was not only the Spanish and Mexican capitals of California for most of the period between 1776 and 1848, but also the stronghold of European civilization on the Pacific coast of the present United States and the hub of social, military, economic, and political activities in California. The Royal Presidio Chapel of San Carlos de Borroméo de Monterey was closely associated with political activities in California; in addition to being used for religious services, which were attended by the Spanish Governors, it was the scene of many colorful ceremonies that were part of the affairs of state. The only remaining presidial chapel in California, it is also the sole extant structure from the Monterey Presidio of Spanish times and the only 18th-century Spanish architectural survival in the present city of Monterey.

Don Gaspar de Portolá, Governor of California, and Father Junípero Serra established the Presidio of Monterey and the San Carlos Mission on June 3, 1770. Within less than 2 weeks, the 60 Spaniards in the pioneer party had erected the rude huts that temporarily constituted the presidio and mission. They then built a stockade around them. The largest hut was utilized as the mission chapel until the next year, when Serra moved his mission to a new site at present-day Carmel, 3 miles south of Monterey; thereafter the hut and the building that replaced

it came to be known as the Royal Chapel (*La Capilla Real*) of the
Presidio of Monterey.

The chapel walls were composed of logs standing on end, the inter-

Royal Presidio Chapel, dating from the late 18th century, is the only extant
building of the Spanish presidio of Monterey. Capital of Spanish and Mexican California, Monterey was the center of political and military activities
and the scene of many colorful ceremonies of state.

stices being filled with twigs and plastered with mud. The roof was supported by a row of wooden beams, covered with layers of sticks,
branches, and leaves, and topped with earth. This rude structure was
replaced in 1773 by an adobe chapel located on the south side of the
presidio plaza, which was used until 1787. In the meantime, Monterey
had been designated as the capital of California, and the Governor rebuilt the presidio.

The new presidio consisted of a stone wall 537 yards in circumference,
12 feet high, and 4 feet thick, which enclosed 10 adobe houses and a
barracks. In 1789, fire destroyed a new log chapel, along with about
half the other buildings, necessitating another building program. This
program was largely completed in 1791, except for the new stone Royal

Presidio Chapel, the present structure, which was not finished until 1795.

When Capt. George Vancouver visited Monterey in 1792, he estimated the garrison at about 100 men and observed that all the soldiers and their families lived within the presidio walls. During the 1800's, the presidio and nearby battery deteriorated. In 1818, Hippolyte de Bouchard, the Argentine pirate, attacked Monterey with 2 ships and 285 men. The Spanish defense force, consisting of only 40 soldiers and 8 rusty, poorly placed cannon, abandoned the presidio and retreated inland after making an initial show of resistance. Before departing, Bouchard ransacked the presidio and burned the battery, the northern side of the presidio, and three houses on the southern side. The chapel was not destroyed, but only adobe walls remained of much of the rest of Monterey. Because repair work proceeded slowly and conditions deteriorated during Mexican rule, by 1841 only the Royal Presidio Chapel remained standing.

Present Appearance. The Presidio of Monterey, active during the period 1770–1841, was bounded by present Webster and Fremont Streets, between Camino El Estero and Abrego Street. No remains are extant except for the Royal Presidio Chapel, erected in 1794–95. The original chapel was about 120 feet long and 30 wide, rectangular in shape and of the basilica type. Between 1855 and 1858, it was enlarged by 30 feet, and transepts were added at the south end, which changed the building's floor plan to that of a cross. Gothic windows with stained glass were also added, and the original flat roof of the belltower was replaced by the present peaked roof. The facade and walls of the original chapel are intact. The front faces north and features a facade of carved sandstone that has ornate columns and a massive arched doorway. The interior is plain, the whitewashed walls being decorated only by a few pictures and images of saints. The altar and the pulpit are at the south end of the building.

After the Mexican Government secularized Carmel Mission in 1834, it was abandoned and many of its relics removed to the Royal Presidio Chapel, where some may still be seen. During this period, the chapel served as a parish church. The chapel reflects the handiwork of Mexican Indians who were imported to construct the building and whose renderings of religious motifs have survived as notable examples of primitive art. The Stations of the Cross are original, as are also the statues of St. John, the Sorrowful Mother, the Spanish Madonna, and the bas-relief of Our Lady of Guadalupe, carved in chalk rock above the entrance.

An adjoining museum houses precious Catholic relics, including the iron safe used by Father Serra, a rudely carved reliquary of Indian manufacture, and Serra's chalice, cape, and dalmatics, together with his altar service of beaten silver.[9]

10. San Diego Presidio, California

Location. San Diego County, in Presidio Park near Old Town, San Diego.

Ownership and Administration. City of San Diego; Park and Recreation Department.

Significance. San Diego Presidio commemorates the beginning of mission effort and European settlement in California and on the Pacific coast of the present United States. Father Junípero Serra said mass at the site on July 1, 1769, before an assemblage of 126 persons, who were the survivors of 300 who had originally set out from Baja California by land and sea to occupy Alta California. After the *Te Deum,* Gov. Don Gaspar de Portolá ceremoniously took possession of California for Spain.

From then until 1776 the San Diego Presidio (a fort until it was legally established as a presidio in 1774) was the base of operations for expeditions that explored new routes and founded new missions and presidios; and from 1776 until 1837 it continued to be the seat of military jurisdiction in southern California. Under Mexican rule, after 1821, it was also the residence of the Governor, from 1825 to 1829.

The religious ceremony of July 1, 1769, was followed by the formal founding at the presidio, on July 16, of the first mission in Alta California, San Diego de Alcalá. The colonists suffered greatly during the first few months. After a damaging Indian attack in August, they erected a crude stockade on Presidio Hill to protect both mission and colony. By January 1770, the settlement was on the point of starvation. On March 19, just when all hope seemed lost, a supply ship sailed into the bay and saved the California venture from total ruin. By the end of the month the colonists had finished the stockade of the presidio, mounted two bronze cannon, and erected wooden houses with tule roofs.

The commandant's residence was situated in the center of the presidio. On the east side of the square were a chapel, cemetery, and storehouses; on the south side were the gate and guardhouse; and around the other two sides were barracks. To remove his Indian charges from the un-

San Diego Mission, the first of the 21 California missions, in 1853. From a lithograph by Charles Koppel. Courtesy, Bancroft Library, University of California.

wholesome influence of the presidial garrison and obtain a better water supply, in 1774 Father Serra moved the mission to another site, 6 miles to the northeast, the present site of San Diego Mission. In 1778, the original wooden walls and buildings of the presidio began to be replaced with adobe structures.

When Capt. George Vancouver reached San Diego in 1793, in the first foreign ship to visit the city, he was not much impressed from a military standpoint. His visit, however, along with others, stimulated the Spanish to strengthen it. In 1795–96, an esplanade, powder magazine, flagpole, and several houses for soldiers were added to the presidio, and Fort Guijarros—the first harbor defense work—was erected on Point Loma. It included an adobe magazine, barracks, and a battery designed to mount 10 cannon.

As the Spanish period drew to a close, the garrison of San Diego Presidio increased, 50 cavalrymen being added in 1819 to the force of about 100 soldiers—some of whom were detached to Los Angeles pueblo and the four missions of the district. The total Spanish population of the San Diego District in that year was about 450, in addition to about 6,800 Indian neophytes. Under the Mexican Government, the size of the military force and the condition of the presidio declined rapidly after 1830. In 1836, Richard Henry Dana found the presidio in a deplorable state and Fort Guijarros in ruins. The following year the Mexicans sent the last of the troops north, and by 1839 the presidio was in complete ruins. Much stone and adobe were removed from it to erect houses in the new pueblo of San Diego, founded in 1835.

Present Appearance. George W. Marston saved the presidio site from complete oblivion in 1929 by donating about 37 acres, including the site, to San Diego for park purposes. The city formally accepted the gift in 1937. Presidio Park, which has been formally landscaped, includes the Serra Museum as its principal architectural feature. This museum, built in 1929, houses a large collection of archeological and historical objects related to early California and Spanish history. The museum library contains both original and published records of the history of the city and the region.

The former site of the presidio is in front of the museum. Construction of the San Diego River dike and the Mission Valley Road destroyed part of the presidio site, and another section lies beneath a park road. However, some vestiges of the structures that once formed the presidio still remain in the form of grass-covered mounds, which suggest part of the outline of former walls and buildings.

In the center of the old presidio stands the Junípero Serra Cross, erected in 1913 from bits of brick and floor tile found on the spot. It bears this inscription: "Here the First Citizen, Fray Junípero Serra, Planted Civilization in California, Here He Raised the Cross, Here Began the First Mission, Here Founded the First Town—San Diego, July 16, 1769." [10]

11. Santa Barbara Mission, California

Location. Santa Barbara County, 2201 Laguna Street, Santa Barbara.

Ownership and Administration. Roman Catholic Church.

Significance. One of the finest and most distinguished of the 21 California missions from an architectural standpoint, this "queen of the missions" is the only one to escape complete secularization throughout its long history. Its sanctuary light has never been extinguished.

Father Fermín Francisco de Lasuén consecrated it on December 16, 1786, as the 10th California mission, located at Santa Barbara Presidio. The first, temporary structure, erected in 1787, was replaced by an adobe church in 1789, and that in turn by a larger building in 1793–94, which

Santa Barbara Mission, in 1875. To the rear and left of the church are the remains of an Indian village that in the first part of the 19th century helped house some 1,800 neophytes. Photograph by C. E. Watkins. Courtesy, Bancroft Library, University of California.

the disastrous earthquakes of 1812 destroyed. In 1815, a labor force of Canalino Indians began to construct the present large stone church, completed for the most part by 1820. The design is classical.

The great church, 179 feet long and 38 feet wide, contained six chapels. The 6-foot-thick sandstone walls were heavily buttressed. The roof and floor were of tile. Two towers were located on the classic facade, the one on the left being completed in 1820 and the other by 1833. Other buildings included a residence for the priests, workshops, and storehouses. In 1803, some 234 adobe huts housing 1,792 Indian neophytes surrounded the mission.

Between 1806 and 1808, the Indians constructed a remarkable irrigation system. It included a large dam across Pedregoso Creek, 1½ miles north of the mission, and a reservoir that was later also used to operate a gristmill, erected in 1827–28. Aqueducts conducted the water first to a filter, or settling, tank and then to a large, stone-walled reservoir 500 feet from the church. The reservoir, 120 feet square and 7 feet high, had a stone fountain and long laundry trough.

In 1834, the Mexicans secularized Santa Barbara Mission and its lands and in 1846 sold them, but the Franciscan fathers continued to occupy the mission in the interim. Indeed, it became the Franciscan capital of California. It was the home of the last father-president, and in 1842

California's first bishop arrived at the mission to establish the seat of his diocese, which included all of Alta and Baja California.

In 1853, the Church founded a Franciscan missionary college at the mission to train English-speaking priests. The buildings were used, and kept in repair, unlike those at the other California missions, during the period of Mexican and early American administration. In 1865, the United States returned some 283 acres of the original mission property, including the buildings, to the Catholic Church.

Present Appearance. Santa Barbara Mission survived virtually intact until June 29, 1925, when a violent earthquake struck the area. Damage was severe, the east tower being destroyed and the interior furnishings battered by falling rock. Only the seven massive buttresses held the walls in place. The following year, restoration began, nearly half of the entire cost being subscribed by the people of California.

Original materials were used as far as possible, and the arches, columns, wall thickness, and all other details were accurately restored. When the reconstruction was completed in 1927, the rebuilt church and convent were little changed from their original construction. A further reconstruction was found necessary during the period 1950–53, when the buildings were discovered to be settling and the towers cracking because of the disintegration of cement and foundations. The facade and towers were de-

Reconstructed in 1926–27, and again in 1950–53, Santa Barbara Mission is one of the best preserved missions in California. The only one to escape complete secularization, it houses valuable Spanish and Mexican relics and documents.

molished and the entire church front carefully rebuilt to duplicate the original appearance.

The mission is not only an architectural gem but also a major museum of Spanish, Franciscan, mission, and California history. It contains a large collection of original records and objects, including the original altar, the beautiful Stations of the Cross brought from Mexico in 1797, 18th-century Mexican paintings and sculptures, and innumerable religious and secular memorabilia of the mission period. The archives contain thousands of original documents, which Father Zephyrin Engelhardt used to write his histories of the California missions.

The fountain and large reservoir near the church, parts of the original mission irrigation system, are perfectly preserved and are part of the present water system of the city of Santa Barbara. Extensive portions of the remainder of the irrigation system are also still visible in the botanic garden.[11]

12. Stanley-Whitman House, Connecticut

Location. Hartford County, 37 High Street, Farmington.

Ownership and Administration. Farmington Village Green and Library Association.

Significance. Built around 1660, apparently by John Stanley, this house is considered to be an almost perfect example of the "added lean-to house" and the New England architectural style. The open setting, tall trees, and picturesque stone wall add greatly to its charm and character. The house is one of the earliest and best preserved of the framed-overhang types, and its ornamental drops are among the finest in the country. The framed front overhang projects 1½ feet beyond the first floor, and the gabled overhang at each end measures 6 inches. The second floor has no overhang. The ornamental drops are carved from the ends of the four second-story posts that project through the overhang.

The interior is characteristic of the early central chimney plan, the parlor and hall being located on the sides of the great central chimney. The chimney below the roof is of well-selected, mostly flat fieldstone, laid in clay mixed with straw in the old English fashion. Above the roof the chimney is of red sandstone, sometimes called "brownstone," laid in small blocks, the wide joints being filled with lime mortar. The large stone fire-

Stanley-Whitman House, Connecticut, built about 1660, illustrates the New England style of architecture.

place in the hall is original, and is 7 feet wide and more than 3 feet high. The lean-to at the rear of the house is an 18th-century addition, possibly about 1760. It includes the central kitchen portion, a "buttery" room at one end and the traditional "birth and death" room at the other. The fireplace in the lean-to is backed against the original central chimney, although it has a separate flue.

In 1735 the Reverend Samuel Whitman, minister in Farmington from 1706 to 1751, purchased the house from Stanley. In 1935, its owner had the house expertly restored by the late J. Frederick Kelly, an authority on early domestic architecture in Connecticut, and then deeded it to the nonprofit association that now administers it.

Present Appearance. Preservation and maintenance of the house are of the highest order. The house is furnished in the style of the period, and in a manner characteristic of the region. Many of the furnishings came from the Farmington area, in which many other 17th- and 18th-century houses are located. A fireproof museum wing, added to the rear of the house, contains especially fine specimens of maps, manuscripts, articles of costume, musical instruments, china, and other items relating to Farmington history. A wagon shed on the grounds houses early farm implements, and the garden in the backyard contains more than 24 varieties of herbs and scented geraniums typical of colonial kitchen gardens. The house is open to visitors throughout the year.[12]

13. Fort Christina, Delaware

Location. New Castle County, near foot of East 7th Street, on Christina River, Wilmington.

Ownership and Administration. State of Delaware; Delaware State Museum.

Significance. The first Swedish expedition to the New World landed at this site about March 29, 1638. It erected the first fortification in New Sweden, Fort Christina, around which grew the first permanent white settlement in the Delaware River Valley and the nucleus of Swedish settlement. Peter Minuit, formerly of New Netherland, headed the expedition of the New Sweden Company, which sent him from Sweden in December 1637 to establish a Swedish foothold in the New World. His assigned destination was the Minquas Kill, which on his arrival he renamed the Christina River in honor of Sweden's young Queen. The expedition of 50 men, in two vessels, landed at a natural wharf of rocks that jutted into the Minquas Kill about 2 miles above its confluence with

Designed by Swedish sculptor Carl Milles, this monument stands on the site of Fort Christina, the first settlement in New Sweden, and commemorates the activities of Swedish colonists in the Delaware Valley. The ship at the top of the monument represents the *Kalmar Nyckel,* one of two vessels that brought the first Swedish colonists to America.

the Delaware. Near the rocks, Minuit erected Fort Christina to guard the settlement and serve as the administrative and commercial center of the colony.

The fort remained the principal center of Swedish settlement even during the period 1643–53, when Gov. Johan Bjornsson Printz ruled from his headquarters on Tinicum Island, some 15 miles north on the Delaware River. When New Sweden fell to the Dutch in the bloodless conquest of 1655, the Dutch posted a few soldiers at Fort Christina, which they called "Altena." Their relations with the Swedish colonists were amicable, but during the peaceful occupation the fort fell into disrepair until Gov. Peter Stuyvesant ordered it repaired for use as the New World headquarters of the Dutch West India Company. The settlement around Fort Christina remained predominantly Swedish despite the annexation to New Netherland. In 1664, when the Delaware Valley fell to the English, English soldiers garrisoned the fort, but the Swedish settlement remained the heart of the village that spread along the banks of the Christina and became the city of Wilmington.

Present Appearance. The 2 acres comprising Fort Christina State Park include the wharf of rocks that was the site of the first landing and near which was the heart of the first Swedish settlement in North America. The ledge of rocks is still partially visible, although much of the natural formation is covered by a plaza that surrounds a striking monument. The monument is a shaft designed by the late Swedish sculptor Carl Milles. It is constructed of black Swedish granite and surmounted by a stylized representation of the *Kalmar Nyckel* (the Key of Kalmar), one of the two ships used by the Minuit expedition.

Treatment of the park is formal. The high brick walls located on two sides, iron fence and ornamental iron gateway on the third, and the Christina River on the fourth separate the site from the surrounding industrial development. Archeological investigation is needed to establish specific information about the fort and surrounding buildings. The park is open to the public throughout the year.[13]

14. Holy Trinity (Old Swedes) Church, Delaware

Location. New Castle County, East 7th and Church Streets, Wilmington.

Ownership and Administration. Protestant Episcopal Church in the United States of America, Diocese of Delaware; maintained by the Holy Trinity (Old Swedes) Church Foundation, Inc., Wilmington.

Significance. This is the oldest surviving church built by a Swedish congregation in the Delaware Valley. No other structure is so closely related historically and geographically to the pioneer Swedish settlement on the Christina River, and none has retained its architectural integrity to so marked a degree. From every standpoint, Holy Trinity is a preeminent survival of the Swedish settlement on the Delaware.

The construction postdates by many years the fall of New Sweden to the Dutch in 1655; largely English in form, the church includes many additions to the original building. Nevertheless, it was built while the Swedish heritage was still a dominant influence in the Delaware Valley. For nearly a century, Swedish Lutheran missionary pastors were assigned. Beneath the church and in the venerable cemetery adjacent to it rest the remains of thousands of early Swedish settlers, many in unmarked graves.

The first churches of New Sweden were of rude log construction, a style later adopted by American frontiersmen. The earliest religious services of the colony were held in Fort Christina. Later, in 1667, the local congregation built a wooden church at Tranhook (Cranehook), on the south bank of the Christina River near its mouth. The new church received little direct supervision from the homeland for the next 32 years. Then, in 1697, three Swedish missionary pastors were sent out to revive

Although its construction postdates the fall of New Sweden by several decades, Holy Trinity (Old Swedes) Church is the oldest surviving Swedish church in the Delaware Valley. Its architecture is primarily English, but the interior contains many Swedish furnishings.

it. As the first step, a new church site was chosen, at the burial ground long used by the settlers around Fort Christina. On May 28, 1698, the builders laid the first foundation stone, and on Trinity Sunday, June 4, 1699, the church was consecrated as *Helga Trefaldighet Kyrcka* (Holy Trinity Church).

The original structure was of the utmost simplicity. Rectangular in shape, it had a brick floor, shingled roof, and gabled ends, without tower, belfry, gallery, or porch. The ceiling was plastered, the pews built of pine, and the altar railing and pulpit carved from walnut. Around 1750, the arched south porch was added; and, in 1774, the gallery, reached by outside stairs. The tower and belfry date from 1802.

After the last Swedish pastor departed, in 1791, jurisdiction over the church was transferred by the Swedish Missionary Society to the Protestant Episcopal Church. After 1830, when the congregation moved to a new building, the old church deteriorated badly. Only one service annually was held until the church was reopened in 1842. At that time, wooden benches were substituted for the pews except in the gallery, wooden flooring placed over the original bricks, and the gallery stairs moved inside. Restoration in 1899 corrected these alterations.

Present Appearance. Holy Trinity is maintained in excellent condition and is open to visitors. In 1946–47, the Garden Club of Wilmington restored the old churchyard. A short distance from the church is the restored Hendrickson House, a fine Swedish stone dwelling dating from about 1690 and recently moved from Essington, Pa. It serves as a museum and library devoted to Swedish colonial life on the Delaware.

Holy Trinity is rich in objects that date from its origin at the end of the 17th century or demonstrate its traditional Swedish ties. The original altar is preserved within a later one of marble; and the aged pulpit, carved in 1698, is still in use. Portraits of the early Swedish pastors, some of whom are buried beneath the church, are hung in the vestry. A former pastor, Eric Bjork, in 1718 donated a silver communion service, which is used upon special occasions. The altar cloth was a gift from the late King Gustav V of Sweden, in 1950. The King himself embroidered the central cross in gold thread. All these objects, displayed in the setting of the 17th-century interior, remind the visitor that this venerable church is one of the most significant and memorable links between Swedish America and the present.[14]

15. Fort San Carlos de Barrancas, Florida

Location. Escambia County, U.S. Naval Air Station, Pensacola.

Ownership and Administration. U.S. Government; Department of Defense.

Significance. Fort San Carlos de Barrancas was originally a semicircular fortification of Pensacola brick, built in 1787 during the last Spanish occupation of West Florida. The high bluff on which it was placed, called by the Spaniards "Barrancas de Santo Tomé," was the site of the earlier Fort San Carlos de Austria, which dated from the first permanent Spanish settlement on Pensacola Bay, in 1698. In 1719, a French force destroyed this first fort and nothing remains of it today. From 1763 to 1781, Pensacola was under British control, and its capture by a Spanish expedition in 1781 marked the beginning of the last period of Spanish rule. The new Fort San Carlos was a defense bastion in West Florida; and, with St. Augustine, a foothold in the Southeastern United States.

Spanish collaboration with the British forces during the War of 1812 led Andrew Jackson to move into Pensacola in 1814. The occupying British force retreated rapidly to their warships after blowing up Fort San Carlos. When Jackson withdrew to New Orleans, the Spanish returned and began to rebuild the fort. During the Seminole Indian War, 4 years later, Jackson again attacked Pensacola. In accepting the surrender of the Spanish Governor, in Fort San Carlos, he in effect seized

Fort San Carlos de Barrancas, Florida. In the late 18th century, the Spanish constructed the fort to guard Pensacola, the capital of Spanish West Florida.

control of West Florida for the United States. He returned as Provisional Governor of the new territory 3 years later.

As a part of the general tightening of coastal defenses during the years 1833–44, U.S. troops strengthened the defenses at the mouth of Pensacola Bay. They constructed a four-sided brick fortification, Fort Barrancas, immediately in the rear of and connected to Fort San Carlos; and, as part of the defensive complex, built Fort Redoubt about 1,000 yards north of Fort Barrancas. During the Civil War, Forts San Carlos and Barrancas were first in the hands of Florida State troops and then the Union forces.

Present Appearance. The forts are in poor condition at present.[15]

16. San Luís de Apalache, Florida

Location. Leon County, near U.S. 90, about 2 miles west of Tallahassee.

Ownership and Administration. Privately owned.

Significance. During the century following the founding of St. Augustine, in 1565, Spanish padres extended their mission system steadily northward along the Atlantic coast into the province of Guale, and westward into the provinces of Timucua and Apalachee. In this way, by the conversion and stabilization of the Indians, they helped make St. Augustine secure. Furthermore, the fertile soils of Apalachee supplied badly needed grain for the inhabitants of St. Augustine. In 1633, the mission system reached Apalachee. San Luís de Apalache (San Luís de Talimali), established sometime during the next two decades, became the administrative center of the province.

By 1675, when the Spanish mission system reached the height of its influence, some 8,000 persons were centered around the 14 flourishing missions of Apalachee. San Luís itself had some 1,400 inhabitants, including the Deputy Governor and a military garrison of infantry and artillery. In 1696, the Spanish built a wooden blockhouse because of the activities of British traders who were stirring up the Indians of the interior against them.

Prior to 1690 Indian war parties, armed and directed by the English, had destroyed two of the Timucua missions. In 1702, the British began a concentrated effort to destroy the Spanish mission system in Florida. A combined English and Creek force from the Ocmulgee trading post area attacked and partially destroyed two more Timucua missions; and the Spanish and Apalachee army, heading north in reprisal, was met and defeated on the Flint River by English-led Creeks. Later that month, Col. James Moore's army of Carolinians sailed south from Charleston, ravaged the Guale missions, and besieged Castillo de San Marcos. All Florida was now in a state of terror.

Only two missions, one in Apalachee and the other in Timucua, were attacked in 1703. In 1704, however, the attacks broke out with renewed fury. In January, an army of 50 Carolinians and 1,000 Creeks, led by Colonel Moore, destroyed 5 of the Apalachee missions—including San Francisco de Oconee—and captured more than 1,000 Apalachee Indians. San Luís escaped destruction, but the province was completely demoralized. Two more Apalachee missions were destroyed in June 1704 and another was attacked. In July, the Spanish evacuated and destroyed San Luís and abandoned the province of Apalachee. More than a decade passed before the Spanish again established a garrison in the province.

Present Appearance. Intermittently since 1948 excavation of the site has been carried out under the auspices of the Florida Park Service and Florida State University. The eastern moat of the fort and postholes indicating one wall of the blockhouse have been uncovered and many artifacts found. Further excavation will no doubt uncover evidence of the whole complex. The site is well preserved.[16]

17. Fort de Chartres, Illinois

Location. Randolph County, at the terminus of Ill. 155, near Prairie du Rocher.

Ownership and Administration. State of Illinois; Division of Parks and Memorials.

Significance. Fort de Chartres was one of France's most imposing fortifications in North America. Though never attacked, in the 18th century it served as the center of French civil and military government of the Illinois country and reflected the aspirations of Frenchmen in the Mississippi Valley.

The present partially reconstructed fort is on the site of the third outpost on the Mississippi to bear the name *de Chartres,* and is preserved as an Illinois State Park. A temporary fort was constructed in 1720. Construction of a permanent fort was begun in 1753 and largely completed

Reconstructed gateway and museum at Fort de Chartres, Illinois. In the 18th century, the fort was the center of French civil and military government in the Illinois country.

3 years later. The fort's massive stone walls, 18 feet high and more than 2 feet thick, enclosed two long barracks, a guardhouse, two officers' quarters, a powder magazine, a kitchen, and outbuildings—all arranged around a 4-acre parade ground. The fort could have accommodated a garrison of 400 men, but less than half that number were usually assigned.

Despite the formal ending of French sovereignty in America in 1763, a French garrison continued to occupy the fort until 1765, when British troops moved in and renamed it Fort Cavendish. It served as the center of British rule of the Illinois country until 1772, when it was evacuated and destroyed.

Present Appearance. The State of Illinois acquired the site in 1915, and since then has reconstructed parts of the fort, including the gateway and the combined guardhouse and chapel. The magazine, which is original, has also been restored. Of even more interest and importance are the extensive foundation remains that have been exposed by archeologists. They present a vivid picture of the nature of the fort when it housed French, and later English, garrisons. A small museum, on the foundations of the fort's original storehouse, displays various artifacts. Standing in a fertile valley free from modern encroachments, the lonely fort is an impressive symbol of the one-time widespread holdings of France in the heartland of North America.[17]

18. Old Kaskaskia Village Site, Illinois

Location. La Salle County, on north side of Illinois River, Utica Township, just upstream from Starved Rock State Park.

Ownership and Administration. Privately owned.

Significance. The Old Kaskaskia Village (or Zimmerman) Site is the best-documented historic Indian site in the Illinois River Valley. It is not to be confused with the Kaskaskia village of French origin below Cahokia. Louis Jolliet and Père Jacques Marquette, in the summer of 1673, as they returned from their pioneering voyage down the Mississippi, noted that it contained 74 houses and was inhabited by the Kaskaskia, a band of the Illinois tribe.

Marquette, who in 1675 established a mission at the village, was replaced 2 years later by Father Claude Jean Allouez, who found a village of 351 houses that was occupied by 7 other bands of the Illinois in addition to the Kaskaskia. René Robert Cavelier, Sieur de la Salle, accompanied by Father Louis Hennepin, visited the village in December 1679 and stated that the 460 houses then located there were "made like long arbors and covered with double mats of flat flags, so well sewed that they are never penetrated by wind, snow, or rain."

La Salle founded Fort Crèvecoeur at the southern end of Lake Peoria, downstream, and left it under the command of Henry de Tonty when he returned north. On his way up the Illinois River, he noted the natural fortification now called Starved Rock and sent Tonty a message to occupy it in case of an Iroquois attack. Tonty moved there in April 1680, but he did not fortify it. In September, a war party of 600 to 700 Iroquois arrived, causing the 7,000 to 8,000 inhabitants of Old Kaskaskia Village to flee downstream immediately. About 500 Illinois warriors fled after a few days of fruitless negotiating. Tonty, forced to leave the area, moved to Green Bay.

After La Salle and Tonty had started construction of Fort St. Louis atop Starved Rock, in December 1682, groups of Miamis and Shawnees joined them. In the latter part of 1683, the Kaskaskia and other Illinois bands returned and settled, probably at the abandoned village, the Old Kaskaskia Village site. In all, about 20,000 Indians gathered in the neighborhood, including some 3,880 warriors.

But the Iroquois attacks continued, and the Miamis and Shawnees departed from Fort St. Louis. As the confederacy fell apart, La Salle's dream of an Indian empire vanished. After a council decided in the fall of 1691 that Starved Rock could not be defended, the bands of Illinois still remaining moved to Lake Peoria. A faction of the Illinois from Lake Peoria that established a settlement near Starved Rock in 1712 and remained in this locality until 1722 probably did not occupy the Old Kaskaskia Village Site.

Archeological investigation at the site has yielded large quantities of European goods in association with Indian items, especially trade goods such as glass beads, copper and brass beads and jinglers, coiled brass wire ornaments, glass bottles, and iron knife and ax blades. Buffalo bones, extremely rare at aboriginal sites east of the Mississippi, are quite common. Either the Illinois hunted west of the Mississippi during the period of occupation, or buffalo roamed over the Eastern prairie.

Present Appearance. The site has been used for agricultural purposes for several generations, but much valuable archeological data probably lie untouched beneath the plow zone. Only a small percentage of the site has been excavated.[18]

19. Starved Rock, Illinois

Location. La Salle County, on Ill. 71, about 6 miles west of Ottawa.

Ownership and Administration. State of Illinois; Division of Parks and Memorials.

Significance. Starved Rock was the first major center of French influence in the Illinois country. La Salle, after his momentous voyage of discovery down the Mississippi to the Gulf of Mexico, in 1682, chose it as a base for his administration and development of the upper Mississippi Valley. With Henry de Tonty, in 1682–83, he constructed Fort St. Louis at Starved Rock (*Le Rocher*), about which La Salle concentrated thousands of Indians as part of his ambitious plan to protect and exploit the vast new territory that he claimed for France. At the lower rapids of the Illinois River, the fort controlled the strategic waterway that was a major connecting link between Canada and the Mississippi Valley. As pressure from their enemies mounted, the Illinois Indians finally deserted Starved Rock for safer territory. This ended the fort's usefulness to the French, who in 1691 abandoned it.

Present Appearance. Starved Rock State Park, dominated by the pin-

On the summit of Starved Rock, in Illinois country, the French explorer La Salle built Fort St. Louis to secure the vast Mississippi Valley for France.

nacle of Starved Rock itself, preserves some of the sites of the Indian communities that clustered around the fort. The pinnacle is a sheer promontory rising 115 feet above the Illinois River in a beautiful natural setting. Use of the park is primarily recreational, but the setting retains much of the feeling of the wilderness as La Salle knew it. Trails give access to various natural and historical features, and plaques on the summit describe the historical significance of the site—a reminder of the great age of French exploration and settlement.[19]

20. El Cuartelejo (Scott County Pueblo Site), Kansas

Location. Scott County, west of U.S. 83 within the boundaries of Scott County State Park, 12 miles north of Scott City.

Ownership and Administration. Kansas State Society, Daughters of the American Revolution.

Significance. This is one of the key sites indicating the far-reaching expansion of Spain beyond New Mexico and her interest in the Great Plains. It consists of the ruins of a seven-room, stone Puebloan structure, probably built by a group of Picurís Indians who in 1696 emigrated from New Mexico to live with the Cuartelejo Apaches. As early as the 1660's, friction between the Pueblo Indians of New Mexico and the Spanish rulers and priests had caused groups of Indians to migrate to El Cuartelejo.

Spanish expeditions under Archuleta (pre-1680 Pueblo Revolt) and Ulibarri (1706) probably came to El Cuartelejo to return groups of Indians to New Mexico. In 1719, Governor Valverde led an expedition northeast from Santa Fe, visited the Cuartelejo Apaches, and learned from them of French penetration into the Plains. As a result, in 1720, the Spanish sent out the Villasur expedition, which passed through El Cuartelejo but was destroyed later by the Pawnees in Nebraska.

Archeological excavation of the site has produced only a few artifacts of Southwestern origin. The pueblo ruin and its typically Southwestern appurtenances—slab-lined hearths, grinding trough, oven, and the like—were directly associated with a material culture complex that was almost entirely Plains Apache. Either the Puebloans stayed in the area only a short time, or they readily adapted themselves to the everyday implements and utensils of the local residents.

Present Appearance. The site has been well preserved, but traces of the pueblo ruin are rather obscure, as would be expected because of climatic factors and the passage of time.[20]

21. Tobias-Thompson Complex, Kansas

Location. Rice County, on the Little Arkansas River, about 4 miles southeast of Geneseo. The Tobias Site is on a ridge south of the river; the Thompson Site is about 450 yards away on a ridge north of the river.

Ownership and Administration. Privately owned.

Significance. Most historians, ethnologists, and archeologists agree that the Quiviran, or Wichita, sites visited by Coronado and later by Bonilla and Humaña were located in present Rice and McPherson Counties, Kans. Fragments of chain mail of ring diameters that fall within the 16th-century pattern have been excavated at the Thompson Site of the Tobias-Thompson Complex. European glass, copper, and iron objects have been obtained from the complex, as well as from the Malone

and Saxman Sites in Rice County, and from the Paint Creek Site in Mc-
Pherson County.

Further evidence of contact between the inhabitants of the Tobias-
Thompson Complex and the Southwest Indians has been provided by the
discovery of turquoise beads, Rio Grande glaze paint pottery, and
Chupadero black-on-white pottery. The glaze paint pottery probably
dates from about the time of Coronado's excursion onto the Great Plains,
in 1541.

Culturally, temporally, and spatially the Tobias and Thompson Sites
are parts of a single community. However, because they are separated by
a small stream and were considered separate sites prior to excavation, they
bear separate designations in archeological literature. Interesting features
of the Tobias-Thompson Complex and associated sites are the so-called
"council circles," low mounds that may have been temples or ritual centers. The "council circle" at the Tobias Site is approximately 60 feet in
diameter and is surrounded by four or possibly five elliptical basins in a
discontinuous circle. Only four similar "council circles" are known, all
in Indian sites culturally related to the Tobias-Thompson Complex.

Present Appearance. The complex is well preserved. It is chiefly in
grassland, but includes some unbroken sod.[21]

22. Cabildo, Louisiana

Location. Orleans Parish, Chartres and St. Peter Streets, on Jackson
Square, New Orleans.

Ownership and Administration. State of Louisiana; Louisiana State
Museum.

Significance. This building, also known as the *Casa Capitular,* was
erected in 1795 to house the *Cabildo* of Spanish Louisiana, the legislative and administrative council for the province. Though fire destroyed
two predecessor buildings, this structure survived during the last 8 years
of Spanish rule in Louisiana and the brief period of French rule in 1803
prior to the transfer of Louisiana Territory to the United States.

Two ceremonies within a period of 3 weeks—November 30 and December 20, 1803—were particularly notable in the Cabildo's history. In
the first, Louisiana Territory was placed under French rule after having
been under Spanish control for 40 years. During the brief period of
French rule, the building was called the *Maison de Ville* (Town Hall).

Representative of Spanish architecture in Louisiana is the Cabildo, or *Casa Capitular.* From 1795 to 1803, it housed the *Cabildo,* the legislative and administrative council for the province of Spanish Louisiana.

In the second ceremony, the transfer of sovereignty of Louisiana from France to the United States took place. For many years, the Cabildo continued to provide public offices, but in 1911 it became the Louisiana State Museum.

Present Appearance. The architectural historian Hugh Morrison has commented that the Cabildo, composed of "a full panoply of Renaissance architectural forms," shows the "most markedly Spanish influence in Louisiana." A massive structure of stuccoed brick, it was altered in the 1850's by the addition of a third floor, and a steep-sided mansard roof.[22]

23. Fort de la Boulaye, Louisiana

Location. Plaquemines Parish, about 1 mile north of Phoenix.

Ownership and Administration. Privately owned.

Significance. Fort de la Boulaye was the first French outpost in the present State of Louisiana. It was established in February 1700 to counter Spanish and English aggression in the region. Pierre le Moyne, Sieur d'Iberville, landed a party of soldiers on a low ridge along the east bank of the Mississippi River, about 18 leagues above its mouth at the "east pass," where his soldiers constructed a 28-foot-square wooden blockhouse and equipped it with six cannon. Iberville left an 18-man garrison, under the command of his brother, Bienville, to hold the fort. Little is known of their experiences, but by 1707 the Indian threat had forced the abandonment of the post. Nevertheless, one Louis Juchereau de St. Denis, who was on amicable terms with the Indians, remained there alone for several years and helped maintain friendly relations with them.

No physical traces of the fort remain above ground, and for many years it was a lost site. However, in the early 1930's four amateur historians of New Orleans achieved virtually certain identification on the basis of geographical evidence and correlation of the previous discovery of hand-hewn cypress logs. Dredging operations in 1923 had produced the hand-hewn logs, although their significance was not realized for some years. A cannonball was found in 1936, after the site had been tentatively identified.

Present Appearance. The site is nearly 1 mile east of the present channel of the Mississippi River on a low ridge surrounded by reclaimed swampland. The ridge is covered by a thick growth of trees and brush, and the site is bisected by a canal. A State historical marker has been erected on the site, but access is difficult.[23]

24. Jackson Square, Louisiana

Location. Orleans Parish, Vieux Carré, New Orleans.

Ownership and Administration. City of New Orleans.

Significance. On December 20, 1803, in this square in the heart of the French capital of Louisiana, the U.S. flag was raised for the first time over the newly purchased Louisiana Territory—the greatest single accession of territory in the history of the Nation. Twice in 3 weeks during late 1803 the allegiance of the inhabitants of New Orleans was shifted, from Spain to France to the United States. At noon on November 30, when the square was known as the Place d'Armes, a crowd gathered to listen to the announcement from the balcony of the Cabildo that Louisiana had passed from Spanish into French possession. On December 20, they heard that their allegiance again had been changed; the flag of France was hauled down and replaced by the Stars and Stripes.

Present Appearance. Jackson Square, a public park, is still the hub of the French Quarter, as it has been throughout the years. It offers a fine view of the Cabildo, St. Louis Cathedral, and other historic buildings. In the center of the square, dominating the park, are the statue of Andrew Jackson and the flagpole marking the site of the symbolic transfer of sovereignty to the United States.[24]

25. Ursuline Convent, Louisiana

Location. Orleans Parish, 1114 Chartres Street, New Orleans.

Ownership and Administration. Roman Catholic Church.

Significance. This convent is not only of historical and religious importance, but is also architecturally significant as a Louis XV public building. It is one of the few remaining links with the beginnings of the great capital of French Louisiana. Shortly after New Orleans was

Ursuline Convent, in New Orleans, constructed in 1748–52, is one of the few extant buildings in the Vieux Carré dating from the French period.

founded, a group of Ursuline nuns arrived from France, in 1727, to establish a convent that would "relieve the poor and sick and provide at the same time for the education of young girls."

The first building of the Ursulines was replaced by the present one, built during the period 1748–52. The nuns abandoned it in 1824 and presented it to the Bishop of New Orleans, who used it as his residence. In 1848, a section of the building was demolished to permit construction of St. Mary's Catholic Church, but it remained the episcopal residence until 1899. Subsequently it served as offices for the archdiocese and as a seminary for priests and in 1924 was extensively remodeled.

Present Appearance. The Ursuline Convent serves today as the rectory for St. Mary's Italian Church, whose parish is responsible for its upkeep. Unfortunately, lack of funds has prevented the rector from doing little more than maintain the status quo. In 1963, some interior refurbishing was done, but no extensive restoration work is planned for the near future. The structure appears to be basically sound.[25]

26. Cole's Hill, Massachusetts

Location. Plymouth County, Carver Street, Plymouth.

Ownership and Administration. Pilgrim Society, Pilgrim Hall, Plymouth.

Significance. The settlement of the Puritans—later to be known as "Pilgrims"—at Plymouth in 1620 looms large in the development of New England and the United States. Unfortunately, virtually all the historic sites relating to the earliest period of the settlement have lost their original character and convey little impression of the colony. One exception is Cole's Hill, which is still the dominant landmark of Plymouth Harbor. The view from the hill of land and harbor and sea conveys a vivid impression of the scene that greeted the *Mayflower's* weary passengers.

The hill rises up from the shores of Plymouth Bay near the foot of Leyden Street, principal thoroughfare of the original settlement. It was the traditional burial place of the Plymouth colonists, Pilgrims, and others, who died during the "starving time," the tragic first winter of 1620–21. The dead were reportedly buried at night, and their graves disguised to prevent the Indians from learning the dangerously weakened state of the survivors. In later years, the colonists occasionally mounted cannons on the hill to ward off possible attack from the sea.

In an early assignment of land tracts, the hill became the site of the home of Deacon Samuel Fuller, the *Mayflower* Pilgrims' "physition & chirurgeon." It was named after the popular tavernkeeper who for many years after 1645 maintained his establishment on a spot overlooking the bay.

Historically, Cole's Hill is perhaps not as significant as other points in Plymouth—Burial Hill, for example, where the colony's first fort was erected, or Leyden Street, where the settlers built the first houses. Unfortunately, the historical character and integrity of these locations have been diminished or wholly obliterated with the passage of time and the growth of the city. Burial Hill, filled with the graves and monuments of many generations, is encroached upon by the present town. Cole's Hill, however, is today relatively open and affords a sweeping view of the bay into which the *Mayflower* sailed and the shore on which its passengers landed.

Present Appearance. Cole's Hill is maintained by the Pilgrim Society as a public park. On its top stands the memorial to the *Mayflower* Pilgrims, erected by the General Society of Mayflower Descendants. In a crypt beneath the monument are bones uncovered during excavations in the 18th and 19th centuries; because no burials were made on the hill after 1637, perhaps some are the unfortunates who braved the terrors of the ocean passage only to die in the first months of the colony's existence. Also located on the hill is the statue of Massasoit, the Wampanoag chief whose friendship shielded the struggling colony from Indian attack in its early years.

At the foot of Cole's Hill is Plymouth Rock, legendary landing site of the Pilgrims and steppingstone to the New World. It has rested in several places over the years, and has been venerated for more than two centuries, first by the people of Plymouth and later by the Nation. Whether or not the Pilgrims actually landed on the rock, it has deep meaning for most Americans. Cole's Hill, the nearby rock, and the curving shores of Plymouth Bay memorably evoke the time more than three centuries past when Englishmen came to the shores of New England to stay.[26]

27. Fairbanks House, Massachusetts

Location. Norfolk County, Eastern Avenue and East Street, Dedham.

Ownership and Administration. Fairbanks Family in America, Inc., Fairbanks House, Dedham.

Fairbanks House, Massachusetts, may be the oldest surviving framehouse in the United States. Jonathan Fayerbanke built the original section of the house about 1637 or 1638.

Significance. This is perhaps the oldest framehouse standing in the United States and an excellent example of the "growing house" of colonial times. The original portion of the house was built about 1637 or 1638 by Jonathan Fayerbanke, who moved to Dedham from Boston in September of 1636. The center portion of the present house is the oldest. As Fayerbanke added to his wealth and land, he added to the size of his home.

The original house consisted of a small porch, hall, and parlor downstairs, and bedchambers upstairs. A lean-to was later added at the back of the house and, perhaps in 1641, a wing on the east side. Still later, around 1654, the west wing was added. The two wings, which have typical New England gambrel roofs, were undoubtedly completed no later than the time of Fayerbanke's death, in 1668.

From the entry porch in the original portion of the house, stairs lead around the chimney to two second-floor bedrooms. The east wing is entered by a small porch in the angle where the wing joins the original house. This wing has a parlor and small bedroom on the lower floor, and a large second-floor room which is reached by a winding stairway.

The west wing, which is entered from the hall of the original house, was probably used as sleeping quarters by laborers on the farm. Some authorities believe that the original house was built with oak timbers brought from England—a custom of emigrants that originated in the need to erect houses quickly for defensive purposes.

Present Appearance. The Fairbanks House, which has always been in the possession of the Fairbanks family, is open to the public. It is furnished with family heirlooms. In spite of interior alterations occasioned by repairs, plastering, painting, and wallpapering, the antiquity and authenticity of the structure is obvious even to the casual observer. The house is excellently maintained—a labor of love on the part of the Fairbanks descendants, for whom the dwelling is a family shrine.[27]

28. Old Ship Church, Massachusetts

Location. Plymouth County, Main Street, Hingham.

Ownership and Administration. First Parish (Unitarian), Hingham.

Significance. Some authorities contend that this church, also known as the Meeting House, erected in 1681, is the oldest English church in continuous use in America. The major rival for this distinction is the Newport Parish Church (St. Luke's) in Smithfield, Va. Old Ship Church is certainly the earliest of New England's churches, and it is a striking survivor of the Puritan settlement of Massachusetts in the 17th century.

The earliest settlement within the bounds of the present town of Hingham dates from 1633, and the major period of settlement began in 1635, when a party arrived under the leadership of the Reverend Peter Hobart and soon built the first meetinghouse. The present structure was erected in 1681, according to tradition by ships' carpenters. This tradition, plus the "look-out," or "captain's walk," surrounding the belfry, and the curved roof timbers which give the interior the appearance of an inverted ship's hull, all probably contributed to the church's name.

For more than a century following its construction, the church was used for town meetings and village gatherings. In 1791, when the congregation voted to raze it and erect a new church, it narrowly escaped destruction. Fortunately, this move was reconsidered, and the church continued to serve its congregation without interruption.

Present Appearance. The plain wooden structure reflects the Puritan rejection of the Gothic architecture of the Anglican tradition and repre-

Old Ship Church, Massachusetts, an early English church. For more than a century after its construction, in 1681, the villagers of Hingham used it for town meetings and gatherings, as well as for religious purposes.

sents a style of building common to New England meetinghouses of the 17th century, for which no Old World precedent existed. The Puritans also abandoned traditional interior arrangements; the pulpit replaced the altar as the focal point of the service, and benches faced it and ran lengthwise of the church. The main entrance was in the rear of the benches, opposite the pulpit.

The church is a unique example of the primitive type of church that has been restored to its original condition. Except for the early 18th-century gallery additions, thanks to careful restoration in 1930, it stands today much as it was originally built. It is handsomely maintained by its Unitarian congregation.[28]

29. Parson Capen House, Massachusetts

Location. Essex County, off the Village Green and Mass. 97, Topsfield.

Ownership and Administration. Topsfield Historical Society, 70 Central Street, Topsfield.

Significance. This house, whose setting and interior are superb, is not only a perfect specimen of a New England colonial residence, but also of the English manor house in America. Erected in 1683, a date verified by inscriptions in two places on the oak frame, it eloquently reflects its English heritage. The skill of workmanship indicates the efforts of craftsmen trained in England. Except for the clapboards in place of half timbers, the house is a faithful counterpart of the English manor house of the 17th century. The Reverend Joseph Capen, minister at Topsfield for many years, had it built on a 12-acre plot given him by the town in 1682.

Present Appearance. The house framework consists of heavy oak timbers mortised and tenoned and held in place by wooden pins. The foundation timbers rest on an underpinning of unmortared field stones. The second story overhangs far out in the front, and the third story projects at each end, the overhangs being supported by wooden brackets. Carved pendants decorate the overhang corners of the building.

The staircase which winds up before the chimney in the entry has its original newel post and turned oaken balusters. The exposed brickwork of the chimney in the entry indicates the early construction of the house. The parlor and somewhat smaller hall, or kitchen, constitute the lower floor. The walls are wainscoted in a fashion typical of the period,

Erected in 1682 by Rev. Joseph Capen, minister at Topsfield, Massachusetts, the Parson Capen House is a noteworthy example of a New England colonial dwelling and 17th-century manor house.

and the hall is dominated by the fireplace, more than 8 feet wide, which has rounded back corners and a large flue. The floor has characteristic wide boards, sanded smooth.

Acquired by the Topsfield Historical Society in 1913, the house was restored under the direction of George F. Dow. The frame timbers are original, but much of the woodwork, inside and out, has been replaced. Furnishings are of the 17th century and include a food hutch, which antiquarians have called unique in America, and a baluster-back armchair inscribed "P. Capen 1708," believed to have been part of the wedding furniture of Priscilla Capen, the parson's daughter. The house is maintained in excellent fashion, and is open to visitors during the summer.[29]

30. Paul Revere House, Massachusetts

Location. Suffolk County, 19 North Square, Boston.

Ownership and Administration. Paul Revere Memorial Association, 19 North Square, Boston.

Significance. This house possesses an unusual combination of historical and architectural interest. Although extensively restored, it retains its original framework and is exceptionally significant as downtown Boston's only surviving 17th-century dwelling and as Revere's home from 1770 to 1800.

John Jeffs probably built the original portion of the house not long after the Boston Fire of 1676, on the site of the Increase Mather parsonage. The house was originally the simple and characteristic one-room type, but by the time Revere moved into it about a century later it had already been enlarged to three full stories. During the 19th century, when the house was a tenement and used as a store, it was considerably altered. An increasing regard for the old house led to its rehabilitation in the present century. In 1908, Joseph Everett Chandler, an architect, directed its careful restoration.

Present Appearance. The exterior of the house is clearly 17th-century in character, featuring typical rooflines, overhang, pendants, windows, and front door. Inside, the kitchen ell at the rear is an early section of the building. Revere probably used the back door in this kitchen when he set out on his famous ride of April 18, 1775; the front door would not have been safe because North Square was full of British soldiers.

In the hall is a recessed fireplace, and a small porch and winding stair are located in front of the chimney. Summer beams span the ceiling of the large room, or hall. The first-floor interior has been restored in 17th-century fashion, but the second-floor chamber is plastered, paneled, and painted as it might have been when occupied by the Reveres. The house is well maintained and is open to the public.[30]

31. Saugus Iron Works, Massachusetts

Location. Essex County, 10 miles north of Boston, on U.S. 1, Saugus.

Ownership and Administration. First Iron Works Association, Saugus.

Significance. The beginnings of the iron industry in the United States may best be traced to New England at Saugus, although some attempts at iron manufacture had been made in Virginia as early as 1619. In 1646, only 26 years after the first permanent settlement had been established in Massachusetts, a partnership bearing the name of the Company of Undertakers for the Iron Works in New England began the construction of an ironworks, under the direction of Richard Leader. The partnership benefited from the initiative of John Winthrop, Jr., and legal encouragement given by the Massachusetts General Court in 1641.

Saugus Iron Works, Massachusetts, in 1650. Courtesy, American Iron and Steel Institute.

The works consisted of a blast furnace, casting house, forge (with two "fineries" and a chafery), a rolling and slitting mill, and various storehouses and other buildings. The works was more than a blast fur-

Reconstructed forge building, at Saugus, Massachusetts, part of a full-scale "working" model of a 17th-century ironworks. In the building, workers reheated cast iron bars and converted them into wrought iron.

nace producing crude pig iron and castware. Its forge manufactured bars of wrought iron, from which could be made the tools and hardware that were needed by colonial farms and enterprises—hoes, shovels, hinges, and other items. Its rolling and slitting mill turned out rod iron that could be shaped into nails, which were much needed in the colonies.

The length of the works' operation (1648–70) and the migration of its workers and technicians to other ironmaking projects make it an important enterprise in U.S. history, even though as a business enterprise it eventually failed. After about 20 years of active and widely distributed production, a growing scarcity of raw materials seriously affected operations. Imported ironwares undercut Saugus iron in the market, and by 1670 the works had been abandoned and had begun falling into ruins. The iron industry did not flower in the colonies until the 18th century.

Present Appearance. The works had completely disappeared by the 1940's, when a project aimed at its reconstruction was begun. Rebuilding involved 6 years of research and construction and funds totaling $1.5 million. The works was opened to the public in 1954. Restored and supported by today's American iron and steel industry, it is a full-scale model of the original 17th-century works and has unique public interest and educational value. It is open daily except Mondays from May 15 through October 15.[31]

32. "Scotch"-Boardman House, Massachusetts

Location. Essex County, Howard Street, Saugus.

Ownership and Administration. Society for the Preservation of New England Antiquities, 141 Cambridge Street, Boston.

Significance. This house, an outstanding survivor of 17th-century New England, has been highly praised by most students of colonial American architecture, particularly because so much of its original finish is unspoiled. Few examples of the typical New England house remain so unmarred.

The exact date of construction is not known. For many years it was believed that the house had been built to shelter Scottish prisoners captured by Oliver Cromwell in the Battle of Dunbar, September 13, 1650, and transported to America to labor in the ironworks at Saugus. Recent scholarship throws some doubt on this contention and suggests that the present house stands near, but not on, the site of the original "Scotch" house and conjectures that the present house was built after 1686. The house followed the normal plan for a typical family dwelling of the period. Its fine decorative detail, characteristic of the best houses of the time, would hardly have been found in prisoners' quarters.

The original form of the present house was the usual two-room central-chimney plan, two-and-a-half stories high, under which a half-cellar was located. The lean-to was a later addition. On the west side of the ground floor is the parlor; on the east side, the hall, or kitchen. Above each of these rooms, on either side of the central chimney, is a sleeping chamber.

Present Appearance. The present exterior of the house—including the clapboards, underboarding, roof covering, windows, and front door—dates almost entirely from a later period than the interior. Formal restoration, during the period 1915–18, was expertly carried out. Little was done to change the condition in which the structure was found, for fear of damaging the integrity of its original finish, so much of which has fortunately survived. Since the restoration, only repairs necessary to preservation and upkeep have been undertaken. The house is open to the public in the summer and is maintained in excellent condition.[32]

33. Whipple House, Massachusetts

Location. Essex County, 53 S. Main Street, Ipswich.

Ownership and Administration. Ipswich Historical Society, 53 S. Main Street, Ipswich.

Significance. This house, one of the earliest surviving in New England, clearly demonstrates the development of a 17th-century dwelling over the centuries. Its three distinct units reflect the evolution of workmanship and architectural detail as the Whipple descendants grew away from their English origins. The original portion of the house may have been built as early as 1638, but the earliest documented date is 1650, when an earlier sale from John Fawn to John Whipple was confirmed.

The original portion of the house was a two-story, two-room structure, which had casement windows and a thatched roof. At one end of the

This 17th-century dwelling, the Whipple House, originally had only two rooms. As the Whipple family grew and prospered, they added to the house.

lower room are the entrance door, great chimney, and stairway to the large sleeping chamber on the upper floor. The sleeping room may have been divided originally by a partition. The original building was the lifetime home of the first John Whipple, a leader of some distinction in the settlement of Agawam, later Ipswich, and in the Massachusetts Colony. He served as deputy of the General Court in Boston, and held the offices of selectman, deacon, and ruling elder at the church in Ipswich.

Whipple's son, also named John, continued the family tradition of public service. He served as a representative to the General Court and as an officer during King Philip's War of 1675–76. In 1670, a year after his father's death, the captain added a second unit to the house, more than doubling its size, as well as a hewn overhang to each story at the east end. The rooms of the addition contained triple-light windows, fine molded framing timbers, and summer beams uniquely crossed at right angles. On the death of Capt. John Whipple, the executors of his will appraised the house, as well as 2½ acres of land, kiln, and outhouse, at £330; even at that early period, the house was an unusually valuable property. The structure assumed today's form when its next owner, still another John Whipple, added a lean-to at the back, sometime after 1700.

Present Appearance. The restoration and preservation of the Whipple House have involved a minimum of alteration. The house is in excellent condition and is exceptionally well furnished from a period standpoint. Maintained as a historic house museum, it is open to the public.[33]

34. Fort Michilimackinac, Michigan

Location. Cheboygan County, on the Straits of Mackinac at the terminus of U.S. 31, Mackinaw City.

Ownership and Administration. State of Michigan; Mackinac Island State Park Commission, Mackinac Island.

Significance. Fort Michilimackinac was an important bastion of French and English power on the Straits of Mackinac and a vital fur-trade center. French hegemony in the American heartland was closely related to its control of the highly strategic straits, the crossroads of the upper Great Lakes connecting Lakes Michigan, Huron, and Superior. In the early interior exploration of North America, the Great Lakes and their related waterways were the main routes into the continent for the French, the first Europeans to penetrate them. The importance of the straits did not escape them.

The earliest French activity on the straits centered on Mackinac Island and at St. Ignace, on their north side. In 1670–71, Père Claude Dablon founded a Jesuit mission on the island, which he named St. Ignace after the founder of his order, St. Ignatius. He was soon joined by Père Jacques Marquette, who came with his Huron flock from the upper end of Lake Superior. In 1672, the mission was moved to the mainland on the north shore of the straits, at which time Marquette took charge, and a fort was added to the mission.

For a few years after 1698, the French officially abandoned the straits, but traders maintained contact with the Indians around the Mackinac area. Early in the 18th century, the French formally returned to the straits and during the years 1715–20 erected a new fort, Fort Michilimackinac, on the south shore of the straits at the site of Mackinaw City. The British took over this fort during the French and Indian War, but the garrison was surprised and most of its occupants massacred in 1763 during the Pontiac uprising.

The British reoccupied the fort in 1764, and it was the only British-garrisoned outpost on the Great Lakes above Detroit until near the close of the War for Independence. In 1781, when U.S. attack appeared imminent, the post was relocated at Mackinac Island. The British remained in control until 1796 and between 1812 and 1815. From 1796 to 1812 and after 1815 the fort belonged to the United States. (The Straits of Mackinac and Mackinac Island are eligible for the Registry of National Historic Landmarks, primarily because of their association with the advance of the frontier, 1763–1830.)

Present Appearance. The restoration of Fort Michilimackinac effectively demonstrates the coordination of archeological and historical research. Modern restoration began in 1932, but the most important work was done after 1959, when the Mackinac Island State Park Commission floated bond issues totaling $125,000 to finance the complete restoration of the fort. In addition to the reconstructed buildings, exhibits at the park include objects found during the excavations and the uncovered foundation outlines of other structures. The park affords a superb view of the Straits of Mackinac.[34]

35. St. Ignace Mission, Michigan

Location. Mackinac County, State and Marquette Streets, St. Ignace.
Ownership and Administration. City of St. Ignace.
Significance. The establishment of St. Ignace Mission on Mackinac

Site of St. Ignace Mission, in St. Ignace, Michigan. The mission served as a base for Marquette and Jolliet's exploratory journey down the Mississippi River. The site is located in a small city park overlooking Lake Huron and Mackinac Island.

Island in 1670–71 marked the beginning of European occupation of the strategically located Straits of Mackinac area [see above description]. At this mission, in 1673, Marquette joined Louis Jolliet on their pioneering journey down the Mississippi River, as far as the Arkansas River. In 1672, the mission was moved to the mainland on the northern shore of the Straits of Mackinac, where it is now commemorated. Inactive during the period 1706–11, in 1712 it was reopened. In 1741, it was again relocated, on the southern shore of the straits, where Jesuits were in charge until 1765.

Present Appearance. The mission site is in a small, 1-acre city park, which overlooks Lake Huron and Mackinac Island. A museum adjacent to the park, maintained by the Catholic diocese of Marquette, interprets the story of Marquette and other French explorers and missionaries. It is open to the public.[35]

36. Kathio Site, Minnesota

Location. Mille Lacs County, along U.S. 169, on Mille Lacs Lake at Vineland, North Kathio Township.

Ownership and Administration. State of Minnesota; Minnesota State Historical Society.

Significance. Kathio (Izatys) was the largest of three villages occupied at the beginning of the historic period by the Mdewakanton band of the Santee (or eastern) division of the Sioux, or Dakota. The first historical mention of the Sioux occurs in Jesuit annals in 1640, at which time nothing was known of them except that they were living in the vicinity of the Winnebagos. They had numerous contacts with the French in the following several decades, but not until 1679 did Daniel Greysolon, Sieur Dulhut (Duluth), make the first definite historical record of Kathio village.

Dulhut stated that he "had the honor to set up the arms of his Majesty in the great village of the Nadouessioux called Izatys." The role of this village in early French-Sioux relations is further demonstrated by the capture of Father Hennepin by the Sioux in the same year. He was freed from another village by Dulhut in 1680, whereupon they went to Kathio and warned the Indians of the danger they faced if they should harm Frenchmen.

Intertribal warfare resulting from European trade and colonization, which produced profound changes in the history of the native peoples of America, is reflected in the subsequent history of Kathio. White settlement impinged upon the Iroquois; at the same time, English and Dutch traders furnished them with firearms. The Iroquois pressed against the Chippewas. The Chippewas in turn, who had the advantage of French arms, attacked the Sioux, farther to the west, who at that time had to rely almost entirely upon the bow and arrow.

As early as the visit of Pierre Charles le Sueur to the Sioux, in 1700, they were moving westward in the face of persistent Chippewa attacks. The showdown, apparently, came in the 3-day Battle of Kathio, about 1740, as a result of which the Sioux lost their territory to the Chippewas. The Sioux moved south and west, where they figured prominently in the history of the Plains and the Rocky Mountain States; they displaced other groups just as they had been displaced by the Chippewas, who still live near Kathio.

Aboriginal materials recovered from the Kathio Site, identified as historic Mdewakanton Dakota-Sioux, corroborate the historic identification of the site as Izatys.

Present Appearance. The site is well preserved. Adjoining it is the Mille Lacs Indian Museum of the Minnesota State Historical Society.[36]

37. Fatherland Plantation Site (Grand Village of the Natchez), Mississippi

Location. Adams County, along the banks of St. Catherine's Creek, 3 miles southeast of Natchez.

Ownership and Administration. Privately owned.

Significance. This is probably the most thoroughly documented historic Indian site in the Southeastern United States. Iberville, in 1700, provided the first description of the village, though it is mentioned in many other early 18th-century sources. Following the establishment of nearby Fort Rosalie after the "First Natchez War" of 1714, Le Page du Pratz sketched scenes of Natchez life, the fort, and the village. French maps of 1725 present detailed information about the Fort Rosalie-Grand Village area; several sources, including Du Pratz, describe the Natchez attack on the French in 1729 and the abandonment of the village in 1730. In addition to its historical significance, the site is extremely important archeologically. Its positive identification has provided a base for inferences concerning prehistoric sites of the Mississippian archeological period.

In the flat bottom land on the west side of St. Catherine's Creek are three mounds. Mound A, almost entirely destroyed by stream erosion, appears to have been a low, truncated pyramid. Mound B is also pyramidal, about 80 feet square at the base and 7 feet high. Excavations of Mound C, a platform mound with burials in the floor of the temple atop it, have yielded extremely significant Indian and European material. The village area, about 5 acres in extent, across the creek from the mounds, has been excavated on a preliminary basis.

Present Appearance. Although the site is within the city limits of Natchez and in an area that has been zoned for commercial use, no development has yet occurred in the vicinity. The site is situated in cutover timberland and covered with brush and second-growth trees. Portions of the village site east of the creek have been badly eroded, but other parts, as well as the village area around the mounds, are well preserved under a covering of alluvium.[37]

38. Ste. Genevieve, Missouri

Location. Ste. Genevieve County.

Ownership and Administration. Various.

Significance. Ste. Genevieve, one of the oldest surviving French settlements in Missouri and in the trans-Mississippi West, is the only place in the upper Mississippi Valley where several buildings of the pre-American period have survived. The oldest European settlement in the region, Cahokia (1699), suffered heavily from floods; Kaskaskia (1703) was entirely washed away by a change in the course of the Mississippi; and the remnants of colonial St. Louis were destroyed either by the fire of 1849 or by urban riverfront development.

The date of the first French settlements in the vicinity of Ste. Genevieve cannot be determined. Lead had been discovered by 1715 about 30 miles to the southwest, and was being mined by primitive means. The earliest known grants of land were made in 1752, when 27 inhabitants owned about 3 miles of Mississippi River frontage. The original site of settlement, probably in the period 1735–40, was in the river bottom on the west bank

Around 1785 Louis Bolduc, a prosperous miner, merchant, and planter, built this house in Ste. Genevieve, Missouri. It has a porch on all four sides, vertical posts on a stone foundation, and Norman roof trusses.

Janis-Ziegler House, or Green Tree Tavern, in Ste. Genevieve. Probably built in the 1790's, the house combines French and American architectural styles. It served as a tavern sometime in the 19th century.

of the Mississippi about 3 miles below the present town. The settlement was probably linked with Kaskaskia, almost directly across the river, then the metropolis of Illinois. Salt springs on Saline Creek, as well as the lead resources, were probably an important factor in the expansion of the settlement, from which shipments were made upstream to St. Louis or downstream to New Orleans. The settlers also grew foodstuffs for export.

Floods, notably one in 1785, caused repeated damage, and the town was moved gradually to the present site on high ground. By 1796, only a few huts of traders remained at the old site. Ste. Genevieve—the principal seat of government in the region for many years after western Louisiana passed from French to Spanish control in 1762—thrived under Spanish administration. It declined, however, as St. Louis gradually grew in importance. In 1803, the Louisiana Territory passed to the United States.

Present Appearance. The current population of Ste. Genevieve is about 4,000. Noteworthy historic buildings include the following:

(1) Bolduc House. Probably erected about 1785 by Louis Bolduc, prosperous lead miner, merchant, and planter, it has been carefully re-

stored by the National Society of Colonial Dames of America and opened to the public. Featuring a porch (*galerie*) on all four sides, construction of vertical posts on a stone foundation, and fine large Norman trusses supporting the roof, it is one of the least changed early French houses in the Mississippi Valley.

(2) Meilleur House, also known as the Old Convent. This two-story frame structure was built about 1815 for the private dwelling of René Meilleur, Louis Bolduc's son-in-law. Around 1837, the Sisters of Loretto bought it and conducted a school there until 1848. The walls are nogged with brick.

(3) Jean Baptiste Valle House. This one-and-a-half story Creole dwelling was the "State House" of the territory up to the time of the Louisiana Purchase and the home of the last commandant under the Spanish administration. It was probably built about 1785. The basic construction is similar to that of the Bolduc House, but it has been more altered. The heavy tapered beams supporting the second floor are exceptionally long.

(4) Mammy Shaw House. This house derives its name from the widow of one Dr. Shaw, a former occupant. Its origins are uncertain, but it is one of the oldest houses in the community. It is now used as a restaurant.

(5) Janis-Ziegler House, or Green Tree Tavern. This attractive structure represents in some respects the architectural transition in Ste. Genevieve from old French to typically American forms. It was probably built in the 1790's, but does not have the Norman roof trusses. The signboard,

Mammy Shaw House, a late 18th-century structure in Ste. Genevieve.

dating from the period sometime in the 19th century when the building was used as a tavern, may be seen in the Ste. Genevieve Museum.

These structures, along with others not listed of equal or slightly less age, constitute an important and unique survival of the French regime in the Mississippi Valley.[38]

39. Utz Site, Missouri

Location. Saline County, on Mo. 122, about 13 miles northwest of Marshall.

Ownership and Administration. Forty-two acres of this 200-acre site are owned by the University of Missouri and used for the Lyman Center for Archaeological Research. The remainder of the site, except for a small portion within Van Meter State Park, is privately owned farmland.

Significance. This site was probably the principal settlement of the Missouri Indians from approximately 1673 until 1728. In 1723, Étienne Veniard, Sieur de Bourgmond, a French trader, built Fort Orleans, a military and trading post, near the site, in present Carroll County. The Indians were apparently friendly with the French. Recovered artifacts include French trading items such as glass beads, brass ear ornaments and rings, and copper and brass for making ornaments.

The Indians probably abandoned their villages shortly after the French left Fort Orleans in 1728, for none of the larger items essential to life in Indian settlements—such as copper and iron kettles, metal knives and axes, and gun parts—have been found during excavations. Early cartography verifies the authenticity of this site. Marquette's map of his exploration of the Mississippi in 1673, as well as maps of La Salle's expedition of 1682, place the Missouri Indians in the area.

Present Appearance. The site is located on a range of low, broken hills along the flat river valley of the Missouri. The slopes, once grassy and treeless, are now covered with timber, except for a few cultivated areas. The 42 acres owned and recently excavated by the University of Missouri were formerly farmland. Excavations are conducted each summer from June through August and may be visited on weekends and holidays. Several buildings are in the area, and a small museum exhibiting excavated materials is open to the public.[39]

40. Pike-Pawnee Village Site (Hill Site), Nebraska

Location. Webster County, on a secondary road, along the south bank of the Republican River, about 7 miles east-southeast of Red Cloud.

Ownership and Administration. Privately owned.

Significance. When Capt. Zebulon M. Pike, U.S. Army, visited this Pawnee village on the Great Plains in 1806, during his famous expedition, he found that the Spanish had been there before him. Thus, the site indicates both the extent of Spanish penetration beyond New Mexico and the initial probing of the United States into the then unknown Southwest. Pike persuaded the Indians to fly the U.S. flag rather than the Spanish.

Among the articles recovered from this site are a Spanish peace medal that dates from 1797; an American peace medal of the type issued by the Government after 1801; a military button bearing the raised figure "1," the regimental number of Pike's infantry; European items such as tools, bridles and stirrups, wooden-backed mirrors, glass beads, and gun parts; and typical Pawnee bone and stone implements. The site coincides with the description in Pike's journal and the official map of his expedition.

Present Appearance. The site is cultivated farmland. All surface indications of the village have been obliterated, but discolored plowed-over areas indicate the location of earth lodges and cache pits.[40]

41. Abó Pueblo and Mission, New Mexico

Location. Torrance County, on north side of U.S. 60, about 10 miles west of Mountainair.

Ownership and Administration. State of New Mexico; Museum of New Mexico.

Significance. The ruins of Abó represent a significant and relatively little-known period in Southwestern aboriginal culture. Occupied from late prehistoric times—about 1300—through early Spanish times, they typify the period in which acculturation began in the Southwest. San Gregorio de Abó Mission was the most important, perhaps the "mother mission," of the Salinas group of pueblos, which also included Quarai, Tenabo, and Tabira. Gran Quivira was a *visita* of Abó, and was not occupied continuously by a priest.

Artist's conception of the San Gregorio de Abó Mission, in 1629. From a painting by Regina Tatum Cooke. Courtesy, Museum of New Mexico.

The first Europeans known to have visited Abó Pueblo were Antonio de Espejo and a small group of Spaniards, in 1583, when the pueblo had a population of about 800. In 1598, Juan de Oñate, first Governor of New Mexico, assigned Father San Francisco de San Miguel to Pecos Pueblo, where he also had the responsibility for neighboring pueblos, including Abó. He departed in 1601, in which year the people of Abó killed two Spanish deserters. When Oñate sent one of his lieutenants, Vicente de Zaldívar, to chastise the residents, a battle occurred.

Missionary efforts at Abó began about 1622. The missionaries brought about several changes in the Indian way of life by introducing a new religion, improving agriculture, introducing new domestic animals and plants, sponsoring new ideas in architecture, and bringing in Spanish goods. The mission and church are believed to have been constructed in 1629–30, under the guidance of Father Francisco de Acevedo. In 1641, the pueblo had a population of about 1,580. Drought and Apache attacks caused its abandonment in the early 1670's, when the inhabitants joined their Piro-speaking relatives on the Rio Grande. At the time of the Pueblo Revolt of 1680, a number of them joined the Spaniards in their southward retreat.

Present Appearance. The ruins lie on a low promontory at the junction of Barranco Arroyo and another unnamed arroyo in the center of a natural amphitheater formed by low-lying hills. They consist of extensive mounds of earth, stone, and debris which cover walls that are

Ruins of San Gregorio de Abó Mission, an influential Spanish mission in New Mexico.

probably several feet high. The mission is built of red sandstone set in adobe mortar. Portions of the church walls survive to roof height, as high as 40 feet above the ground. The *convento* was covered with debris prior to excavation, in 1938–39. The ruins of both pueblo and mission are in good condition.[41]

42. Acoma Pueblo, New Mexico

Location. Valencia County, on N. Mex. 23, about 13 miles south of U.S. 66.

Ownership and Administration. Acoma Tribal Council and Roman Catholic Church.

Significance. This pueblo, spectacularly perched on a prominent mesa

357 feet above the plains of western New Mexico, is believed to be the oldest continuously inhabited settlement in the United States. Probably occupied as early as A.D. 1200, it possesses important historic and prehistoric values. Several 16th-century Spanish exploring expeditions visited it, including Alvarado, one of Coronado's lieutenants, in 1540; Rodríguez and Chamuscado, in 1581; Espejo, in 1583; and Oñate, in 1598.

In part because of their defensible location, the Acoma Indians were persistently hostile during the Spanish period. This pueblo, probably more than any other in the Southwest except Taos, exemplifies native resistance to Spanish rule. In December 1598, the residents lured Capt. Juan de Zaldívar, one of Oñate's officers, into the pueblo and murdered him and 14 of his men. Two months later the Spanish retaliated. Capt. Vicente de Zaldívar, brother of the slain Juan, led a force of 70 soldiers against the fortress-like rock. In a bitterly fought battle, the Spaniards stormed the mesa, captured and partially burned the pueblo, and killed about 1,500 of the inhabitants.

Although Acoma was assigned a mission in 1598, the hostility of the Indians prevented its construction for 30 years. In 1629, Fray Juan Ramírez, a Franciscan, founded Estévan del Rey Mission. During the Pueblo rebellion of 1680, the Acomas murdered the resident priest, Fray

Acoma Pueblo, New Mexico, dates from prehistoric times. In the 16th and 17th centuries, it was a center of native resistance to Spanish rule. Only a handful of Indians live in the pueblo today. Courtesy, New Mexico State Tourist Bureau.

Lucas Maldonado. Following the reconquest, in 1692, they successfully resisted an attack by Don Diego de Vargas and held out until induced to surrender in 1699. The mission of San Estévan had suffered relatively little damage during the rebellion, and continued to serve the pueblo during the remainder of the Spanish period.

Present Appearance. Acoma today is nearly deserted, only a handful of people residing there; the rest of the Indians live at Acomita, 15 miles distant, and gather at Acoma for periodic festivals. The pueblo is little altered from its prehistoric character. Recent construction blends with the old. The church of San Estévan, still used at festival time, is constructed of plastered stone and adobe, as are the adjacent *convento* and other mission buildings, which are partially in ruins. San Estévan is one of the least altered of New Mexico missions. Measuring 150 by 40 feet, it is also one of the largest. The Acoma Indians keep the church and pueblo in good repair. Admission fees are charged to visit the pueblo and church and to take pictures. Guide service is provided.[42]

43. Hawikuh, New Mexico

Location. Valencia County, 12 miles southwest of Zuñi Pueblo, on a graded road, along the opposite side of the Zuñi River, northwest of the village of Ojo Caliente.

Ownership and Administration. Zuñi Indian Tribal Council; and U.S. Department of the Interior, Bureau of Indian Affairs.

Significance. The now-abandoned Zuñi pueblo of Hawikuh was once the largest of the fabled "Cities of Cíbola," at which the early Spanish explorers hoped to find wealth. Probably at Hawikuh, or possibly Kia-kima, the Negro Estévan died at the hands of the Indians in May 1539, and Fray Marcos de Niza viewed one of these pueblos from a distance. In July 1540, Coronado and his army arrived at Hawikuh, the first pueblo they visited. After a sharp skirmish with the inhabitants, during which a few Spaniards were wounded and a few Indians killed, Coronado stormed the pueblo and took possession. The ill treatment that he and his men accorded the Indians set the pattern for Spanish-Indian conflict in the Southwest for the duration of Spanish rule.

From Hawikuh, Tovar and Cárdenas journeyed to the Hopi country and the Grand Canyon; Alvarado, north and east to Taos and Pecos. Coronado made his headquarters at Hawikuh for several months during the summer and autumn of 1540 before moving east to winter on the Rio Grande. Subsequent Spanish explorers, including Chamuscado and Rodríguez (1581), Espejo (1583), Oñate (1598 and 1604–05), and Zaldívar (1599), also visited the pueblo.

In 1629, the Spanish founded a mission, La Purísima Concepción de Hawikuh, at the pueblo. The Zuñis in 1632 murdered the resident priest, Fray Francisco Letrado, and fled to another pueblo. They returned in 1635, when the mission was reestablished as a *visita* of the mission at Halona Pueblo. In 1672, Apaches raided Hawikuh, killed the priest, and burned the church. The church was rebuilt, only to be destroyed during the Pueblo rebellion of 1680, in which the Zuñis participated whole-heartedly, and during which they abandoned the pueblo. When they submitted to Don Diego de Vargas during the reconquest of 1692, they returned to the Zuñi country but reoccupied only one of the six pueblos, Halona. Hawikuh has thus been abandoned since 1680.

Present Appearance. The ruins of Hawikuh cover the top of a long, low ridge on the Zuñi Indian Reservation. The site was excavated during the period 1917–23 by an expedition of the Heye Foundation under the leadership of Frederick Webb Hodge. Sandstone rock walls, in places several feet high, outline the foundations and rooms of part of the pueblo; and mounds of earth littered with rocks mark the locations of other portions. Mounds of eroded adobe, 2 or 3 feet high, are all that remain of the mission church and part of the monastery.[43]

44. Palace of the Governors, New Mexico

Location. Santa Fe County, north side of plaza, Santa Fe.

Ownership and Administration. State of New Mexico; Museum of New Mexico.

Significance. The Palace of the Governors, also known as the "Adobe Palace," is the oldest public building in the United States. It embodies much of the heritage and spirit of the historic Spanish capital of New Mexico, Santa Fe. Built about 1610, it has served as the Spanish, Mexican, and American capitols of New Mexico and the residence of its Governors. Even during the period 1680–92, when the Spaniards were ejected by the Indians from New Mexico, it apparently served as the residence and headquarters of the leaders of the Pueblo Revolt.

Don Pedro de Peralta, second royal Governor of New Mexico, had the palace constructed as part of the royal presidio of Sante Fe. The palace

Palace of the Governors, in Santa Fe, is the oldest public building in the United States. Built about 1610, for nearly three centuries it served as capitol of New Mexico and as the residence of Spanish, Mexican, and American Governors. Courtesy, New Mexico State Tourist Bureau.

housed administrative offices and living quarters of the Spanish Governors until the Indian rebellion of 1680. When the Spanish defenders abandoned the palace and broke through the Indian lines to make their escape to the south, Santa Fe fell. The Indians held it for a dozen years, until Don Diego de Vargas subjugated them once again, in 1692. The palace again became the seat of Spanish authority in New Mexico and continued to be so throughout the 18th and early 19th centuries.

Mexican Governors replaced the Spanish after the successful Mexican revolution in 1821, and resided in the building until Gen. Stephen Watts Kearny's "Army of the West" occupied Santa Fe and raised the U.S. flag in 1846. From then until 1885, except for a brief Confederate occupation during the Civil War, the palace housed the American Territorial government of New Mexico. A new State capitol building was occupied for offices and legislative uses in 1885, but until 1909 the Governors continued to use the palace as their residence.

Present Appearance. For more than 350 years, the palace has evolved through cycles of damage, repair, reconstruction, modification, and restoration. The present structure occupies the original site. Despite modern reconstruction and restoration, much of it is the original building. It occupies the entire northern side of the historic plaza of Santa Fe—end of the Santa Fe Trail and site of romance and adventure in the minds of generations of Americans who have been enthralled with the stories about Kit Carson and others associated with the American development of the Southwestern United States.

The front of the building is a block-long *portal*. Behind the palace is a large and attractive patio, fully enclosed by connecting parts of the building and walls. The pueblo architectural style—plastered adobe, flat roof, viga ceiling—is typical of the 17th century, when the palace, as an integral part of the presidio, covered and enclosed about 2 acres. Operated by the Museum of New Mexico, the palace houses an excellent display of exhibits relating to the prehistoric, Spanish, and Territorial periods of New Mexico history.[44]

45. Pecos Pueblo, New Mexico

Location. San Miguel County, on N. Mex. 63, about 4 miles north of U.S. 84–85.

Ownership and Administration. State of New Mexico; Museum of New Mexico.

Significance. The pueblo, whose ruins are among the most impressive

Ruins of Nuestra Señora de los Angeles de Porciúncula Mission, at Pecos Pueblo, New Mexico. The pueblo, visited by many Spanish explorers, figured prominently in the Pueblo Revolt of 1680. By the mid-19th century, it had fallen into ruins.

in the Southwest, is of exceptional historical importance because it was visited by many early Spanish explorers, it supported a mission for nearly the entire period of Spanish settlement, and it figured prominently in the Pueblo Revolt of 1680.

One of the largest pueblos of New Mexico in the 16th and 17th centuries, Pecos served as the gateway to the buffalo plains for several of the Spanish explorers. Plains tribes brought buffalo hides, "alibates flint," and other items to the pueblo to exchange for cloth, turquoise, and corn. Hernando de Alvarado, one of Coronado's lieutenants, and a few of his men were the first Spaniards to visit it, in 1540. At this pueblo Alvarado obtained the services of a Plains Indian slave—called "The Turk"—whose tales of wealth in a land called Quivira drew Coronado and his followers far out into the Plains, as far as present Kansas, in a fruitless quest; Ysopete, another Plains Indian who joined the Spaniards at Pecos Pueblo, denied these claims. One of Coronado's friars remained at the pueblo.

Castaño de Sosa and Oñate visited the pueblo in the 1590's. In the early 1600's, when the pueblo had about 2,000 inhabitants, the mission of Nuestra Señora de los Angeles de Porciúncula was established. Its church, on the south end of the mesa, was partially destroyed during the Pueblo uprising of 1680. The inhabitants of Pecos joined wholeheartedly in the war against the Spanish and against the Tewa and Tano people who remained too friendly to the Spanish. They also participated in the lesser rebellion of 1696.

The mission was reestablished on orders of Gov. Don Diego de Vargas, but by the middle of the 18th century the pueblo had declined notably. The attacks of the Comanches, who began moving south through eastern New Mexico in the early 1700's, were damaging, as were also the diseases that they introduced. As a result, by 1749 the population had dropped to 1,000. After further decline and especially a smallpox epidemic in 1788, only 152 inhabitants remained in 1792. The pueblo was then made a *visita* rather than a mission. In 1838, the surviving 17 residents departed to join their linguistic kinsmen at Jémez, to the west. The ruins were a well-known landmark to travelers on the Santa Fe Trail, which passed close by.

Present Appearance. In the 1500's, the pueblo was a quadrangle surrounded by houses four stories high, the upper stories of which were surrounded by covered walkways. The nearby mission church was large; even today its walls, in ruins, stand 50 feet high in places. These walls have been stabilized by the State, but heavy rains in recent years have done further damage. The church has been excavated, but adjacent mission buildings have not. Low walls, however, outline the pattern of the *convento*.

The pueblo, north of the mission, was partially excavated and stabilized during the period 1915–29. The exposed portions, of stone construction, are typical of pueblo architecture, but most of the pueblo still lies underground. Mounds indicate terraced houses, which were at one time four stories high. One large kiva has been restored and is open to visitors, and the stone defensive wall that once surrounded the entire pueblo has been rebuilt to a height of 3 or 4 feet. The ruins are open to the public.[45]

[On June 28, 1965, the President signed the act of Congress authorizing Pecos National Monument as a unit of the National Park System.]

46. Quarai Pueblo and Mission, New Mexico

Location. Torrance County, just west of N. Mex. 10, about 8 miles north of Mountainair.

Ownership and Administration. State of New Mexico; Museum of New Mexico.

Significance. The ruins of Quarai Pueblo and Nuestra Señora de la Concepción de Quarai Mission reflect the involvement of Indians in the sharp church-state rivalry of the mid-17th century in New Mexico. Like those at nearby Abó, they represent an important and relatively little-known period in Southwestern aboriginal culture, the period in which the native inhabitants began to become Europeanized.

Quarai may have been visited by Chamuscado and Rodríguez in 1581 and by Espejo in 1583. It is certain that Oñate visited it in 1598, while making a trip to the salt lakes on the west side of the Sandia Mountains. In that year, Fray Francisco de San Miguel was assigned to Pecos Pueblo, from where he also ministered to Quarai and other nearby villages. In 1628, Quarai received its first resident priest, Fray Juan Gutiérrez de la Chica. Until the 1670's, various Franciscans were in residence at the pueblo.

Serving as the seat of the Holy Inquisition in New Mexico during the 1630's, Quarai became a focus for the next several decades in the conflict of religious and secular authority in the province. In the late 1660's, its inhabitants, weary of being in the middle of the controversy, planned to revolt with Apache help. The Spanish discovered the plot, however, and executed the leader, Estévan Clemente.

The droughts of this period also weakened the pueblo, and in 1672 some 600 residents joined relatives living at Tajique, 12 miles to the north. In 1674, the residents of Tajique abandoned it in turn and moved to Isleta, another Tiwa-speaking pueblo, on the Rio Grande below present Albuquerque. At the time of the Pueblo Revolt of 1680, many Isleta residents moved south with the fleeing Spanish survivors; they settled near the site of El Paso, Tex., and established another community called Isleta. After the abandonment of Quarai in 1672, Indians never again occupied it. The only known subsequent residents were Spanish troops who were based there in the 1750's to ward off attacks launched through Abó Pass by Apaches.

Present Appearance. Like several other pueblos in the region, Quarai contains two churches: A small early one, of which only wall outlines remain; and a large structure, in ruins, whose walls still stand to a height of 40 feet in places. Dates of construction and related data are not known for either church. During the period 1934–36, the Museum of New Mexico excavated and stabilized the massive sandstone walls of the large church and monastery and in 1938 and 1939 accomplished additional work. A small amount of archeological effort had earlier been expended on the pueblo ruins in 1916 and the 1930's. Quarai became a State monument in 1935.[46]

47. San Gabriel de Yungue-ouinge, New Mexico

Location. Rio Arriba County, on San Juan Pueblo Grant, across the Rio Grande from San Juan Pueblo.

Ownership and Administration. Privately owned by Indians of San Juan Pueblo.

Significance. The ruins of San Gabriel de Yungue-ouinge mark the site of the first capital of New Mexico, established by the Spanish colonizer Don Juan de Oñate late in 1598 or early in 1599. Although French, Spanish, and English colonies in the Southeast predate San Gabriel, the San Gabriel ruins include the oldest European church and house remains yet found in the continental United States.

Just above the junction of the Rio Chama and the Rio Grande, Oñate and his party discovered two pueblos. They named the one on the east bank of the Rio Grande, San Juan de los Caballeros; the other, on the west side, was known by its Indian name of Yungue-ouinge. The party

Excavations at San Gabriel de Yungue-ouinge. Established by Don Juan de Oñate in 1598 or 1599, San Gabriel served as capital of Spanish New Mexico until about 1610. Courtesy, University of New Mexico.

occupied San Juan Pueblo, and hurriedly erected a church dedicated to St. John the Baptist. No trace of the church has ever been found.

After a few months, the Spaniards took over Yungue-ouinge from the Indians. The new site of Spanish occupation, renamed San Gabriel, had about 400 "houses," or rooms. Recent excavations by the University of New Mexico have revealed that San Gabriel de Yungue-ouinge was originally built in a large **U**-shape, the opening facing to the south. The Spaniards evidently leveled the west wing and built some rooms. To the east wing, they apparently added peripheral rooms, built over thickly studded cobblestone foundations. Near the mouth of the **U** they built a permanent church of white tufa blocks. Excavation has yielded many Spanish artifacts, including mail and armor, ceramicware, ecclesiastical furnishings, hinges, and various personal accouterments.

San Gabriel remained the capital of Spanish New Mexico until a new Governor, Don Pedro de Peralta, arrived in 1609. Probably the following year he established Santa Fe as a royal presidio and the capital of the province. Some Spaniards may well have remained in the San Gabriel area, but the pueblo seems to have been reoccupied at least in part by San Juan Indians. Eventually it fell into disuse, except for a few Spanish-American and Indian dwellings that stood on top of the old mounds. This was its condition until the recent excavations were undertaken.

Present Appearance. Some of the old mounds marking the site of San Gabriel de Yungue-ouinge have been bulldozed away for enlargement of modern fields, and a considerable section of the east mound remains unexcavated. In the southern part of the east wing, however, the foundations and lower walls of the Spanish-occupied section, as well as the church, have been excavated and stabilized by archeologists from the University of New Mexico. This area is fenced and the owner, a San Juan Indian who acts as caretaker, shows visitors through the site.[47]

48. Taos Pueblo, New Mexico

Location. Taos County, 3 miles northeast of Taos.

Ownership and Administration. Taos Tribal Council.

Significance. This famous, much-pictured, multistoried pueblo, more than any other Indian community of the Southwest, exemplifies native resistance to the Spanish and American invaders of New Mexico. From the earliest times it was of great importance because of its size, strategic location, and trading activities with the Plains Indians. It was visited by most of the Spanish explorers of New Mexico, including Hernando de Alvarado, one of Coronado's officers, in 1540; another member of his expedition, the next year; and the explorer-colonizer Oñate in 1598.

About 1620, Franciscan friars built the first church, San Gerónimo de Taos, at the pueblo, one of the earliest in New Mexico. At that time, the population of the pueblo was estimated at 2,500 persons. In 1639, the inhabitants destroyed the church, and tension mounted to the point that 2 years later the Spanish sent a punitive expedition against Taos. Almost a decade later, some Taos residents fled to the Plains, in present Scott County, Kans., where they took refuge among the Apaches, with whom they had long had trading contacts. When Spanish officials later induced many of these refugees to return from the Plains, they rebuilt the church and mission.

Popé, a medicine man, plotted and directed the Pueblo Revolt of 1680 from Taos. Before the Taos warriors descended the Rio Grande to join other Puebloans, attack Santa Fe, and drive the Spaniards out of New

Taos Pueblo exemplifies native resistance to Spanish and American invaders of New Mexico, especially during the Pueblo Revolt of 1680. Still inhabited, it has changed little throughout the years. Courtesy, New Mexico State Tourist Bureau.

Mexico, they again razed the Church of San Gerónimo de Taos and murdered the priest. Popé and other Taos Indians apparently held positions of leadership in Santa Fe during the dozen years of the Spanish expulsion, and they were among the last to submit when Don Diego de Vargas returned in 1692 to reassert Spanish authority. The Taosenos fled twice rather than submit, and De Vargas sacked the pueblo. In 1696, the Indians revolted again, but De Vargas pursued them into a nearby canyon, where finally they surrendered. The population of the pueblo declined from about 2,000 in 1680 to 505 by 1760.

Relationships improved during the 18th century, as Spaniards and Taosenos drew together for protection from Ute and Comanche raids. Something of this cooperative spirit was rekindled in 1847 when, instigated by Mexicans who resented the U.S. occupation of New Mexico, Taos led another rebellion. Governor Bent and other Americans were killed at the nearby Spanish-Mexican village of Taos. When troops arrived from Santa Fe, the Taos Indians took refuge behind the thick walls of San Gerónimo Mission, only to be blasted out by American artillery fire. The church has never been rebuilt, but has been replaced by a new structure at another site. Indian graves are located all around and within the crumbling walls of the ruined church, which has a roofless bell tower.

Present Appearance. The pueblo, still inhabited, has a population to-day of more than 1,200. It appears much the same as it always has, mainly because of the conservatism of its residents. It is divided into two compact units, northern and southern, by a small stream that flows from the nearby rugged mountains. Each unit is still five or six stories high, built now entirely of adobe and featuring many doors and windows. In earlier times, the upper stories were largely constructed of wood, and ceiling hatchways provided the only exterior entrances and illumination of the chambers. Each story is still terraced back, about 15 feet, from the story below. Few of the *portales,* or wooden porches, which formerly covered the terraces, remain.[48]

49. Boughton Hill (Gannagaro) Site, New York

Location. Ontario County, on Holcomb-Victor Road, 1¼ miles south of Victor.

Ownership and Administration. Privately owned.

Significance. Boughton Hill is the site of Gannagaro, an important 17th-century Seneca village, from which the Senecas struck at the French and their Indian allies. Braves from Gannagaro ranged as far west as the Illinois country, where they attacked Fort St. Louis and harried French traders. The Seneca Indians, the westernmost of the five-nation League of the Iroquois, were mainly dependent upon Dutch and English trade goods, although they rarely dealt directly with the traders. The Mohawks, an eastern Iroquois tribe, acted as middlemen in the extensive beaver fur trade between the Senecas and the Dutch.

After the beaver supply was exhausted in the Iroquois country about 1640, the League of the Iroquois attempted to gain control over the tribes engaged in the fur trade with the French. The French were angered, and conflict ensued for many years; in 1666, they invaded the Mohawk country twice. In 1683, a war party of Seneca braves sacked seven canoes filled with French goods and attacked Fort St. Louis. Wary of an Iroquois-English alliance, the French refrained from retribution until 1687, after the Marquis de Denonville became Governor of Canada. To further his ambition to secure New York for France, Denonville attacked the Seneca and drove them away from Gannagaro. Though weakened and defeated, they soon returned to the area but decentralized and lived in small family clusters.

Gannagaro was apparently a town of several hundred dwellings, but no definite pattern of settlement has been established. The site has yielded a large quantity of trade items and artifacts; few of the artifacts are aboriginal. No excavations have been carried out at the nearby Fort Hill Site, where the Seneca are said to have built a palisaded fort, or at the Battlefield Site, where Denonville is believed to have been ambushed.

Present Appearance. This site is located on farmland. No structural remains or evidence of Indian occupation are visible.[49]

50. Dutch Reformed (Sleepy Hollow) Church, New York

Location. Westchester County, on U.S. 9, at the northern outskirts of North Tarrytown.

Ownership and Administration. First Reformed Church of North Tarrytown.

Significance. This church, a distinguished relic of Dutch America, is notable for its architectural and historical associations with colonial life on the Hudson. The exact date of construction is not known, but it was probably between 1697 and 1699. Frederick Philipse I, Lord of Philipsburg Manor, erected the church for his tenants. The congregation had organized by 1697, when a pastor assumed his duties and the building was dedicated.

Dutch Reformed (Sleepy Hollow) Church, New York, is a notable reminder of Dutch influence in colonial America. In the late 17th century, Frederick Philipse I, Lord of Philipsburg Manor, erected the church for his tenants. It was an active church until after the Civil War.

The first significant changes in the church occurred during the War for Independence, when the special pews of the Lords of the Manor were removed, and high-backed, soft-pine pews were substituted for the plain oak tenant benches. In 1837, the building was struck by lightning and partially destroyed, and certain alterations resulted. Around 1840, the congregation built a new church in Tarrytown to serve as a branch of the old one, and after the Civil War it came to replace the original structure as the place of regular worship. From that time on, the Sleepy Hollow Church has been used only for occasional services and special programs.

Present Appearance. A partial restoration of the interior of the church—beams, quartered oak ceiling, and pulpit—was undertaken prior to the bicentennial observance; this corrected much of the 1837 alteration. The interior is barren of decoration and somewhat bleak in character. However, the charm of the original design remains, and the building and grounds are carefully maintained by the congregation of the First Reformed Church, which owns the property. The adjacent burial ground is also well kept. Included among the graves is that of Washington Irving, who perpetuated the name of "Sleepy Hollow" for the church. The church is open to the public only on special occasions.[50]

51. Fort Crailo, New York

Location. Rensselaer County, on Riverside Street south of Columbia Street, Rensselaer.

Ownership and Administration. State of New York; Department of Education, University of the State of New York, Albany.

Significance. Fort Crailo, a brick manor house on the east bank of the Hudson River, was probably built around the beginning of the 18th century. Standing near the center of what was once the 700,000-acre estate of Kiliaen Van Rensselaer, who managed the first and only successful patroonship established by authority of the Dutch West India Company, its role in Dutch life in the Albany region was a major one. The architectural changes that have taken place over the years merely emphasize the wealth of the various socially prominent Dutch owners, who enlarged and altered their residence as the need arose.

The immense Van Rensselaer estate was founded in 1630. Van Rensselaer was a wealthy diamond merchant of Amsterdam, whose agents obtained a vast tract that extended from the mouth of the Mohawk

Fort Crailo, probably built in the first part of the 18th century, was headquarters of the immense Van Rensselaer estate, at one time a 700,000-acre patroonship.

River southward for 20 miles along both sides of the Hudson, and a total width of almost 50 miles. Fort Crailo, headquarters of this empire, was built on the site of Rensselaer, known then as "Greenen Bosch"—"Pine Forest" in Dutch and corrupted later to "Green Bush."

Some authorities believe that Fort Crailo dates from 1642, but others contend that it was constructed later of material from an earlier house, or that it stands on the foundation of the 1642 residence built by Rensselaer's first agent. The State of New York, however, credits the building to Hendrick Van Rensselaer, younger brother of the patroon, and dates it about 1704. It is known that the Van Rensselaer family occupied the house as early as that year and continued to live in it until 1871.

In 1740, Col. Johannes Van Rensselaer added a cross hall and dining room, upstairs rooms, and the remainder of the ell extending behind the main building. A grandson of Johannes made other alterations early in the 19th century. In 1924, a Van Rensselaer descendant donated the old house to the State of New York. During restoration, the State eliminated most of the 19th-century alterations.

Present Appearance. Fort Crailo consists of two and one-half stories and a cellar; the earliest portion includes two rooms and a hall on the first and second floor. The heavy brick walls are laid in Dutch crossbond.

The loopholes on the lower floor indicate the original defensive nature of the house. In keeping with the house's significance as the manorial seat of a foremost Hudson Valley Dutch family, it is furnished with care. Maintained in good condition, it is open throughout the year.[51]

52. Fort St. Frederic, New York

Location. Essex County, junction of N.Y. 8 and U.S. 9N, Crown Point Reservation.

Ownership and Administration. State of New York; Department of Conservation.

Significance. This fort symbolizes the bitter struggle between France and England for mastery of North America. The French built it in 1731 to guard Lake Champlain—the key to the defense of Canada. It served in this capacity for the next 28 years, after which it was of vital importance to the British in defending the Hudson Valley and the northern colonies. Originally, it had high 18-foot-thick walls of limestone, quarried about one-half mile away. The eastern side of the four-story fort had a high watchtower that had thick walls and was equipped with a number of cannon. The fort was served by a battery of 62 guns. It was about 300 feet square and had four bastions; three were diamond-shaped, and the fourth, on the northwest, quadrangular shaped. The fort included a small church and stone quarters for officers and troops.

Some years after the fort's construction, the French erected a second fort, Carillon, 12 miles to the south to further protect the Lake Champlain approach to Canada. In 1759, British forces under Maj. Gen. Jeffrey Amherst captured Carillon and renamed it Ticonderoga. It later figured prominently in the War for Independence. At the time of Amherst's invasion, the French abandoned and destroyed Fort St. Frederic. The British did not rebuild it, but erected a new fort about 200 yards away and named it Crown Point, or Amherst.

Present Appearance. Though fragmentary, the ruins of Fort St. Frederic, consisting of walls and earthworks, make possible a mental recreation of the original stone fort. Nearby in the picturesque setting are the ruins of Fort Amherst. Chimney Point, on the opposite shore of Lake Champlain, sheltered a French settlement that was contemporary with Fort St. Frederic. An adjacent museum contains a number of relics that were found in and near the forts.[52]

53. Old Fort Niagara, New York

Location. Niagara County, on N.Y. 18, just north of Youngstown.

Ownership and Administration. State of New York; leased to the Old Fort Niagara Association, Youngstown.

Significance. At this strategic fort, in the eastern Great Lakes region, as much or more fighting occurred as at any other outpost during the colonial period and the early years of the United States. The fort was at various times controlled by the Iroquois Federation, France, England, and the United States. Situated at the mouth of the Niagara River, it commanded the Great Lakes route between Lakes Erie and Ontario and protected the approaches to New York's western frontier.

Built in 1679 by order of La Salle, the fort was rebuilt twice by the French, the last time in 1725–26. The notable Stone House, or "Castle," in reality a fort built to resemble a French provincial chateau so as to delude the Indians, was erected during this period. Between 1750 and 1759, the French enlarged the fort and converted the Stone House and temporary buildings into an elaborate stronghold with earthworks, moats, magazines, and gun emplacements. Much of this later improvement remains.

In 1759, as the struggle between England and France neared its climax in America, a British force captured Fort Niagara. William Pitt, the English Prime Minister, regarded the fort as second in importance only to Quebec. In English hands during the War for Independence, the fort was a base for combined British-Indian expeditions against the American frontier. The British held it until 1796 when, under the Treaty of 1794, the United States took it over. Recaptured by the British during the War of 1812, it was restored to the United States by the Treaty of Ghent, at the end of the conflict.

Present Appearance. The fort is today one of the best restored and preserved in America. Restored features include the famous "Stone House," moat, drawbridge, blockhouse, earthen ramparts, parade grounds, and a cross symbolic of one planted on the site in 1688 by Father Pierre Millet. Millet had accompanied a French column sent to the relief of the dozen survivors of the 100-man garrison that had been almost wiped out by hunger and disease the preceding winter. The fort is adjacent to the Fort Niagara Military Reservation, a Regular Army post. Restorations of the Old Fort Niagara Association, which were aided by the survival of several buildings and fortifications, clearly portray the fort's history.[53]

54. Old House, New York

Location. Suffolk County, on N.Y. 25, Cutchogue, Long Island.

Ownership and Administration. Congregational Society of Cutchogue.

Significance. This house, which notably commemorates English settlement on Long Island, is undoubtedly one of the most distinguished but least known examples of English domestic architecture in the United States. It was erected in 1649 by John Budd at Southold, some 10 miles northeast of its present site. A decade later, Budd built a more imposing home and gave his original house as a wedding gift to his daughter, Anna, bride of Benjamin Horton, who moved it to its present location and re-erected it. It subsequently passed into the hands of Joseph Wickham, a master tanner, who lived in it until his death, in 1734. Later, in 1784, it was confiscated from Parker Wickham, who had been a Loyalist during the War for Independence, after which its owners in turn were Jared Landon and William Harrison Case. The Case heirs donated it to the Congregational Society of Cutchogue.

Present Appearance. The house has two floors and an attic. On the first floor are the kitchen and "hall," and on the second floor are two bedrooms. The great brick chimney, whose top is pilastered, lies to the left of the center of the house. A steep winding stair leads to the second story. The stair from the second floor branches to give access to the attic, which is split in two by the great chimney.

The kitchen, on the left of the entrance, features a huge fireplace. The fireplace in the "hall," on the right of the entrance, is the same size. Both fireplaces have been somewhat reduced by the construction of smaller fireplaces inside the originals. The smaller fireplaces were added around the middle of the 18th century, probably when paneling was placed over the original walls.

The original random-width wallboards were removed and used on the exterior to replace the original hand-rived oak boards. The exterior was then lathed and plastered. Construction details throughout the house are unusually fine and reflect the work of a master builder. The three-part casement window frames on the north wall of the second floor are especially notable. Traces have also been found of the casement windows that were originally on the first floor.

The house was restored in 1940 in connection with the Southampton Old Town Tercentenary Celebration, through the efforts of the Tercentenary Committee, the Case family, and the Independent Congregational Church of Cutchogue. The church purchased the land and the Case family donated the building. Church funds and private contributions made the restoration possible. When the house was restored, the plastered walls and a saltbox roof were removed. The gunstock posts on the second floor and all interior framework were left exposed. Furnishings are of the 17th and 18th century. Among the historic items displayed is the original confiscation deed of 1784. The structure is in very good condition and is open to visitors on a regular schedule.[54]

55. Philipsburg Manor, Upper Mills, New York

Location. Westchester County, 381 Bellwood Avenue, off U.S. 9, north of intersection with N.Y. 117, North Tarrytown.

Ownership and Administration. Sleepy Hollow Restorations, Inc., Tarrytown.

Significance. This simple stone house authentically portrays a great 17th-century manor and presents a remarkable picture of Dutch settlement in the lower Hudson Valley before 1750. Frederick Philipse, First Lord of the manor of Philipsburg, built the older portion about 1683, although he used the more pretentious manor house at the site of Yonkers, a few miles south, as his main residence when away from the city of New York.

When the First Lord died, in 1702, the northern section of the manor passed to his second son, Adolphus, who made the house at North Tarrytown his permanent home. From the more imposing manor house at Yonkers, Frederick Philipse II ruled the southern section of the manor. When Adolphus died, in 1750, Frederick II inherited the northern portion of the estate and reunited the entire manor under a single owner. Frederick II continued to live in the more elaborate manor house at Yonkers, and the building at North Tarrytown fell into obscurity. In 1785, Gerard Beekman added the frame wing to the original stone structure. The house was much abused over the years until its restoration was undertaken in 1943. It is now a project of Sleepy Hollow Restorations.

Present Appearance. When all restoration work is completed and the house opened to the public, 24 rooms will be furnished in period style from the date of the earliest construction to the opening of the 19th century. These rooms will present a vivid cross section of the continuity of Dutch life and tradition on the Hudson. Further adding to the interest and historical integrity of the property is the nearby Dutch Reformed (Sleepy Hollow) Church, built around 1697 by Frederick Philipse I for his tenants.[55]

56. Philipse Manor Hall, New York

Location. Westchester County, Warburton Avenue and Dock Street, Yonkers.

Ownership and Administration. State of New York; State Education Department, University of the State of New York, Albany.

Significance. This house is an outstanding representative of the 18th-century Dutch manorial system in the lower Hudson Valley. It served as the social and administrative center of the great manor of Philipsburg, created under English rule in 1693. Governed successively by Lords of the Manor Frederick Philipse I, II, and III, the manor of Philipsburg was closer to the colonial capital of New York and was more intimately associated with its social and political institutions than any of the other Hudson River baronies.

The first Frederick Philipse came to New Netherland in 1647. Although well born, he had little more than his good name when he arrived in New Amsterdam and became a "carpenter" for the Dutch West India Company. In 1657, he acquired the "Small Burgher Right of New Amsterdam," which made him eligible to become a merchant and to occupy certain public offices in the colony. Thereafter his rise was rapid as he acquired houses and land, and profited highly in colonial trade. His marriage in 1662 to Margaret de Vries, a wealthy widow, paved the road to further advancement.

Soon Philipse was one of New Netherland's leading citizens. In 1672, he and two partners bought a large section of the former patroonship of Adriaen Van der Donck, on the site of Yonkers. Several years later Philipse bought out his partners and in succeeding years amassed holdings up the Hudson River Valley as far as the Croton River. By 1693, his estate extended more than 20 miles along the east side of the Hudson and embraced some 156,000 acres. Out of this vast empire, a royal patent in 1693 created the manor of Philipsburg and designated Frederick Philipse as its First Lord.

Philipse's domain then became an important unit in the political and

Philipse Manor Hall, New York, whose construction began in the 17th century, served as social and administrative center for the Philipse family's manor of Philipsburg. In the 19th century, it was the village and city hall of Yonkers.

social development of provincial New York. His grandson, Frederick Philipse II, inherited the manor and maintained the family's role of leadership in the colony. Frederick III, however, remained loyal to the Crown when the colonies declared for independence, and in 1776 he was arrested on orders of General Washington and the manor of Philipsburg confiscated. When Philipse and his family fled to England, a colorful chapter in the story of colonial America came to an end.

Sometime in the 1680's, perhaps before the creation of Philipsburg Manor, Frederick Philipse I built a sturdy stone house on the site of Yonkers. Many authorities have asserted that this structure is preserved today as the south wing of the present building. One expert investigator has concluded that part of the foundation may antedate 1682; that part of the southern wing dates from about the period 1682–94; and that the remainder and larger part, constructed by the Second Lord of the Manor, dates from about 1725 or 1730, or possibly as late as 1745.

After the War for Independence, Philipse Manor Hall passed through several hands. For some years following 1868, it served Yonkers as the village hall and later the city hall. Threatened with demolition at the end of the 19th century, it was saved through the efforts of local citizens and organizations. Finally, in 1908, the State of New York accepted an

endowment of the house from Mrs. William F. Cochran which specified that it be maintained by the American Scenic and Historic Preservation Society. Within 4 years, the house was completely renovated. The
notable Cochran collection of portraits of presidents and other historical
figures was also assembled and exhibited. It includes works by Stuart,
Copley, the Peales, Trumbull, and Vanderlyn.

Present Appearance. As restored, Philipse Manor Hall is an outstanding representation of the early Georgian style. The original stone portion
of the building forms the base of the L-shaped plan; the later brick addition, a long north arm. The interior is distinguished by intricate plaster-
work on the ceilings of a number of rooms in both sections. The older
portion of the house probably received this embellishment when the new
section was added by the Second Lord.

The manor hall is structurally sound and the exterior is in good condition. The interior walls and ceilings need plastering, and additional period furnishings would be highly desirable. The important Cochran
portrait collection is well displayed. The house is open to the public, and
tours are conducted. The grounds immediately adjacent to the hall are
well kept, but the setting is somewhat marred by surrounding commercial
development.[56]

57. Van Cortlandt Manor, New York

Location. Westchester County, on U.S. 9, north of intersection with
N.Y. 9A, Croton-on-Hudson.

Ownership and Administration. Sleepy Hollow Restorations, Inc.,
Tarrytown.

Significance. This stone manor house, along with its grounds and outbuildings, is the most authentic and significant survival of the 18th
century Dutch-English manor house of the Hudson Valley. Its oldest
portion was constructed between 1665 and 1681. Simplicity of line and
detail set the house apart from more pretentious manor houses such as
Philipsburg Manor, Upper Mills, at North Tarrytown, and Philipse
Manor Hall, in Yonkers. Van Cortlandt Manor was remodeled in the
mid-18th century, the period which is reflected in its recent restoration.

The Van Cortlandt family in America was founded by Oloffe Stevense
Van Cortlandt, a soldier who in 1638 came from the Netherlands. In

Representative of an 18th-century Dutch-English manor house in the Hudson Valley is the Van Cortlandt Manor, once the home of the influential Van Cortlandt family and center of their 86,000-acre estate.

1677, his son, Stephanus, started acquiring land in the lower Hudson Valley, on the Croton River. A few years later he began the construction of his country house, likely on the foundation of an earlier fort-trading post that may have been erected as early as 1665.

William III recognized Stephanus' semifeudal estate, amounting to 86,000 acres, as the Manor of Cortlandt on June 16, 1697. It was not until 1749, however, that the manor became a dwelling in fact as well as name. In that year, Pierre Van Cortlandt, Third Lord of the Manor, occupied it on a permanent year-round basis. Before moving his family to the manor, Pierre enlarged it; he added a second story and otherwise modified the earlier building to the extent seen by today's visitor.

Pierre added new lustre to the family name. A foremost leader of colonial New York, he was an active patriot in the War for Independence and became the first Lieutenant Governor of the State, 1777–95. During the war, the family abandoned the estate, which was damaged by passing troops and vandals. When it was safe for the family to return, the damage was repaired. Until 1940, the property was the home of succeeding generations of Van Cortlandts.

Present Appearance. The house and a small portion of the original manor lands were purchased in 1953 by John D. Rockefeller, Jr., and the property is now a unit of Sleepy Hollow Restorations, Inc. Under these auspices, the house and 175 acres of the original estate have been expertly restored. In addition to the manor house, the restoration includes the estate office building built by the Third Lord; the Ferry House, an 18th-century tavern that served travelers on the old Albany Post Road; and the gardens, orchards, and outbuildings of the manor. The house is furnished largely with Van Cortlandt family items, which date from the 17th to the early 19th century. Excellent guide service is provided.[57]

58. Voorlezer's House, New York

Location. Richmond County, Arthur Kill Road opposite Center Street, Staten Island.

Ownership and Administration. Staten Island Historical Society, Richmondtown, Staten Island, N.Y.

Significance. This framehouse, built before 1696, is not only the oldest known elementary school building in the United States but also one of the most important surviving relics of 17th-century Dutch settlement in New York. The earliest documented reference to it is dated 1696; and the date of the patent on which it is located is 1680. The house was probably erected some time between those dates. How long it served as a school is not known. It passed through several hands, but remained in the possession of one family for more than 150 years. Though well maintained for many years, by 1936 it had fallen into disrepair and was threatened with demolition. Fortunately, a member of the Staten Island Historical Society purchased the building and donated it to the organization.

Present Appearance. The two-story house is clapboarded. The roof has an unequal pitch because the front of the house is 2 feet higher than the rear. The foundation walls are 2 feet thick, of rough, undressed field stone laid up in mud and mortar. All timbers are of oak or white wood, cut in nearby forests and hewn to size with a broadax. A massive stone-and-brick chimney is at the northeast end of the house. Around 1800, the present staircases were substituted for the straight ladder-like stairs believed to have been used originally.

The first floor contains a small room used as living quarters and a large room for church services. The second floor has a small bedchamber and a large room, believed to be the one used for the school. The extra set of floor beams indicate that the room was designed to accommodate a large number of persons. The floors in the house are of white pine boards, 14 to 16 inches wide. The windows and doors, which have been replaced, have the low and wide proportions of the originals. The building is open by appointment; a custodian is on the premises.[58]

59. Big Hidatsa Village Site, North Dakota

Location. Mercer County, on an improved road, along the north bank of the Knife River, 2½ miles north of Stanton.

Ownership and Administration. Privately owned.

Significance. The largest of the three Hidatsa villages was located at this site, also known today as the Olds Site, from about 1740 to 1845. During that period, these villages, and two later Mandan villages nearby, were important in the Northern Plains fur trade. As early as 1738, La Vérendrye, the French fur trader and explorer, may have contacted the Hidatsas when he visited the Mandans on the Heart River. During the next decade, the French began to trade with the two tribes.

This trade flourished until the beginning of the French and Indian War, in 1754. After 1766, British traders were active in the area. Meriwether Lewis and William Clark spent the winter of 1804–5 at nearby Fort Mandan and described the Hidatsas in their journal. George Catlin, Prince Maximilian, and Karl Bodmer described and sketched the villages in the years 1832–34. These descriptions and sketches are especially valuable because the Mandans were nearly destroyed and the Hidatsas seriously weakened by a smallpox epidemic in 1837. Shortly after 1845, the surviving Hidatsas moved upstream and established a new village near the newly constructed Fort Berthold.

Archeological excavation of the site has revealed lower levels primarily of aboriginal materials and a large number of European trade items mixed with aboriginal items in the upper levels.

Present Appearance. This site, which is not open to the public, embraces approximately 15 acres. Because most of it has not been cultivated, it is exceptionally well preserved. The depressions of more than 100 circular earth lodges and several fortification trenches can be seen clearly.[59]

60. Menoken Indian Village Site, North Dakota

Location. Burleigh County, just off U.S. 10–83, about 1¼ miles north of Menoken.

Ownership and Administration. State of North Dakota.

Significance. The Mandan village located at this site was probably the one visited by the French explorer La Vérendrye in 1738. He described it as a fort built on a small hill in the open prairie. It contained about 130 dwellings and was surrounded by a palisade that had four bastions, outside of which was a defensive ditch 15 feet deep and 15 to 18 feet wide. While at the village, La Vérendyre heard of five other villages located nearby on "the river," and sent his son to visit them. After visiting only the nearest village on a 1-day trip, the son reported that it was situated "on the bank of the river," and that it was twice as big as the one they were in. He added that "the palisade and fortification there are . . . built in the same style as that in which we were."

The references are undoubtedly to the Missouri River and to the five earth lodge villages dating from the La Vérendrye period whose sites have been found at the mouth of the Heart River in North Dakota. The Menoken Indian Village is the only known fortified Mandan village of the period that is located eastward and within 1 day's journey of the Heart River villages. The ditch surrounding the site is still clearly visible, and archeological investigation has produced evidence of a palisade that had four bastions. Thus, this village was probably the one visited by La Vérendrye.

Present Appearance. The site has been well preserved by the State of North Dakota, which calls it the Menoken Indian Village Archeological Site.[60]

61. Forks of the Ohio, Pennsylvania

Location. Allegheny County, "The Golden Triangle," Point State Park, Pittsburgh.

Ownership and Administration. Commonwealth of Pennsylvania; Department of Forests and Waters.

Significance. From about 1750 until 1815 the Forks of the Ohio, where the Monongahela and Allegheny Rivers join to form the Ohio

River at Pittsburgh, was a strategic key to the Ohio Valley and the vast territory drained by the upper Mississippi River. Men of three nations fought and died struggling for control of this strategic location, where the bustling city of Pittsburgh—one of the first permanent settlements by the English west of the Allegheny Mountains—arose in the shelter of a series of fortifications. Still later, the forks was a major gateway to the West for waves of settlers pushing into the Ohio and Mississippi Valleys.

The growing French influence in the Ohio Valley region during the 1750's was incompatible with the westward thrust of England's seaboard colonies. George Washington visited the forks in November 1753, while en route to the French-held Fort Le Boeuf to warn the French away from the Ohio country. Washington strongly endorsed the forks as the most strategic position to command the rivers, and in February 1754 Englishmen began to construct the first outpost there. Two months later, however, a combined force of French and Indians seized the weak stockade. The French proceeded to build a fort, which they named after Duquesne, the Governor-General of New France. This heightened the tensions that led to the 9-year conflict known in America as the French and Indian War and abroad as the Seven Years' War.

When Washington learned that the French had seized the post at the forks, he returned with a small force, which on May 28 surprised and defeated a French scouting party near Great Meadows, 11 miles east of the present city of Uniontown. Troops from Fort Duquesne besieged the hastily built Fort Necessity and forced Washington to surrender on July 4. The French beat off a more threatening English effort the next year, when they shattered Gen. James Braddock's force several miles east of the forks. Thus, for 3 years longer, Fort Duquesne continued to serve as a French base for raids against the English frontier.

In 1758, 6,500 British and colonial troops under Gen. John Forbes made a remarkable forced march through the rugged Pennsylvania wilderness and found Duquesne destroyed and abandoned by the French because of pressures elsewhere and the desertion of their Indian allies. Col. Hugh Mercer was left with 200 men to secure the position for England. In 1759, the English began to construct a major permanent fortification, named Fort Pitt in honor of the Prime Minister of England. The exterior walls of the pentagonal fort were earthen ramparts faced with brick. Frame and brick buildings were constructed inside, parallel to the interior walls. A town that subsequently became Pittsburgh began to take shape in the surrounding vicinity as settlers, mostly Virginians, followed Braddock's trail to take advantage of whatever opportunities might be available.

Fort Pitt was one of the few English forts to withstand attack during the Pontiac uprising of 1763–64. As the French and Indian threat receded, the fort deteriorated, while the settlement of Pittsburgh prospered as a base for traders, backwoodsmen, and westward-moving settlers. The United States built a fifth and last fort, LaFayette or Fayette, at the forks in the winter of 1791–92, when war with the Indians in the old Northwest flamed anew. Located a quarter of a mile above the site of Fort Pitt, which had fallen into ruin, the fort supplied troops during the Whisky Rebellion, in 1794, and served as a supply and training depot in the War of 1812.

Present Appearance. A few years ago the point of land at the forks lay beneath a clutter of commercial structures and railroad tracks. However, development of the 36-acre Point State Park in the shadow of modern Pittsburgh's skyscrapers on the city's "Golden Triangle" has removed the most objectionable modern intrusions and will provide an eloquent historical interpretation. Archeological investigation has provided much useful information about Fort Pitt, whose flag bastion has been restored. Careful plans have been laid for rebuilding the Monongahela Bastion, including a museum under the administration of the Pennsylvania Historical and Museum Commission. The original Bouquet Blockhouse, preserved for years by the Allegheny County Chapter of the Daughters of the American Revolution, will remain at its original site. Attractive promenades have been laid out along the shores of both rivers, and stone bleachers seating 3,000 persons have been placed along the Allegheny River. In summer the city of Pittsburgh anchors a barge at the park, and free concerts and other programs are presented.[61]

62. The Printzhof, Pennsylvania

Location. Delaware County, near the junction of Pa. 291 and 420, corner of Taylor Avenue and Second Street, Essington.

Ownership and Administration. Commonwealth of Pennsylvania; Pennsylvania Historical and Museum Commission.

Significance. The site and remains of the Printzhof, home and headquarters of Gov. Johan Printz and the "capital" of New Sweden during the period 1643–53, comprise one of the most notable preservations relating to the story of Sweden in America. The site is also significant as the first permanent white settlement in what became Pennsylvania.

The first Swedish expedition to America, in 1638, planted a settlement on the banks of the Minquas Kill, now the Christina River, at the site of modern Wilmington. The infant colony of New Sweden limped along for a few years, virtually ignored by the homeland, until the energetic autocrat Johan Printz arrived in 1643 to direct affairs. After exploring the Delaware River as far north as the site of Trenton, N.J., "Big Guts," as the Indians admiringly called the Governor, chose small Tinicum Island as the best location for his dwelling place because of its fertile soil and because it was well protected by the surrounding Darby and Bow Creeks, and the Delaware itself.

Printz immediately erected a fort, New Gothenburg, and within it a commodious log house, the Printzhof, for himself and his family, as well as a log chapel, storehouse, and brewery. Two years later, in 1645, a fire and the explosion of the fort's powder magazine destroyed the buildings. With characteristic energy, Printz rebuilt the fort and the Printzhof. Until his departure from New Sweden in 1653, he ruled his struggling colony with an iron hand. At Tinicum Island he held court; acted as prosecutor, judge, and jury; and conducted a holding action against the claims to the Delaware of his Dutch counterpart in New Amsterdam, Peter Stuyvesant. At Tinicum were located the first mills, church, and school in the territory that would one day be Pennsylvania.

Present Appearance. The site of the Printzhof and a portion of the surrounding settlement has fortunately been spared from the intensive modern development on the banks of the Delaware, and is preserved in the 7 acres of Governor Printz Park. Archeological investigation in 1937 by the Pennsylvania Historical and Museum Commission disclosed the stone foundations of Printz's house, and uncovered thousands of artifacts of Swedish origin. The foundations of the Printzhof are the only visible remains of the settlement. The present park was created through the donation of land by the Swedish-Colonial Society to celebrate the 300th anniversary of the founding of New Sweden in 1938. The park was formally dedicated by Prince Bertil of Sweden on June 29, 1939.[62]

63. Wanton-Lyman-Hazard House, Rhode Island

Location. Newport County, 17 Broadway, Newport.

Ownership and Administration. Newport Historical Society, 82 Touro Street, Newport.

Significance. This house, probably built around 1695 and one of New England's best Jacobean houses, illustrates the architectural transition from the 17th to the 18th century. Its sturdy frame construction is typical of the earliest New England houses, and its elaborate structural detail and ornamentation reflect the changes that began early in the 18th century and developed into the Georgian style of the middle colonial period. Although other 17th-century structures may still stand in Newport, the Wanton-Lyman-Hazard House best reflects the architecture of the century.

The first known mention of the house dates from 1724, when Stephen Mumford transferred ownership over to Richard Ward, who in 1740 became Governor of the Colony of Rhode Island. In 1765, the house, then occupied by Martin Howard, the Tory Stamp Master of Newport, was extensively damaged during the Stamp Act riots. Subsequent repairs probably included the casing of the beams and the installation of the mantel paneling.

Present Appearance. Originally a two-and-one-half story structure, the house had rooms on both sides of the massive chimney and probably a kitchen ell on the rear. The chimney is of brick rather than stone. Because brick was not common in Rhode Island before the 18th century, the

Wanton-Lyman-Hazard House, in Newport, Rhode Island, is a combination of 17th- and 18th-century architectural styles.

chimney represents a unique example of brickwork in the colony. The characteristically steep pitch of the roof remains unchanged. The only major changes in the house's original exterior are the addition of a lean-to across the back; the installation of dormers and sash windows; and the building of the classic doorway, which dates from 1782. The huge plaster coved cornice in the front of the roof indicates an attempt on the part of the original builder to break away from the simple treatment of the 17th century.

Purchased by the Newport Historical Society from the Hazard family in 1927, the house was restored under the direction of Norman M. Isham. In the north bedchamber may be seen the original ceiling beams and the massive corner posts. The house and its garden are maintained in excellent condition. Furnishings are of the 18th century, but a few earlier pieces are included. The house is open to the public from May 15 to October 15.[63]

64. Adam Thoroughgood House, Virginia

Location. Princess Anne County, on Lynnhaven Bay, just off Va. 166, about 4 miles east of Norfolk.

Ownership and Administration. Adam Thoroughgood House Foundation, Norfolk.

Significance. This restored house, one of the oldest in Virginia, is a fine example of the central-hall house of 17th-century Virginia. Adam Thoroughgood came to Virginia in 1621 as an indentured servant. After working off his indenture, he rose rapidly in position and in 1629 became a member of the House of Burgesses. By the time of his death, in 1640, at the age of 35, he owned some 7,000 acres of land in Princess Anne County.

In 1636, Thoroughgood bought the tract on which the present house stands. The Adam Thoroughgood House Foundation does not believe that this house is the one listed in his will in 1640, but that he may have built it for one of his sons, or that it may have been built by a son or grandson. In any event, it is of authentic 17th-century design and workmanship. Of brick, it measures 45 by 22 feet. Three walls are laid in English bond and one in Flemish. The house is a low-eaved, one-and-a-half story structure and has a steep gabled roof. Of the two huge end chimneys, one is projecting and one set inside the wall. A hall, 10 feet wide, separates the two rooms below, the one to the north being the larger. The house was altered in 1745, when the original leaded glass

Adam Thoroughgood House, a fine example of a 17th-century central-hall house, is one of the oldest brick structures in Virginia.

panes in the parlor were replaced with Georgian windows; the exposed ceiling beams were covered with plaster; and paneling was added to the walls.

Present Appearance. Under the auspices of the foundation, the Thoroughgood House was restored to its 17th-century condition and opened to the public in 1957. The restoration included removal of dormers, reduction in the size of windows, return of leaded glass panes, and the removal of plaster and other later additions. In several places, glass inserts show details of the original construction. The original 5,350-acre estate has been subdivided through the years, and a recent housing development has reduced the house tract to 4½ acres. The grounds, which have been nicely landscaped, include a 17th-century garden donated by the Garden Club of Virginia.[64]

65. Bacon's Castle, Virginia

Location. Surry County, on Va. 10, between Surry and Rushmore.

Ownership and Administration. Privately owned.

Significance. Bacon's Castle is one of the most important existing buildings of 17th-century Virginia, on both historical and architectural grounds. Earliest extant example of the Virginia cross-plan houses and a remarkable architectural monument of the colonial period, it was built by Arthur Allen about 1655 and figured prominently in Bacon's Rebellion of 1676. A number of the rebel followers of Nathaniel Bacon seized Major Allen's house and fortified it; the house was thereafter known as Bacon's Castle.

This house is the earliest extant example of a 17th-century Virginia cross-plan house. In 1676, Nathaniel Bacon's rebel followers seized and fortified it for about 3 months. Thereafter it was known as Bacon's Castle.

The garrison, commanded at various times by William Rookings, Arthur Long, Joseph Rogers, and John Clements, retained control of the house for more than 3 months, but their cause was declining. The death of Bacon in October left his forces under the leadership of Joseph Ingram, who proved to be unsuited to the command. Ingram dispersed his army in small garrisons. As the demoralized troops began to plunder indiscriminately, conditions in the colony became deplorable.

Gov. William Berkeley began to conquer the isolated posts one by one, some by force and some by persuasion. A loyal force from the vessel *Young Prince* captured an unidentified "fort" on December 29 that many historians have identified as Bacon's Castle. After withstanding a brief siege early in January 1677, the Loyalists used the "fort" as a base of operations for the last engagements of the rebellion, which ended before the month was out.

Bacon's Castle is a fine extant example of the Virginia cross plan. A two-story brick structure laid in English bond, it has a 10-foot-square, two-story porch in front and a larger stair tower in the rear. The main floor originally had a great hall and smaller parlor. The stair tower afforded access to a large cellar containing several rooms and an 8-foot-wide fireplace, as well as two large bedrooms on the second floor and three more in the garret.

Exterior features of note are the Flemish gables at each end of the house; large triple chimneys stand barely free of the gables. The chimneys, set diagonally and joined only at the caps, rise from a straight stack 10 feet wide and 4 feet deep. The house is a unique example of Jacobean architecture.

Present Appearance. Bacon's Castle has been altered at various times, and until a few years ago was in poor condition. About the middle of the 19th century, a brick addition was annexed to the east side of the house; it replaced an earlier frame addition that was moved some distance away and is still standing. Many original features remain unaltered, and the present owner has renovated the house so carefully as to permit a restoration at some future time. The home is privately owned and is not ordinarily open to visitors.[65]

66. St. Luke's Church, Virginia

Location. Isle of Wight County, on U.S. 258, at Benns Church.

Ownership and Administration. Historic St. Luke's Restoration, Inc., Smithfield.

Significance. This venerable structure, originally called the "Old Brick" or "Newport Parish" Church, is probably the best surviving example of 17th-century Gothic architecture in the United States. Its construction may have begun in 1632, for that year is incised on some of the bricks. In any event, the church doubtless replaced a wooden structure built a decade earlier.

Laid in Flemish bond in a single nave plan approximately 24 by 60 feet, the brick church took about 5 years to complete. Installation of the permanent interior fittings took longer, possibly as much as 25 years. About 1657, Col. Joseph Bridger, a prominent parishioner, brought over several artisan members of the Driver family from England to complete this work. During the last quarter of the century, a third story was added to the existing church tower, possibly by second-generation members of the Driver family.

Various architectural changes were made during the 18th century. When the Anglican Church in Virginia was disestablished, in 1785, St. Luke's was used only for occasional services and was not properly maintained. Rehabilitated in 1821, it remained in use for 15 years, being abandoned a second time when Christ Church in Smithfield, 5 miles away, was completed. After a half-century of disuse, a violent storm in 1887 collapsed the roof and part of the east gable. A partial restoration was made soon after under the auspices of the Reverend David Barr, but

St. Luke's Church, Virginia, begun about 1623, is a noteworthy example of 17th-century Gothic architecture. It has been carefully restored to its original condition.

in 1953 the foundations were discovered to be crumbling. During the next 4 years, the foundations were repaired and the church was completely restored.

Present Appearance. The church has been carefully restored to its 17th-century condition, except that the commemorative stained glass windows added in the late 19th century have not been replaced. The exterior work included permanent shoring of the foundations, reopening the base of the tower, altering the east stepped gable, and repointing the masonry. Interior restoration was extensive, including a timber roof erected with Gothic tie-beams; a floor of square brick; 17th-century rood-screen, chancel rail, and pews; and a triple-decker pulpit. The church has been furnished with a number of rare items, including a pair of silver wine flagons dated 1683, a silver trencher-plate of 1696, chancel furnishings of 17th-century cut-velvet, a 17th-century Bernard Smith organ, and a font made from a tree trunk. Occasional memorial services are held at the church, which is open to visitors daily.[66]

67. La Fortaleza, Puerto Rico

Location. Between Calle Recinto Oeste and San Juan Bay, southwest side of San Juan Island, San Juan.

Ownership and Administration. Commonwealth of Puerto Rico.

Significance. La Fortaleza (The Fortress) was the first true fortification in San Juan, established in 1521. The Spanish built it between 1533 and 1540 for protection against raids by Carib Indians and by English and French freebooters. Because of its comparatively poor location, however, it soon occupied a position of only secondary importance in the defenses of San Juan. Nevertheless, at the end of the 16th century the Earl of Cumberland, who led a successful English attack on the city, described it as "a strong castle, built of stone, square, and commonly called the King's Palace . . . and where we found a great stock of ammunition." In 1625, a Dutch force under Gen. Bowdoin Hendrick captured La Fortaleza, along with the rest of the town. However, the major defensive position, El Morro, succeeded in holding out; and, when the invaders retreated, they burned everything they could, including a large part of La Fortaleza. Since reconstruction of the fortress on a larger scale, which occurred soon after, it has been used chiefly as the residence of the Governors of Puerto Rico, as well as offices of the Treasurer and Intendant.

Present Appearance. One of the oldest structures in the New World, La Fortaleza is a fine example of Spanish colonial architectural style. It has tiled roofs; galleries, staircases, and doorways liberally decorated with wrought iron; sunlit patios; and graceful arches. Originally it was a simple, two-towered fortress. By 1580, additional rooms had been erected; they were arranged to form a patio and to serve more as a residence for the military commandant and officers than as a fortification. The reconstruction in the first half of the 17th century involved a considerable enlargement of the fortress. In 1846, the Spanish thoroughly renovated La Fortaleza and altered some of the interior decorations. In 1939, the U.S. Army also thoroughly rehabilitated the structure. Many historical features were lost during these renovations, but the basic identity of the structure is intact, including elements traceable to its original construction more than 400 years ago.[67]

68. Columbus Landing Site, Virgin Islands

Location. St. Croix Island, 4 miles west of Christiansted, west side of Salt River Bay.

Ownership and Administration. Privately owned, except for 5 acres of Fort Sale site, which are owned by the Government of the Virgin Islands.

Significance. This site is the earliest one now under the U.S. flag that is associated with Columbus. On November 14, 1493, on his second voyage to the New World, Columbus discovered an island with the Indian name of *Ay Ay,* which he named Santa Cruz. Landing in a small boat from the fleet anchorage in the bay, a party of Columbus' men attacked a small group of Indians, killing one and capturing the others. This is apparently the first recorded armed conflict between Europeans and aboriginal Americans. After the men named a nearby cape the "Cape of the Arrow," the fleet sailed on.

Little is known of the subsequent history of the island until the French conquered it in 1650 and renamed it St. Croix. During their 4- to 5-year occupation of the island, they built Fort Sale on the west side of Salt River Bay. The residence of the French Governor was on the east side, as well as a small village called Bassin, on the site of Christiansted. At the time of the French exodus in 1695, the population was only 147 white persons and 623 Negro slaves.

Present Appearance. The site, a prominent knoll on the west side of the bay, is unimproved and covered with brush and some trees. It embraces the remains of Fort Sale and an aboriginal site. The latter, 6 acres covered by potsherds and shells, has been excavated extensively. Fort Sale was an earthwork fortification, and the site is now covered with sod. It has not been investigated archeologically.

In 1958, the Legislature of the Virgin Islands passed a bill providing for the acquisition of two tracts of land on Salt River Bay totaling 50.05 acres that would encompass the entire historic and archeological area. The Government of the Virgin Islands planned to develop and maintain this land as a historical and public recreational area. Five acres of land at the old fort site were purchased in 1961.[68]

D. Historic Districts Eligible for the Registry of National Historic Landmarks

In some instances, groups of historic buildings located in proximity, when considered collectively, provide outstanding illustrations of a past era. These groups are designated Historic Districts and declared eligible for the Registry of National Historic Landmarks. Such districts sometimes include individual structures that are eligible on their own merits for Landmark designation. The following Historic Districts illustrate the phases of history treated in this volume.

1. Vieux Carré Historic District, Louisiana

Location. Orleans Parish, the section of the city of New Orleans bounded by the Mississippi River, Rampart Street, Canal Street, and Esplanade Avenue.

Ownership and Administration. Various.

Significance. Covering some 85 blocks, the Vieux Carré is the nucleus of the original city of New Orleans and the scene of many historic events—from the initial French settlement through the French, Spanish, and early American eras. Many of its buildings represent a unique fusion of architectural styles, which reveal the growth of New Orleans in the late 18th and first part of the 19th centuries and the blending of diverse national influences into a cosmopolitan metropolis.

The Frenchman Jean Baptiste le Moyne, Sieur de Bienville, founded New Orleans in 1718, and 3 years later military engineers platted the town into 80 rectilinear blocks. In 1722, it became the capital of French

[282

Louisiana and, because of its location 100 miles above the mouth of the Mississippi, thrived as a trade center. By the mid-18th century, it had gained a reputation for glamorous living and was the cultural center of Louisiana. In 1762, when western Louisiana passed from France to Spain, it became the capital of Spanish Louisiana and grew rapidly. Although fires in 1788 and 1794 nearly destroyed it, its residents erected substantial buildings to replace the old ones.

In 1803, New Orleans officially passed from Spain back to France, and 20 days later from France to the United States. During the War of 1812, the British failed to capture the city. After the war, it continued to prosper, particularly because it became the major port for the newly developing steamboat traffic on the Mississippi and its tributaries. The influx of U.S. settlers and traders, Latin American political refugees, and European immigrants made ante bellum New Orleans one of the most cosmopolitan cities in the United States. By mid-century, it had become the commercial and financial emporium of the entire Mississippi Valley, the fourth largest city in the United States, and the second most active port. Today it is a thriving port city and center of culture.

Present Appearance. Most of the buildings in the Vieux Carré date from between 1794, when the second of two disastrous fires swept the town, and 1850. They are a mixture of various European styles of architecture, primarily French and Spanish. To some extent, however, they also reflect the Greek Revival style, which swept the country in the 19th century. Sites and buildings in the Historic District dating from the French and Spanish periods that are eligible for the Registry of National Historic Landmarks and are described elsewhere in this volume with the other Landmarks include: The Cabildo, Jackson Square, and the Ursuline Convent. St. Louis Cathedral, also located in the Historic District, is described in the "Other Sites Considered" section.

Listed below are some other buildings that date back to the French and Spanish periods:

(1) The Presbytère, 713 Chartres Street. Built between 1795 and 1813, the Presbytère was intended to be the rectory for St. Louis Cathedral, but shortly after its completion the Catholic Church rented it to the city for a courthouse. In 1853, the city purchased it. It is now a part of the Louisiana State Museum.

(2) Madame John's Legacy, 632 Dumaine Street. Rebuilt after a fire destroyed the original house in 1788, this house is one of the oldest in New Orleans. Of "brick between posts" construction on a raised base-

ment, it is typical of the French colonial period. It is owned by the Louisiana State Museum.

(3) Montegut House, 731 Royal Street. Built about 1795 and extensively remodeled about 1830, this house is a fine example of a Vieux Carré residence.

(4) Bosque House, 617 Chartres Street. Built in 1795, this residence is noted for its monogrammed balcony, one of the finest examples of Spanish colonial ironwork in the Vieux Carré.

(5) Le Petit Theatre, 616 St. Peter Street. A pink stuccoed building that is now a part of the Little Theatre, Le Petit Theatre was constructed between 1789 and 1796.

(6) Lafitte's Blacksmith Shop, 941 Bourbon Street. This building is constructed of "brick between posts," a type of architecture introduced by French builders soon after the founding of the city. The shop is mentioned in city records as early as 1772.

(7) Bank of the United States, 339 Royal Street. Probably built in 1800, this building was subsequently occupied by the Planters' Bank, a branch of the United States Bank of Philadelphia, and the New Orleans Gas Light and Banking Company. It is now owned by another private company. Its wrought-iron balconies are among the finest in New Orleans.

(8) Maspero's Exchange, 440 Chartres Street. Built in 1788, this building, originally known as the Exchange Coffee House, was a meeting place for soldiers, planters, merchants, and buccaneers. Jean and Pierre Lafitte used the second floor for their headquarters.

Many other interesting sites and buildings that pertain to later periods of history are also included in the Historic District.[69]

2. Colonial Annapolis Historic District, Maryland

Location. Anne Arundel County; the area bounded by Spa Creek, Duke of Gloucester Street, Church Circle, College Avenue, and King George, Hanover, Randall, and Prince George Streets; Annapolis.

Ownership and Administration. Various.

Significance. Though this Historic District was declared eligible for the Registry of National Historic Landmarks primarily because of its 18th-century significance, it also has important associations with the phases of history treated in this volume. In 1649, the same year that

The majority of historic buildings in Annapolis, Maryland, date from the 18th century. One exception is the Sands House, the oldest frame building in the town, built in 1690's.

Lord Baltimore's Religious Toleration Act made Maryland a haven for nonconformists, about 300 dissatisfied Puritans emigrated from Virginia to the mouth of the Severn River, near the site of Annapolis. Soon afterward, some of them settled at the site of Annapolis—which they gave various names, including Proctor's Landing, Arundelton, Severn, and Anne Arundel Town, until 1695, when they renamed it Annapolis in honor of Princess Anne, Protestant daughter of James II.

The year before, the town had been designated the capital of Maryland in place of St. Marys City. A political and mercantile center, the town also had an active social and cultural life. Merchants and planters built elegant homes and entertained legislators. Theaters, horseraces, and taverns provided entertainment. After the turn of the 18th century, the affluence of the city increased and during the War for Independence reached its pinnacle. Near the end of the war, the Continental Congress met in the Maryland State House (a Registered National Historic Landmark, relating primarily to political and military affairs, 1783–1830), where in 1783 George Washington resigned his commission. Soon after this period, Baltimore began to gain the ascendancy as the commercial center of the State of Maryland.

Present Appearance. More pre-Revolutionary brick buildings are preserved in Annapolis than in any other U.S. city. Most of the historic buildings date from the 18th century. Some of the more important are the Maryland State House, Old Treasury Building, William Reynolds Tavern, Peggy Stewart House, Christopher Hohne-Holland House, and Brice House. The few buildings remaining from the 17th century include: the Little Photo Studio, originally the Kentish Inn, constructed in 1696–1700 as a tavern; and the Sands House, the oldest frame building in the town, built in the 1690's.[70]

3. Huguenot Street Historic District, New York

Location. Ulster County, on the Walkill River, New Paltz.

Ownership and Administration. The Huguenot Historical Society, New Paltz, New York, Inc., owns the Abraham Hasbrouck House, Bevier-Elting House, Hugo Freer House, and Jean Hasbrouck House. The Daniel du Bois House is privately owned.

Significance. The settlement of Huguenots, both French and Walloons, was a significant facet of U.S. development in the 17th and 18th centuries. Nowhere is this more graphically illustrated by historic buildings than at New Paltz, where five stone houses clustered along Huguenot Street constitute a remarkable picture of an early Huguenot community. The original settlement at New Paltz was made during the latter part of the 17th century, but most of the five houses date from the first part of the 18th century, although they incorporate 17th-century elements.

Surrounded by the Dutch and friendly with them, the Huguenot settlers of New Paltz nevertheless resisted intermarriage and for many years preserved their own way of life. For all practical purposes, they were an independent, self-governing body that was tolerated by the Crown and later the State of New York. In 1785, the State legislature confirmed the ancient grants and petitions, and incorporated the town into the State government. The original system of government for New Paltz, established in 1728, consisted of a council of 12 heads of families, the *Duzine*. Descendants of the original 12 governed until 1826.

Even without its Huguenot associations, the existence of five early buildings on one continuously inhabited street would justify recognition of the New Paltz community as an outstanding survivor of colonial America. When it is also considered that Huguenot Street was a haven for European refugees, New Paltz is unique in terms of its period and historical significance.

Present Appearance. The five Huguenot houses, all strongly reflecting Dutch architectural influence, are described below:

(1) Jean Hasbrouck House (Memorial House). Built around 1712 by one of the original patentees of the settlement, it has been remarkably well preserved. Its rough stone walls, topped by a high, steep-pitched roof, give it a medieval appearance. The interior has a center-hall plan; two rooms are on each side. Over the entrance door is an early shed-stoop. The house is open to the public.

(2) Abraham Hasbrouck House. This house is also relatively unaltered. Its rough-faced stone walls and gabled roof with sloping shed dormers and three chimneys are typical Dutch colonial. The north portion dates to 1694; additions were made in 1700 and 1712.

(3) Bevier-Elting House. The center portion of this house, the home of an original New Paltz patentee, dates from the end of the 17th century, although the house was substantially enlarged around 1735.

(4) Daniel du Bois House. This house was built around 1705 on the site of a log fortress, the walls of which are said to have been incorporated in the newer dwelling. Fifty years later, the second story was added, and in the 19th century the house was enlarged and its interior altered.

(5) Hugo Freer House. In addition to thick stone walls and steep-pitched roof, this house has solid shutters on the windows and divided door with overhang hood—both common in Dutch colonial architecture. The north end was built about 1694 and the south end about 1735.

Besides these five houses, the Deyo House may be mentioned. Portions of the walls of the present house are all that remain of the original structure, built by Pierre Deyo, another of the New Paltz patentees. The house was extensively remodeled in the 19th century, little of its original construction being spared. It is also owned by the Huguenot Historical Society, New Paltz, New York, Inc.[71]

4. Hurley Historic District, New York

Location. Ulster County, on U.S. 209, about 3 miles west of Kingston and the New York Thruway.

Ownership and Administration. Privately owned houses.

Significance. Preserved in this little town, which lies between the Hudson River and the Catskills, is a collection of stone houses that still preserves the Dutch heritage of the region to an unusual degree. Ten of these houses, some still occupied by descendants of early Dutch settlers, extend along Hurley Street, the town's principal thoroughfare. Scattered nearby are other houses that have survived for two centuries and more. A few of these have characteristics more English than Dutch, attesting to the changes in settlement after the fall of New Netherland—changes that occurred despite the stubborn, if nonviolent, resistance of the original settlers to the English and their alien ways.

Hurley, or *Nieuw Dorp* (New Village), as it was then known, was founded in 1662 by a few Dutch and Huguenot settlers from nearby Wiltwyck (Kingston). With the permission of Dir. Gen. Peter Stuyvesant, the settlers laid out the new town on the fertile bottom land of Esopus Creek. Construction had scarcely started when the Esopus Indians burned it to the ground. The prisoners taken in the raid were soon released. After a short, ruthless campaign by troops of New Netherland, peace was made in May 1664.

In a matter of months, the victors were themselves conquered by the English, who seized New Netherland in the name of the Duke of York. English rule was not harsh, but the Dutch of *Nieuw Dorp* stubbornly resisted any change in their way of life. In 1669, Gov. Francis Lovelace

Ten stone houses of Dutch origin on Hurley Street and more than a dozen others in the town make Hurley, New York, an unmatched example of a Hudson Valley Dutch settlement of the 18th century. The Van Deusen House, in the foreground, built in 1723, was a temporary capitol of New York during the War for Independence.

renamed the town Hurley after his ancestral home, Hurley-on-Thames. Despite its English name, for the next century and more, Hurley remained a Dutch provincial town—in language, customs, and architecture.

During the War for Independence, the town was shaken from its accustomed serenity by the passing of the armies and the influx of refugees from Kingston, when the British set the torch to that Hudson River settlement in October 1777. The people of Hurley treasure incidents of this period, and also the town's importance as a station on the "Underground Railroad" and residence of the antislavery leader Sojourner Truth. But it is the town of Hurley, its quiet streets and sturdy houses, that is distinguished—a representative of the time when Dutch America flourished in the valley of the Hudson.

Present Appearance. All the most interesting houses except one lie along two historic roads—Hurley Street and the Hurley Mountain Road. These include the Jan Van Deusen House; the Du Mond, or Guard, House; the Houghtaling House; and the Elmendorf House, or Half Moon Tavern. The exception is the Hardenbergh House, on Schoonmaker Lane a short distance south of Hurley Street.

The old cemetery north of Hurley Street is the resting place of many of the town's earliest settlers, as revealed by the Dutch names on the worn gravestones. Not only Hurley's houses, but also the fertile flood lands of Esopus Creek, west of the town, recreate the story of the early settlers and reveal why they chose this spot for their "New Village." [72]

E. Other Sites Considered

In the process of selecting the comparatively few historic sites of such outstanding character as to merit recognition as Registered National Historic Landmarks for the phases of history treated in this volume, a great many throughout the Nation were carefully studied, compared, and evaluated. The sites described below were among those deemed by the Advisory Board to possess noteworthy historical value but not "exceptional value" (national significance) within the special Landmark criteria. Some of them, however, may satisfy the criteria for other volumes in this series. In addition to Landmark sites and those described below, many others—too numerous to list—were evaluated and judged to be of lesser importance.

1. Dauphin Island, Alabama

Location: Mobile County, at the entrance to Mobile Bay.

Pierre le Moyne, Sieur d'Iberville, sent by Louis XIV in 1699 to found a colony at the mouth of the Mississippi, was the first European known to have visited this island. He called it "Massacre Island" because he discovered a huge pile of bleaching human bones on its sandy beach. Bienville, Iberville's brother, established a post on the island in 1702, and it served as port of entry to the settlement at Fort Louis de la Mobile, 30 miles upriver, and later to the colony at the site of Mobile. A settlement grew up around the post, and in 1711 Bienville renamed the island "Dauphine" in honor of Marie Adelaide of Savoy, wife of the Dauphin Louis, Duke of Burgundy. In spite of near-destruction by hurricanes and attacks by British privateers, the colony survived.

Until about 1720, the island served as the main port of the Mobile area. In 1762, France ceded it to Spain, which retained possession until the following year, when England gained title by the Treaty of Paris. Spain reoccupied the island 20 years later and held it until 1813, when Gen. James Wilkinson, learning that a British base was located there, seized it for the United States.

The island is now connected to the mainland by an oversea highway and has undergone considerable residential development. Partially restored Fort Gaines, built in 1822 on the eastern tip of the island and prominent during the Civil War, is the most notable existing historic site today.

2. Fort Condé (Fort Charlotte) Site, Alabama

Location: Mobile County, Mobile.

In 1710, Jean Baptiste le Moyne, Sieur de Bienville, built Fort Condé on the site of Mobile. The temporary, wooden fort, first known as Fort Louis, evolved into a stone-and-brick structure that was for a time considered to be the most formidable in French Louisiana. In 1702, Bienville had moved his settlement from Fort Maurepas, near present Ocean Springs, Miss., to a site near present Mount Vernon, Ala., where he had erected Fort Louis de la Mobile, also called Fort Louis de la Louisiane. The settlers remained at this fort until floods forced them to relocate, at Fort Condé.

At the end of the French and Indian War, France yielded all territory east of the Mississippi, except New Orleans, to England. This cession included Mobile, and the English took over Fort Condé; they renamed it Fort Charlotte. They held it until 1780, when the Spanish captured it; the Spanish maintained possession until the War of 1812, when Gen. James Wilkinson of the United States ousted them. Concerned about possible attacks from the sea, the United States at this time also built defenses, such as Fort Gaines, at the entrance to the harbor. After the United States purchased Florida, in 1819, Fort Charlotte was of no further importance and gradually fell into ruins.

The site was eventually sold and used for various modern buildings. However, Fort Condé is commemorated by a bronze plaque at the rear of the Mobile County Courthouse, on Church Street, where part of an alleged original wall is also located.

3. Fort Louis de la Mobile (Fort Louis de la Louisiane) Site, Alabama

Location: Mobile County, on U.S. 43, at Twenty-Seven Mile Bluff, on the outskirts of Mount Vernon.

This fort, the second capital of French Louisiana, was established in 1702 by Jean Baptiste le Moyne, Sieur de Bienville. Also known as Fort Louis de la Louisiane, it was located on the Mobile River in the heart of the French Empire in the lower Mississippi Valley. During the first few years, the colonists were plagued by sickness, floods, and near-starvation, but by 1704 supply ships were arriving from Canada regularly. As more immigrants arrived, including brides for the colonists, the colony grew.

La Salle's lieutenant, Henry de Tonty, died at the fort during a yellow fever outbreak and was buried nearby in an unmarked grave. Most of the colonists, however, survived and stayed on until a series of floods, in 1710, forced them to abandon Fort Louis de la Mobile and move to the site of present Mobile, where they founded Fort Condé, first known as Fort Louis.

In 1902, the people of Mobile erected a monument at the site of Fort Louis de la Mobile, on property now owned by the Alabama Power Company.

4. Fort Tombigbee Site, Alabama

Location: Sumter County, on the Tombigbee River, just off U.S. 11, near Epes.

Fort Tombigbee, whose spelling varies widely in historical records, was constructed as a military-trading post by the French in 1735 above the confluence of the Tombigbee and Black Warrior Rivers, in Choctaw and Chickasaw Indian country. It served as an advanced French base during the Chickasaw War, as a base for trade with the Choctaws, and as a check against British influence in the area. After the French and Indian War, the British occupied it for 5 years and renamed it Fort York. Then abandoned, it fell into ruins. In 1794, the Spanish rebuilt and renamed it Fort Confederation. They remained until 1797, the year before Congress designated the Mississippi Territory. In 1802–3, one of a series of treaties by which the United States absorbed the Choctaw lands was negotiated at the fort. Subsequently, it was abandoned and fell into ruins. The National Society of Colonial Dames of America has placed a marker on the site.

5. Hano Pueblo, Arizona

Location: Navajo County, near Ariz. 264, north of Walpi and Sichomovi on First Mesa, Hopi Villages.

Hano is the only pueblo inhabited today that exemplifies the shifts of the native New Mexican population resulting from Spanish pressures. During the first part of the 17th century, the Tewa-speaking people of Hano lived in the Galisteo Basin south of Santa Fe. During the Pueblo Revolt of 1680–92, they moved to a new pueblo near Santa Cruz. In 1696, they rebelled again, burned their church, killed two padres, and abandoned their pueblo, Tsanwari, as they fled west, as had other Rio Grande groups during earlier periods of unrest.

To help protect Walpi from Ute inroads, the Hopi Indians at that pueblo invited the Tewas to settle to the north, at the head of the trail leading from First Mesa. As time passed, other Rio Grande groups that had taken refuge in Hopiland returned to New Mexico, but the people of Hano remained. They still retain their language and ceremonies, although their kivas and some other aspects of their culture have been influenced by contact with the Hopis. They are noted as producers of fine pottery. Their population is more than 300 today.

6. Tubac, Arizona

Location: Santa Cruz County, on U.S. 89, about 40 miles south of Tucson.

Tubac Presidio was the most northerly Spanish military outpost of Pimería Alta between 1752 and 1776, and was the base from which Capt. Juan Bautista de Anza opened an overland route from Sonora to California and founded the colony that grew into the city of San Francisco. The Spanish established the presidio in 1752, on the site of a Pima Indian village, to protect Jesuit missionaries who had been driven from the area during a Pima rebellion the preceding year. Settlers, attracted by mining and agricultural possibilities, built the pueblo of Tubac and the church of Santa Gertrudis de Tubac.

Because of Apache depredations, in 1776 Spanish officials replaced

Ruins at Tubac, Arizona. From 1752 to 1776, Tubac Presidio was the northernmost Spanish military outpost in Pimería Alta.

the presidio at Tubac with one at Tucson. In the first years of U.S. occupation and acquisition of Arizona, Tubac and Tucson were about the only towns in the region. Until recently Tubac resembled a typical small Mexican village of adobe huts, but the present artists' colony has done much to foster interest in its early history. Tubac Presidio State Historical Monument is located in the plaza where the presidio once stood. Archeological excavation and restoration is planned at the presidio and at the nearby site of the church. The park contains an excellent museum.

7. John Law Colony (lost site), Arkansas

Location: On Arkansas River in the general vicinity of Arkansas Post National Memorial.

John Law was an ill-starred financial wizard who, in 1717, obtained a monopoly of commerce in Louisiana from Louis XV. He also obtained a grant of about 12 square miles on the Arkansas River at Arkansas Post, where he intended to create a duchy. He agreed to settle 1,500 colonists and to provide a sufficient military force to protect them from the Indians. By April 1721, more than 700 Germans, including wives and families, had been settled and were building homes and storehouses, plowing, and sowing crops. Prospects seemed good, although there were many difficulties. Nevertheless, when news arrived that Law's

"Mississippi Bubble"—a financial house of cards—had collapsed, the colonists departed. They sailed down the Mississippi intent upon returning to Europe, but French officials persuaded them to settle along the Mississippi near New Orleans, in a district thereafter known as the "German Coast." The exact site of the colony on the Arkansas River has never been determined.

8. Menard, Wallace, and Related Sites, Arkansas

Location: Arkansas County, left bank of Arkansas River, about 5 miles below Arkansas Post National Memorial.

This extensive multicomponent group of sites has yielded increments of relatively late date, including European trade goods, and revealed native burials. One of the sites may have been that of the original Arkansas Post, the trading post founded in 1686 by Henry de Tonty on the site of an Indian village—probably Quapaw—that had contact with Europeans at an early date. Archeologists have comprehensively investigated the sites. Tonty's post was more likely at the Menard site—the Arkansas River then having had its main channel in today's Menard Bayou—but the evidence is not conclusive. The area is now mixed pastureland, orchard, cultivated acreage, and woodland.

9. Angel Island, California

Location: Marin and San Francisco Counties, in San Francisco Bay.

This island was discovered by the Portolá expedition on November 4, 1769. It was used as a base by the Ayala expedition, which in 1775 conducted the first detailed exploration of San Francisco Bay—discovered in 1769. This exploration resulted in official recognition of the bay's merits as a harbor by Spain and its first use as a port. In the early 19th century, the island was used occasionally by Russian and Aleut sea otter hunters, and also by whaling and trading vessels as a fueling and watering place. In 1839, the Mexican Government granted it to Antonio Mario Osio for use as a ranch. In 1863, the U.S. Army utilized it for harbor defense. No surviving structures date from the Spanish or Mexican periods, but much of the island is relatively unspoiled. It is being developed as a California State Historical Park.

10. Anza-Borrego Desert State Park, California

Location: Eastern side of San Diego County, extending into Imperial County; traversed by Calif. 78.

This 455,525-acre park commemorates a portion of the route twice followed during the period 1774–76 by Capt. Juan Bautista de Anza, pioneer of the 700-mile overland route from Tubac, in Pimería Alta, now in Arizona, to San Gabriel Mission, in California. Three campsites of the two expeditions are identified in the park. The desert in the region is little changed from the days of the pioneering expeditions.

Anza was commandant of Tubac in 1773, when he volunteered to find an overland route to the California missions. Accompanied by 35 volunteers, he left on January 8, 1774. Traveling by way of Caborca and Sonoita to the Yuma villages, where he crossed the Colorado River, he moved on some distance to the southwest and then turned westward into the Colorado desert. He marched south of and roughly parallel to the present international boundary until he struck the mountains on the western edge of the desert, and then turned north to Borrego Valley and traversed San Carlos Pass into the Cahuilla Valley. He then pushed on to near the site of Riverside, and reached San Gabriel Mission on March 22.

Anza's second expedition, which arrived at San Gabriel on January 4, 1776, consisted of 240 settlers, 695 horses and mules, and 355 cattle. The route was closed after the revolt of the Yuma Indians in 1781 for about 45 years, but it was used again during the period of Mexican administration; and it was followed in part by some of the gold seekers and emigrants to California in 1849 and later years.

11. Cajon Pass, California

Location: San Bernardino County, on U.S. 66–91–395, about 22 miles northeast of San Bernardino.

This pass was a major southeastern gateway into California from about 1830 to 1846. Through it passed the packhorse trail to California known as the Old Spanish Trail, which originated in Santa Fe, New Mexico. Father Francisco Garcés, who was attempting to find a California-New Mexico route, was evidently the first European to cross the San Bernardino Mountains, in 1776. He probably used an Indian trail a few miles to the east of Cajon Pass. Starting at the confluence of the Colorado and Gila Rivers, he had gone up the Colorado to the Mojave villages near the present city of Needles before turning westward across the desert.

Jedediah Smith and other American fur trappers apparently used the same Indian trail in 1826 and 1827. However, the trail over the entire distance from Santa Fe to California was not completely effective until William Wolfskill and George C. Yount utilized Cajon Pass. These well-known traders made the trip in 1830–31; they were followed by other traders, as well as by forty-niners and emigrants. The Old Spanish Trail was important, although not as heavily traveled as the more southerly Gila Trail. Cajon Pass has been substantially altered by the construction of a superhighway. The Indian trail, a Registered State Historical Landmark, is 8½ miles northwest of Crestline, on Calif. 2.

12. Dana Point, California

Location: Orange County, on U.S. 101 Alt., 7 miles south of Laguna Beach.

This point, overlooking a precipitous 400-foot-high cliff near San Juan Capistrano Mission, is one of many that were utilized in the international hide and tallow trade. Active in this trade, which flourished in the decades

Dana Point, one of many such points along the California coast, was important in the hide and tallow trade. It was named after the American author Richard Henry Dana, who participated in the trade and described it in *Two Years Before the Mast*.

just prior to the war with Mexico, were France, Russia, England, various South American nations, and the United States. Mission Indians prepared the hides and bags of tallow at the mission tanneries. The hides were soaked in salt water and brine, scraped, stretched, dried, and beaten to remove all dust. Mission Indians then transported the hides and bags on pack mules and carts to the point, from where they were thrown over the cliff to the beaches below, transported by small boats to the waiting ships, and carried to Boston, London, and other world ports.

The point was named after Richard Henry Dana, Jr., the American author who served for 2 years as a crew member on the *Pilgrim*, which was actively engaged in the hide and tallow trade. In *Two Years Before the Mast*, published in 1840, he vividly and accurately describes the trade, especially at this point.

13. De la Guerra Adobe, California

Location: Santa Barbara County, State and De la Guerra Streets, Santa Barbara.

Don José Antonio Julián de la Guerra Noriega, who founded one of California's oldest and most prominent families, built this large, one-story adobe structure about 1826 during his long period of service (1815–42) as commandant of the Presidio of Santa Barbara. Because of his prominence, his home was the center of social life in the Santa Barbara region. Richard Henry Dana, Jr., who visited the home in the 1830's, described in *Two Years Before the Mast* the colorful ceremonies during the daughter's wedding. The home was built around three sides of a spacious patio, where such occasions as the wedding and state ceremonials often took place. Many of the roof timbers and door and window lintels were constructed of local sycamore, but others were probably brought in by sailing vessels.

An *altito,* a three-story, tower-like element, used for office and library purposes, has been razed. A group of other white-plastered, tile-roofed structures, which have been built around the old house, make a sizable complex that is now occupied by shops and studios and the offices of the Santa Barbara Chamber of Commerce. The local "Old Spanish Days" fiesta is held annually, the events centering around El Paseo, the "Street in Spain," which adjoins the De la Guerra Adobe.

14. Los Angeles Pueblo, California

Location: Los Angeles County, Los Angeles.

El Pueblo de Nuestra Señora la Reina de los Angeles de Porciúncula—
or Los Angeles for short—was established on September 4, 1781, by 4
soldiers, 12 settlers, and their families, who settled on a 17,500-acre tract
on the orders of Spanish Gov. Felipe de Neve. During the Spanish and
Mexican periods, the population grew slowly but steadily, totaling 1,250
in 1845. Los Angeles was the largest settlement in California when it
became a part of the United States.

The present Los Angeles plaza, laid out in 1818, replaced the 1781
plaza. The 1818 plaza survives as a city park, near which are situated
two structures dating from the Spanish period; the plaza is surrounded
by Main, Los Angeles, Arcadia, and Macy Streets. The adobe Plaza
Church (535 North Main Street) was designed by José Antonio Ramírez
and built between 1818 and 1822 by Indians under the supervision of
José Chapman. Its dimensions were originally 90 by 75 feet. It had a
choir loft, deep glassless windows, earthen floor, and tar-covered flat
roof. Little remains today of the original structure or design.

The Avila Adobe, just off the plaza at 14 Olvera Street, is the oldest
surviving house in Los Angeles. Erected in 1818 by Don José María
Avila, later mayor of the town, it contained 18 rooms in an L-shape and

Los Angeles, in 1853. From a lithograph by Charles Koppel. Courtesy,
Bancroft Library, University of California.

included a wing extending across present Olvera Street. The sturdy adobe walls were 2½-feet thick, the ceilings 15 feet high, and the flat roof covered with black asphalt from the Brea pits. Restored from a ruinous condition after 1930, the house is now part of the Pueblo de los Angeles State Historical Monument.

15. El Molino Viejo, California

Location: Los Angeles County, 1120 Old Mill Road, Pasadena.

El Molino Viejo (The Old Mill), probably constructed during the period 1810–12 for San Gabriel Mission by Father José María de Zaldivéa, was the first water-powered gristmill in California. The only others built there during the Spanish period were at Santa Cruz Mission and at San José Pueblo. Built with massive stone-and-adobe walls, some 5 feet thick, it measured 20 by 50 feet. It was abandoned in 1823, but the ruins provided the basis for a reconstruction in 1929. A private residence until recently, it is now owned by the California Historical Society, which plans to restore it and use it as a southern California headquarters and museum.

16. Monterey (Old Town), California

Location: Monterey County, Monterey.

Monterey abounds in historic sites and structures that illustrate the political, economic, religious, and social life of Spanish and Mexican California. Of special note is the Vizcaíno-Serra Landing Site, at the foot of Pacific Street near the entrance to the U.S. Presidio of Monterey, which commemorates Sebastián Vizcaíno's landing in 1602 and the founding of the presidio and mission of Monterey in 1770 by Fray Junípero Serra and Gov. Gaspar de Portolá. The Royal Presidio Chapel is a Registered National Historic Landmark.

Monterey as a town, or pueblo, was formally authorized in 1827 by the Mexican Government. People had already begun to construct homes outside of the walls of the presidio, and by 1830 the population was about 500. Richard Henry Dana, Jr., who visited the town a few years later, praised its appearance, especially the green lawns of the hundred or so houses.

Among the many historic sites and buildings in Monterey, in addition

Presidio and town of Monterey, California, in 1841. The town, founded in 1827 by the Mexican Government, grew up around the presidio. Courtesy, Bancroft Library, University of California.

to the Vizcaíno-Serra Landing Site and the Royal Presidio Chapel, the following are of particular interest:

(1) Site of Town Plaza, bounded by Munras, Pearl, and Tyler Streets. This is the original site of the central plaza of Monterey, a triangular area now much reduced in size and considerably altered.

(2) Old Custom House, Main and Decatur Streets. This Registered National Historic Landmark (relating primarily to the War with Mexico, 1846–48) is the oldest Government building extant in California. The original section was constructed in 1827; it was extensively enlarged during the period 1841–46. A State historical monument, it is open to the public.

(3) Larkin House, 464 Main Street. Another Registered National Historic Landmark (relating primarily to the War with Mexico, 1846–48) and a State historical monument, this two-story adobe-and-frame residence was built during the period 1835–37 by Thomas O. Larkin. It is the prototype of the architectural style known as Monterey colonial, a combination of Spanish adobe style with New England frame construction that was widely adopted in California. Larkin was the U.S. consul in California and a key figure in events of the 1830's and 1840's.

(4) Casa de Soto, 816 El Dorado Street. This residence is probably

One of many historic buildings in Monterey (Old Town), California, the Larkin House illustrates the Monterey colonial style of architecture.

the best extant architectural example of the traditional Spanish-Mexican one-story adobe residence. It was built about 1820.

(5) The French Consulate, Franklin Street and Estero. This one-story adobe, built about 1840, has been removed from its original location and restored. It is owned by the city of Monterey.

(6) The First Theater, southwest corner of Pacific and Scott Streets. Built about 1843 and used as a theater by U.S. troops in 1847, it is now owned by the State of California.

17. Placerita Canyon, California

Location: Los Angeles County, along an improved road, 6 miles east of Newhall.

While looking in this canyon for stray cattle, in 1842, Francisco López y Arballo first discovered gold, near the surface, in commercial quantities in California. Fortune-seekers swarmed to the area. The placer fields were mainly worked by Francisco García, an experienced miner who brought in other miners from Sonora, Mexico. By the end of 1843, they had mined about $42,000 worth of gold nuggets from nearby San Feliciana Canyon in the San Fernando Hills, as well as an unknown amount from Placerita

Canyon. The deposits were exhausted after being worked about 5 years. The canyon is a Registered State Historical Landmark.

18. La Purísima Concepción Mission (Lompoc), California

Location: Santa Barbara County, on Calif. 1, about 4 miles north-east of Lompoc.

Of the 21 Spanish missions in California, this one is probably the most accurately restored and gives the best picture of mission life in Spanish California. Founded on December 8, 1787, by Father Fermín Francisco de Lasuén, by 1804 it had 1,520 Indian neophytes. It was destroyed by the major earthquakes of 1812, and rebuilt at its present site, 4 miles to the northeast, between 1813 and 1821. Secularized by the Mexican Government in 1834, it quickly went to ruin. During the period 1935–42 the

Ruins of the first La Purísima Concepción Mission (Lompoc), California, prior to 1925. After a disastrous earthquake in 1812, padres abandoned the mission and built a new one about 4 miles to the northwest. Courtesy, Bancroft Library, University of California.

The second La Purísima Concepción Mission (Lompoc), constructed after the 1812 earthquake. One of the most colorful missions in California, it has been carefully restored.

Civilian Conservation Corps, under the direction of the National Park Service, carefully restored most of the buildings, as well as a portion of the irrigation system. In 1941, the mission became a State historical monument, and further reconstruction has been accomplished recently.

19. La Purísima Concepción Mission Site (Fort Yuma), California

Location: Imperial County, on U.S. 80, just across the Colorado River from Yuma, Ariz.

In the fall of 1780, Padre Francisco Garcés, three other Franciscan friars, and a small band of soldiers founded on the Colorado River two new experimental colonies, combination missions-presidios-pueblos. One colony, which included Purísima Concepción Mission, was situated on the California side near the point where the Gila River enters the Colorado River. The other colony, including the San Pecho y San Pablo Mission, was 12 miles to the south in present Mexico. The experiment in combining religious, military, and civil functions did not work well because of friction among the different factions.

Anyway, not long after a fresh group of settlers arrived in June 1781, the Yuma Indians attacked and destroyed both colonies, killed all but six men, and captured the women and children. The Indians blocked travel to California by the Yuma route until 1826, when the Mexicans established a garrison at the La Purísima Concepción site to protect mail carriers and traders. The U.S. Army constructed Fort Yuma at the site in 1850, for which purpose it utilized some stones from the destroyed mission. No surface traces of the mission remain today.

20. Rancho Guajome, California

Location: San Diego County, on Calif. 76, about 8 miles east of Oceanside.

This is one of the best unaltered examples of the California rancho of the Mexican period. Many of the original outbuildings have survived, unlike those at most other ranchos, and the rural setting in the vicinity is unimpaired. The acreage, however, has been reduced in extent. The original Rancho Guajome grant comprised 1 square league, which in 1852 its two mission Indian owners, Andrés and José Manuel, sold to an American, Abel Stearns. The latter immediately presented it as a wedding gift to his sister-in-law, Ysidora Bandini, upon her marriage to a U.S. Army officer, Cave J. Couts. In 1852–53, this couple built the one-story ranchhouse.

The house is U-shaped. The doors of the approximately 20 rooms open into the inner patio. Sleeping rooms occupy one wing, and kitchen and bakehouse the other; the living quarters stretch across the front of the house. The patio, planted with flowers and orange trees, is closed on the upper side of the U by an outer courtyard surrounded by high adobe walls, which at one time had heavy wooden gates. Within the walls were a blacksmith shop, chapel, school, jail, carriage house, and other farm buildings. The house, which is not open to the public, is now privately owned.

21. Rancho Los Alamos, California

Location: Santa Barbara County, on U.S. 101, about 3 miles north of Los Alamos.

Rancho Los Alamos, in an unaltered rural setting, is probably the finest surviving example of the traditional one-story Mexican ranchhouse in

One-story Mexican ranchhouse at Rancho Los Alamos, California.

California. The original grant of 1839 to José Antonio de la Guerra y Carrillo consisted of almost 50,000 acres. In an era noted for lavish hospitality, Los Alamos was a favorite overnight stopping place for travelers between Santa Barbara and Monterey. The house, which has been carefully restored, has some American features; it has plank floors, board ceilings, paneled doors, six-paned window sashes, and central heating and electricity. The general appearance of the house, however, has not been changed greatly, and many of the original furnishings are still being used.

22. Rancho Los Cerritos, California

Location: Los Angeles County, 4600 Virginia Road, Long Beach.

The Los Cerritos ranchhouse was probably the largest and most impressive in southern California during the Mexican period, and is today the largest restored adobe house in the region. The 27,000-acre Rancho Los Cerritos was part of one of the first two provisional land grants made in California by the King of Spain in 1784 for ranching purposes. It came into the possession of John Temple, a young New Englander who married a granddaughter of the original owner and later acquired Mexican citizenship. Temple, soon a wealthy rancher, also profited in the hide trade. In the 1850's, he became an important builder in the city of Los Angeles. In 1882, the new owners subdivided the rancho for real estate and town development purposes.

The magnificent ranchhouse was built in 1844 in the Monterey colonial style. The central two-story portion, containing the family rooms, is 100 feet long, and at each end are one-story wings, each 145 feet long. A large patio is enclosed by an adobe wall, which joins the ends of the wings. In 1955, the city of Long Beach purchased the restored adobe structure and now exhibits it as a historic house and museum. The original ranch setting has been destroyed by urban growth and the intrusion of Signal Hill district oil wells.

Ranchhouse at Rancho Los Cerritos, California. The ranch figured prominently in the California cattle industry during the Mexican period.

23. Rancho Petaluma, California

Location: Sonoma County, near Calif. 116, about 4 miles east of Petaluma.

The headquarters building of the former vast Rancho Petaluma is the largest adobe structure in California. Owner of the rancho was Gen.

This building, once the headquarters of Rancho Petaluma, is the largest adobe structure in California.

Mariano Guadalupe Vallejo, in the 1840's the richest man in California and one of the most powerful politically. The building from which the 67,000-acre rancho was administered—although Vallejo actually resided in Sonoma, 12 miles distant—was built between 1835 and 1844 under the supervision of the owner's younger brother, Sálvador. Oxen hauled redwood timber some 50 miles from the north, and Indians manufactured adobe bricks on the spot.

    The large two-story adobe, in the Monterey colonial style, typically **U**-shaped, was 200 by 150 feet in size. The walls were 3 feet thick and 20 feet high, and a broad veranda ran around the interior and exterior. Iron grills and solid wooden shutters covered the windows and doors. Living quarters were on the second floor, and storerooms and Indian workshops on the ground floor. The building had fallen into a bad state of repair by 1910, when the Native Sons of the Golden West purchased it and the surrounding 5 acres. In 1951, the property became a California State Historical Monument, and is being carefully repaired and reconstructed.

24. San Antonio de Padua Mission, California

Location: Monterey County, on the Hunter Liggett Military Reservation, 5 miles northwest of Jolon.

The picturesque rural setting of this mission has remained almost unchanged since the day it was founded—the third of the California missions. Father Junípero Serra established the mission on July 14, 1771, and the following year moved it 1½ miles to the present location because of a shortage of water at the original site. At its peak in 1805, it had 1,296 Indian neophytes.

Ruins of San Antonio de Padua Mission, California, in 1875. Photograph by C. E. Watkins. Courtesy, Bancroft Library, University of California.

Construction of the present church was begun in 1810 and finished in 1813; other structures on the large adjoining quadrangle were rebuilt during the period 1813–21, including Indian quarters, workshops, walls, and storage areas. The mission's irrigation system, begun as early as 1774, ultimately consisted of several dams, reservoirs, and some 20 miles of

Chapel of San Antonio de Padua Mission, California.

open flumes and masonry conduits. In addition, wells dug near the mission supplied water for the orchard, vineyard, and gardens.

Secularized by the Mexican Government in 1834, the property was acquired by the United States Government at the end of the Mexican War, and returned to the Roman Catholic Church in 1862. Of the original buildings, only the church remained; most of the other structures were marked only by the grass-covered mounds into which the adobe structures had crumbled. Restoration, aided by the Hearst Foundation, has been underway since 1948.

Portion of restored quadrangle at San Antonio de Padua Mission, California. Restoration, aided by the Hearst Foundation, began in 1948.

Casa de Bandini, a historic structure in San Diego. Juan Bandini erected the first story in 1827–28. When the building began to be used as a hotel and stage station, in 1869, a second story was added.

25. San Diego Pueblo (Old Town), California

Location: San Diego County, west of Presidio Park and bounded approximately by Rosecrans, Frontier, and Condé Streets, San Diego.

The Mexican Government formally established San Diego Pueblo (Old Town) in 1835, although old soldiers of the Presidio of San Diego had begun to build their homes on the flats below Presidio Hill perhaps a dozen years earlier. Richard Henry Dana, Jr., who visited the town in 1836, commented: "The small settlement lay directly below the fort, composed of about 40 dark brown looking huts, or houses, and two larger ones, plastered, which belonged to two of the 'gente de razon.' The town is not more than half as large as Monterey . . . and has little or no business." The population in 1840 was only about 150, but by 1845 it had increased to about 350.

A number of Mexican sites and structures have survived, including:

(1) Old Town Plaza, bounded by Calhoun, Wallace, and Mason Streets, and San Diego Avenue. Formerly the political and social center, it is now a city park, somewhat smaller than it originally was.

(2) Casa de Bandini, 2660 Calhoun Street. This one-story residence was built in the years 1827–29 by a leading citizen, Juan Bandini. The second story and veranda were added in 1869, when the structure began to be used as a hotel and stage station.

(3) Casa de Estudillo, 4000 Mason Street between Calhoun Street and San Diego Avenue. This 12-room, one-story, U-shaped adobe was built in 1827 or 1828 by Prefect Don José Antonio Estudillo. Reconstructed from ruins in 1910, it is now a privately operated museum.

(4) Casa de Carrillo, at Presidio Hill Golf Course. The present caddy house of the golf course includes the greatly altered remnants of what is reputed to be the oldest house of San Diego Pueblo, built perhaps as early as 1824 by Don Francisco María Ruíz.

Also of interest are Casa de López (3890 Twiggs Street), Casa de Machado (2545 San Diego Avenue), Casa de Stewart (Congress Street north of Mason Street), and Casa de Pedrorena (2616 San Diego Avenue).

26. San Francisco Bay Discovery Site, California

Location: San Mateo County, on Sweeney Ridge, 4 miles west of Millbrae.

For more than 225 years, from 1542 until 1769, San Francisco Bay escaped the notice of Spanish explorers of the Pacific coast—probably because the Golden Gate is narrow and frequently obscured by fog; and islands and mountains are visible behind the low-lying bay as viewed from the ocean. It was finally discovered in 1769 by Capt. Gaspar de Portolá, whose party set out overland from San Diego for Monterey Bay. Missing that place, it pushed on to the north. Sighting Point Reyes from San Pedro Mountain, Portolá determined to move on to Drakes Bay. From a camp in San Pedro Valley, near present Shelter Cove, he sent out a scouting expedition that returned with news that a large body of water lay over the hill to the east.

The main party later followed the beach to the north and then marched to the northeast into the mountains. From a summit, the crest of present Sweeney Ridge, the men beheld San Francisco Bay, one of the great anchorages of the world. Father Juan Crespi noted in his diary: "It is a very large and fine harbor, such that not only all the navy of our most Catholic Majesty but those of all Europe could take shelter in it." After further exploration of the area in subsequent years, in 1776 the Spanish established the presidio and mission of San Francisco. The discovery site, in unaltered surroundings, is privately owned but is a Registered State Historical Landmark.

27. San Gabriel Arcángel Mission, California

Location: Los Angeles County, Junípero Street and West Mission Drive, San Gabriel.

This mission was established in 1771 by a band of missionary priests sent from San Diego de Alcalá Mission by Father Junípero Serra. The present rectangular stone church, built between 1791 and 1805, replaced an earlier adobe one that had been destroyed by floods, along with other adobe mission buildings. In 1812, an earthquake severely damaged the church and other new buildings, which were subsequently repaired and restored. Much of the interior of the church is original. The church does not have front towers, like most other California mission churches. The exterior, relatively unadorned, features only the slender buttresses that line the long sidewalls, which rise above roof level to form pointed finials.

San Gabriel Mission was the western terminus of the overland trail that Capt. Juan Bautista de Anza founded from Tubac in 1776, as well as of the Old Spanish Trail and the Salt Lake-Los Angeles Trail. It was also known to Jedediah Smith in 1826–27, to many forty-niners who camped nearby, and to the patrons of the Butterfield Southern Overland Mail. The setting has been considerably altered by urban growth.

28. San José Pueblo Site, California

Location: Santa Clara County, Jefferson Schoolground, Hobson Street, San José.

San José Pueblo, or village, was the first of three the Spanish founded in Alta California, the other two being Los Angeles and Branciforte. Founded in 1777 by Lt. José Moraga, who led a party of 65 soldiers and settlers, it first consisted of temporary houses of palisaded logs and earthen roofs. The next year, the residents constructed two dams for irrigation purposes. The population grew slowly; it totaled only about 80 in 1790, and about 900 by the end of the Mexican period, in the mid-19th century. About 1797, to avoid winter floods, the village had moved to an area near what is now the corner of Market and San Fernando Streets. Nothing remains today of any Spanish or Mexican house; a school is on the first site of the pueblo.

29. San Juan Bautista Pueblo, California

Location: San Benito County, San Juan Bautista.

The Mexican Government established this pueblo in 1835, just after it secularized San Juan Bautista Mission. The pueblo had a population of only about 75 at the end of the Mexican period. Grouped around the original plaza today are several structures dating from the Spanish and Mexican periods. The residence and office of Gen. José Castro is a large, well preserved, two-story adobe building, built during the period 1839–41, on the west side of the plaza. North of it is the Plaza Hotel, whose first story the Spanish built about 1814 as a barracks for the soldiers from Monterey Presidio who guarded the mission. The second floor and balcony were added in 1858, when the structure was converted to hotel use. Both of these buildings are a part of San Juan Bautista State Historical Monument, and are open to visitors.

At Third and Franklin Streets is Casa de Juan Anza, a private residence, altered but in excellent condition, believed to have been built about 1799. On the north side of the plaza is San Juan Bautista Mission. It was founded in 1797, and its church built during the period 1803–12. The church is one of the largest in California; it measures 210 by 77 feet.

San Juan Bautista Mission sits on the north side of a historic plaza in San Juan Bautista, California. Centered around the plaza are a number of structures dating from the Spanish, Mexican, and early American periods.

The outer walls are largely original. The mission, open to the public, houses a museum that contains numerous historic relics.

30. San Juan Capistrano Mission, California

Location: Orange County, just off U.S. 101 Alt., about 3 miles north of San Juan Capistrano.

This mission, named after St. John of Capistrano, was founded in 1776 by Father Junípero Serra. Until 1794, when enlargement of the mission began, a small adobe building served as a chapel. Two adobe granaries and 40 houses for neophytes were built, followed by a cruciform church. The church, a semi-Moorish stone structure, took 9 years to complete and was regarded as the finest in California. It featured a lofty tower,

Ruins of the patio at San Juan Capistrano Mission, California. In 1776, Father Junípero Serra founded the mission. In 1812, an earthquake destroyed it, but in recent years much of it has been restored. Photograph by C. E. Watkins. Courtesy, Bancroft Library, University of California.

five interior arches of irregular stone, and massive stone walls. In 1812, a major earthquake toppled the tower and killed 40 Indians. Ruined, the church was never rebuilt. Until 1834, when the Mexicans secularized the mission, the congregation used the small adobe chapel for services. The mission participated in the international hide and tallow trade that flourished just prior to the war with Mexico.

Although the great church is in ruins, the chapel, living quarters, corridors, and gardens have been restored. Owned by the Roman Catholic Church, the mission is open to the public. A museum features Spanish and Mexican artworks and artifacts.

31. San Luis Rey de Francia Mission, California

> *Location: San Diego County, just off Calif. 76, about 5 miles east of Oceanside.*

Architecturally, this mission is probably second only to Santa Barbara Mission in its design, beauty, and extent of surviving original remains. It was established in 1798 by Father Fermín Francisco de Lasuén. The church, built during the period 1811–15, combines Spanish, Moorish, and Mexican elements in a distinguished and picturesque baroque style.

One of the most beautiful missions in California—San Luis Rey de Francia, near Oceanside. Its baroque style of architecture, a combination of Spanish, Moorish, and Mexican elements, is unique.

Secularized in 1834, the mission was turned over to Capt. Pablo de la Portilla and Pío Pica, who later became Governor.

In 1865, the mission was returned to the Roman Catholic Church by the U.S. Government, which had acquired it at the end of the war with Mexico. When the Catholic Church rededicated it as a Franciscan college, in 1893, the surface remains of the church and other mission buildings were quite extensive. Since that time, a careful program of reconstruction and restoration has been carried forward.

32. Santa Barbara Presidio and Pueblo, California

Location: Santa Barbara County, Santa Barbara.

The Presidio of Santa Barbara was the fourth and last to be founded in Alta California under Spanish authority—the others being located at San Diego, Monterey, and San Francisco. Its construction was begun on April 21, 1782, by 55 soldiers under the direction of Gov. Felipe de

Presidio and pueblo of Santa Barbara, in 1829. From a lithograph by G. & W. Endicott. Courtesy, Bancroft Library, University of California.

Neve, Capt. José Francisco Ortega, and Father Junípero Serra; shortly thereafter, Santa Barbara Mission was constructed. Log huts and a stockade 80 yards square were erected first, as well as some irrigation works

Santa Barbara Mission, in 1829. From a lithograph by G. & W. Endicott. Courtesy, Bancroft Library, University of California.

in preparation for small-scale farming. Next, the temporary wooden structures and walls were replaced by adobe buildings and walls. In August 1793, the fort was finally completed. In 1826, the town, or pueblo, of Santa Barbara was established formally by the Mexican Government. The following year from 60 to 80 one-story adobe houses, each of which had its own garden, were reportedly outside the presidio walls.

The former site of the presidio is now in an area bounded approximately by Garden, Anacapa, Carrillo, and De la Guerra Streets in the heart of the modern city. Only two relics of the presidio have survived, both considerably altered: El Cuartel, 122 Cañon Perdido Street, a small one-story, two-room house erected before 1790; and El Cañada, 121 Cañon Perdido Street, another small pre-1790 structure, that was once part of the presidio wall. In addition to the two relics of the presidio, other early structures in Santa Barbara include the De la Guerra Adobe, State and De la Guerra Streets; Casa Carrillo, 11 East Carrillo Street; and the Covarrubias Adobe, 715 Santa Barbara Street.

33. Sonoma Pueblo, California

Location: Sonoma County, Sonoma.

Sonoma Pueblo was the chief military base of the Mexican Government in Alta California from 1835 to the end of the Mexican period. Established in June 1835 both to check possible Russian expansion from Fort Ross and to control the Indians, it was founded by Lt. Mariano Guadalupe Vallejo, Military Commander and Director of the Northern Frontier and Commandant of the Presidio of San Francisco, who acted under orders from Gov. José Figueroa. Transferring his garrison from San Francisco to Sonoma, Vallejo conducted a series of successful campaigns against the Indians and his force served as a buffer to Russian expansion until the Russians withdrew from California, in 1841. Promoted to colonel in 1836 and general by 1840, Vallejo was one of the most powerful figures in Alta California.

During the years 1836–41, Lt. Mariano Guadalupe Vallejo built Sonoma Barracks, shown above, at Sonoma Pueblo. The pueblo was the chief military base of the Mexican Government in Alta California from 1835 to the end of the Mexican period.

In 1846, Sonoma Plaza was the site of the raising of the Bear Flag, the beginning of the revolt of "Yankee" settlers and others against Mexican authority. It is a Registered National Historic Landmark (relating primarily to the war with Mexico, 1846–48). Near the plaza are a number of interesting Mexican-period restored buildings, including:

(1) Sonoma Barracks, northwest corner at the intersection of Spain Street and First Street East. This large, two-story adobe structure was erected during the period 1836–41 by Vallejo. It is now a part of Sonoma State Historical Monument.

(2) Site of Vallejo's Home, *Casa Grande,* north side of Spain Street west of the barracks. The home has been demolished, but behind the

San Francisco Solano (Sonoma) Mission in the 1890's, before restoration. Courtesy, De Young Museum.

modern frame buildings still stands a two-story adobe structure that was once the servant quarters.

(3) "Swiss" Hotel, 18 West Spain Street. This two-story, balconied adobe residence was built about 1840 by Vallejo's brother Sálvador, whose residence it was until about 1865. It became a hotel in 1881.

(4) Fitch House, southwest corner of plaza (First Street West and Napa Street). Jacob P. Leese built this two-story adobe house in 1841.

San Francisco Solano (Sonoma) Mission, founded in 1823, was the last of the 21 California missions to be established.

(5) San Francisco Solano (Sonoma) Mission, northeast corner of plaza. Founded in 1823, this was the last of the 21 California missions and the only one to be established during the Mexican period. As the northernmost, its purpose was to counter Russian advances. Secularized in 1834, it soon fell into ruins. The present mission "church" is actually the chapel that was built in the years 1840–43 for use as the town church. It and the nearby *convento,* or padres' residence, have been restored and are open to the public as part of Sonoma State Historical Monument.

(6) Blue Wing Inn, 133 East Spain Street. Built in 1840, this is an excellent example of a two-story adobe hotel constructed in the Monterey colonial style.

34. Trinidad Head, California

> *Location: Humboldt County, U.S. Coast Guard Station, just off U.S. 101, about 1½ miles from Trinidad.*

The Spanish explorers Bruno Heceta and Juan Francisco de la Bodega y Cuadra visited Trinidad Bay on June 9, 1775, in their vessels, the *Santiago* and the *Sonora.* They erected a huge pine cross on the promontory and took formal possession for Charles III of Spain; they named the promontory Trinidad because it was the day following the feast of the

Holy Trinity. After briefly exploring the region and replacing a broken mast, they sailed northward. In 1793, the English explorer George Vancouver also visited the bay. The site of the original Spanish pine cross is marked by a massive granite cross, 9 feet high and weighing 2 tons, that was erected in 1913. The cross is near the lighthouse, about 400 feet above the ocean. The rugged coast area has changed little since Spanish times.

35. Villa de Branciforte (Santa Cruz), California

Location: Santa Cruz County, along North Branciforte Street, Santa Cruz.

Villa de Branciforte was established in July 1797 at the mouth of the San Lorenzo River on its east bank by 17 colonists, 9 soldiers and their families. It was the last of the three pueblos, or villas, that the Spanish founded in Alta California—the other two being San José and Los Angeles. The site, selected by engineer Lt. Alberto Córdoba, especially because of its advantages for coastal defense, was 1 mile east of Santa Cruz Mission, on the west bank of the river. Branciforte grew slowly, and it absorbed the mission when it was secularized, in 1834. However, in 1912, Branciforte gave up its historic name when the modern city of Santa Cruz annexed it. North Branciforte Avenue, originally about 1 mile long, was the only street in the old village. No remains of original Spanish or Mexican structures are extant in Santa Cruz today.

36. Yerba Buena Pueblo, California

Location: San Francisco County, on Kearny between Clay and Washington Streets, San Francisco.

This pueblo, on San Francisco Bay and not far from the Presidio of San Francisco, developed into the city of San Francisco after California officially became a part of the United States in 1848; its central plaza became Portsmouth Square. The Mexican Government established it in 1835, when a single settler, William A. Richardson, was residing there. After 5 years, the population was still only 50, and by 1846 only 200. By that time, a one-story adobe Custom House had been constructed to accommodate the growing commerce. Nothing remains today of pre-

Anchorage at Yerba Buena Pueblo (San Francisco), in 1846. From a lithograph by G. & W. Endicott. Courtesy, Bancroft Library, University of California.

1848 structures. The present plaza (Portsmouth Square), a small city park, replaces one that was destroyed several years ago to permit the construction of an underground public garage.

37. Buttolph-Williams House, Connecticut

Location: Hartford County, Broad and Marsh Streets, Wethersfield.

This house was erected by David Buttolph during the 1690's. The next owner, Benjamin Beldon, probably used it as a tavern. In 1721, Daniel Williams purchased it and his family retained possession for many years. Recognizing the house as a striking example of a 17th-century Connecticut home, in 1947 the Antiquarian and Landmarks Society of Connecticut acquired it. During restoration, the relatively recent clapboards were removed, and the original thin, pine clapboards were uncovered. The house features the typical large central chimney, overhangs, and small windows. Inside is an excellent collection of early colonial furniture and kitchen furnishings. The house is open to the public during the period May 15–October 15.

38. Henry Whitfield House, Connecticut

Location: New Haven County, Whitfield Street, Guilford.

This restored massive stone house dates from about 1639, 3 years after Henry Whitfield established Guilford. Whitfield erected it not only to shelter his wife and seven children but also to serve as a community meetinghouse and a garrison house during Indian attacks. Greatly damaged by fire in 1865, the house was reconstructed in 1868. However, only about a third of it is original—the rear wall, huge chimney on the north, and foundation.

The style, that of an English Midlands manor of the 16th or 17th centuries, is notable for steep roof and thick walls. On the first floor are the kitchen and a spacious hall, 33 by 15 feet, which has a large fireplace at each end. Living quarters are upstairs. The house is furnished with 17th-century pieces, and features exhibits of early weaving and metalworking. An herb garden outside the house is also of interest. Owned and operated by the State of Connecticut, the house is open to the public throughout the year except during the period December 15 to January 15.

39. Nehemiah Royce House, Connecticut

Location: New Haven County, 538 N. Main Street, Wallingford.

This house, erected in 1672, retains many of its 17th-century characteristics: Massive central chimney, gable-end overhang, and clapboarded sides. It is a sharp-peaked saltbox house, furnished with period pieces. Moved to its present location in 1924, it is owned by the Society for the Preservation of New England Antiquities and is open to the public during July and August.

40. Thomas Lee House, Connecticut

Location: New London County, west of Niantic on Conn. 156, near entrance to Rocky Ned State Park, East Lyme.

About 1660 Thomas Lee II built this single-room residence, to which additional rooms were later added—in 1695 and during the period 1730–35. It is perhaps the oldest frame building in Connecticut. The

Lee family occupied an important position in the life of the colony. Thomas Lee II served as constable and held a seat in the General Assembly in 1676; he also owned a considerable amount of land. Thomas Lee III, a justice of the peace for more than 40 years, used the house as his office.

The front of the house is dignified by a cornice and a handsome doorway, over which are five small window-lights. The east room, the original room, is sheathed with shadow-molded boards. The rooms to the west are plastered and paneled. All parts of the structure benefited from a 1914 restoration. The house, which contains period furnishings, is open to visitors between June 15 and September 15.

41. Hendrickson House, Delaware

> *Location: New Castle County, East Seventh and Church Streets, on the grounds of Holy Trinity (Old Swedes) Church, Wilmington.*

This is one of the few extant Swedish colonial houses. Erected some time before 1690 by Hendrick Johnson as a wedding present for his son Andrew, it was originally located on the father's property on Crum Creek at Essington, Pa. The property was sold in 1958 to an aircraft corporation, which offered the house to any group that would remove it. The house was later moved to the grounds of Holy Trinity Church, where it now serves as a museum and library commemorating Swedish settlement. Of stone construction, measuring 40 by 15 feet, it has one large and one small room on the first floor and a single large room with dormer windows on the second floor. A narrow, winding stairway connects the two levels. Both first-floor rooms have fireplaces. Originally, the house had 3 small windows, which contained 48 panes of glass.

42. McIntire House, Delaware

> *Location: New Castle County, 8 Strand, New Castle.*

This house is probably the oldest in New Castle, which contains many colonial buildings of historical and architectural interest. Evidently built around 1690, it is a superlative specimen of a small townhouse of the 17th century. Fortunately, it survived the disastrous New Castle fire of 1824. The design and excellence of paneling and fireplace treatment delight devotees of colonial buildings. Privately owned, the house is open only on New Castle Day, in the spring.

43. New Castle, Delaware

> *Location: New Castle County, on the Delaware River, 6 miles south of Wilmington.*

New Castle, one of the oldest towns in the Delaware Valley, still reflects the heritage of some of its earliest citizens, the Dutch. In 1651, Peter Stuyvesant, Governor of New Amsterdam, assumed control over a Finnish and Swedish settlement farther upriver. He erected Fort Casimir—the counterpart of New Amsterdam on the Hudson—on a spit of land since carried away by the South (Delaware) River. In 1656, the fort and the surrounding settlement was renamed New Amstel. When the British

Amstel House, erected in the early 18th century, is one of many historic structures preserved in New Castle, Delaware. Courtesy, Delaware State Development Department, Dover.

captured it in 1664 and gave it its present name, it consisted of about 100 buildings. William Penn acquired the settlement as part of Delaware in 1682, and it was there that he first set foot in America. New Castle was a seat of government in Penn's colony and later briefly the capital of Delaware.

Among the historic places in New Castle are the McIntire House and the Old Dutch House [see entries directly above and below]; the Amstel House, built before 1730; Immanuel Episcopal Church, constructed between 1703 and 1710; the Gov. Gunning Bedford House of about 1730; and the Presbyterian Church, erected in 1707.

The Green—bounded by Delaware, Market, Harmony, and Third Streets—was laid out at the order of Stuyvesant when he assumed control of the settlement, and it remains the center of the historic town. One of the interesting old buildings situated on it is the Old Court House, on the north side of Delaware Street. A 20-foot section of its east wing may have existed when William Penn assumed rule of the Delaware region. One of the best times to sightsee in New Castle is on New Castle Day, on the third Saturday in May, when most of the historic buildings are open to visitors.

44. Old Dutch House, Delaware

Location: New Castle County, 32 East Third Street, New Castle.

This house is a fine example of a small, early Dutch colonial dwelling.

Old Dutch House, in New Castle, Delaware, is a charming survivor of Dutch settlement in the Delaware River Valley.

Apparently erected during the latter half of the 17th century, when New Castle was still a small village, it may be the oldest house in Delaware. The unknown builder provided exceptionally low and wide eaves, a single dormer, and a huge central chimney. Beneath the unusual front eave is a stout door, which is flanked by two shuttered, low-lying windows. The simplicity and smallness of the house contrast sharply with the grander and larger buildings of New Castle's later days. The house, which is also known as the Dutch House Museum, contains an excellent collection of Dutch furniture. Restored by the Delaware Society for the Preservation of Antiquities in 1938 and now owned by the New Castle Historical Society, it is open to the public throughout the year.

45. Swedish Blockhouse, Delaware

Location: New Castle County, on Naaman's Creek, just west of U.S. 13, about ½ mile south of Delaware-Pennsylvania boundary.

This two-story stone structure was probably erected in 1654 by the Governor of New Sweden, Johan Rising. It has a steep hip roof. The small loopholes beneath the eaves enabled muskets to be fired at attackers. A narrow stairway leads from the first to the second floor. A corner chimney and brick oven are located on the first floor. Dutch soldiers took over the blockhouse in 1655, when New Sweden fell into Dutch hands, but 6 years later it fell to the Indians. It changed hands twice during the War for Independence. During the 18th century, it was incorporated into an inn, and remains part of a public house to this day.

46. St. Augustine, Florida

Location: St. Johns County.

The first permanent European settlement within the present United States and a longtime seat of Spanish power in the New World, St. Augustine was established in 1565 by Don Pedro Menéndez de Avilés. His purpose, which was successfully executed, was to drive out the French, who had founded a settlement at Fort Caroline the previous year. From his strategically located and easily defended new base, Menéndez destroyed the fort and massacred a French force, led by Jean Ribaut, which had set out from Fort Caroline to attack the Spanish but had been shipwrecked south of St. Augustine. As a result, France lost its hold in the region.

Old Spanish Kitchen, photographed from the "Oldest House," in St. Augustine. Courtesy of J. Carver Harris, Photographer.

The Spanish controlled St. Augustine during two periods: 1565–1763 and 1783–1821. During the first period, when their power in the New World was at its zenith, the city was a vital center of imperial activity. It was the military base of operations for countering British and French influence in the region and headquarters of the missionary effort to convert the Indians, which involved the establishment of a series of missions in the present States of Georgia, South Carolina, and Florida.

As the focal point of Spanish power in the region, St. Augustine was frequently attacked—particularly by the principal antagonists of the Spanish in the region, the English. In 1586, Sir Francis Drake raided and burned the city, but the colonists returned and rebuilt it. Throughout the following century, English buccaneers, Indians, and other raiding parties harassed it; as a defense, in 1672 the authorities began to build the major fortification, Castillo de San Marcos.

The first period of Spanish influence in the region ended in effect in 1742, when Gen. James Oglethorpe, British commander in Georgia and South Carolina, who 2 years earlier had seriously threatened St. Augustine, defeated the Spanish when they tried to capture Fort Frederica. In 1763, the Treaty of Paris confirmed British control of Florida. When the British occupied St. Augustine, most of the colonists fled to Cuba, whose sovereignty had been transferred back to Spain by the British in exchange

Dining Room of "Oldest House," in St. Augustine. The house, constructed about 1703, now serves as headquarters of the St. Augustine Historical Society. Courtesy, J. Carver Harris, Photographer.

for Florida. Yet the city prospered under British rule. During the War for Independence, it was a refuge for Tories and an important base for British operations against the southern colonies.

By 1783, when Spain regained Florida, her international influence was waning, especially in the New World. In 1819, she ceded Florida to the United States by treaty; and, in 1821, the same year the treaty was finally ratified, she lost all her territory in North America because of the Mexican Revolution. For these reasons, and also because of the initial encroachment of American frontiersmen, Spanish reoccupation of St. Augustine in 1783 was little more than nominal.

St. Augustine still reveals much of its Spanish inheritance. It has many narrow, winding streets, which end abruptly in cross streets. Of particular note is the Plaza de la Constitución, which contains a public market and is lined by important civic buildings. Established in 1598, it is the oldest public square in the United States. Its name commemorates the Spanish liberal constitution of 1812. Many extant or reconstructed buildings reflect Spanish influence. Some of these are described below:

(1) The "Oldest House," 14 St. Francis Street. This house, which

features coquina walls and hand-hewn beams, was constructed about 1703 on a site occupied since at least the early 1600's. The St. Augustine Historical Society owns it and uses it for its headquarters. Adjoining the house is the Webb Memorial Library and Museum.

(2) Llambias House, 31 St. Francis Street. Built during the first Spanish occupation, this house was constructed of coquina. It is named after one of its owners, T. Llambias, one of a group of Minorcan immigrants who relocated from New Smyrna to St. Augustine during the British occupation in 1777. Now restored, it is operated by the St. Augustine Historical Society.

(3) Old Spanish Treasury, corner of St. George and Treasury Streets. This is one of the best examples of Spanish architecture of the later period. It is a flat-roofed house, which has white shutters. The first story is of yellow stuccoed stone; the second, of wood. The house is furnished with 19th-century pieces. The Woman's Exchange maintains it as a museum and operates an adjoining shop.

(4) Old Spanish Inn, 43 St. George Street. One of St. Augustine's oldest surviving buildings, it has been restored to resemble an early 18th-century inn in Spain. Nine rooms are furnished with authentic Spanish pieces brought from Madrid, Toledo, Seville, Granada, and Barcelona.

(5) Fatio House, on Aviles Street just south of the public library. This is a two-story stuccoed building of coquina which has a red tile roof. In excellent condition, it was built by Andrew Ximenez between 1806 and 1821 in a style associated with the second Spanish occupation. The old slave quarters, kitchen, patio, and balconies provide space for gift-shops, painters' studios, and apartments.

Celebrating its 400th anniversary in 1965 with special ceremonies and programs throughout the year, St. Augustine launched additional reconstruction projects.

47. San Francisco de Oconee (Scott Miller Site), Florida

Location: Jefferson County, about 2½ miles southeast of Waukeenah.

Archeological study suggests that a Spanish mission—thought to be San Francisco de Oconee—was founded at this site around 1650. About 1633, intensive Spanish mission activity began among the Indians of present northwest Florida. By 1702, when Spanish influence was at its height, the Spanish had established 14 missions in Apalachee Province, but 2 years later destroyed or abandoned all of them because of English and Creek raids. Excavation has uncovered remains of two buildings, constructed by the wattle and daub technique, which had floors of packed red clay. Items of Spanish origin were quite common, including sherds of majolica and tinaja, pistol flintlocks, a spur rowel, beads, hinges, locks, an anvil, axes, and hoes, as well as fragments of Chinese porcelain. The site is now in farmland.

48. San Marcos de Apalache (Fort St. Marks), Florida

Location: Wakulla County, on Fla. 363, about 2 miles south of U.S. 98, at the junction of the Wakulla and St. Marks Rivers, just south of the village of St. Marks.

San Marcos de Apalache was of great importance in the mid-17th century, when Spain occupied the Province of Apalachee, centered in the Florida Panhandle. Apalachee's fertile soil provided grain, sorely needed at St. Augustine, and the Wakulla-St. Marks River junction was the logical shipping point. A flimsy, wooden fortification built in 1660 at the site by the Spanish was captured in 1682 by a raiding party of French, English, and Indians. Repossessed by the Spanish, who built a stronger wooden fort, the site became the nucleus of a sizable settlement, but the Spanish abandoned it after Col. James Moore of South Carolina raided Apalachee in 1704.

In 1718, Capt. José Primo de Rivera arrived with a new force and rebuilt a third wooden fort on the site. A few years later, the Spaniards began to construct a stone fort, but it had not been completed when England acquired Florida in 1763, holding it until 1783. The British firm of Panton, Leslie & Co. established a trading center at the site and remained after the Spanish reoccupation, in 1787. San Marcos, as a result, became a thriving center of Indian trade. Gen. Andrew Jackson captured it in 1818 during the Seminole campaign and executed two British traders near the fort, one of the episodes that brought United States-Spanish relations to a crisis and influenced the Spanish to sign the Adams-Onís Treaty, by which the United States acquired Florida.

During the Civil War, the Confederates superimposed entrenchments and fortifications upon the ruins of the earlier Spanish forts. The tract, in State ownership, is heavily wooded, and only a portion of the stonework from the late Spanish fort stands above ground. The fort site is open to the public. A museum houses artifacts found in the area and exhibits prepared by the Florida State Museum.

[When this volume was in an advanced stage of publication, the Advisory Board declared Fort San Marcos de Apalache to be eligible for the Registry of National Historic Landmarks.]

49. Santa Catalina de Guale Mission Site, Georgia

Location: Liberty County, on St. Catherine's Island.

The Spanish Franciscan mission of Santa Catalina de Guale was the most important on the coast of present Georgia during the 17th century. It had been constructed by the time Gov. Pedro de Ybarra visited Guale (Georgia) in 1604, following the Guale revolt of 1597, although the precise date is uncertain. It continued to be the most significant mission in the area until its abandonment in 1686 in the face of continued English inspired and directed raids from the Carolinas. No surface indications of the mission buildings are visible today, but excavation has uncovered Spanish and Indian pottery sherds of the period and a few iron nails. The site, well preserved, is owned by a private foundation. Now in forest and underbrush, it is used for grazing.

50. Spanish Mission Site, Georgia

Location: McIntosh County, on Altamaha River, just east of Darien.

This site was probably the location of Santo Domingo de Talaje Mission, one of the Spanish missions to the Guale Indians during the period 1600–1675. Excavation of the site has revealed large, square postholes outlining a rectangular building 70 by 35 feet that was obviously not of Indian design. Three burials in the cemetery of nearby Fort King George, which was active during the period 1721–26, were superimposed over some of the postholes. Because the postholes contained only Indian and 17th-century Spanish materials, they undoubtedly were dug, used, and refilled before Fort King George was established.

A wall enclosed the rectangular building as well as a small, Indian-type house to its rear. Outside the wall to the east were shallow wall trenches and small, round postholes of 15 Indian houses. Nearly 200 sherds of Spanish majolica and tinaja, dating from the first half of the 17th century, substantiate the dating and verify Spanish occupation of the mission. Most of the site is in a State-owned tract that includes the sites of Fort King George and Fort Darien.

51. Cahokia Courthouse, Illinois

Location: St. Clair County, just off Ill. 3, Cahokia.

Capt. Jean Baptiste Saucier, the builder of Fort de Chartres, shortly after 1737 built this log-and-stone structure for his residence. It is a unique monument to the early French settlers of the Illinois country and an excellent example of French colonial architecture. The oldest house in Illinois, possibly the earliest surviving dwelling in the Midwest, and without doubt the oldest courthouse west of the Allegheny Mountains, it has been completely reconstructed.

Old Holy Family Church, Cahokia, Illinois, dates from about 1799. Restored in 1951, it is used regularly for religious services. Courtesy, *Evening and Sunday Journal,* East St. Louis.

An excellent example of French colonial architecture, Cahokia Courthouse, Cahokia, Illinois, was originally a residence. Between 1793 and 1814, it served as a U.S. courthouse.

The construction is of special interest because of the vertical placement of the wall logs; the interstices contain stone and mortar. The building measures about 35 by 43 feet—unusually large—and consists of four rooms and a large attic. The builder's son sold it to the United States in 1793, after which it served as a U.S. courthouse and a center of political activity in the old Northwest. After the county seat was moved from Cahokia in 1814, it was used as a saloon, storehouse, public hall, and finally as a home again.

In 1904, the building was exhibited at the Louisiana Purchase Exposition in St. Louis, and was then purchased by the Chicago Historical Society. Part of it was exhibited in Jackson Park, Chicago, until 1938, when Illinois State archeologists excavated the original foundation site and discovered a number of objects relating to the building. In 1939, as part of a WPA program, the building was reerected on the original site, and much of the original material employed. The State of Illinois maintains the Cahokia Courthouse as a State memorial.

52. Fort Kaskaskia State Park, Illinois

Location: Randolph County, on Ill. 3, about 5 miles north of the village of Chester.

The area memorialized by this park has been under the flags of three nations: France, Great Britain, and the United States. Kaskaskia, established by the French in 1703, prospered as an important outpost on the Mississippi and a source of agricultural commodities. During the French and Indian War, the French erected a palisaded fort on the hill across the Kaskaskia River. Apparently it was never attacked, and the inhabitants destroyed it themselves after the Treaty of Paris in 1763, when the British assumed control of the Illinois country.

During the American War for Independence, George Rogers Clark captured Kaskaskia. From 1809 to 1818, the town served as the first capital of Illinois Territory. When Illinois became a State in 1818, it served as the capital for 2 years, but after 1820 began to decline. A disastrous Mississippi flood in 1844 destroyed most of the town, and in 1910 another flood completely obliterated the site.

Fort Kaskaskia State Park includes the home of Pierre Menard, built in 1802, which stands just below the hill on which the fort stood. The home is an excellent example of French colonial architecture. Nearby, close to the fort site, is the Garrison Hill Cemetery, which contains the remains of many early settlers. Some of the ramparts of Fort Kaskaskia are still visible, and on Kaskaskia Island the State of Illinois has erected a memorial to the pioneer French settlement.

53. Fort Massac, Illinois

Location: Massac County, on U.S. 45, about 1 mile southeast of Metropolis

The original Fort Massac, named Fort Ascension, was erected in 1757 by the French to thwart British encroachment into the lower Ohio Valley. The following year, the French renamed it Fort Massiac. Cherokee Indians made the only known attack upon the fort, in the fall of 1757. At the end of the French and Indian War, when the French lost the area east of the Mississippi River to England, they abandoned the fort and it steadily declined. It was soon destroyed by the Cherokees, and the ruins were left untouched by the British.

In 1794, the United States rebuilt the fort to guard against Spanish attack and renamed it Fort Massac. After the War of 1812, it was abandoned. In 1903, when little more than the site remained, the Daughters of the American Revolution preserved part of the original site and made possible some reconstruction. The State of Illinois maintains the area now as a State memorial. Wood posts outline the first fort and its buildings, and a moat has been rebuilt.

54. Père Marquette State Park, Illinois

Location: Jersey County, on Ill. 100, about 6 miles west of Grafton.

Père Marquette State Park, the largest in Illinois, commemorates the beginning of European exploration of the rich Illinois country and its subsequent settlement and development. The Illinois and Potawatomi Indians were occupying the area of the park when Père Marquette, along with Louis Jolliet and five other companions, passed by in the fall of 1673. At the confluence of the Illinois and Mississippi Rivers is located a large, plain cross in honor of Père Marquette's party. The park provides extensive accommodations for visitors, including a lodge and guesthouses, a nature museum, and interesting roadways.

55. Vincennes, Indiana

Location: Knox County.

The oldest town in Indiana, Vincennes retains to this day something of its French inheritance. The initial date of settlement is not known, but a French trading post may have been located at the site as early as 1683. Settlers were known to have been residing there by 1727, and a fort was constructed about 1732. The early settlement was called by various names, such as Au Poste, Post Ouabache (Wabash), and Post St. Francis Xavier. After Indians captured and executed the commander of the fort, Francois Marie Bissot, Sieur de Vincennes, in 1736, the settlers named the town after him. Of the three earliest French settlements in present Indiana—the other two being Fort Ouiatenon and Fort Miami—only Vincennes survived and prospered.

After the French and Indian War, the British took over the settlement and built a new fort, Fort Sackville. In 1779, George Rogers Clark, recognizing Vincennes' strategic location, captured it for the United States. When Indiana Territory was created in 1800, Vincennes became the seat of government, and William Henry Harrison was appointed Governor. In 1813, the capital was moved to Corydon.

The most tangible remaining evidence of French influence in Vincennes today is the Old French Cemetery, located on the grounds of the St. Francis Xavier Cathedral, at Second and Church Streets. This cemetery contains the remains of many early settlers; the earliest burial was in

1741. The cathedral, construction of which began in 1825, was built on or near the site of a chapel that had been erected when Vincennes was established.

56. Arkansas City Country Club Site, Kansas

Location: Cowley County, on the bluffs east of Walnut River, about 1 mile east of Arkansas City.

Most historians, ethnologists, and archeologists agree that the area referred to by the early Spanish explorers as "Quivira" is the central and south-central Kansas of today, especially along the Smoky Hill and Arkansas Rivers and their immediate tributaries. Quiviran sites have been excavated in Cowley, Rice, and McPherson Counties. Coronado visited the area in 1541, Fray Juan de Padilla in 1542, the Bonilla-Humaña expedition about 1590, and the Oñate expedition in 1601.

The Arkansas City Country Club Site, one of the most interesting sites, is unique among Quiviran sites because it contains two relatively large mounds as well as smaller ones. No artifacts of European origin have been found during the limited excavations carried out to date, but other evidence reveals contact with the Pueblo Indians of the Rio Grande Valley. The Quiviran culture represented at the Arkansas City Country Club Site and at other Cowley County sites is very similar to that of the Rice and McPherson County sites. The site, located on a golf course, is well sodded and excellently preserved.

57. Fanning Site, Kansas

Location: Doniphan County, on a ridge between Wolf Creek and the Missouri River Valley, about 1 mile north of Fanning.

This site, the location of a late 17th-century Kansa Indian village, reflects early contact between the Indians and European traders and trappers. Small quantities of iron, glass beads, and brass items have been discovered in trash-filled cache pits, including a few knife blades that were undoubtedly obtained from some of the small parties of French traders and trappers which ventured up the Missouri and its tributaries late in the 17th century.

The identification and significance of the Fanning Site is strengthened by its apparent relationship with the Doniphan Site, 16 miles to the north, which was the principal village of the Kansa tribe in 1724, when the French trader Étienne Veniard de Bourgmond visited them. European goods found at the Doniphan Site are believed to have come from Bourgmond's trading post, Fort Orleans, established in 1723 near present Malta Bend, Mo. The Fanning Site, now in farmland, is well preserved.

58. Fort St. Jean Baptiste de Natchitoches Sites, Louisiana

Location: Natchitoches Parish, New Second Street and vicinity, Natchitoches.

Fort St. Jean Baptiste, which the French began to construct in 1715, was the first fortified outpost on the frontier between French Louisiana and New Spain. Its location remained internationally significant for well over a century. In 1719, the garrison, commanded by Philippe Blondel, destroyed the Spanish mission at Los Adaes, 15 miles away, which had been established in 1716. As a result, in 1721–22 the Spanish founded a presidio at Los Adaes. In 1731, the Natchez Indians, fresh from slaughtering the Fort Rosalie garrison in Natchez, attacked Fort St. Jean Baptiste. With the help of friendly Indian reinforcements, the French wiped out the attackers.

In 1737, because of recurrent floods, a new fort was built on high ground, in what is now the American Cemetery, and the old fort abandoned. The latter fort is known to have been in existence in 1769. No evidence of the forts remains above ground, however, and further archeological investigation will be required to authenticate the sites and provide additional information. The earlier site, 200 yards east of the new site, is owned by the Association of Natchitoches Women for the Preservation of Historic Natchitoches, and local leaders are planning to reconstruct the original fort.

59. Fort St. Philip, Louisiana

Location: Plaquemines Parish, on the left bank of the Mississippi River, opposite Triumph.

Francisco Luís Hector, Baron de Carondelet, Governor of Louisiana and West Florida, built this fort in 1795, as a part of his plan to extend

Spain's dominion over the entire Mississippi Valley and to prevent the encroachment of American frontiersmen. His plan included the instigation of Indian attacks on the frontiersmen; a fleet of gunboats patrolling the Mississippi River; and a series of forts along the border area of the territory, including Fort St. Philip.

The fort figured prominently in the Civil War, along with Fort Jackson across the river, when Adm. David Farragut and his Union fleet bombarded the two forts in 1862 and then was able to seize the city of New Orleans. (Fort St. Philip has been designated as eligible for the Registry of National Historic Landmarks, relating primarily to the Civil War.) The Army did not garrison the fort after 1871, although it made repairs during World War I with a view to possible use. After the war, the Government sold the fort and it has remained in private ownership. The 1,100 acres of the former St. Philip Military Reservation stretch along the Mississippi River for 2 miles and are accessible only by boat. The site, covered with orange trees, is privately owned. Ruins of the early fort may be seen, along with some World War I buildings.

60. Longfellow-Evangeline State Park, Louisiana

> *Location: St. Martin Parish, on the Bayou Teche, 1 mile east of St. Martinsville.*

This park commemorates the migration of the Acadians—now called Cajuns—who first settled in the British seaboard colonies and from 1760 on eventually settled on an irregular basis in Louisiana after being exiled from Nova Scotia because of their religious beliefs. In his poem "Evangeline," Longfellow popularized the migration and the many years of hardships the Acadians faced while searching for a homeland. The people living in the immediate vicinity of the park, and in the surrounding communities, are their direct descendants and speak with an Anglo-French dialect. The museum in the park—a house once reputedly occupied by Louis Arceneaux, the "Gabriel" of Longfellow's poem—commemorates the story of Gabriel and Evangeline and Acadian history.

61. Presidio of Los Adaes Site, Louisiana

> *Location: Natchitoches Parish, just north of La. 6, about 2 miles northeast of Robeline.*

Concerned by the threat of French encroachment into Spanish-claimed territory, the Spaniards in 1716 established San Miguel de Linares Mission a few miles southwest of the French settlement and fort at Natchitoches. In 1719, the mission was attacked and destroyed by a French force from Fort St. Jean Baptiste de Natchitoches, but in 1721–22 the Spanish returned and rebuilt, on an adjoining hill, the Presidio of Nuestra Señora del Pilar de los Adaes (Adais).

For the next half-century, the presidio was an important outpost and the capital of the frontier province of Texas, the seat of 13 Spanish Governors down until 1773. In the last decade of its existence, it consisted only of a hexagonal fort, defended by 6 cannons and 100 soldiers, and a village of about 40 "miserable houses constructed with stakes driven into the ground."

Long after the presidio had been abandoned, in 1806, the site's strategic importance was still recognized by the signing there of a preliminary treaty between Ens. Joseph María Gonzales and Capt. Edward Turner of the U.S. Army. Gonzales agreed to retreat to Spanish-owned Texas and to cease sending Spanish patrols across the border into the United States. This treaty led to the formal establishment, a few weeks later, of "neutral ground" between Texas and the United States by Gen. James Wilkinson and Spanish Lt. Comdr. Simon de Herrera. The two nations honored the boundary for 14 years.

Only a few unidentified mounds of earth are visible today on the attractive ridge where the presidio stood. Of the 40 acres or so encompassing the presidio, mission, and village sites, about 9 acres are in public ownership as a historical park. The National Society of the Daughters of American Colonists and the State of Louisiana have commemorated the site with markers.

62. St. Louis Cathedral, Louisiana

Location: Orleans Parish, Jackson Square, New Orleans.

The site of this cathedral, facing the historic Place d'Armes, or Jackson Square, has been consecrated to the Roman Catholic Church from the earliest days of New Orleans. The stately cathedral now occupying the site honors the patron saint of Bourbon France, who was also the patron of *Nouvelle Orléans*. The first church on the site, a small adobe-wood structure called the Parish Church, was erected by Bienville soon after 1718, when he founded the city, but in 1723 a hurricane destroyed it.

Although extensive alterations have obscured its original appearance, St. Louis Cathedral, constructed between 1789 and 1794, exemplifies the Spanish period in the Vieux Carré, New Orleans.

The second church, of brick and wood, served from 1727 until destroyed in the great fire of 1788, which damaged most of the city.

The present St. Louis Cathedral, built between 1789 and 1794, originally resembled other Spanish-built churches in Mexico and South America. Extensive alterations made in 1851, however, included enlargement of the building and addition of steeples and the present columned and pilastered portico. These alterations, along with two subsequent renovations, have obscured the original appearance of the church.

63. Sang pour Sang Hill, Louisiana

Location: Natchitoches Parish, just south of Cloutierville.

This high, rocky, tree-studded hill is located adjacent to and named after a former lake called *Sang pour Sang,* which is now completely dry. In 1732, a group of Natchez Indians took refuge on the shores of this lake after fleeing down the Red River from Fort St. Jean Baptiste de Natchitoches. In 1731, they had besieged the fort unsuccessfully but burned a captive Frenchwoman alive in full view of the garrison. In retaliation, St. Denis, the commander of the fort, led 40 of his soldiers and 100 Indian allies against the Natchez and killed 92 warriors and 4 chiefs. The surviving Indians fled to the shores of the lake, where the Frenchmen found and annihilated them.

64. Norridgewock Site, Maine

Location: Somerset County, on U.S. 201 Alt., about 7 miles north of Norridgewock Town, at Old Point.

Norridgewock, or *Nanrantsouak,* is the site of an Abnaki Indian village, where a French Jesuit mission was established in 1646 and served the Indians for decades. Enmity later arose between the English and French, and in 1701 English officials ordered that the mission be closed. In 1704–5, the British destroyed the mission buildings, but Father Sebastian Rasle had a temporary structure built while work was carried forward on a new church, completed in 1718.

In 1722, however, the English returned again; 200 Englishmen under Capt. John Harmon pillaged the church and carried off the manuscript of a dictionary of the Abnaki language on which Father Rasle had been working for many years. Two years later, Father Rasle was killed during another English attack, when the church and Indian village were destroyed. In fear of further attacks, the Indians abandoned the site, part of them going to Canada. Nothing remains of the settlement today. The site is now a camping area that is owned by the State of Maine and includes some privately owned land.

65. Popham Colony Site (lost site), Maine

Location: Sagadahoc County, just off Maine 209, near Popham Beach in Phippsburg Town.

The first English colony in New England was founded at this site late in the summer of 1607 by the Plymouth Company in its effort to settle "North Virginia." Unlike the London Company's similar venture in "South Virginia," at Jamestown in the same year, this attempt was unsuccessful. The party of more than 100 colonists, led by George Popham and Raleigh Gilbert, landed on a point at the mouth of the Kennebec (then the Sagadahoc) River. They immediately constructed Fort St. George, after which they built a small ship. Severe weather and bad luck, however, plagued them. A fire during the winter destroyed most of their provisions, George Popham died, and Raleigh Gilbert had to return to England. This left the colony vulnerable and without effective leadership. Defeated, the survivors returned to England late in 1608.

The colony was located in the general area of Popham Beach on Sabino Head. The assumed site is on a 45-acre tract of land owned by the State. It is virtually unspoiled by modern intrusions, except for a few scattered framehouses and the concrete remains of Fort Baldwin, a World War I coast defense installation.

66. St. Croix Island, Maine

Location: Washington County, in the mouth of the St. Croix River.

In 1604, Pierre du Guast, Sieur de Monts, a French Huguenot, aided by Samuel de Champlain, established a colony on this island. It was one of the first French New World settlements and, though unsuccessful, was a challenge to England for the colonization of North America. The colonists suffered a disastrous winter; lack of food and water caused a scurvy epidemic, and many of them died. After a month of searching for a better site, in 1605 the leaders moved the colony across the Bay of Fundy to the site of Port Royal, Nova Scotia. In 1613, the British destroyed all of the buildings left on the island. Archeological investigation by the National Park Service has revealed burials and other traces of the original French settlement. Public Law 87, 81st Congress, approved June 8, 1949, authorized establishment of St. Croix Island National Monument.

Built in 1653 by the townspeople of York, Maine, York Gaol now serves as a museum and contains colonial and Indian relics. A portion of the original stone wall may be seen in this photograph. Photograph by Douglas Armsden. Courtesy, Old Gaol Museum Committee, York.

67. York Gaol, Maine

Location: York County, Long Lands Road, York.

This is one of the oldest public buildings in New England. York was established in 1624 by the Plymouth Company. In 1641, it formed a government and adopted a city charter, and in 1652 reorganized into a town. The townspeople then constructed many public buildings, such as the gaol, which is the oldest extant building in York. Built of stone in 1653, its walls are now covered with wood siding, and a large gambrel roof has been added. The original prisoners' cells may be seen in the old part of the structure. The gaol, now a museum containing colonial and Indian relics, is open to the public during the summer.

68. Cross Manor, Maryland

Location: St. Marys County, just off Md. 5, about 1 mile below St. Inigoes.

Built about 1643, Cross Manor is probably the oldest house in Maryland.

Constructed of brick on a 2,000-acre grant that Thomas Cornwallis obtained in 1639, it originally had a gambrel roof. The roof was later changed to a gabled design and other alterations were made. The gardens, about as old as the residence, are of interest; some of the ancient boxwood are at least 35 feet in circumference. The house is privately owned, but may be visited by appointment.

69. Hill Farm, Maryland

Location: Calvert County, just northwest of Md. 266, below Lusby.

This frame farmhouse, situated on a hill overlooking St. Leonard's Creek, is a superlative specimen of an unpretentious early farm dwelling. Dating from about 1670, it still has the original pine siding. Three small dormer windows jut from the steep roof, and brick chimneys are located at each end of the house. A log cabin, added sometime after the original construction, now forms an attractive wing. The house has been restored and furnished with period furniture. Though privately owned, it may be visited by appointment.

70. Holly Hill, Maryland

Location: Calvert County, 1½ miles from Friendship.

This is one of Maryland's most appealing and lovely early colonial houses, both on the interior and exterior. The original section of the **T**-shaped residence was constructed about 1667, and the most recent wing about 1720. The one-story brick house has gabled ends, a steeply pitched roof, and several imposing chimneys. Boxwood and flower borders complement the exterior. Inside, two original murals are especially noteworthy, one located over a mantel and the other over the dining room door. After the house was restored, the owners installed a collection of early 18th-century American and French antiques. The house is privately owned, but it is open by appointment.

71. St. Marys City, Maryland

Location: St. Marys County.

This city, presently the location of St. Marys College, is the site of the first English settlement in Maryland. When Leonard Calvert, brother of the Lord Proprietor of the colony, sailed into the mouth of the Potomac River and up the St. Marys River in 1634, his two ships dropped anchor near an Indian village whose inhabitants were moving away because of fear of other Indians. The 200 colonists settled in the abandoned Indian village and soon erected a fort. Later, a town evolved and grew along with other newer nearby settlements. In 1676, it was the capital of a bustling colony. In that year, a statehouse was erected for the use of the colonial assembly.

In 1694, however, the capital was moved to Anne Arundel Town, renamed Annapolis the following year, and shortly thereafter St. Marys City lost even its county seat status. As a result, it rapidly declined. No original 17th-century building has survived, though foundations of some of the 60 houses built in the 1600's lay under shallow coverings of dirt. The present reconstruction of the early statehouse, on Middle Street, was inspired by the Maryland Tercentenary Celebration of 1934. It is furnished with copies of period furniture. Nearly all the land of the old central city is privately owned. In 1965, the State was examining the possibility of reconstructing parts of the city.

72. House of Seven Gables, Massachusetts

Location: Essex County, 54 Turner Street, Salem.

Long known as the Turner House, the House of Seven Gables is now identified—perhaps inaccurately—with the novel of the same name, published in 1852, by Nathaniel Hawthorne. The earliest section of the weatherbeaten, rambling house was probably built about 1668, and it

House of Seven Gables, Massachusetts. Courtesy, Eric H. Muller, Photographer.

shows medieval influence. The house has been expanded at various times and the number of gables increased from the original four to seven. In 1910, it was restored. Numerous pieces of furniture used by various owners are exhibited, as well as items associated with Hawthorne. The House of Seven Gables Settlement Association owns the house, which is open to the public throughout the year.

73. Jethro Coffin House, Massachusetts

Location: Nantucket County, Sunset Hill Road, Nantucket Island.

This is one of the few extant 17th-century houses of the long-popular Cape Cod style and is one of the best examples. Built about 1686, it features the characteristic steeply pitched roof, having an unusually long rearward slope, and the typical massive central chimney. Small, medieval-type windows indicate the house's great age. The tall chimney has an exceptionally interesting flue device, and inverted horseshoe, which was supposed to ward off witches. In 1927, the house was completely restored. Maintained by the Nantucket Historical Society, it is open to the public between June 15 and October 1.

74. John Ward House, Massachusetts

Location: Essex County, 132 Essex Street, Salem.

This clapboard-covered house, built in 1684, reflects the architectural mode of the era. It originally had only one room, but was later expanded into a two-story structure that was distinguished by cross gables and an overhang. Moved to the present location in 1909, where it was restored and furnished, it includes colonial furnishings. The exposed beams of the kitchen and the fascinating collection of early kitchenware and utensils are of special interest. The Essex Institute owns the house, which is open to the public from June through September.

75. Peter Tufts House, Massachusetts

Location: Middlesex County, 350 Riverside Avenue, Medford.

This is probably the oldest brick house in New England. Built in 1678,

Peter Tufts House, Massachusetts, built in 1678. It is maintained by the Society for the Preservation of New England Antiquities.

it is a two-story, gambrel-roof structure that has two rooms in each story. The builders placed portholes for muskets in the front wall on both floors because Indians still posed a threat when the house was erected. Despite a remodeling of the house in the 1890's, the exterior and the great oak beams inside make it one of New England's most interesting colonial dwellings. Maintained by the Society for the Preservation of New England Antiquities, it is open to the public throughout the year on a limited schedule.

76. Plymouth Rock, Massachusetts

Location: Plymouth County, just off Water Street, Plymouth.

This great granite rock—incised with the date 1620—commemorates the landing of the Pilgrims in New England. Resting under a portico of classical design, surrounded by an iron fence, and lying two-thirds underground, it is located at the foot of Cole's Hill. Historians have not been able to determine definitely whether or not it was the actual point where the first exploring party came ashore. No mention of the

The landing of the Pilgrims in the New World is commemorated at Plymouth Rock, Massachusetts. The rock, surrounded by an iron fence, lies under this portico, at the bottom of Cole's Hill.

landing place was made in the official records of the Pilgrims. In any event, as the traditional symbol of the landing, the rock is venerated by the people of the United States.

77. Rebecca Nurse House, Massachusetts

Location: Essex County, 149 Pine Street, Danvers.

Built in 1678, this is an interesting 17th-century clapboard house whose simple lines and basic workmanship demonstrate colonial building skills. The builder was Francis Nurse, but the house derives its name from his wife Rebecca, who in 1692 was condemned and hanged as a witch during the witchcraft hysteria. She stoutly maintained her innocence, yet could not satisfy her accusers. The house has been restored and is furnished with period pieces. Owned by the Society for the Preservation of New England Antiquities, it is open to the public between June 15 and October 15. At other times, it may be visited by appointment.

78. William Harlow House, Massachusetts

Locqtion: Plymouth County, corner of Sandwich and South Streets, Plymouth.

This house is one of several extant 17th-century structures in Plymouth. When Sgt. William Harlow built it in 1677, he used lumber taken from the fort on Burial Hill. Now restored, the house is owned by the Plymouth Antiquarian Society. Costumed hostesses perform spinning, weaving, candlemaking, and other household arts of the 17th century. The house is open from May 30 to September 30.

79. Fort L'Huillier Site, Minnesota

Location: Blue Earth County, right bank of Blue Earth River, near its junction with the Le Sueur River, just southwest of Mankato.

Pierre Charles le Sueur established Fort L'Huillier in 1700 as a headquarters for trading and mining. The fort consisted of three or four log cabins surrounded by a palisade. When Le Sueur returned to France the following year he carried with him much geographical data—such as the location of Indian villages and streams—that were incorporated in various maps and travel accounts. He also reportedly had 2 tons of the local blue earth transported to Paris at great expense, only to find that it was merely clay instead of the valuable copper ore he believed it to be. The site of Fort L'Huillier is on a large natural mound, about 60 to 75 feet high, on the top of which are a few acres of fairly level ground. The site is in farmland, and evidence of the fort's structures has been destroyed by cultivation.

80. Fort St. Charles Site, Minnesota

Location: Lake of the Woods County, Magnusson Island, on the southern shore of the Northwest Angle Inlet, near Penasse.

In 1732, Pierre Gaultier de Varennes, Sieur de la Vérendrye, established Fort St. Charles as his westernmost headquarters, and it became the focal point for French fur trade and exploration in a large region. The fort consisted of an oblong palisade of posts, about 12 to 15 feet high, within which were located several rough cabins, a missionary's residence, commandant's house, chapel, powder magazine, storehouse, and other structures. Two gates were located opposite each other, and the fort had an observation tower.

In 1736, La Vérendrye sent a relief party from the fort to Michilimackinac Island—1,500 miles away—for supplies. The party of 19 voyageurs and 3 canoes, led by La Vérendrye's son, Jean Baptiste, and Jesuit Father Aulneau, camped on a small island in the Lake of the Woods (now called Massacre Island), where Indians massacred them. The elder La Vérendrye brought the bodies back to the fort and buried them beneath the chapel. In the early 1750's, the fort was abandoned.

In 1908, an archeological expedition under the auspices of the Historical Society of St. Boniface discovered the site. Excavation revealed the ruins of a large fireplace; the locations of the chapel, the priest's house, and the commandant's quarters; remnants of the palisade; and apparently some skeletal remains of the Jean Baptiste de la Vérendrye party. In 1951, the Knights of Columbus placed a granite altar on the spot where the original chapel stood. Today, Fort St. Charles is marked by a conjecturally reconstructed stockade of cedar poles. The foundations of the original huts have been marked, and the chapel reconstructed of concrete "logs." The site is owned by the Minnesota Fourth Degree Knights of Columbus.

81. Davion's Bluff (Loftus Heights), Mississippi

Location: Wilkinson County, Fort Adams Road, Fort Adams.

In 1698, a French mission was established by Fathers Davion and Montigny at this bluff, on the bank of the Mississippi River. The site is of considerable historic interest in relation to the changing fortunes of the European powers in the lower Mississippi Valley in the 18th century, and in the later growth and development of the United States. Davion's Bluff became known as Loftus Heights following the ambush there in 1764 of an English force under Maj. Arthur Loftus.

In 1799, the United States constructed Fort Adams on the heights after the Spanish withdrew from the Natchez district. This fort helped to mark and defend the boundary between Spanish and American lands east of the Mississippi River. Aaron Burr sought to enlist the support of Gen. James Wilkinson, the fort's first commander, in his scheme to found an empire in the old Southwest. No remains are extant of the early mission and few of the fort. The town of Fort Adams, a small farming center, is now on the site of the mission. The site's historic environment has been changed by the altered course of the Mississippi River, which now lies about 1 mile away.

82. Fort Rosalie (Fort Panmure) Site, Mississippi

Location: Adams County, foot of South Broadway, Natchez.

Fort Rosalie was established in 1716 at present Natchez by the French, 3 years after a trading post was opened, for protection against the Indians. The wooden structures—officers' quarters, guardhouse, barracks, and powder magazine surrounded by a palisade—soon fell into ruin, and plans for rebuilding a permanent brick structure came to naught because in 1729 the Natchez tribe massacred most of the inhabitants. The following year, the French built another provisional post at the site.

When the British took over at the end of the French and Indian War and found the post in ruins, they rebuilt it and renamed it Fort Panmure. Seized by an American force during the War for Independence, the post was recaptured by the British, occupied by the Spanish during the period 1783–98, and then passed again into American hands. Finally, it was abandoned after Fort Adams was constructed, in 1799, nearer the crucial United States-Spanish boundary.

Peter Little built the present Rosalie Mansion in 1820 on part of the fort tract, and in 1930 the mansion was acquired by the Mississippi State Society of the Daughters of the American Revolution.

83. Old Spanish Fort, Mississippi

Location: Jackson County, on Krebs Lake, 1 mile outside of Pascagoula.

This house, known as the Old Spanish Fort, is probably the oldest in Mississippi. Yet it has changed little with the passage of time. It was built about 1718 by Joseph Simon de la Pointe on land given to his aunt, the Duchess of Chaumont, by Louis XIV. Fortified by its French occupants for defense against the Indians and Spanish, it was sturdily built of hewn timbers, shell lime, and shells. The Spanish, who took over the area in 1783, utilized it both as a fort and a chateau.

Richard Jackson House, in Portsmouth, New Hampshire, is the oldest house in the town and perhaps in the State. Its original section dates from the year 1664.

84. Richard Jackson House, New Hampshire

Location: Rockingham County, Jackson Hill Street, Portsmouth.

This two-story house is the oldest in Portsmouth, and perhaps in the State. The present central section is the original part, built in 1664. The two wings and the rear lean-to are later additions. As restored by the Society for the Preservation of New England Antiquities, which owns the property, it reflects well the architecture of its period. Plain and unpainted, the exterior is in the original state except for the casement windows. The interior also retains much of the original flavor; it has exposed beams, sheathed or crudely plastered walls, and broad floorboards. The house is open to the public from June 1 to October 15.

85. William Dam Garrison House, New Hampshire

Location: Strafford County, 182–192 Central Avenue, Dover.

This small log cabin, erected about 1675 by William Dam (Damme), is an excellent representative of the fortified residence, or garrison, that was once common in New England. It is one of the few such structures in the area that escaped destruction by the Indians. It consists of two rooms and has a central chimney. The walls are hand-hewn oak logs, some of them more than 20 feet long, which have lapped joints at the ends. The original small windows have been replaced by larger ones. The house has been preserved under a private trusteeship as a historic residence since 1915, when it was moved from its original site on Back River Road to its present location. Open to the public, it contains colonial household articles and clothing.

86. Nothnagle House, New Jersey

> *Location: Gloucester County, on Paulsboro-Repaupo Road, ¼ mile north of Repaupo.*

A section of this house dates from the early colonial period. Evidently constructed by Swedes or Swedish-Finns, the house was originally a one-story, typical Swedish log structure, whitewashed and built of cross-piled, dovetailed logs. The fireplace was located in the corner. The date of construction cannot be determined.

87. Swedish Log Cabin, New Jersey

> *Location: Gloucester County, 1 mile north of Swedesboro.*

This cabin, one of the few extant Swedish log cabins in the United States, stands on a plot of ground bought by Marten Martensson on March 9, 1685, some years after New Sweden had been conquered by the Dutch and then by the English. It was built in the 1680's, measures 12 by 15 feet, and is seven logs in height. The logs are dovetailed at the corners. A door, about 3 feet high, affords the only access. The cabin is located on a privately owned farm.

88. Trinity Episcopal (Old Swedes) Church, New Jersey

> *Location: Gloucester County, on King's Highway at Raccoon Creek, Swedesboro.*

The congregation of this church consisted of some of the first Swedish settlers, who arrived in the area before 1650. Dependent at first upon occasional ministerial visits, it later obtained permission for the schoolmaster to conduct regular services in a log cabin. After the War for Independence, the congregation constructed the present handsome edifice. The date of construction, 1784, is given on a circular stone set in the wall over the entrance, below the sloping eaves of the gabled roof.

The church was constructed of brick and stone, and the facade incorporates a striking Palladian window. At the opposite end of the building is a graceful white spire. When the Swedish Lutheran mission ended in 1789, the Episcopal Church fell heir to the building and has used it ever since. The Swedish heritage is attested to by several items in the church, including the old registers, a 1730 silver communion service, and a Swedish Bible and flag. Old tombstones in the churchyard bear the names of early Swedish settlers.

89. Zabriskie-Von Steuben House, New Jersey

> *Location: Bergen County, on New Bridge Road, ½ mile off N.J. 4, North Hackensack.*

John and Peter Zabriskie, millers, built this interesting house between 1739 and 1752. An excellent example of early Dutch colonial construction, it is built of stone. It has a gambrel roof, front porch, and two front doors. Nine slender columns support the roof over the porch. The west wall contains a square stone plaque bearing the Zabriskies' initials, the date 1751, and a millwheel indicating the owners' business.

The house was confiscated during the War for Independence because the Zabriskies remained loyal to the Crown, and it served as headquarters for both armies during campaigns in New Jersey; it housed Gen. George Washington and Lord Charles Cornwallis. Gen. Frederick William Von Steuben, who was awarded the house and surrounding land in return for his services during the war, later sold it to the Zabriskies, after they had become citizens of the United States. The property is now owned by the State of New Jersey, and it is used as a museum and headquarters by the Bergen County Historical Society.

90. Coronado State Monument, New Mexico

> *Location: Sandoval County, just off N. Mex. 44, about 5 miles northwest of Bernalillo.*

This monument preserves the extensive ruins of the ancient pueblo of

Kuaua, believed to have been besieged by Coronado in the winter of 1540–41. A sister pueblo 1 mile to the south may have been the site of Coronado's winter quarters during that period. The ruins include a restored square kiva, on whose interior walls are represented prehistoric Indian murals. The murals depict masked dancers, and are based on partially preserved originals found by archeologists when the University of New Mexico excavated the kiva in the 1930's. An adjacent museum exhibits Pueblo Indian and Spanish colonial artifacts. Operated by the Museum of New Mexico, the monument is open to the public throughout the year.

91. San Felipe de Neri Church, New Mexico

Location: Bernalillo County, northwest side of Old Town plaza, Albuquerque.

Construction of this church was begun by Fray Manuel Moreno, at the northwest corner of the plaza, almost as soon as Gov. Cuervo y Valdez, in 1706, established the villa of Albuquerque. The facade has been rebuilt and minor repairs have been made, but the church today differs little from the original. The most imposing and historically significant edifice in Old Town Albuquerque, it is still used by the Catholic Church for religious purposes.

92. San José de Giusewa Mission, New Mexico

Location: Sandoval County, on N. Mex. 4, Jémez Springs.

This Franciscan mission was founded around 1620 at the Pueblo of Giusewa, probably by Fray Gerónimo Zarate Salmerón, and ministered actively to the Jémez Indians for at least 10 years. The pueblo sheltered some 800 inhabitants. The Jémez pueblos and missions had stormy histories—revolt, abandonments, and reestablishments at various sites. By 1658, Giusewa had definitely been abandoned, perhaps because of Navajo aggression.

The ruins of the mission church, now part of Jémez State Monument, are unusually impressive. Walls of stone, 4 to 8 feet thick, rise as high as 30 feet in places, and the ruins of an octagonal tower stand 50 feet high. Extensive remains of the *convento,* especially the monastery, adjoin the church. A small private chapel in the monastery is the best preserved room. West of the church are the ruins of the pueblo, including dwelling rooms and kivas.

93. San Juan Pueblo, New Mexico

Location: Rio Arriba County, on U.S. 64, about 27 miles north of Santa Fe.

The northernmost of the several pueblos of the Tewa group, San Juan was the first Spanish base in New Mexico, and thus the temporary first capital when Oñate occupied the region in 1598. The Spanish invaders occupied a large part of the pueblo—which they called "San Juan de los Caballeros"—while they built permanent quarters and a church across the Rio Grande at the neighboring pueblo that was known by its Indian name of Yungue-ouinge. Existence at San Juan was apparently uneventful during the 17th century until the Pueblo Revolt of 1680, in which the pueblo was deeply involved. Popé, the leader of the uprising, directed it chiefly from Taos Pueblo, but he was a native of San Juan. In 1692, the Spanish reconquered the Rio Grande Valley around San Juan.

North section of the plaza at San Juan Pueblo, the first Spanish base in New Mexico.

94. Santa Fe, New Mexico

Location: Santa Fe County.

The second oldest city in the United States, Santa Fe still reflects to a remarkable degree—in its architecture, customs, people, and language— its Indian-Spanish-Mexican heritage.   Site of an ancient Indian village and since 1610 capital of New Mexico under Spain, Mexico, and the United States, *La Villa Real de la Santa Fé de San Francisco* (The Royal City of the Holy Faith of St. Francis) is truly the "Cradle of the Southwest." As in few other places in the United States, the blend of cultures that resulted from Spanish settlement can be seen and experienced.

Pueblo- and Territorial-style buildings line the narrow streets; Spanish language and customs predominate; historic sites and buildings abound.   Santa Fe—also a modern art and cultural center—has made special efforts to preserve its heritage. A number of excellent museums, most of them units of the Museum of New Mexico, trace the history of this ancient city and its environs from the days of prehistoric Indians, through the Spanish and Mexican periods, to the present.

The focal point on the plaza in Santa Fe is the Palace of the Governors, a Registered National Historic Landmark. The plaza itself—also a Registered National Historic Landmark (relating primarily to the Santa Fe Trail)—has significant associations with early Indian-Spanish history.   The Spanish used it for official, religious, and military functions. In fact, the entire pageantry of 17th-century Spanish conquest and settlement, Pueblo Revolt, and Spanish reconquest reached their climax in or near the plaza.

Among the many other important sites and buildings throughout the city of Santa Fe associated with the Spanish period are:

(1) Chapel of San Miguel. Originally built by Fray Alfonso de Benavides in 1626, this chapel is one of the oldest in the United States. It was partially destroyed during the Pueblo Revolt of 1680. After the reconquest, in 1692, it was rebuilt on the same site and for the next 50 years served as the military chapel of Santa Fe. Impressive carved altar decorations, historic paintings—some dating from the 13th century—and a bell said to have been cast in Spain in 1536 are interesting features. An excellent example of an 18th-century Spanish chapel, San Miguel still serves as a parish church.

(2) Rosario Chapel. Standing in the old Spanish cemetery northwest of Santa Fe, this chapel was originally built by De Vargas on the spot where his army camped while besieging Santa Fe during the reconquest of 1692. Rebuilt in 1807 and still used as a church, it is the starting point for the De Vargas procession, which commemorates the reconquest annually during Fiesta.

(3) Guadalupe Church. Built about 1795, this still-active parish church is the oldest shrine in the United States dedicated to the Virgin of Guadalupe.

(4) Barrio de Analco. This district, which surrounds the Chapel of San Miguel, was occupied by Mexican Indians who came north with the Spaniards. During the Pueblo Revolt it was razed, but after the reconquest it became the residential section for soldiers, servants, Indians, and *genízaros* (halfbreeds). Its historic buildings and narrow, winding streets make it one of the most picturesque sections of the city.

Numerous residences and commercial buildings also date from the Spanish period. Among them are the Gregorio Crespin House, the so-called "Oldest House," El Zaguan, and the Borrego House. Many of these fine old buildings have been marked with plaques by the Historic Santa Fe Foundation.

95. Billou-Stilwell-Perine House, New York

Location: Richmond County, 1476 Richmond Avenue, Dongan Hills, Staten Island.

This house is an interesting illustration of a Dutch-type house greatly modified by numerous additions in different styles, particularly in the 18th century. Pierre Billou, a Huguenot who arrived at New Amsterdam in 1661 and subsequently received a land grant on Staten Island, erected the original stone section about 1665. In 1679, Thomas Stilwell, a well-to-do landowner, enlarged the house. His descendants owned it until the mid-18th century, at which time Edward Perine acquired it. The Perine family owned it until 1913. It has a shingled, sloping roof, and an unusual jambless fireplace, which is very high and has a large stone hearth. A secret chamber opens into a room that features a ceiling with exceptionally large beams. Owned by the Staten Island Historical Society, the house is open to the public on a limited weekend schedule or by appointment.

96. Bowne House, New York

Location: Queens County, corner of Bowne Street and Fox Lane, Flushing, Long Island.

John Bowne erected this simple, two-story frame residence in 1661, some 10 years after he had migrated to New Netherland from Derbyshire, England. The house not only has general historic interest but is notably associated with the growth of religious freedom in America. Bowne and his wife were jailed and deported to Holland for trial because they held Quaker gatherings in their home. Bowne pled the cause of individual freedom of worship so successfully before the court that the Bownes were permitted to return to Flushing, and the Dutch West India Company declared that henceforth freedom of worship would prevail in its New World colony.

The Bowne family occupied the house until 1946, when the Bowne House Historical Society took it over and restored it. The kitchen is of particular interest for it was the meeting place of John Bowne and his Quaker friends. It is dominated by a gigantic fireplace. The house is open to the public throughout the year for a few hours each week.

97. Brett-Teller House, New York

Location: Dutchess County, 50 Van Nydeck Avenue, Beacon.

This house was erected by Catharyna and Roger Brett in 1709, the year after Catharyna inherited 28,000 acres of an 85,000-acre tract of land along the Hudson River, originally purchased from the Indians in 1663. It was a typical Dutch structure, one-and-a-half stories high, having a low gambrel roof extending downward over the porch. The original section of the house still retains some of the roundheaded shingles that were used on the exterior. Both the wing and the present kitchen were added after 1709, the latter probably after 1790. In 1790, Isaac De Peyster Teller acquired the house and it remained in the Teller family for seven generations. During the War for Independence, prominent guests included Washington, Lafayette, and Von Steuben. The house is now owned by the Melzingah Chapter, Daughters of the American Revolution, and is open daily.

98. Caughnawaga Site, New York

Location: Montgomery County, west side of Cayadutta Creek, one-quarter mile west of Fonda.

Caughnawaga, the last Mohawk village in the present United States before the tribe moved to Canada, illustrates European missionary influence on the Indians. Occupied during the period 1667–93, it was the site of a French Jesuit mission for about 10 years, 1668–79. The Indian girl Kateri Tekakwitha, known as "Lily of the Mohawks," was baptized and confirmed at this mission; she died at the age of 19. Because of her exemplary Christian life, she has gone through several stages of canonization, the first aboriginal North American to be so honored, and her influence has made the site a Catholic shrine.

Comprehensive excavation has revealed the entire circumference (1,016 feet) of the double stockade and the outlines of 12 lodges. White stakes in each of the 3,041 post molds help the visitor visualize the pattern of the village. The site is pleasantly situated on a bluff overlooking the Mohawk River. Nearby is the town of Fonda, founded in 1775 by a group of Dutchmen and named Caughnawaga until 1851.

99. Dyckman House, New York

Location: New York County, 204th Street and Broadway, New York.

This Dutch-style residence, typical of the final phase of Flemish colonial architecture, is the only 18th-century farmhouse still standing in Man-

Dyckman House, the only 18th-century framehouse extant in Manhattan, is a typical example of Flemish colonial architecture.

hattan. William Dyckman's first house on this site was burned during the War for Independence, but in 1783 Dyckman erected the one that is still carefully preserved today. The house is a white, two-story residence, the lower walls of fieldstone and the upper of clapboard. A gambrel roof in the front extends over a rail-enclosed porch. Descendants of the original owner rehabilitated the house and in 1915 presented it to New York City, which keeps it open to the public throughout the year.

100. Fort Ste. Marie de Gannentatha, New York

Location: Onondaga County, on N.Y. 57, about 1½ miles north of Syracuse.

Fort Ste. Marie de Gannentatha was erected for protection against the Dutch and Indians by 50 French colonists who in 1656 attempted to settle near the present city of Syracuse. The colony eventually failed. The present stockade is a reconstruction. The exterior is of unfinished logs and the interior of roughhewn boards; reproduced period furnishings help recreate the appearance of the original stockade. Many French and Indian relics are displayed. Near the stockade is the Jesuit Well, the site of a salt spring visited in 1654 by Father Simon le Moyne, a Jesuit missionary. The stockade is open to the public all year.

101. Lefferts Homestead, New York

Location: Kings County, on Empire Boulevard, Prospect Park, Brooklyn.

This house was built in 1777 by Lt. Peter Lefferts, descendant of a New York Dutch family, on the site of his previous home, destroyed by fire in a military action at the beginning of the War for Independence. The original site was at 563 Flatbush Avenue, from which the building was moved to the present location in 1918, when Lefferts' descendants presented it to the city of New York.

The design of the house reflects Lefferts' Dutch heritage. A low gambrel roof ends in a deep overhang in front, which is supported by several columns. The handsome front door is surmounted by a richly carved entableture of sunburst designs. Inside, an arch on the north side of the main hall separates the dining and living rooms. The parlor and bedrooms are on the south side of the hall; a children's room occupies the second floor along with a maple room and a workroom. The attic has a smokeroom. The house is furnished with period furniture and is maintained as a museum by the city of New York. It is open to the public on a limited schedule throughout the year.

102. National Shrine of North American Martyrs, New York

Location: Montgomery County, on N.Y. 58, Auriesville.

This shrine, which memorializes all Roman Catholic clerics put to death by Indians, illustrates European missionary efforts. Father Isaac Jogues, a French Jesuit missionary who first arrived in North America in 1636, was captured by the Mohawk Indians in 1642, and suffered terribly before he was helped to escape by a Dutch minister. Returning in 1646 from a voyage to France, he was again captured by unfriendly natives, who executed him on October 18, 1646, in the Mohawk village of *Osseruenon*, where the National Shrine of North American Martyrs is now located. Jogues and seven other priests who were killed by Indians were canonized in 1925. Adjoining the shrine is a statue of Kateri Tekakwitha, "Lily of the Mohawks," an Indian girl of exceptional Christian devotion, who was born in *Osseruenon*. Open from May 6 to October 28, the shrine includes an Indian museum, a cafeteria, and an inn.

103. Nichols Pond Site, New York

Location: Madison County, 10 miles south of U.S. 20, Fenner Township.

This well-preserved site is believed by some historians to have been the location of the fortified Oneida village that Champlain and his Huron allies attacked in 1615—even though pottery sherds recovered from the site are prehistoric Mohawk rather than 17th-century Oneida. The topography of the area, however, conforms generally with that described by Champlain. Excavation has revealed about 120 feet of a quadruple stockade that has ample room between the walls for the galleries mentioned by Champlain. The site has been leased to the Champlain Battle Park Association by the County of Madison and is being developed on a limited scale.

104. Old Stone Fort, New York

Location: Schoharie County, at the northern edge of Schoharie.

The Old Stone Fort was originally a church of the Reformed Protestant High Dutch Church Society. The congregation that constructed it had worshipped in two previous structures, built in 1724 and 1737, a little to the northeast of the Old Stone Fort site. The present structure was built in 1772 of local stone, hauled by the parishioners themselves. Many carved their names on the stones, but during the War for Independence the names of Tories were obliterated. In 1830, a tower and spire that had dominated the church were removed.

The church came to be called the Old Stone Fort after 1778, when the State of New York converted it into a fort by erecting a stockade around the building and blockhouses at the southwest and northeast corners. In 1780, Sir John Johnson attacked it with a force of some 800 British soldiers, Indians, and Tories, but was repulsed. The stockade was not removed until 1785. In 1844, the congregation moved to a new edifice, and in 1857 the State purchased the old church and used it as an arsenal until 1873, when it was deeded to Schoharie County. A museum today, the Old Stone Fort is administered by the County Board of Supervisors and the Schoharie County Historical Society. It is open to the public from April through October.

105. Pieter Bronck House, New York

Location: Greene County, on U.S. 9W, 1½ miles south of West Coxsackie.

This house is outstanding among Dutch colonial houses in the Hudson Valley. It was built in two sections by descendants of Jonas Bronck, who settled on Manhattan Island in 1639 and after whom the Bronx is named. In 1663, Pieter Bronck, a stepson, built a stone house on land purchased from the Indians. About 1738 his grandson, Leendert Bronck, added a larger brick house, connected to the original house by a doorway. Their descendants lived in the duplex house until 1938, when the owner presented it to the Greene County Historical Society.

The stolid, plain character of the original house exemplifies Dutch

Pieter Bronck House, New York, consists of two parts, a stone section erected in 1663 and a larger brick section erected about 1738. It is outstanding among surviving Dutch colonial houses in the Hudson River Valley.

pioneer construction. The loopholes on the second floor were used for muskets. The addition reflects the grandson's prosperity as well as more settled conditions in the area. It also consists of two stories and has a gabled roof. The living room has massive ceiling beams that are supported by nautical curved knees, a technique rather common in the area's farmhouses. This room also has a steep stairway, Dutch door, and broad floorboards, all typical of Dutch houses of the era. The house, which is open to the public throughout the year, exhibits colonial furnishings and historical memorabilia.

106. Pieter Wyckoff Homestead, New York

> *Location: Kings County, southwest corner of Ralph Avenue and Canarsie Lane, Brooklyn.*

Because Pieter Wyckoff, who arrived in New Amsterdam in 1637, probably built this house between 1639 and 1641, it is one of the oldest extant on Long Island. Wyckoff lived in it for 44 years, while superintendent of Peter Stuyvesant's estate and also as a large landowner in his own right. The original building was only about a little more than half as deep as the present one, and it probably had a steep roof. The existing gable roof is low and sweeping and has projecting front and rear eaves. A wing was added to the house, perhaps around 1784, and some very old shakes are still on the exterior. The house is maintained and exhibited by the Wyckoff House Foundation.

107. Senate House, New York

Location: Ulster County, 312 Fair Street, Kingston.

Erected as a residence by Col. Wessel Ten Broeck between 1676 and 1695, when Kingston was a small village called Esopus, this building remained in his family until 1888, when the State acquired it for preservation as a historic shrine. The first New York State Senate used it in 1777, soon after the State constitution was adopted, during the British occupation of New York City. The senators deliberated in the end of the building where the door opens directly onto the street. When the British subsequently burned Kingston, the building was gutted along with other structures, but it was later rebuilt. Maintained as a historic structure, it exhibits period pieces and furnishings, most of them donated by descendants of early settlers in the vicinity. An adjacent museum,

Col. Wessel Ten Broeck erected this structure in Esopus (Kingston), New York, between 1676 and 1695. During the War for Independence, when the New York State Senate met in the house, it came to be known as the Senate House. Courtesy, New York State Education Department.

erected in 1927, contains historic objects relating to the Kingston area and a collection of paintings by John Vanderlyn, a Kingston-born artist. The house and museum are open to the public throughout the year.

108. Van Alen House, New York

Location: Columbia County, on N.Y. 9H, about 6 miles east of Kinderhook.

Built by Luycas Van Alen in 1737, this house is regarded today as an exceptional example of Dutch architecture in America. The site was well situated on what later became the post road between Albany and New York. The brickwork was laid up in Dutch crossbond, on a fieldstone foundation, which enclosed a cellar. The walls were plastered and the ceilings beamed with heavy timbers. The first floor consisted of living room and kitchen, each of which had a great tiled and hooded fireplace at the gable end. A large brick wing was added to the original structure on the north end, probably before 1750. The addition had its own cellar; the first floor consisted of a hall with staircase, small bedroom or larder, and parlor; and the second floor included a hall, storage room, and bedroom.

Changes in the 19th century involved interior partitions and window and door openings, as well as the erection of a front porch across the north wing. The house is now owned by the Greene County Historical Society. Vacant since 1938, it is in poor condition; major stabilization and restoration are required to stave off imminent collapse. The outbuildings have disappeared and the grounds have become unkempt, yet the house still retains to a considerable degree the flavor of a bygone age.

109. Grand Assembly of the Albemarle (lost site), North Carolina

Location: Monument in Pasquotank County, on N.C. 170, about 1 mile north of Nixonton.

At least 100 settlers were already living in the region just north of Albemarle Sound in 1663, when Charles II granted Carolina to a group of proprietors. In 1664, they appointed William Drummond as Governor, and early the next year they promulgated the "Concessions and Agreement," which provided for a unicameral legislature having broad powers and composed of the Governor, his council, and 12 deputies. The first such legislature met early that year on Halls Creek, about 7 miles southwest of present Elizabeth City. According to tradition, it assembled beneath a large oak tree because no building was large enough to accommodate it. Among the business transacted was a petition asking that land be granted to settlers on the same terms as in Virginia—resulting in the Great Deed of Grant in 1668. The exact site of the first meeting of the Grand Assembly of the Albemarle is not known, but the stone monument adjacent to Halls Creek Church is probably not far away.

110. Cape Meares, Oregon

> *Location: Tillamook County, south side of Tillamook Bay, just west of U.S. 101.*

This rocky headland, 700 feet high, was discovered in 1778 by Capt. John Meares, an English explorer, who found the bay closed by a sand

In 1778, the English explorer Capt. John Meares discovered this headland, now Cape Meares, Oregon. It is wild and beautiful and looks today much the same as when first discovered.

barrier and called it "Quicksand Bay." The cape probably had been sighted in 1775 by the Spanish explorer Bruno Heceta. The north side is still wild and beautiful, unchanged except for an unobtrusive Coast Guard station. On the south side are a number of summer beach cottages.

111. Caleb Pusey House, Pennsylvania

Location: Delaware County, Race Street, Upland.

Built in 1683, this house is the oldest extant English-constructed house in Pennsylvania. Pusey, a Quaker, migrated from England to manage a gristmill in which William Penn was a partner. Becoming a warm friend of Penn, who apparently visited this home, he became a member of the assembly, served on the colony's Executive Council, and in 1701 sat on the Governor's Council. Selling his interest in the milling business in 1708, he moved to Chester, after which his former home had various owners. By the 1930's, the house seemed destined for eventual loss. Interest in it increased after World War II, however, and in the early 1960's the Friends of the Caleb Pusey House came to its rescue and began restoration.

112. Fort Le Boeuf, Pennsylvania

Location: Erie County, on the north bank of French Creek, Waterford.

The French built Fort Le Boeuf in the spring of 1753 as part of a major effort to strengthen their hold over the vast lands in Canada and the Mississippi-Ohio Valleys that they claimed. The fort resembled Fort Presque Isle, built a bit sooner, although it was somewhat smaller. Four log buildings stood within a log stockade. The Governor of Virginia sent a young officer, George Washington, to protest the incursion into British-claimed territory, but the French rebuffed him. During the French and Indian War, a British force laid siege to a major French stronghold, Fort Niagara, and the garrisons of Fort Le Boeuf and other minor posts were summoned as reinforcements. Fort Niagara fell, and in 1759 the French themselves destroyed Fort Le Boeuf.

Great Britain used the site of Fort Le Boeuf for a depot, and in 1794 the Americans built a blockhouse nearby, but all these buildings fell into ruins and disappeared as the area became a settled and prosperous section of modern Pennsylvania. The Commonwealth of Pennsylvania today operates a museum illustrating the history of Fort Le Boeuf on its site. Across the street are the foundations of the 1794 blockhouse. Many interesting artifacts of French, Indian, British, and American origin have been recovered in the area.

113. Fort Presque Isle Site, Pennsylvania

Location: Erie County, at 6th and Parade Streets, Erie.

In 1753, a French force under Sieur Marin from Montreal, recognizing the strategic possibilities afforded by the sheltering arm of the Presque Isle peninsula, built a fort there, about the same time as Fort Le Boeuf. The stockade of chestnut logs measured about 120 feet square and 15 feet high, and enclosed several buildings. After the British captured Fort Niagara, the French abandoned and destroyed Fort Presque Isle. The English rebuilt the fort and garrisoned it, but later abandoned it. No remains are extant today.

114. Lower Swedish Cabin, Pennsylvania

Location: Delaware County, on Creek Road, 1 mile south of Clifton Heights.

This cabin, erected during the period 1640–50, is one of the earliest extant examples of Swedish log construction in the United States. The walls

An early example of Swedish log construction, Lower Swedish Cabin, Pennsylvania, built in the period 1640–50.

consist of logs about 12 inches in diameter, notched at the corners. The cabin originally consisted of only one room, but another was added later; a low door connects the rooms. The ceiling rafters can be touched by the upraised hand. Each room contains a Swedish-style corner fireplace, above which rises a large stone chimney. The roof is gabled.

115. Pennsbury Manor, Pennsylvania

Location: Bucks County, 3½ miles east of U.S. 13, just outside of Tullytown.

This is the re-created country estate of William Penn, the founder of Pennsylvania. He purchased the lands in 1682, on his first visit to Pennsylvania, and began construction the following year. During the next 15 years, he directed the development in a stream of correspondence from England. He stayed at the manor frequently while he resided in the New World during the period 1699–1701 and entertained many colonial personages and Indian visitors. The manor fell into a deplorable state after he finally returned to England, and by the end of the century was in ruins. The Pennsylvania Historical Commission acquired it on the 250th anniversary of his first trip to America and subsequently carefully re-created the manor house, bake and brew houses, stable, other outbuildings, and gardens and grounds. The manor is open to the public all year.

116. Swedish Cabin (Morton Homestead), Pennsylvania

Location: Delaware County, on Pa. 420, near Darby Creek Bridge, about 2 miles south of Glenolden.

This hewn-log structure was probably built in 1654, a year before New Sweden fell to the Dutch, and is the best preserved and most carefully documented of the few known remains of Swedish settlement in the 17th century. About 1698, a second cabin was erected a few feet distant, and around 1806 the two structures were connected by a third one, built of stone. Marten Martensson built the original cabin shortly after he arrived in New Sweden.

The long-time tradition that the cabin was the birthplace of John Morton, a signer of the Declaration of Independence, has not been verified.

Swedish Cabin (Morton Homestead), Pennsylvania. It consists of two log cabins connected by a stone building. The three structures were built between 1654 and 1806.

Morton's great-grandfather did, however, once own the land on which the cabin stands. Since 1935, when the cabin was in a dilapidated condition and surrounded by modern framehouses, the Commonwealth of Pennsylvania has carefully restored it. It is furnished with period pieces. The setting is now preserved by a small park of approximately 3 acres, which is open to visitors throughout the year.

117. Eleazar Arnold House, Rhode Island

Location: Providence County, 449 Great Road, near Lincoln Woods Reservation State Park.

This house is representative of the Rhode Island "stone-ender" type, a regional variation in construction stemming from Rhode Island's abundant supply of building stone, as compared to Massachusetts and Connecticut. When first built, it had only one room, which had a fireplace at one end. When a rear lean-to was added later, for a kitchen, a new chimney was joined to the original one; the whole was so wide that it almost covered that end of the house.

Composed of numerous pilasters, the chimney top is one of New England's most imposing. The remainder of the two-story structure is of clapboard, and features a sharp-peaked front gable and a long roof over the kitchen. The outstanding interior feature is the huge hall fireplace, which has an oak mantel more than 12 feet long. The house is owned by the Society for the Preservation of New England Antiquities, under whose aegis it was restored in the 1930's. It is open daily except Monday from June 15 to October 15; at other times, by applying to the custodian in an adjacent house.

118. Great Swamp Fight Site (lost site), Rhode Island

Location: Washington County, on R.I. 2, about 2 miles southwest of West Kingston.

This site illustrates New England's struggle with the Indians in the 17th century. On December 19, 1675, during the bloody King Philip's War, forces of the United Colonies stormed a formidable fort of the Narragansett Indians in Rhode Island's Great Swamp and crushed the Indians for all time. Many warriors escaped the disaster, but hundreds of older Indians, including women and children, were slaughtered, and the Narragansetts' winter food supply was destroyed. It was a decisive blow against King Philip's effort to overwhelm white settlements in New England. A marker on the Great Swamp indicates the approximate location of the Indian fort.

119. Roger Williams Spring and House Sites, Rhode Island

Location: Providence County, North Main Street and Alamo Lane (Spring Site), and 233 North Main Street (House Site), Providence.

These sites, which are associated with the founding of Rhode Island in 1636 by Roger Williams and a group of dissenters from the strict religious practices of the Massachusetts Bay Colony, commemorate the struggle for freedom of conscience in colonial America. The group founded the settlement of Providence near a fresh spring at the junction of the Woonasquatucket and Moshassuck Rivers, at the base of a hill. The colony was a refuge for persecuted religious groups and freedom seekers. As the colony grew, the spring provided inadequate water. In 1869, it was walled up and replaced by a pump. In 1892, the site was filled in to accommodate urban development, but in 1930 a private citizen bought it and donated it to the city, which created a small memorial park. Roger Williams' house was destroyed by fire during King Philip's War, in 1673. Excavation of the site in 1906 revealed some hearthstones, evidences of a fireplace and a wall, and a jamb. A new commercial building has since been erected on the site. It is unfortunate that no structure or site with integrity associated with the life and work of so outstanding a leader as Roger Williams is extant.

[On October 22, 1965, the President signed the act of Congress authorizing the establishment of Roger Williams National Memorial, to consist of not more than 5 acres at the Spring Site.]

120. Albemarle Point (Old Town), South Carolina

Location: Charleston County, just off S.C. 61, about 2 miles north of Charleston.

In 1670, a group of English settlers founded a colony at this point, where the seat of government remained until the founding a decade later of Charleston, originally known as Charles Town, the first permanent white settlement in present South Carolina. The colonizing expedition had left England in August 1669 in three vessels, two of which (the *Port Royall* and *Albemarle*) were lost en route. The third, the *Carolina,* was repaired at Bermuda and in March 1670 reached Port Royal Harbor. The leaders felt that the location was too exposed to Spanish and Indian attack, and sailed up the coast to Albemarle Point. They landed and erected wooden fortifications and homes. The colony's business was conducted at this location under three Governors until, in December 1679, the proprietors designated Oyster Point (Charleston), at the junction of the Cooper and Ashley Rivers, as port town for the colony. Within 1 year, Albemarle Point was deserted. All surface traces of the Albemarle settlement have disappeared. The site is included in the privately owned Old Town Plantation. A monument, erected in 1909, stands near the plantation house, which is some distance from the point.

121. Medway Plantation, South Carolina

Location: Berkeley County, 2.1 miles east of U.S. 52, at Mt. Holly.

Medway is the oldest recorded house in South Carolina. It was built of brick in 1686 by Jan Van Arrsens, Seigneur de Weirnhoudt, leader of a small group of Hollanders who came to Carolina to settle. The original

In 1686, a Dutchman built Medway, the oldest recorded house in South Carolina. The central part, featuring crow-stepped gables, is original.

house, which measured 27 by 38½ feet and had one-and-a-half stories, followed a plan described by William Penn in a 1684 broadside for prospective settlers of Pennsylvania. It had a partition near the middle and another to divide one end into two smaller rooms. Indicative of its Dutch origins, it had stepped gable ends and end chimneys.

Alterations and additions were made to the original structure. A second story was added, as well as unsymmetrical major wings on both the east and west sides and several smaller additions. Though the integrity of the original has been impaired, these changes have not spoiled the esthetic effect of the house. Consciously or otherwise, the taste of the original Dutch builder has dominated succeeding owners. None of the numerous outbuildings antedates the 19th century. The plantation, privately owned and beautifully maintained, is not open to visitors.

122. Middleburg Plantation, South Carolina

Location: Berkeley County, 2½ miles southwest of Huger.

Probably the oldest extant wooden house in South Carolina, Middleburg was built about 1699 by Benjamin Simons, whose descendants have owned it ever since. One-room deep, it resembles the distinctive Charleston "single house." The first-floor interior walls, redecorated about 1800, are finished with wide boards. In the lovely formal garden are tunneled walks of age-old camellia japonicas.

123. Parris Island, South Carolina

Location: Beaufort County, in Port Royal Sound, near Port Royal.

On this island are the sites of the first French settlement within the present United States and two later Spanish posts. In 1562, under the command of Jean Ribaut, a group of French Huguenots built a small earth-and-log post and named it Charlesfort. During Ribaut's absence in France to seek reinforcements, and lacking support from the mother country, the colonists soon abandoned the fort. After incredible hardships, they returned home.

In 1566, the Spaniards established Fort San Felipe on the island, but the Indians destroyed it about 1576. Within 1 year, the Spanish returned and built a stronger post, Fort San Marcos, which became the center of a substantial settlement of some 60 houses and the capital of the province of Santa Elena. The Spanish abandoned it in 1587 during the general retrenchment that followed Sir Francis Drake's attack on St. Augustine.

Archeological excavations under the auspices of the U.S. Marine Corps in 1923 at the southern end of the island revealed the remains of a stockade and yielded a substantial number of artifacts. The excavators identified the site as Charlesfort, and it has been so marked by a granite monument; a marker also indicates that the Spanish forts were probably on Pilot or Means Creek. However, a more recent investigator has concluded that the excavated site was probably Fort San Marcos. Owned by the U.S. Government, the island is used by the U.S. Marine Corps as a recruit depot.

124. La Vérendrye Site, South Dakota

Location: Stanley County, Third Avenue near Third Street, Fort Pierre.

On February 16, 1913, a lead plate inscribed with the names of four 18th-century French explorers, and dated March 30, 1743, was found at this site, although the location of its original placement has been questioned by some historians. Louis-Joseph and Francois de la Vérendrye and two companions, returning eastward from the Black Hills region, deposited the plate to commemorate their attempt to find a Northwest Passage to the "Western Sea." Their expedition was one of two organized and financed by Pierre Gaultier de Varennes, Sieur de la Vérendrye, the famous French explorer. The South Dakota Historical Society and the Fort Pierre Commercial Club have placed a marker at the site. The plate itself is in the possession of the society.

125. Fort Assumption Site, Tennessee

Location: Shelby County, E. H. Crump Boulevard, near the eastern end of the Mississippi River bridge, Memphis.

Fort Assumption was erected in 1739 by Jean Baptiste le Moyne, Sieur de Bienville, who landed with a French force at the Wolf River to establish a base of operations against the Chickasaw Indians, allies of the English. The fort was named in honor of the day on the church calendar that construction began. The French abandoned and destroyed it in 1740, when they made peace with the Chickasaws and Bienville disbanded the Choctaws and his other Indian allies. Though the remains have been obliterated by modern urban construction, a State historical marker indicates the site.

126. Fort Loudoun, Tennessee

Location: Monroe County, off U.S. 411, about 1 mile southeast of McGhee.

The first English settlement west of the Smoky Mountains, Fort Loudoun figured prominently in the French and Indian War. Started in 1756, the year before the French began construction of Fort Massac, near the confluence of the Ohio and Tennessee Rivers, it was completed in 1757 and occupied until 1760. Its primary purpose was to protect and support the Cherokees against the French and their Indian allies, and thus to protect the English frontier. Relations between the English and the Cherokees deteriorated, however, and in 1760 the Indians laid siege to Fort Loudoun. When Capt. Paul Demere, commander of the fort, surrendered, he obtained a promise of safe conduct to Fort Prince George, in present South Carolina, for all the soldiers and their families. Less than 15 miles from Fort Loudoun, the Indians attacked, killed 27 soldiers and 3 women, and took all the survivors as prisoners.

Extensive archeological excavations at the fort have yielded exact information on its size, shape, and construction—not only concerning the palisade but also many of the structures inside. Portions of the fort have been reconstructed, and it is open to the public daily from March through October. The site is administered by the Fort Loudoun Association. Fort Loudoun is eligible for the Registry of National Historic Landmarks (relating primarily to the development of the English colonies, 1700–1783).

127. Fort Prudhomme Site, Tennessee

> *Location: Tipton County, Second Chickasaw Bluff, just below the mouth of the Hatchie River, off Tenn. 59, between Randolph and Richardson's Landing.*

La Salle built Fort Prudhomme in 1682, on his first voyage down the Mississippi. One of the first forts or habitations of any kind built in the Tennessee country by Europeans, it was named after Pierre Prudhomme, armorer of the expedition. After Prudhomme failed to return from a hunting trip, La Salle built the fort for temporary protection during the search. After Prudhomme was found, La Salle left him in charge of the fort and continued to explore the Mississippi. On La Salle's return trip, he became ill and remained at the fort for 40 days before being able to continue upriver. The fort was then abandoned and fell into ruins. No remains are visible today.

128. Fort St. Louis Site, Texas

> *Location: Victoria County, head of Lavaca Bay, west bank of Garcitas Creek, about 10 miles east of Placedo.*

This site commemorates the first French attempt to colonize the gulf coast, which created special Spanish interest in Texas. In 1685, La Salle, intending to plant a colony near the mouth of the Mississippi, led 400 colonists and soldiers instead into present Texas, where he founded Fort St. Louis on Lavaca Bay, an inlet of Matagorda Bay. A month later, he moved it to a new location 5 miles above the mouth of Garcitas Creek. A temporary wooden structure, it served as a base for his exploration of the surrounding country.

Hunger and Indian attacks disheartened the colonists, and the venture was a failure from the beginning. La Salle, after reconnoitering to the south and west, started north, hoping to reach Fort St. Louis in Illinois country, but mutineers murdered him. Two years later, Indians attacked the fort and wiped out most of the remaining Frenchmen. The survivors were captured 3 months later by the Spanish expedition of Capt. Alonso de León, which had been sent to investigate reports of French encroachment in Texas. De León burned the fort to the ground.

The failure of La Salle's colony ended French attempts to colonize Texas. The French established themselves at the mouth of the Mississippi and continued to threaten Texas along the Louisiana frontier, but they never again seriously contested Spain's hold on Texas. In 1722, the Spanish built the mission of Nuestra Señora del Espíritu Santo de Zuñiga and the presidio of Nuestra Señora de Loreto near the site of Fort St. Louis, but abandoned them 4 years later.

Pinpointed by the late Prof. Herbert Eugene Bolton, the site has been accepted by most historians and substantially confirmed by archeological investigation. Positive proof of authenticity may never be obtained. On private ranch property, the site is marked on the surface only by traces of ancient walls constructed of adobe.

129. La Bahía (Goliad), Texas

Location: Goliad County, on U.S. 77A–183, just south of Goliad.

In the 18th century, the Goliad vicinity was known as La Bahía del Espíritu Santo. One of the oldest municipalities in Texas, La Bahía has its origins in the Spanish response to French advances into Texas beginning in 1685. In 1722, the Spanish founded the mission of Nuestra Señora del Espíritu Santo de Zuñiga and the presidio of Nuestra Señora de Loreto on Matagorda Bay near the abandoned site of La Salle's Fort St. Louis. They were commonly called the mission and presidio of La Bahía (The Bay). The settlement retained this name even after it moved inland, first to a site on the Guadalupe River, and in 1749 to its present location on the San Antonio River. The new mission and presidio attracted Spanish ranchers and farmers to the area, and a sizable colony soon grew up.

Espíritu Santo Mission, near Goliad, Texas, was a part of the Spanish settlement La Bahía, which reached its peak during the last half of the 18th century.

La Bahía reached its peak of influence during the last half of the 18th century, when hundreds of converted Indians farmed surrounding fields and tended huge herds of cattle. By 1790, however, Franciscan missionary activity in Texas began to ebb. Within a few years, La Bahía's prosperity faded and the mission Indians fled. The missions were secularized and the Franciscans returned to Mexico. In 1829, the Congress of Coahuila and Texas declared La Bahía a town and its name was changed to Goliad. A few years later, it was the site of the Goliad Massacre, during the Texas Revolution.

Espíritu Santo Mission, authentically restored under the supervision of the National Park Service, is an imposing example of 18th-century mission architecture; it resembles San Xavier del Bac, in Arizona, and San Juan Capistrano, in California. It is the central feature of Goliad State Park, which also contains a small museum illustrating Spanish colonial history. To the east, on a hill overlooking the San Antonio River, are the chapel and crumbling compound walls of La Bahía presidio. The chapel is still in use as a Catholic parish church. The compound is now being excavated and stabilized under private auspices, in cooperation with the Catholic Church, with a view toward future restoration.

West of Goliad are the ruins of the mission of Nuestra Señora del

Crumbling walls and chapel of La Bahía Presidio, Texas. It is now being accurately restored.

Rosario de los Cujanes. Twenty-nine miles south of Goliad, at the town of Refugio, is the site of the mission of Nuestra Señora del Refugio. La Bahía presidio also protected these two missions.

130. San Antonio, Texas

Location: Bexar County.

In 1718, San Antonio de Bexar was founded as part of a Spanish effort to forestall French designs on Texas. Destined to become the most important Spanish settlement in Texas, it was the capital during the latter part of Spanish rule. When it was founded, a new mission, San Antonio de Valero—which later became known as the Alamo—was established nearby. This mission carried out the first successful missionary effort in Texas. San Antonio was the political, religious, military, and population center of the Spanish province.

The rich heritage of the city has been largely preserved through the efforts of the San Antonio Conservation Society, the Daughters of the Republic of Texas, the Roman Catholic Church, the Texas State Parks Board, and the city of San Antonio. As a result, San Antonio has retained an old-world atmosphere equaled by few American cities and expressed by a wealth of significant historic sites and buildings.

The most famous historic site in Texas is the Alamo, which is eligible for the Registry of National Historic Landmarks (relating primarily to the Texas Revolution), originally known as San Antonio de Valero Mission. First of the five Franciscan missions at San Antonio, San Antonio de Valero prospered for nearly a century. At one time, members of scores of different tribes were enrolled as neophytes. Another significant mission in San Antonio, San José y San Miguel de Aguayo, is commemorated by the San José National Historic Site.

The Alamo, the most famous historic site in Texas, was originally San Antonio de Valero Mission. Courtesy, San Antonio Chamber of Commerce.

Spanish Governors Palace, in San Antonio, was the residence and headquarters of 18th-century Spanish Governors and Vice-Governors of Texas. It has been restored and now serves as a museum.

South from the central city are the other three San Antonio missions, relocated in 1731 on the San Antonio River following abandonment of the east Texas missions: Nuestra Señora de la Purísima Concepción de Acuna, San Francisco de la Espada, and San Juan Capistrano. During the middle of the 18th century, all five missions were extremely active. They were self-sufficient communities, islands of civilization in the surrounding wilderness. The Franciscans, in addition to indoctrinating Indian neophytes in the Christian religion, trained them in trades, and taught them the Spanish language.

Though the missions eventually failed, were secularized, and then abandoned, their remains are tangible evidence of Spanish colonial policy. Some are still used for special religious observances. The city of San Antonio plans a "Mission Parkway" to make the missions more accessible to visitors and students.

The Spanish Governors Palace on Plaza de las Armas was the residence and headquarters of 18th-century Spanish Governors and Vice-Governors of Texas. Over the entrance arch are the Hapsburg arms, and the date 1749 is carved on the keystone. A Spanish map, however,

Chapel of San Francisco de la Espada Mission, south of San Antonio.

shows that the palace occupied the same location as early as 1722. When Spanish sovereignty ended, it passed into private hands and was neglected. In 1929, the city of San Antonio purchased it to avert complete ruin. The present structure is an outstanding and authentic restoration. Of plastered adobe, it consists of 10 rooms, furnished with Spanish furniture. A patio in the rear, which features cobbled walks, fountain, and well, is planted with native flowers and shrubs. The palace is operated as a public museum.

Another important site, which illustrates the techniques of 18th-century mission agriculture, is the Espada Aqueduct, a Registered National Historic Landmark (relating primarily to agricultural development). Once part of an integrated irrigation system that served the five missions in the area, it is the best preserved section and is still functioning. Franciscans built the dam, aqueduct, and acequia during the period 1731–45. The most spectacular of the associated structures is the graceful, double-span aqueduct over Piedro Arroyo. The site, on Espada Road, is maintained as a park by the San Antonio Conservation Society.

Many other sites in San Antonio are associated with the Spanish period, including the restored historic district "La Villita."

Nuestra Señora de la Purísima Concepción de Acuna Mission—one of five 18th-century Franciscan missions in the San Antonio area.

131. San Francisco de los Tejas Mission (lost site), Texas

Location: Houston County, about 3 miles northwest of Weches.

This mission, the first established by Franciscans in Texas, was originally built on the west bank of the Neches River during a Spanish colonization expedition led by Alonso de León into east Texas in 1690 to discourage French encroachment. The Spanish abandoned the mission in 1693 because the Tejas Indians were uncooperative.

In 1716, the mission was reestablished at another site 8 miles away, but on the east bank of the river. It was one of seven set up by the Franciscans, again to counter a French threat, during a second expedition, led by Domingo Ramón. In 1719, the French invaded east Texas from Louisiana and forced the Spanish to again abandon the mission and retreat to San Antonio.

Two years later, after the French withdrew, the mission was again reestablished in the same location and renamed San Francisco de los Neches by Father Felix de Espinosa, who was a member of the Aguayo expedition. When the Spanish abandoned nearby Dolores presidio, the Neches mission was moved farther inland to the site of Austin and later to San Antonio.

The exact locations of the various mission sites are not known. A one-room log chapel has been constructed by the State in Davy Crockett National Forest on the approximate site of the first mission.

132. San Saba Mission and San Luís Presidio, Texas

Location: Menard County. Mission site, at the southern edge of Menard; presidio site, on Tex. 29, about 3 miles northwest of Menard.

San Sabá de la Santa Cruz Mission represents a disastrous Franciscan attempt to convert the Lipan Apache Indians. Established in 1757 by Fray Alonso Giraldo de Terreros on the south bank of the San Sabá River, it was protected by the San Luís de las Amarillas Presidio, just north of the river. The mission failed to convert the Apaches, whose only interest in it was hope of obtaining Spanish aid against their Comanche enemies. In 1758, the Comanches and their allies set fire to it; only

In 1757, the Spanish founded this presidio, San Luís de las Amarillas, to protect nearby San Sabá Mission. In 1758, Comanches destroyed the mission, and, in 1769, the Spanish abandoned the presidio. The presidio has been partially restored.

three inhabitants survived.

Although the presidio was maintained until 1769, the mission was never rebuilt. No remains of the mission are extant, but the presidio has been partially restored on the original foundations. The State of Texas is considering a proposal that the present San Sabá Historic Park, containing the ruins of the restored presidio, be connected by a scenic drive to the nearby frontier post, Fort McKavett, and redesignated the San Sabá River State Historic Park.

133. Spanish Fort Site, Texas

Location: Montague County, both sides of Red River, near village of Spanish Fort.

An important village of the Taovayas, a band of the Wichitas, was located at this site in the latter half of the 17th and most of the 18th centuries. The Wichitas were known as early as the time of Coronado, but the first known reference to the Taovayas was made in 1719 by Bernard de la Harpe, a French trader, who encountered them on the

Canadian River in present Oklahoma. They were among the tribes who in 1758 destroyed San Sabá Mission; this resulted in Diego Ortíz Parilla's retaliatory expedition the following year. The Taovaya village—protected by a stockade and moat, armed with French guns, and displaying a French flag—repulsed the Spaniards. A smallpox epidemic in 1812 decimated the village, and the survivors joined other groups of Wichitas. The site is located in privately owned cottonfields, and few surface remains are apparent. In 1936, the Texas Centennial Commission erected a marker near the site.

134. Crossing of the Fathers (lost site), Utah

> *Location: Kane and San Juan Counties, 1½ miles below Ute Ford, in Glen Canyon of the Colorado River.*

The Domínguez-Escalante expedition, consisting of the 2 fathers and 12 companions, discovered and used the ford now known as the Crossing of the Fathers on November 7, 1776, after searching 2 weeks for a way to cross the Colorado River. The party, on the trail for 5 months, had unsuccessfully attempted to blaze a trail through Colorado, Utah, and Arizona to connect New Mexico with the missions and settlements of California; and was forced to return to Santa Fe by the lateness of the season. The steps its members chiseled into the canyon wall on their return trip were still visible until recently, when completion of the Glen Canyon Dam submerged these last vestiges of an important Spanish exploration in the Lake Powell Reservoir.

135. Chimney Point, Vermont

> *Location: Addison County, at the Champlain Bridge, on Vt. 17, about 8 miles southwest of Addison.*

Chimney Point is a promontory in Lake Champlain, where Samuel de Champlain reportedly stood in 1609, after a battle with the Iroquois Indians on the western shore of the lake, and gave his name to the beautiful inland sea stretching before him. The battle marked the beginning of continued hostilities between the Iroquois and the French. In 1690, a French expedition under Jacobus de Warm built a small, temporary fort at the site, but the first important settlement was made in 1730 by some French colonists. who renovated the fort and renamed it Fort de Pieux.

The settlement that grew up around the fort became one of the most important of the French in the New World. In 1759, its inhabitants abandoned it because of a threatened Indian invasion, and in 1760 raiding Mohawks destroyed it completely. The grim picture of chimneys rising from blackened ruins gave the point its name. Many cellar holes of the ancient French town are still visible. Chimney Point is privately owned and is not open to the public.

136. Fort Ste. Anne Site, Vermont

Location: Grand Isle County, on West Shore Road, about 3 miles north of Isle La Motte Village, on Isle La Motte.

Fort Ste. Anne was the oldest European settlement in Vermont. In 1666, a group of French soldiers, led by Capt. Pierre de la Motte, built it for protection against the Mohawks. Settlers located around the fort, and the Jesuits built a chapel nearby, where the first mass in Vermont was held. The settlement proved to be a temporary one, and no remains exist. The site is outlined by cedars and spaced rock mounds.

137. Belle Air, Virginia

Location: Charles City County, on Va. 5, just east of Charles City Courthouse.

This early frame plantation house was built about 1670. Despite 18th- and 19th-century additions, it still retains its rare original structural interior framework of heart pine. Plainly visible today are the summer beams, intermediate and corner posts, and an unusual staircase. Situated on a knoll and surrounded by a 4-acre lawn and a grove of old trees, the house overlooks more than 200 acres of rolling farmland. Restored in the 1950's, it is furnished with 18th-century antiques. A smokehouse, old laundry-kitchen, and a new herb garden are interesting adjuncts to the house, which is privately owned and not open to the public.

138. Bladensfield Estate, Virginia

Location: Westmoreland County, 1.8 miles northeast of junction of Va. 3 and 203, near Warsaw.

The original Bladensfield Estate, of 1,000 acres, was patented by John

Jenkins in 1653, and the present house was built for Jenkins by Nicholas Rochester, who came from England in 1689. At Jenkins' death, in 1719,

Late in the 17th century, John Jenkins built this mansion on his 1,000-acre Bladensfield Estate, in Virginia.

Bladensfield was added to the Nomini Hall estate. The house is a large frame building on a brick basement. The walls of nogging covered with clapboards rise two stories to a gabled roof, which has several dormers. The largest of the dormers is over the entrance. Mantels and cornices are hand-carved, and the flooring is dowel-pinned. The house is privately owned and is not open to the public.

139. Fort Monroe, Virginia

> *Location: On U.S. 258, east of 64 and 60, Old Point Comfort, on the eastern outskirts of Hampton.*

Fort Monroe is located on the site of some of the first fortifications built by the English in North America. At this site, in 1609, the Jamestown settlers built Algernourne Fort, a wooden structure, against possible attack by the Spanish. This fort was occupied by 50 settlers and equipped with 7 cannon. During the period 1630 to 1632, it was reconstructed by Col. Samuel Mathews and renamed Point Comfort. It was again reconstructed, this time in brick, during the years 1728–30, and called Fort George, but in 1749 was destroyed by heavy winds. During the Siege of Yorktown, Count de Grasse strengthened his defenses by placing batteries on the point.

Construction of the present Fort Monroe was begun in 1819 and was largely completed in 1836. The fort was completely surrounded by a water-filled moat and a 40-gun water battery, which stood between the outer banks of the moat and the shore of Chesapeake Bay. In 1865, President Lincoln held an unsuccessful peace conference at the fort with Confederate commissioners. After the collapse of the Confederacy, Jefferson Davis, its President, was captured and held prisoner for 2 years at the fort, which is a Registered National Historic Landmark (relating primarily to the Civil War).

For more than 350 years, the site of Fort Monroe has been occupied continuously—having been garrisoned longer than any other Army post in the United States. Through the years the fort has grown from a crude frontier stockade to one of our major Army posts. Fort Monroe, the last and most important of the defenses built on this site, is now the headquarters for the Continental Army Command.

140. Grace Church, Virginia

Location: York County, 1 block off Main Street, Yorktown.

York-Hampton Parish was formed about 1680 by uniting the two parishes. In 1697, a new church was erected at Yorktown, the two earlier churches being abandoned. Built of native marl, it was T-shaped and had a steeple. During the War for Independence, the windows and furnishings were destroyed by fire, and the British used the church as a magazine. After being restored and used for many years, it was again burned during the War of 1812. It was then rebuilt, but the transept was pulled down, leaving the nave, the rectangular building of today.

During the Civil War, the church was used again for military purposes; the furnishings were destroyed, and the bricks from the old wall around the churchyard taken away. The old bell was removed in 1865, but in 1889 it was recast and returned. The marl walls have been hardened by the two fires that have gutted the building. The cupola and carved doorway are late additions. Services are still held every Sunday.

141. Green Spring Plantation Site, Virginia

Location: James City County, junction of Va. 5 and 415.

Sir William Berkeley, Royal Governor of Virginia during the periods 1641–52 and 1660–77, began construction of the mansion at Green Spring about 1646. When completed, it was the largest and most imposing in 17th-century Virginia and a forerunner of later pretentious colonial mansions. A road ran directly from the estate—where considerable colony business was transacted—some 3 miles to Jamestown. Unfortunately, little more than the foundations of the once great house and its dependencies now remain. Because the extensive archeological remains, complicated by later construction, are difficult to interpret, the exact outside appearance and interior arrangement of the house in Berkeley's time can only be conjectured.

Berkeley's activities at Green Spring were diverse. They included winemaking, cultivation of rice and flax, production of silk from mulberry trees, maintenance of a large fruit orchard, the raising of oranges in a hothouse, and the harvesting of timber products. Berkeley also raised livestock, including racehorses, and had a windmill and pottery kiln.

An act of Congress, approved June 5, 1936 (49 Stat. 1483), authorized the inclusion of the Green Spring site in Colonial National Historical Park.

142. Henricus (Henricopolis) Site, Virginia

Location: Henrico County, on Farrar's Island, in the James River.

In the fall of 1611, Sir Thomas Dale and 350 workmen from Jamestown, of which Dale was later Governor, built the city of Henricus about 10 miles below present Richmond at the great bend of the James River. Dale's orders were to move the inhabitants of Jamestown to the new city and to make it the capital of the colony. The proposed city was situated on 7 acres of ground in the neck of Farrar's Island, where it then joined the mainland. In 1618, Gov. Sir George Yeardley was instructed to choose a suitable site at the city for a University of Henrico, already imposed in the town's charter. Accordingly, 10,000 acres were set aside and money was collected in England to finance the college. The Indians, however, destroyed the city in 1622, and the migration from Jamestown never occurred. Nevertheless, Henricopolis marked the first notable expansion of the colony upriver from Jamestown. A small tract of the original city of Henricus is owned today by the Virginia Society of the Colonial Dames of America, and it is marked by two stone monuments.

143. Hill Farm, Virginia

Location: Accomack County, about 6 miles off County 661, via Va. 177, southwest of Accomac.

This farm was patented about 1663 by Capt. Richard Hill. The well-proportioned, one-and-a-half story brick house was built in the last half of the 17th century; one of the bricks is dated 1697. Frame additions are of a later period. The first story sets on a high foundation; the half story is lighted by dormers set closely together on the tall gabled roof. In the center of the house is a wide cross hall, from which rises a fine stairway. On the left is the parlor, which has handsomely restored paneling and moldings. Privately owned, the house is not open to the public.

144. Keeling House, Virginia

Location: Princess Anne County, on County 615, about 5½ miles north of U.S. 58, overlooking the Lynnhaven River.

When Adam Keeling I made his will in 1683, he bequeathed to his son Thomas the land on which this story-and-a-half house was soon built, apparently by Thomas. Especially notable is the fine colonial brickwork, which is a good example of Flemish bond. The design is worked out in the gables by the use of blue headers. The end chimneys give height, and dormers relieve the severity of the steep-pitched roof. A kitchen wing has been added to the original house. Privately owned, the house is not open to the public.

145. Merchant's Hope Church, Virginia

> *Location: Prince George County, on County 641, about ½ mile from Va. 10, some 6½ miles east of Hopewell.*

This gaunt, rectangular church takes its name from a grant of land made in 1635 to the owners of *The Merchant's Hope,* a bark that plied between England and Virginia. The interior has been greatly altered, though the floors are still paved with the original flagstones. The year 1657, carved in one of the huge rafters of the barrel-vaulted roof, has been considered the date of construction, although the design is of a later period.

Like most of the old colonial churches, Merchant's Hope suffered depredations during later wars. The interior was destroyed during the Civil War, when the church was used as a picket station, but the beautiful colonial brick exterior is practically the same as when it was built. The church, a member of the Episcopal Diocese of Southern Virginia, holds services only during the summer months.

146. Old Mansion, Virginia

> *Location: Caroline County, on Va. 301, just south of Bowling Green.*

Old Mansion was the seat of the original Bowling Green Estate. Maj. John Hoomes built the house on land he patented in 1670. The early brick portion of the one-and-a-half story house, built not later than 1675, has balanced dormer windows. The brick walls are in good condition, though they are somewhat concealed by a weathered coat of white paint. During the century following construction, a frame portion was added at the rear. It continues the steep-hipped gambrel roof, now covered with modern roofing. A small porch added along the side and a wide screened porch across the front further obscure the original appearance.

The grounds are distinctive. A large tree-lined oval—a well-kept bowling green—stretches from the entrance gate to near the front of the house. This is ringed by cedar trees, some of which are apparently original. An unusual walk, lined by old English boxwoods, leads from the top of the green to the house entrance. At the rear are remnants of a terraced garden. An avenue of ancient holly trees approaches the south side of the house. The house is privately owned and is not open to the public.

147. Rosegill Estate, Virginia

Location: Middlesex County, on Va. 227, about 1½ miles north of Va. 33, east of Saluda.

Ralph Wormeley patented this estate and began construction in 1649. The house contained a chapel, picture gallery, large library, and 30 guest chambers. One immense attic room provided 14 beds for bachelor guests.

This mid-17th-century mansion, at Rosegill Estate, was once the temporary seat of the colony of Virginia.

Two Governors—Sir Henry Chicheley and Lord Francis Howard—lived in the house, which was once the temporary seat of the colony. The present main house contains part of the first. The long, many-windowed building has one brick and one frame story beneath a gabled roof. Green shutters flank the numerous windows and accent the white walls. Privately owned, the house is not open to the public.

148. Sheild House, Virginia

Location: York County, Main Street, Yorktown.

Thomas Sessions built this one-and-a-half story house, an outstanding example of 17th-century brick construction, in the 1690's. Walls of large brick rise from a high basement to a gabled roof. Outside chimneys and five dormers provide character. The front door is a so-called "Christian door," although not of the same type as in the Old North Church in Boston. This one has two upright crosses, but the same tradition clung to it—that it was good for driving witches away. The house also has many HL hinges, which were chiefly used in New England. The Siege of Yorktown, in 1781, raged around the house, which was also used during the Civil War by one of Gen. George B. McClellan's staff for a headquarters. Privately owned, the house is not open to the public.

149. Smith's Fort Plantation Site (Rolfe House), Virginia

Location: Surry County, on Va. 31, about 2 miles north of Surry.

This is the site of a fortification built by Capt. John Smith on the south side of the James River as a refuge in the event that enemy attack forced evacuation of Jamestown, across the river. Constructed early in

Possibly the oldest brick residence in Virginia, the "Rolfe House," or "Warren House," dates from about 1652. It is located on the site of a fortification built in 1609 by Capt. John Smith to protect Jamestown.

1609, the fort was the first extension of Jamestown, but was hardly used because no attacks occurred. The generally accepted site is marked by a few mounds of earth and is on property owned by the Association for the Preservation of Virginia Antiquities. The site has been called both "Smith's Fort Plantation" and "The Rolfe Property," for the site also contains a small brick residence that was built on property owned by John Rolfe. The property was part of a grant made to Rolfe by Powhatan when Rolfe married Pocahontas, Powhatan's daughter. The house, called the "Rolfe House," "Warren House," and "Fifty-Foot Brick House," was reportedly built by Thomas Warren in 1652 and is the oldest brick house in Virginia. It has been restored, furnished in 17th-century style, and is open to the public.

150. Discovery Bay, Washington

Location: Jefferson County, along U.S. 101, at the eastern entrance to the Strait of Juan de Fuca.

This bay was discovered by the Spanish explorer Alférez Manuel Quimper, on July 11, 1790, and named Bodega y Quadra Bay in honor of the famous Spanish explorer. Francisco de Eliza, another Spaniard, used it in 1791 as a temporary base of operations while he explored the San Juan Islands. The following year, during an expedition along the Pacific coast and into the Strait of Juan de Fuca, the English explorer Capt. George Vancouver anchored his vessels, including the *Discovery,* in the bay and named it Discovery Bay. After a few weeks, he set out eastward in his longboats for a 2-month exploration of the Puget Sound area. Except for present farming uses, the appearance of Discovery Bay has changed little since the 18th century.

151. Neah Bay, Washington

Location: Clallam County, on the south side of the entrance to the Strait of Juan de Fuca, at the western terminus of Wash. 9A.

The first European settlement on the present Pacific Northwest coast of the United States was made on the shores of this bay. The bay was discovered in 1790 by the Spanish explorer Alférez Manuel Quimper, who called it Bahía de Nuñez Gaona. In May 1792, the Spanish frigate *Princesa* landed on its shore a group of settlers, led by Lt. Sálvador

Fidalgo. The settlers built a fortified village of about 10 houses, which they called Nuñez Gaona, but they abandoned it after about 5 months, when Quimper moved them to Nootka.

The present settlement at Neah Bay, as the bay was later called, was initiated in 1851, when Samuel Hancock, an American wagonmaker, erected a trading post. The appearance of Neah Bay has changed little since the 18th century, except for the small village located there, which is the administrative and trading center of the Makah Indian Reservation and a fishing center. No remains of the early Spanish settlement are visible, but brick and tile used by the Spanish builders are occasionally found and are displayed by the Washington State Historical Society museum in Tacoma.

152. Point Grenville, Washington

Location: Grays Harbor County, 8 miles west of Wash. 9C, Quinault Indian Reservation.

The Spanish explorers Bruno Heceta and Juan Francisco de Bodega y Quadra anchored their vessels, the *Santiago* and *Sonora*, off this point on July 13, 1775. The next day Heceta and 23 of his men landed on

Point Grenville, Washington. In 1775, the Spanish explorers Heceta and Quadra landed at the point and claimed the area for Spain. They were the first Europeans known to set foot in the State of Washington.

the promontory and claimed the area for Spain; these men were apparently the first Europeans to set foot in the present State of Washington. They were ambushed by Indians and seven of them killed. Heceta named the point "Punta de los Martires" in honor of the slaughtered sailors. In 1792, the English explorer Capt. George Vancouver sighted the promontory and renamed it Point Grenville. Little changed since 1775, the point is now utilized for a U.S. Coast Guard Station.

153. Green Bay, Wisconsin

Location: Brown County.

Green Bay, located along the banks of the Fox River, is the oldest settlement in Wisconsin. Early French voyageurs and *coureurs de bois* probably knew about the site and named it *Baye des Puants* because the Puants, a Winnebago tribe, resided there. Not until 1634, however, did Jean Nicolet, commissioned by Champlain, arrive at *La Baye* and claim the region for France. For more than 30 years little happened at *La Baye,* but in 1669 Father Claude Allouez, a Jesuit missionary, founded a mission there. In 1673, Marquette and Jolliet left St. Ignace to open up a water route to the Mississippi. They sailed from Lake Michigan to Green Bay and then went down the Fox and Wisconsin Rivers to the Mississippi. After this journey, because of its strategic position on the water route to the Mississippi, *La Baye* became an important fur trading center and rendezvous. In 1684, the French Government appointed Nicolas Perrot commandant of the region, and he built a crude frontier fort and trading post at *La Baye.* Soon, many traders, trappers, Indians, missionaries, and French soldiers settled there.

During the first half of the 18th century, the settlement was involved in constant warfare with the Fox Indians, and the French built Fort La Baye in 1716 to keep the area open for trade. In 1728, the Indians destroyed it, but the French rebuilt it 5 years later. At the end of the French and Indian War, in 1763, the British occupied Fort La Baye. They called the settlement Green Bay (*La Baye Verte*) because the water and shore assumed green tints early in the spring. During the British regime, the fur trade reached its height and Green Bay developed into a prosperous farming community. After 1783, when the United States acquired the Northwest Territory from the British, French and British traders continued to live in the settlement and opposed American interference. Not until after the War of 1812 did Americans share fully in the fur trade of the region, when John Jacob Astor's American Fur Company gained control.

Located at Green Bay is the oldest extant house in Wisconsin, the Roi-Porlier-Tank Cottage.

154. Prairie du Chien, Wisconsin

Location: Crawford County.

Located on a broad terrace overlooking the Mississippi, 3 miles north of the confluence of the Mississippi and Wisconsin Rivers, Prairie du Chien is the second oldest settlement in Wisconsin—the first being Green Bay. Prairie du Chien was a vital station on the route between Canada and the vast French-claimed heartland of North America.

Soon after Louis Jolliet and Père Jacques Marquette passed nearby in 1673 while journeying down the Wisconsin and Mississippi Rivers, the site became an important gathering place for French and Indian trappers, traders, and hunters. In the mid-1680's, Nicolas Perrot erected Fort St. Nicolas there, but a permanent French garrison was never assigned. In the mid-1700's, French stragglers may have settled at the site and named it for a Fox Indian chief whom they called *Le Chien* ("the dog"). A land claim made by three French Canadians in 1781, however, is usually considered the date of the first permanent settlement.

For more than a century, the settlement was a base for the French commercial exploitation of the entire region west of the Great Lakes. In spite of the British occupation during the War for Independence and for a short time in 1814, and subsequent American rule, no notable change occurred in commercial activities at Prairie du Chien. Both British and American trading companies prospered, even though the settlement changed hands.

No structure survives from the French period. The important surviving buildings date from the late 18th and early 19th centuries. Historical interest is centered in the older part of town, on St. Feriole Island; at Villa Louis, administered by the State Historical Society of Wisconsin; the Brisbois House; and the Astor Warehouse. Other more recent sites of interest include the second Fort Crawford, the Dousman Hotel, and the Diamond Jo Steamship Line warehouse. All of these buildings, as well as the city of Prairie du Chien, are eligible for the Registry of

National Historic Landmarks (relating primarily to the advance of the frontier, 1763–1830).

155. Roi-Porlier-Tank Cottage, Wisconsin

Location: Brown County, 10th Avenue and 5th Street, Green Bay.

This cottage in Green Bay is the oldest extant residence in Wisconsin. It is typical of those built by early fur traders in the old Northwest. The original section was built in 1776 by Francis Roi, a French trapper, several years after France had lost Wisconsin to Great Britain. Roi incorporated a huge fireplace, built of wattle and daub—an unusual method of construction in French America, but quite common in Canada. In 1805, Jacques Porlier bought the cottage and used it as his residence. During the War of 1812, English officers used it to hold conferences. Nils Otto Tank, a Norwegian, purchased it in 1850 and had it clapboarded, plastered, and painted. He also added low wings on each side. Originally located on the west bank of the Fox River, the cottage was moved to its present site by the Green Bay Historical Society and the South Side Improvement Association. It is open to the public all year.

156. Fort San Geronimo, Puerto Rico

Location: On the Boquerón, the opening into Condado Lagoon, San Juan.

This small fort occupies a strategic site that the Spanish early utilized to defend the eastern land approaches to San Juan and to support the harbor defenses. The earlier fort or forts—depending on whether or not rebuilding or new building was carried on in 1608—at this site served from the 16th through most of the 18th centuries. The Spanish designed the present masonry structure in 1791; built it in the period 1792–96; and identically reconstructed it during the years 1799–1801, after the British partially destroyed it in 1797. The fort rests on a sandstone bedrock that juts out into the sea. It has two main levels, or tiers. The upper one, the gundeck, is connected by two ramps with the forecourt. Inside are storerooms, magazines, dungeon, kitchen, and other facilities. The fort is administered by the Institute of Puerto Rican Culture, which in 1961 restored it and installed a military museum.

SUGGESTED READING

General Works

BAKELESS, JOHN E. *The Eyes of Discovery—The Pageant of North America as Seen by the First Explorers.* Philadelphia: Lippincott, 1950. Includes numerous and extensive quotations relating the marvels of discovery in the words of those who first saw the Western Hemisphere. Consists mainly of descriptions of flora, fauna, and geographical features.

BOLTON, HERBERT E. and THOMAS M. MARSHALL. *The Colonization of North America, 1492–1783.* New York: Macmillan, 1936. A concise but thorough account of the exploration and colonization of the continent and the international rivalries that were involved.

BREBNER, JOHN B. *The Explorers of North America, 1492–1806.* New York: Macmillan, 1933; reprinted in paperback 1955. A well-written work of careful scholarship that views as a whole the significant explorations of the continent. Includes quotations from contemporary narratives.

CROUSE, NELLIS M. *In Quest of the Western Ocean.* New York: Morrow, 1928. Studies European attempts to find a water passage through or around the American continental block. Also sheds light on motivations for European expansion.

DE VOTO, BERNARD A. *The Course of Empire.* Boston: Houghton Mifflin, 1952. One of a number of attempts to tie the various explorations of North America into a meaningful whole, this book is written with power and persuasion and is often considered to be De Voto's major work. It has literary merit, but its historical value has been highly praised and disparagingly criticized.

FOLMER, HENRY. *Franco-Spanish Rivalry in North America, 1524–1763.* Vol. VII of the *Spain in the West* series. Glendale: Arthur Clark, 1953. Excellent work. Stresses international rivalries and diplomatic maneuverings.

[403

Newton, Arthur P. *The Great Age of Discovery.* London: University of London, 1932. Contains monographs by various British historians on a number of explorers, from Vasco da Gama to Frobisher. Analyzes explorers against the background of their own times.

Priestley, Herbert I. *The Coming of the White Man, 1492–1848.* Vol. I of *A History of American Life,* ed. by Arthur M. Schlesinger and Dixon R. Fox. New York: Macmillan, 1929. A history of European contacts with the New World that emphasizes social rather than military and political aspects.

The Spanish

Bolton, Herbert E. *Coronado, Knight of Pueblos and Plains.* Albuquerque: University of New Mexico Press, 1949. An enjoyable biography of Coronado and an extensive survey of his exploration of the Southwest.

———. *Rim of Christendom—A Biography of Eusebio Francisco Kino, Pacific Coast Pioneer.* New York: Macmillan, 1936. Not only the definitive biography of Padre Kino, the famous missionary, but also the best available account of early Spanish efforts in Arizona.

———. *The Spanish Borderlands—A Chronicle of Old Florida and the Southwest.* Vol. XXIII of *The Chronicles of America* series, ed. by Allen Johnson. New Haven: Yale University Press, 1921. A compact and readable volume that is still popular with students and laymen alike.

Bourne, Edward G. *Spain in America, 1450–1580.* Vol III of *The American Nation* series, ed. by Albert B. Hart. New York: Harper, 1940; reprinted in paperback 1962. Probably the most widely read scholarly work on the foundations of the Spanish Empire in North America.

Carter, Hodding and Betty W. *Doomed Road of Empire—The Spanish Trail of Conquest. American Trails* series. New York: McGraw-Hill, 1963. An interesting and scholarly work on the Spanish borderlands by a Pulitzer prizewinner and his wife. Tells the stories of the Spaniards, Mexicans, and Americans who traveled the *Camino Real* (Royal Highway) from Saltillo to Natchitoches and its parallel trails in Texas between 1568 and the Battle of Buena Vista, in 1847.

Caughey, John W. *History of the Pacific Coast of North America.* New York: Prentice-Hall, 1938. An excellent one-volume history of the Pacific coast—from Mexico to Alaska—that emphasizes the period before 1850.

HARING, CLARENCE H. *The Spanish Empire in America.* New York: Oxford, 1947. An authoritative summary, stressing institutional development, that is equally valuable to the specialist and nonspecialist.

HORGAN, PAUL. *Great River—The Rio Grande in North American History.* 2 vols. New York: Rinehart, 1954. Vol. I, *Indians and Spain.* A Pulitzer-prize-winning history that is particularly readable. Devoted as much to life along the Rio Grande as to the river itself. Discusses various phases of Indian and Spanish life and their interrelationships.

MADARIAGA, SALVADOR DE. *The Rise of the Spanish American Empire.* New York: Macmillan, 1947. This and the following volume provide an excellent synthesis of the history of the Spanish Empire in America.

——— . *The Fall of the Spanish American Empire.* New York: Macmillan, 1948.

MORISON, SAMUEL E. *Admiral of the Ocean Sea—A Life of Christopher Columbus.* Boston: Little, Brown, 1942. A condensation of a two-volume work, published the same year, that was awarded a Pulitzer prize for biography.

SPICER, EDWARD H. *Cycles of Conquest—The Impact of Spain, Mexico, and the United States on the Indians of the Southwest, 1533–1960.* Tucson: University of Arizona Press, 1962. A comprehensive, specialized work that should nevertheless be of interest to the layman who is interested in delving beyond the surface of history. Includes the findings of recent scholarship on Indian-Spanish relationships.

The French

BISHOP, MORRIS. *Champlain—The Life of Fortitude.* New York: Knopf, 1948. A scholarly and probably the most readable biography of the famed French explorer. The author's admiration of Champlain enhances rather than detracts from the presentation.

MUNRO, WILLIAM B. and GEORGE M. WRONG. *Adventures of New France.* Vol. III of *The Chronicles of America* series, ed. by Allen Johnson. New Haven: Yale University Press, 1918. One of the better volumes of this series. Divided into two parts: "Crusaders of New France," by Munro, and "The Conquest of New France," by Wrong.

NUTE, GRACE L. *The Voyageur.* St. Paul: Minnesota Historical Association, 1931, reprint 1955. Although most of this work concentrates on the period after 1763, when the French had been driven off the continent, it is valuable for its portrayal of the French voyageur.

PARKMAN, FRANCIS. *La Salle and the Discovery of the Great West.* Vol. III of his collected *Works.* Boston: Little, Brown, 1902; available in paperback. First issued in 1869, this volume is a monument to La Salle's achievements in the Mississippi Valley. The style is somewhat more labored than usual for Parkman.

———. *Pioneers of France in the New World.* Vol. I of his collected *Works.* Boston: Little, Brown, 1902. Originally published in 1865, this classic provides a fascinating account of the activities of the early French pioneers—from Fort Caroline, in Florida, to Quebec, in Canada. It has never been surpassed as an account of the Huguenot ventures in North America, although its principal purpose is to describe the foundations of New France.

———. *The Battle for North America.* Ed. by John Tebbel. Garden City: Doubleday, 1948. A rather extensive (746 pages) condensation of Parkman's massive study of the French in North America and their struggle to hold the continent's heartland.

———. *The Jesuits in North America in the Seventeenth Century.* Vol. II of his collected *Works.* Boston: Little, Brown, 1902. This classic narrative of missionary tenacity was first published in 1867. Relates the martyrdom and zeal of the Jesuit fathers in spreading European culture and influence among the Indians and settlers in New France.

THWAITES, REUBEN G. *France in America, 1497–1763.* Vol. VII of *The American Nation* series, ed. by Albert B. Hart. New York: Harper, 1905. This book remains an outstanding summary of the French period. Like several other volumes in the series, it surpasses in literary merit and historical skill more recent works in the field.

WRONG, GEORGE M. *The Rise and Fall of New France.* 2 vols. New York: Macmillan, 1928. The story of France in America told by a Canadian historian. Neither as readable nor as perceptive as Parkman's works, but it is based on more recent scholarship and presents a different viewpoint and organization.

The Dutch and Swedes

BENSON, ADOLPH B. and NABOTH HEDIN. *Americans from Sweden. The People of America* series. Philadelphia: Lippincott, 1950. Discusses all phases of Swedish colonial history and the role of the Swedes in America, including religion and education.

NISSENSON, SAMUEL G. *The Patroon's Domain.* New York: Columbia University Press, 1937. Although this work is designed to trace the history of Rensselaerswyck and the vicinity of Albany, it is the best analysis of the patroon system available. Places colonization of New Netherland in the context of the commercial growth of the Dutch Republic.

RAESLY, ELLIS L. *Portrait of New Netherland.* New York: Columbia University Press, 1945. Originally a doctoral dissertation, this socially oriented history competently treats government, religion, culture, political ideas, literature, and other aspects of New Netherland.

The English

ANDREWS, CHARLES M. *Colonial Folkways—A Chronicle of American Life in the Reign of the Georges.* Vol. IX of *The Chronicles of America* series, ed. by Allen Johnson. New Haven: Yale University Press, 1921. Emphasizing social aspects of colonial history, this widely read book has contributed much to general understanding of the American heritage.

——— *Colonial Self-Government, 1652–1689.* Vol. V of *The American Nation* series, ed. by Albert B. Hart. New York: Harper, 1904. In the field of Andrews' specialty, this volume is still the best single one on the subject.

CHITWOOD, OLIVER P. *A History of Colonial America.* New York: Harper, 1931. One of the best works of its kind available. Presents a thorough and factual résumé of European colonization of North America, but emphasizes the area of the present United States and the activities of the English.

CRAVEN, WESLEY F. *The Southern Colonies in the Seventeenth Century, 1607–1689.* Baton Rouge: Louisiana State University Press, 1949. Vol. I of *A History of the South* series, ed. by Wendell H. Stephenson and Ellis M. Coulter. Carefully examines the cultural development of colonial Virginia, Maryland, and the Carolinas.

ELLIS, GEORGE E. *The Puritan Age and Rule in the Colony of the Massachusetts Bay, 1629–1685.* Boston: Houghton Mifflin, 1888. This study, one of the first of its kind, is still probably the most inclusive and is basically sound. Recent advances in social and intellectual history, however, have resulted in modifications of Ellis' ideas.

GREENE, EVARTS B. *The Foundation of American Nationality.* New York: American Book Co., rev. ed. 1935. A review of American colonial history as a part of that of the British Empire, from the foundations of the colonies to the adoption of the Federal Constitution. Written for laymen and students, it synthesizes modern scholarship relating to the period.

——— . *Provincial America.* Vol. VI of *The American Nation* series, ed.

by Albert B. Hart. New York: Harper, 1905. Focusing on the British settlements that became part of the United States, this volume tells the story of their expansion, government, religion, culture, and commerce.

MILLER, PERRY. *The New England Mind—The Seventeenth Century.* New York: Macmillan, 1939. An intellectual history of Puritanism in New England. The theological doctrines and philosophical roots of the colonial leaders are cogently synthesized and thoroughly analyzed.

————. *Roger Williams—His Contributions to the American Tradition.* Indianapolis: Bobbs-Merrill, 1953. Of a number of biographies of Roger Williams, this one seems to present the best-rounded portrait.

MORISON, SAMUEL E. *Builders of the Bay Colony.* Boston: Houghton Mifflin, 1930. Illuminates with literary skill the lives of a number of individuals who contributed to the early development of Massachusetts—from Richard Hakluyt to Anne Bradstreet. Provides a sympathetic account of New England Puritanism.

————. *The Intellectual Life of Colonial New England.* New York: New York University Press, 2d ed. 1956. Not so much a history of ideas as a history of intellectual endeavor. It surveys such subjects as education, bookselling, libraries, sermons, political tracts, poetry, and science.

NETTELS, CURTIS P. *The Roots of American Civilization.* New York: Crofts, 1946. Crofts' *American History* series, ed. by Dixon R. Fox. Treats theoretical and practical aspects of British colonial policy from the standpoint of the British Government and the colonists. Illuminates economic, political, and social facets of the American heritage.

PEARE, CATHERINE O. *William Penn—A Biography.* Philadelphia: Lippincott, 1957. Probably the most perceptive of all the biographies of this prominent Anglo-American.

STARKEY, MARION L. *The Devil in Massachusetts—A Modern Inquiry into the Salem Witch Trials.* New York: Knopf, 1949. A modern psychological study of the witch trials. Their history is clearly told, and it is related to the social and religious background in Massachusetts. Of the numerous studies on the subject, this is probably the most interesting to the average reader.

SWEET, WILLIAM W. *Religion in Colonial America.* New York: Scribner's, 1942. The definitive general work on the subject. Examines religious motivation for colonization, the effect of the colonial experience on Old World religious thought, and the great variety and diversity of religious opinions in the colonies.

WERTENBAKER, THOMAS J. *The First Americans, 1607–1690*. Vol. II of
    A History of American Life, ed. by Arthur M. Schlesinger and
    Dixon R. Fox. New York: Macmillan, 1927. Like other volumes
    in the series, this one emphasizes social aspects, Wertenbaker's field
    of specialty.
————— . *The Founding of American Civilization—The Middle Colonies.*
    New York: Scribner's, 1938. This volume and the two listed immedi-
    ately below comprise one of the finest overall studies available on
    our colonial heritage. Like the others, it is written from the colonial
    rather than the British viewpoint. Surveys the founding of New
    York, New Jersey, and Pennsylvania.
————— . *The Founding of American Civilization—The Old South.* New
    York: Scribner's, 1942. Treats the establishment of Virginia, Mary-
    land, and the Carolinas with well-rounded historical scrutiny.
————— . *The Founding of American Civilization—The Puritan Oligarchy.*
    New York: Scribner's, 1947. Primarily a study of Massachusetts,
    but discusses the other Puritan colonies in New England. Provides
    an excellent analysis of the development of the Bay Colony.
WILLIAMSON, JAMES A. *The Age of Drake*. London: Black, 3d ed. 1952.
    Tells the tale of Drake and the "sea dogs" with vigor, taste, and
    authenticity. Contributes much to an understanding of the back-
    ground of U.S. colonial history.
————— . *A Short History of British Expansion.* 2 vols. New York: Mac-
    millan, 2d ed. 1931. Possibly no other single work so effectively places
    the development of the British seaboard colonies in the perspective
    of empire.
WILLISON, GEORGE F. *Saints and Strangers*. New York: Reynal and Hitch-
    cock, 1945. A lively story of the Pilgrims and the founding of
    Plymouth colony. Drawn largely from original material—Brad-
    ford's journal, letters, and other manuscripts of the colonists—it is
    written with sympathetic understanding.
WRIGHT, LOUIS B. *The Cultural Life of the American Colonies, 1607–1763*.
    New York: Harper, 1957. A short but outstanding survey of our
    colonial cultural heritage.

NOTES

1. Apalachicola Fort, Ala.: Herbert E. Bolton, ed., *Arredondo's Proof of Spain's Title to Georgia* (Berkeley, 1925); Verner W. Crane, *The Southern Frontier, 1670–1732* (Durham, N.C., 1928); David L. DeJarnette, "Archeological Salvage in the Walter F. George Basin of the Chattahoochee River in Alabama," MS Report, National Park Service (1963).

2. Fort Toulouse (Fort Jackson), Ala.: Crane, *Southern Frontier;* Dunbar Rowland and Albert G. Sanders, *Mississippi Provincial Archives, French Dominion* (3 vols., Jackson, 1927–32); Daniel H. Thomas, "Fort Toulouse—In Tradition and Fact," *The Alabama Review*, XIII, 4 (October 1960).

3. Awatovi, Ariz.: Herbert E. Bolton, *Spanish Exploration in the Southwest, 1542–1706* (New York, 1916); R. G. Montgomery, Watson Smith, and J. O. Brew, *Franciscan Awatovi*, Papers of the Peabody Museum of Archaeology and Ethnology, XXXVI (Cambridge, 1949); Erik K. Reed, "Special Report on Awatovi, Arizona" and "Supplementary Report on Awatovi, Arizona," MS Reports, National Park Service (1938); Edward H. Spicer, *Cycles of Conquest* (Tucson, 1962).

4. San Xavier del Bac Mission, Ariz.: Herbert E. Bolton, *Rim of Christendom—A Biography of Eusebio Francisco Kino, Pacific Coast Pioneer* (New York, 1936); Herbert E. Bolton, *Kino's Historical Memoir of Pimería Alta* (Cleveland, 1919); Cleve Hallenbeck, *Spanish Missions of the Old Southwest* (New York, 1926); Aubrey Neasham, "Special Report on the Mission of San Xavier del Bac," MS Report, National Park Service (1940).

5. Carmel Mission, Calif.: Hubert H. Bancroft, *History of California* (7 vols., San Francisco, 1884–90), I–IV; John A. Berger, *The Franciscan Missions of California* (New York, 1941); Father Zephyrin Engelhardt, *Mission San Carlos Borroméo*, ed. by Father Felix Pudlowski (Santa Barbara, 1934); Mrs. Francis N. Smith, *The Architectural History of Mission San Carlos Borroméo* (Berkeley, 1921); Kurt Baer, *Architecture of the California Missions* (Berkeley and Los Angeles, 1958).

6. Fort Ross, Calif.: Bancroft, *History of California,* II and IV; Bancroft,

History of Alaska (San Francisco, 1886); John W. Caughey, *California* (Englewood Cliffs, N.J., 1957); Mildred B. Hoover, Hero E. and Ethel G. Rensch, *Historic Spots in California,* rev. by Ruth Teiser (Stanford, 1958); Olaf T. Hagen, "Historic Sites Survey Report: Fort Ross, California," MS Report, National Park Service (1941).

7. Old Mission Dam (Padre Dam), Calif.: Bancroft, *History of California,* I and II; Father Zephyrin Engelhardt, *San Diego Mission* (San Francisco, 1920); Baer, *Architecture of the California Missions.*

8. Presidio of San Francisco, Calif.: Bancroft, *History of California,* I–IV; George Vancouver, *Voyage of Discovery to the North Pacific Ocean and Around the World* (6 vols., London, 1801), III.

9. Royal Presidio Chapel, Calif.: James Ladd Delkin, *Monterey Peninsula,* American Guide Series (Stanford, 1946); Bancroft, *History of California,* I–IV; Father Zephyrin Engelhardt, *Missions and Missionaries of California* (4 vols., San Francisco, 1908–15); Rexford Newcomb, *The Old Mission Churches and Historic Houses of California* (Philadelphia, 1925).

10. San Diego Presidio, Calif.: Richard F. Pourade, *The History of San Diego—The Explorers* (San Diego, 1960); Winifred Davidson, *Where California Began* (San Diego, 1929); Bancroft, *History of California,* I–III; Engelhardt, *San Diego Mission;* William E. Smythe, *History of San Diego, 1542–1907* (San Diego, 1907).

11. Santa Barbara Mission, Calif.: Father Zephyrin Engelhardt, *Mission Santa Barbara* (San Francisco, 1923); Bancroft, *History of California,* I–IV; John A. Berger, *The Franciscan Missions of California* (New York, 1941); Baer, *Architecture of the California Missions.*

12. Stanley-Whitman House, Conn.: Anthony N. B. Garvan, *Architecture and Town Planning in Colonial Connecticut* (New Haven, 1951); J. Frederick Kelly, *The Early Domestic Architecture of Connecticut* (New Haven, 1924); Hugh Morrison, *Early American Architecture—From the First Colonial Settlements to the National Period* (New York, 1952); Bertha C. Trowbridge and Charles M. Andrews, *Old Houses of Connecticut* (New Haven, 1923).

13. Fort Christina, Del.: Rogers W. Young, "Site of the Swedish Fort Christina, Wilmington, Delaware," MS Report, National Park Service (1940); Letter, Leon de Valinger, Jr., State Archivist, Dover, Del., to Northeast Regional Office, National Park Service, Mar. 24, 1961; *Delaware—A Guide to the First State,* American Guide Series (rev. ed., New York, 1955); Esther C. Meixner, *Swedish Landmarks in the Delaware Valley* (Bridgeport, Pa., 1960).

14. Holy Trinity (Old Swedes) Church, Del.: Letter, Rev. H. Edgar Hammond, Holy Trinity (Old Swedes) Church Foundation, Inc., Wilmington, Del., to Northeast Regional Office, National Park Service, Apr. 18,

1961; Historic American Buildings Survey, National Park Service, 7 sheets and 8 photos (1934) ; Meixner, *Swedish Landmarks;* Amandus Johnson, *Swedish Settlements on the Delaware—Their History and Relation to the Indians, Dutch, and English, 1638–1664* (2 vols., New York, 1911) ; Rogers W. Young, "Holy Trinity (Old Swedes) Church, Wilmington, Delaware," MS Report, National Park Service (1940).

15. Fort San Carlos de Barrancas, Fla.: Albert Manucy, "Report on Historic Sites at Pensacola, Florida," MS Report, National Park Service (1939) ; Herbert E. Bolton, *The Spanish Borderlands* (New Haven, 1921).

16. San Luís de Apalache, Fla.: Mark F. Boyd, Hale G. Smith, and John W. Griffin, *Here They Once Stood—The Tragic End of the Apalachee Missions* (Gainesville, Fla., 1951) ; Ralston B. Lattimore, "San Luís de Apalache," MS Report, National Park Service (1939) ; Venila L. Shores, "The Ruins of San Luís near Tallahassee," *Florida Historical Quarterly,* VI (1927) ; Mark F. Boyd, "Mission Sites in Florida," *ibid.,* XVII (1939).

17. Fort de Chartres, Ill.: *Fort de Chartres State Park,* pamphlet, State of Illinois, Division of Parks and Memorials (n.p., n.d.) ; Clarence W. Alvord, *The Illinois Country, 1673-1818,* Vol. I (1920), *The Centennial History of Illinois* (6 vols., Chicago, 1917–20).

18. Old Kaskaskia Village Site, Ill.: Wayne C. Temple, *Indian Villages of the Illinois Country, Historic Tribes,* Illinois State Museum Scientific Papers, Vol. II, Part 2 (Springfield, Ill., 1958) ; Donald E. Wray, "Archeology of the Illinois Valley, 1950," in J. B. Griffin, *Archeology of Eastern United States* (Chicago, 1952) ; K. G. Orr, "The Historic Upper Mississippi Phase in Northern Illinois—La Salle County Excavations, 1947," *Proceedings of the Fifth Plains Conference for Archeology,* Laboratory of Anthropology, University of Nebraska (Lincoln, 1949).

19. Starved Rock, Ill.: *Starved Rock State Park,* pamphlet, State of Illinois, Division of Parks and Memorials (n.p., n.d.) ; Charles W. Paape, "Starved Rock in the History of Illinois," MS Report, National Park Service (1937) ; Francis Parkman, *La Salle and the Discovery of the Great West* (Boston, 1903) ; John B. Brebner, *The Explorers of North America* (New York, 1933). *See also* Note 18.

20. El Cuartelejo (Scott County Pueblo Site), Kans.: Waldo R. Wedel, *An Introduction to Kansas Archeology,* Bureau of American Ethnology Bulletin 174 (Washington, 1959) ; James H. Gunnerson, "An Introduction to Plains Apache Archeology—The Dismal River Aspect," *Anthropological Papers,* Bureau of American Ethnology Bulletin 173 (Washington, 1959) ; A. B. Thomas, *After Coronado* (Norman, Okla., 1935).

21. Tobias-Thompson Complex, Kans.: Wedel, *Introduction to Kansas Archeology;* Waldo R. Wedel, "Archeological Remains in Central Kansas and Their Possible Bearing on the Location of Quivira," *Smithsonian Mis-*

cellaneous Collections, Vol. 101 (Washington, 1942); Herbert E. Bolton, *Coronado, Knight of Pueblos and Plains* (Albuquerque, 1949).

22. Cabildo, La.: Morrison, *Early American Architecture;* C. P. Dimitry, "The Story of the Ancient Cabildo," *Louisiana Historical Quarterly,* III (1920); [H. P. Dart], "The Cabildo of New Orleans," *ibid.,* V (1922); J. A. Robertson, ed., *Louisiana under the Rule of Spain, France, and the United States, 1785–1807* (2 vols., Cleveland, 1911).

23. Fort de la Boulaye, La.: Maurice Ries, "The Mississippi Fort Called Fort de la Boulaye," *Louisiana Historical Quarterly,* XIX, No. 4 (Oct. 1936); Dunbar Rowland and Albert G. Sanders, *Mississippi Provincial Archives, French Dominion* (3 vols., Jackson, 1927–32).

24. Jackson Square, La.: Stanley C. Arthur, *Old New Orleans* (New Orleans, 1936); A. P. Whitaker, *The Mississippi Question, 1795–1803* (New York, 1934); Robertson, ed., *Louisiana.*

25. Ursuline Convent, La.: Samuel Wilson, Jr., "An Architectural History of the Royal Hospital and the Ursuline Convent of New Orleans," *Louisiana Historical Quarterly,* XXIX, No. 3 (July 1946); Henry C. Semple, *The Ursulines in New Orleans and Our Lady of Prompt Succor— A Record of Two Centuries, 1725–1925* (New York, 1925); Gabriel Gravier, *Relation du Voyage des Dames Religieuses Ursulines de Rouen á la Nouvelle-Orleans, avec une Introduction et des Notes* (Paris, 1872).

26. Cole's Hill, Mass.: William T. Davis, *Ancient Landmarks of Plymouth* (Boston, 1889); Alvin P. Stauffer, "Historic Sites in or near Plymouth, Massachusetts, Relating to Pilgrim History," MS Report, National Park Service (1941); Samuel E. Morison, *By Land and By Sea* (New York, 1953); George F. Willison, *Saints and Strangers* (New York, 1945).

27. Fairbanks House, Mass.: Alvin L. Jones, *Ye Old Fayerbanks House* (Boston, 1894); Morrison, *Early American Architecture;* Harold R. Shurtleff, *The Log Cabin Myth—A Study of the Early Dwellings of the English Colonists in North America* (Cambridge, 1939); Samuel Chamberlain, *Open House in New England* (Brattleboro, Vt., 1937); Historic American Buildings Survey, National Park Service, 24 sheets (1939), 2 photos (1936).

28. Old Ship Church, Mass.: George F. Marlowe, *Churches of Old New England* (New York, 1947); Morrison, *Early American Architecture;* Edward F. Rines, *Old Historic Churches of America* (New York, 1936).

29. Parson Capen House, Mass.: George F. Dow, *The History of Topsfield* (Topsfield, Mass., 1940); Historic American Buildings Survey, National Park Service, 3 photos (1936); Chamberlain, *Open House in New England;* Fiske Kimball, *Domestic Architecture of the American Colonies and of the Early Republic* (New York, 1922); Donald Miller, "A Seventeenth Century New England House," *The Architectural Record,* XXXVIII, No. 3 (Sept. 1915); Morrison, *Early American Architecture.*

30. Paul Revere House, Mass.: Morrison, *Early American Architecture;* Esther Forbes, *Paul Revere and the World He Lived In* (Boston, 1942).

31. Saugus Iron Works, Mass.: *The Saugus Ironworks Restoration,* pamphlet, American Iron and Steel Institute (*ca.* 1955); E. N. Hartley, *Ironworks on the Saugus* (Norman, Okla., 1957).

32. "Scotch"-Boardman House, Mass.: Abbott Lowell Cummings, "The Scotch-Boardman House—A Fresh Appraisal," *Old Time New England,* XLIII, Nos. 3 and 4 (Winter and Spring 1953); Morrison, *Early American Architecture.*

33. Whipple House, Mass.: Thomas F. Waters, "The John Whipple House," *Publications of the Ipswich Historical Society,* XX (Ipswich, Mass., 1915); Morrison, *Early American Architecture;* Lathrop, *Historic Houses;* Dorothy and Richard Pratt, *A Treasury of Early American Homes* (New York, 1949; rev. ed. 1956).

34. Fort Michilimackinac, Mich.: Moreau S. Maxwell and Lewis R. Binford, "Excavation at Fort Michilimackinac, Mackinaw City, Michigan, 1959 Season," *Michigan State University Cultural Series,* Vol. I, No. 1; Louise P. Kellogg, *The French Regime in Wisconsin and the Northwest* (Madison, 1925); Francis Parkman, *A Half-Century of Conflict* (2 vols., Boston, 1914); Howard H. Peckham, *Pontiac and the Indian Uprising* (Princeton, 1947).

35. St. Ignace Mission, Mich.: Thomas M. Pitkin, "Mackinac Island and Associated Sites," MS Report, National Park Service, 1937; Kellogg, *French Regime;* Parkman, *Half-Century of Conflict;* Francis Parkman, *The Jesuits in North America* (2 vols., Boston, 1909).

36. Kathio Site, Minn.: Russell W. Fridley, "Preserving Historic Sites," *Minnesota History,* XXXVII, No. 2 (1960); Lloyd A. Wilford, "The Prehistoric Indians of Minnesota—The Mille Lacs Aspect," *ibid.,* XXV, No. 4 (1944); Brebner, *Explorers of North America.*

37. Fatherland Plantation Site (Grand Village of the Natchez), Miss.: James A. Ford, *Analysis of Indian Village Site Collections from Louisiana and Mississippi,* Anthropological Study No. 2, Department of Conservation, Louisiana Geological Survey (New Orleans, 1936); John R. Swanton, *Indian Tribes of the Lower Mississippi Valley and Adjacent Coast of the Gulf of Mexico,* Bureau of American Ethnology Bulletin 43 (Washington, 1911).

38. Ste. Genevieve, Mo.: John Drury, *Historic Midwest Houses* (Minneapolis, 1947); Charles E. Peterson, "Early Ste. Genevieve and Its Architecture," *The Missouri Historical Review,* XXXV, No. 2 (Jan. 1941); *Missouri: A Guide to the 'Show Me' State,* American Guide Series (New York, 1954).

39. Utz Site, Mo.: Robert T. Bray, "The Missouri Indian Tribe in Ar-

chaeology and History," *Missouri Historical Review,* LV, No. 2 (1961) ; Carl H. Chapman, "A Preliminary Survey of Missouri Archaeology—Part I: Historic Indian Tribes," *The Missouri Archaeologist,* X, No. 1 (1946).

40. Pike-Pawnee Village Site (Hill Site), Nebr.: Elliott Coues, ed., *The Expeditions of Zebulon Montgomery Pike, 1805–1807* (3 vols., New York, 1895) ; William D. Strong, "An Introduction to Nebraska Archeology," *Smithsonian Miscellaneous Collections,* Vol. 93 (Washington, 1935) ; Waldo R. Wedel, *An Introduction to Pawnee Archeology,* Bureau of American Ethnology Bulletin 112 (Washington, 1936).

41. Abó Pueblo and Mission, N. Mex.: Joseph H. Toulouse, Jr., *The Mission of San Gregorio de Abó,* School of American Research Monograph No. 13 (Albuquerque, 1949) ; Erik K. Reed, "Special Report on Abó State Monument, New Mexico," MS Report, National Park Service (1940) ; George Kubler, *The Religious Architecture of New Mexico* (Colorado Springs, 1940) ; Paul A. F. Walter, *The Cities That Died of Fear* (Santa Fe, 1931).

42. Acoma Pueblo, N. Mex.: Leslie A. White, *The Acoma Indians,* Bureau of American Ethnology, 47th Annual Report, 1929–30 (Washington, 1932) ; William R. Hogan, "Brief Special Report on Acoma, New Mexico," MS Report, National Park Service (1938) ; Erik K. Reed, "Supplementary Report on Acoma, New Mexico," MS Report, National Park Service (1942) ; Stanley A. Stubbs, *Birds-Eye View of the Pueblos* (Norman, Okla., 1950) ; George P. Hammond and Agapito Rey, *Oñate, First Colonizer of New Mexico* (2 vols., Albuquerque, 1940) ; Kubler, *Religious Architecture of New Mexico.*

43. Hawikuh, N. Mex.: Frederick W. Hodge, *The History of Hawikuh* (Los Angeles, 1937) ; Erik K. Reed, "Special Report on Hawikuh, New Mexico," MS Report, National Park Service (1938) ; Herbert E. Bolton, *Coronado, Knight of Pueblo and Plain* (New York and Albuquerque, 1949) ; George P. Hammond and Agapito Rey, eds., *Narratives of the Coronado Expedition* (Albuquerque, 1940).

44. Palace of the Governors, N. Mex.: Clinton P. Anderson, "The Adobe Palace," *New Mexico Historical Review,* XIX (April 1944) ; Aubrey Neasham, "Special Report Covering the Governor's Palace in Sante Fe, New Mexico," MS Report, National Park Service (1939) ; Ralph E. Twitchell, ed., *The Spanish Archives of New Mexico* (2 vols., Cedar Rapids, 1914) ; Ralph E. Twitchell, *The Leading Facts of New Mexican History* (5 vols., Cedar Rapids, 1912) ; Ralph E. Twitchell, *The Palace of the Governors, the City of Sante Fe, Its Museums and Monuments,* Historical Society of New Mexico Publication No. 29 (Santa Fe, 1924) ; Paul A. F. Walter, *Old Sante Fe and Vicinity* (Santa Fe, 1930).

45. Pecos Pueblo, N. Mex.: Alfred V. Kidder, "The Story of the Pueblo

of Pecos," *El Palacio,* Museum of New Mexico, LVIII (1951) ; Kubler, *Religious Architecture of New Mexico;* Edgar L. Hewett and Reginald G. Fisher, *Mission Monuments of New Mexico* (Albuquerque, 1943) ; Clarence W. Hackett, *Historical Documents Relating to New Mexico, Nueva Vizcaya, and Approaches Thereto, to 1773* (Washington, 1937) ; Frederick W. Hodge, George P. Hammond, and Agapito Rey, eds., *Fray Alonso de Benavides' Revised Memorial of 1634* (Albuquerque, 1945).

46. Quarai Pueblo and Mission, N. Mex.: Walter, *The Cities That Died of Fear;* Kubler, *Religious Architecture of New Mexico;* Hewett and Fisher, *Mission Monuments.*

47. San Gabriel de Yungue-ouinge, N. Mex.: Hammond and Rey, *Oñate;* Hodge, Hammond, and Rey, eds., *Benavides' Memorial;* Gilberto Espinosa, *Villagra's History of New Mexico, 1610* (Los Angeles, 1933) ; George M. Foster, *Culture and Conquest* (New York, 1960).

48. Taos Pueblo, N. Mex.: Forrest, *Missions and Pueblos;* Frederick W. Hodge, *Handbook of American Indians* (Washington, 1910) ; Hewett and Fisher, *Mission Monuments;* Charles W. Hackett, "The Revolt of the Pueblo Indians of New Mexico in 1680," Texas State Historical Association *Quarterly,* XV (1911) ; J. Manuel Espinosa, *Crusaders of the Rio Grande: The Story of Don Diego de Vargas and the Reconquest and Refounding of New Mexico* (Chicago, 1942) ; Kubler, *Religious Architecture.*

49. Boughton Hill (Gannagaro) Site, N.Y.: William N. Fenton, "Problems Arising from the Historic Northeastern Position of the Iroquois," *Smithsonian Miscellaneous Collections,* Vol. 100 (1940) ; George T. Hunt, *The Wars of the Iroquois* (Madison, 1960) ; Reuben G. Thwaites, *France in America* (New York, 1905) ; Charles F. Wray and H. L. Schoff, "A Preliminary Report on the Seneca Sequence in Western New York, 1550–1687," *Pennsylvania Archaeologist,* XXIII, No. 2 (1953).

50. Dutch Reformed (Sleepy Hollow) Church, N.Y.: Rogers W. Young, "Dutch Reformed (Sleepy Hollow) Church, North Tarrytown, New York," MS Report, National Park Service (1940) ; John K. Allen, *The Legendary History of the Old Dutch Church of Sleepy Hollow, Tarrytown, N.Y.* (Tarrytown, N.Y., 1891) ; Helen W. Reynolds, *Dutch Houses in the Hudson Valley Before 1776* (New York, 1929).

51. Fort Crailo, N.Y.: Harold D. Eberlein and Cortlandt Van Dyke Hubbard, *Historic Houses of the Hudson Valley* (New York, 1942) ; Morrison, *Early American Architecture;* Reynolds, *Dutch Houses.*

52. Fort St. Frederic, N.Y.: Charles S. Marshall, "Crown Point and Plattsburg," MS Report, National Park Service (1937) ; "Interim Report of the Joint Legislative Committee to Study Historic Sites," Legislative Document, State of New York (Albany, 1950) ; Hoffman Nickerson, *The Turning Point of the Revolution* (Boston, 1928) ; W. Max Reid, *Lake*

George and Lake Champlain (New York, 1910).

53. Old Fort Niagara, N.Y.: Claud H. Hultzén, Sr., *Old Fort Niagara—The Story of an Ancient Gateway to the West,* pamphlet, Old Fort Niagara Association (n.p., 1933) ; Frank H. Severance, *An Old Frontier of France: The Niagara Region and Adjacent Lakes Under French Control* (New York, 1917) ; Thor Borresen, "Father Millet Cross," MS Report, National Park Service (1939).

54. Old House, N.Y.: *The Old House . . . Cutchogue, N.Y.,* pamphlet (n.p., n.d.) ; Letter, Mrs. Roland C. Horton, Custodian, The Old House, to Northeast Regional Office, National Park Service, Aug. 18, 1961; Dorothy and Richard Pratt, *A Guide to Early American Homes, North* (New York, 1956).

55. Philipsburg Manor, Upper Mills, N.Y.: Eberlein and Hubbard, *Historic Houses;* "Sleepy Hollow Restorations," pamphlet, Sleepy Hollow Restorations, Inc. (Tarrytown, N.Y., n.d.) ; Reynolds, *Dutch Houses.*

56. Philipse Manor Hall, N.Y.: Rogers W. Young, "Philipse Manor Hall, Yonkers, New York," MS Report, National Park Service (1940) ; Eberlein and Hubbard, *Historic Houses;* Morrison, *Early American Architecture;* Reynolds, *Dutch Houses.*

57. Van Cortlandt Manor, N.Y.: *Sleepy Hollow Restorations* and *Van Cortlandt Manor, Croton-on-Hudson,* pamphlets, Sleepy Hollow Restorations, Inc. (Tarrytown, N.Y., n.d.) ; Merrill Folsom, "Old Croton House Is Being Restored," *New York Times,* Aug. 11, 1958; Rogers W. Young, "Van Cortlandt Manor House, Harmon, New York," MS Report, National Park Service (1940) ; Eberlein and Hubbard, *Historic Houses;* Reynolds, *Dutch Houses.*

58. Voorlezer's House, N.Y.: *The Story of the Voorlezer's House,* pamphlet, Staten Island Historical Society (n.p., 1956) ; Loring McMillen, "The Voorlezer's House," *The Staten Island Historian,* I (Jan. 1938) and ff. *passim.*

59. Big Hidatsa Village Site, N. Dak.: Edward M. Bruner, "Mandan," in Edward H. Spicer, ed., *Perspectives in American Indian Culture Change* (Chicago, 1961) ; Frank G. Roe, *The Indian and the Horse* (Norman, Okla., 1955) ; William D. Strong, "From History to Prehistory in the Northern Great Plains," *Smithsonian Miscellaneous Collections,* Vol. 100 (Washington, 1940) ; George F. Will and Thad C. Hecker, "The Upper Missouri River Valley Aboriginal Culture in North Dakota," *North Dakota Historical Quarterly,* XI, Nos. 1 and 2 (1944).

60. Menoken Indian Village Site, N. Dak.: G. Hubert Smith, "Explorations of the La Vérendryes, 1738–43, With Special Reference to Vérendrye National Monument," MS Report, National Park Service (1951) ; Russell Reid, "Report on Vérendrye's Journey to North Dakota in 1738, With

Special Reference to the Location of the Indians and Village Sites He Visited," MS Report, National Park Service (1942); Will and Hecker, "The Upper Missouri River Valley Aboriginal Culture in North Dakota"; Strong, "From History to Prehistory in the Northern Great Plains."

61. Forks of the Ohio, Pa.: John P. Cowan, "Fort Pitt, Pittsburgh, Pennsylvania," MS Report, National Park Service (1937); Letter, John J. Grove, Coordinator, Point State Park, Pittsburgh, Pa., to Northeast Regional Office, National Park Service, Dec. 28, 1961; Alfred P. James and Charles M. Stotz, *Drums in the Forest* (Pittsburgh, 1958); "Part One of the Report of the Point Park Commission," mimeo. (Pittsburgh, 1943); *Report on Forests and Waters—Land and People,* pamphlet, Pennsylvania Department of Forests and Waters (n.p., 1958).

62. The Printzhof, Pa.: Letter, Donald H. Kent, Chief, Research and Publications Division, Pennsylvania Historical and Museum Commission, to Northeast Regional Office, National Park Service, Apr. 6, 1961; Sylvester K. Stevens and Donald H. Kent, *Conserving Pennsylvania's Historical Heritage,* pamphlet, Pennsylvania Historical and Museum Commission (Harrisburg, 1947); Johnson, *Swedish Settlements.*

63. Wanton-Lyman-Hazard House, R.I.: Maud L. Stevens and Jonas Bergner, "Two Papers on the Wanton-Lyman-Hazard House," Newport Historical Society *Bulletin,* LIX (Oct. 1926); Antoinette F. Downing, *Early Homes of Rhode Island* (Richmond, 1937); Historic American Buildings Survey, National Park Service, 6 photos (1936); Morrison, *Early American Architecture.*

64. Adam Thoroughgood House, Va.: Morrison, *Early American Architecture;* Kimball, *Domestic Architecture;* Henry C. Foreman, *The Architecture of the Old South—The Medieval Style, 1585–1850* (Cambridge, 1948).

65. Bacon's Castle, Va.: Robert H. Land, "Bacon's Castle, Surry County, Virginia," MS Report, National Park Service (1937); Kimball, *Domestic Architecture;* Morrison, *Early American Architecture;* Thomas J. Wertenbaker, *Bacon's Rebellion, 1676,* Jamestown 350th Anniversary Booklet No. 8 (Williamsburg, 1957).

66. St. Luke's Church, Va.: James G. Van Derpool, "The Restoration of Old St. Luke's," *The Commonwealth,* Sept. 1955; *Historic St. Luke's Restoration,* pamphlet, Historic St. Luke's Restoration, Inc. (n.p., n.d.): Raleigh C. Taylor, "Historic Sites Survey Report on St. Luke's Church, Isle of Wight County, Virginia," MS Report, National Park Service (1937); Henry I. Brock, *Colonial Churches in Virginia* (Richmond, 1930); Morrison, *Early American Architecture;* Historic American Buildings Survey, National Park Service, 10 sheets and 15 photos (1890–1940); George C. Mason, *Colonial Churches of Tidewater Virginia* (Richmond, 1945);

Henry C. Foreman, *Virginia Architecture in the Seventeenth Century* (Williamsburg, 1957).

67. La Fortaleza, P.R.: Ricardo T. Reyes, "The Harbor Defenses of San Juan in the Sixteenth Century," MS Report, National Park Service (1955); Adolfo de Hostos, *Ciudad Murada* (San Juan, 1948); E. A. Hoyt, *A History of the Harbor Defenses of San Juan* (San Juan, 1944); Inigo Abbad y Lasierra, *Historia Geográfica, Civil y Natural de la Isla de San Juan* ([San Juan or Madrid?], 1782); A. P. Newton, *The European Nations in the West Indies, 1493–1688* (London, 1943).

68. Columbus Landing Site, V.I.: David J. Jones and Clarence L. Johnson, "Report on Historic Sites of St. Croix, Virgin Islands, of the United States—Part Two: Salt River Bay Area," MS Report, National Park Service (1951); Samuel E. Morison, *Admiral of the Ocean Sea* (Boston, 1942); Samuel E. Morison, *The Second Voyage of Christopher Columbus from Cadiz to Hispaniola* (London, 1939); José Gonzales Ginorio, *El Descubrimiento de Puerto Rico* (San Juan, 1936); Theodoor de Booy, *Archeology of the Virgin Islands—Indian Notes and Monographs*, Vol. I, No. 1 (New York, 1919).

69. Vieux Carré, La.: Arthur, *Old New Orleans;* E. Wilson Lyon, *Louisiana in French Diplomacy, 1759–1804* (Norman, 1934); Morrison, *Early American Architecture;* Robertson, ed., *Louisiana;* Christopher Tunnard and Henry H. Reed, *American Skyline—The Growth and Form of Our Cities and Towns* (New York, 1956); Whitaker, *The Mississippi Question;* Samuel Wilson, Jr., *A Guide to Architecture of New Orleans* (New York, 1959).

70. Colonial Annapolis, Md.: Matthew P. Andrews, *The Founding of Maryland* (Baltimore, 1933); Historic Annapolis, Inc., *Three Ancient Blocks of Annapolis, Maryland's Capital City* (Annapolis, 1963); Henry P. Hopkins, pamphlet, "Colonial Houses of Annapolis, Maryland, and Their Architectural Details" (Baltimore, 1963); Newton D. Mereness, *Maryland as a Proprietary Province* (New York, 1901); Morrison, *Early American Architecture;* Lyman P. Powell, *Historic Towns of the Southern States* (New York, 1900); Thomas J. Wertenbaker, *The Old South* (New York, 1942); Paul Wilstach, *Tidewater Maryland* (Indianapolis, 1931).

71. Huguenot Street, N.Y.: Eberlein and Hubbard, *Historic Houses of the Hudson Valley;* Morrison, *Early American Architecture;* Historic American Buildings Survey, National Park Service, various sheets and photos.

72. Hurley, N.Y.: Eberlein and Hubbard, *Historic Houses; The Hurley Historian,* periodical of the Hurley-Hudson-Champlain Festival Committee, I (1959) and ff. *passim;* Reynolds, *Dutch Houses;* Augustus H. Van Buren, *A History of Ulster County Under the Dominion of the Dutch* (Kingston, 1923).

CRITERIA FOR SELECTION
OF HISTORIC SITES
OF EXCEPTIONAL VALUE

1. Structures or sites at which events occurred that have made a significant contribution to, and are identified prominently with, or which outstandingly represent, the broad cultural, political, economic, military, or social history of the Nation, and from which an understanding and appreciation of the larger patterns of our American heritage may be gained.

2. Structures or sites associated importantly with the lives of persons nationally significant in the history of the United States.

3. Structures or sites associated significantly with an important event that outstandingly represents some great idea or ideal of the American people.

4. Structures that embody the distinguishing characteristics of an architectural type specimen, exceptionally valuable for a study of a period style or method of construction; or a notable structure representing the work of a master builder, designer, or architect.

5. Objects that figured prominently in nationally significant events; or that were prominently associated with nationally significant persons; or that outstandingly represent some great idea or ideal of the American people; or that embody distinguishing characteristics of a type specimen, exceptionally valuable for study of a period style or method of construction; or that are notable as representations of the work of master workers or designers.

6. Archeological sites that have produced information of major scientific importance by revealing new cultures, or by shedding light upon periods of occupation over large areas of the United States. Such sites are those which have produced, or which may reasonably be expected to produce, data affecting theories, concepts, and ideas to a major degree.

7. When preserved or restored as integral parts of the environment, historic buildings not sufficiently significant individually by reason of historical as-

sociation or architectural merit to warrant recognition may collectively compose a "historic district" that is of historical significance to the Nation in commemorating or illustrating a way of life in its developing culture.

8. To possess national significance, a historic or prehistoric structure, district, site, or object must possess integrity:

For a historic or prehistoric structure, integrity is a composite quality derived from original workmanship, original location, and intangible elements of feeling and association. (A structure no longer on the original site may possess national significance if the person or event associated with it was of transcendent importance in the Nation's history and the association consequential.)

For a historic district, integrity is a composite quality derived from original workmanship, original location, and intangible elements of feeling and association.

For a historic or prehistoric site, integrity requires original location and intangible elements of feeling and association. (The site of a structure no longer standing may possess national significance if the person or event associated with the structure was of transcendent historical importance in the Nation's history and the association consequential.)

For a historic object, integrity requires basic original workmanship.

9. Structures or sites which are primarily of significance in the field of religion or to religious bodies but are not of national importance in other fields of the history of the United States, such as political, military, or architectural history, will not be eligible for consideration.

10. Birthplaces, graves, burials, and cemeteries, as a general rule, are not eligible for consideration and recognition except in cases of historical figures of transcendent importance. Historic sites associated with the actual careers and contributions of outstanding historical personages usually are more important than their birthplaces and burial places.

11. Structures, sites, and objects achieving historical importance within the past 50 years will not as a general rule be considered unless associated with persons or events of transcendent significance.

12. Structures, sites, and objects proposed for addition to the National Park System must also meet standards of suitability and feasibility.

ACKNOWLEDGMENTS

Advisory Board on National Parks, Historic Sites, Buildings, and Monuments (1959–61)

Stanley A. Cain, University of Michigan
Edward B. Danson, Jr., Museum of Northern Arizona
Harold P. Fabian, Utah State Park and Recreation Commission
E. Raymond Hall, University of Kansas
Walter L. Huber, San Francisco, Calif.
John A. Krout, Columbia University
Frank E. Masland, Jr., Carlisle, Pa.
John B. Oakes, New York City
Sigurd F. Olson, Ely, Minn.
Earl H. Reed, American Institute of Architects
Fred Smith, Newark, N.J.
Robert G. Sproul, Berkeley, Calif.
Robert L. Stearns, Denver, Colo.
Harold S. Wagner, Akron, Ohio
Carl I. Wheat, Menlo Park, Calif.

Consulting Committee for the National Survey of Historic Sites and Buildings (1958–61)

J. O. Brew, Peabody Museum of Archaeology and Ethnology
Eric Gugler, American Scenic and Historical Preservation Society
Richard Howland, Smithsonian Institution
Frederick Johnson, Robert S. Peabody Foundation for Archaeology, Phillips
    Academy
Waldo G. Leland, American Council of Learned Societies
Earl H. Reed, American Institute of Architects
S. K. Stevens, Pennsylvania Historical and Museum Commission
Louis B. Wright, Folger Shakespeare Library

[423

National Park Service

Frederick R. Bell, Picture Librarian, Office of Information

Mrs. Eleanor S. Calhoun, Publications Branch, Division of Interpretation and Visitor Services

Vincent L. Gleason, Chief of Publications, Division of Interpretation and Visitor Services

Herbert E. Kahler, Chief (retired), Division of History and Archeology

Robert E. MacKay, Student Research Assistant

Charles W. Porter III, Chief Historian (retired), Division of History Studies

Rogers W. Young, Staff Historian, Division of History Studies

Other Individuals

E. O. Baum, President, Pasquotank County Historical Society, Elizabeth City, N.C.

Mrs. H. Beal, Photographic Library, Museum of the City of New York

Mrs. Gordon C. Berryman, Directress, Thomas Rolfe Branch, Association for the Preservation of Virginia Antiquities, Surry.

Mrs. Margaret C. Blaker, Office of Anthropology, Smithsonian Institution, Washington, D.C.

Mrs. Peter Bolhouse, Executive Secretary, Newport Historical Society, Newport, R.I.

Frederick A. Bonsal, formerly Resident Director, Saugus Iron Works Restoration, Saugus, Mass.

Dr. Mark F. Boyd, Tallahassee, Fla.

Dr. Peter A. Brannon, Director, Department of Archives and History, Montgomery, Ala.

Orin M. Bullock, Jr., Supervisor of Architectural Research, Colonial Williamsburg, Williamsburg, Va.

Miss Charlotte Capers, Director, Department of Archives and History, Jackson, Miss.

Waldo S. Carrell, Pensacola Chamber of Commerce, Pensacola, Fla.

Dr. H. Bailey Carroll, Editor, *Southwestern Historical Quarterly*, University of Texas, Austin.

Robert D. Christie, Director, Historical Society of Western Pennsylvania, Pittsburgh.

Walter A. Coldwell, Assistant Director, Florida Park Service, Tallahassee.

Dr. Ernest A. Connally, Associate Professor of Architecture, University of Illinois, Urbana, Ill.

Dr. Albert B. Corey, State Historian, Division of Archives and History, New York State Education Department, Albany.

Dr. Walter L. Creese, President, Society of Architectural Historians, Urbana, Ill.

Abbott L. Cummings, Society for the Preservation of New England Antiquities, Boston, Mass.

Miss Anna K. Cunningham, Supervisor of Historic Sites, University of the State of New York, State Educational Department, Albany.

Dr. Donald C. Cutter, Department of History, University of Southern California, Los Angeles.

Miss Elizabeth Dawson, Curator, Adam Thoroughgood House Foundation, Norfolk, Va.

Leon de Valinger, Jr., State Archivist, Hall of Records, Dover, Del.

Charles L. Dufour, New Orleans, La.

Harold J. Dyer, Director of State Parks, State Park Commission, Augusta, Maine.

Jack Dyson, Historian, California Division of Beaches and Parks, Sacramento.

Thomas S. Eader, Assistant Librarian, Maryland Historical Society, Baltimore.

Claude Evanhamm, Director, Museum of Man, San Diego, Calif.

Mason Foley, Town Historian, Hingham, Mass.

Mrs. F. E. Freeman, Custodian, Fairbanks House, Dedham, Mass.

Peter Geldof, Jr., Superintendent of State Parks, Wilmington, Del.

Dr. Benjamin Gilbert, Department of History, San Jose State College, San Jose, Calif.

Mrs. Alice B. Good, Director of Library and Archives, State of Arizona, Phoenix.

E. W. Gravolet, Pointe-ala-Hache, La.

Miss Pearl V. Guyton, Natchez, Miss.

Mrs. Ethel W. Harris, Custodian, San José Mission National Historic Site, San Antonio, Tex.

J. Carver Harris, Business Manager, St. Augustine Historical Society, St. Augustine, Fla.

Dr. Emil W. Haury, Arizona State Museum, Tucson.

Miss Gertrude Hill and the staff of the Library of the Museum of New Mexico, Santa Fe.

David S. Hugg, Information Office, Delaware State Development Department, Dover.

Wesley A. Johnson, Courtaulds (Alabama), Inc., Mobile.

Rupert S. Jones, Plant Manager, Courtaulds (Alabama), Inc., Mobile.

Douglas F. Jordan, Wakefield, Mass.

Miss Elizabeth Jordan, Fort Boykin-on-the-James, Smithfield, Va.

Miss Ella Jordan, Fort Boykin-on-the-James, Smithfield, Va.

Donald H. Kent, Chief, Research and Publications Division, Pennsylvania Historical and Museum Commission, Harrisburg.

ACKNOWLEDGMENTS

Richard G. Kimball, Minister, New North Church, Hingham, Mass.

Dr. Lawrence Kinnaird, Department of History, University of California, Berkeley.

Mrs. Walter Kyers, Whitman House–Farmington Museum, Farmington, Conn.

Mrs. Sidney J. Legendre, Medway Plantation, Mount Holly, S.C.

Miss Bessie Lewis, Pine Harbor, Ga.

Maj. Gen. R. B. Luckey, Commandant, U.S. Marine Corps Recruit Depot, Parris Island, S.C.

Thomas W. Martin, Chairman of the Board, Alabama Power Co., Birmingham.

Dr. George May, Historic Sites Specialist, Michigan Historical Commission, Lansing.

Dennis McCarthy, Director, Arizona State Parks Board, Phoenix.

James Messer, Sr., Tallahassee, Fla.

Mrs. Florence Miller, Office Manager, U.S. Capitol Historical Society, Washington, D.C.

John B. Morrill, Forest Preserve District of Cook County, River Forest, Ill.

Dr. A. Russell Mortensen, Director, Utah State Historical Society, Salt Lake City.

Dr. Aubrey Neasham, Historian, California Division of Beaches and Parks, Sacramento.

Vrest Orton, Chairman, Vermont Historic Sites, Weston.

C. H. Overman, Jr., Pensacola, Fla.

Glenn Price, Historian, California Division of Beaches and Parks, Sacramento.

Anthony Ragusin, Biloxi Chamber of Commerce, Biloxi, Miss.

Dr. Frank D. Reeve, Editor, *New Mexico Historical Review,* Albuquerque.

Mrs. Mary F. Rhymer, Curator of Prints and Photographs, Chicago Historical Society.

Dr. Rupert N. Richardson, Department of History, Hardin-Simmons University, Abilene, Tex.

Richard S. Rodney, President, New Castle Historical Society, New Castle, Del.

C. H. Schaeffer, former Director of the Florida Park Service, Tallahassee.

Henry I. Shaw, Jr., Editor-in-Chief, Company of Military Historians, Washington, D.C.

Albert Simons, F.A.I.A., Charleston, S.C.

O. K. Sistrunk, Biloxi, Miss.

Capt. Pete Skrmetta, Biloxi, Miss.

Miss Eleanor Sloan, Secretary, Arizona Pioneers Historical Society, Tucson.

Dr. S. K. Stevens, Executive Director, Pennsylvania Historical and Museum Commission, Harrisburg.

W. S. Tarlton, Historic Sites Superintendent, State Department of Archives and History, Raleigh, N.C.

John O. Theobald, Phoenix, Ariz.

William Thomas, President, Fort Toulouse Memorial Park Association, Wetumpka, Ala.

William G. Tyrrell, Historian, Division of Archives and History, New York State Education Department, Albany.

Stephen S. Waligurski, Town Historian, Hurley, N.Y.

Dr. Clyde Walton, State Historian, Illinois State Historical Library, Springfield.

Dr. Joseph Waring, Old Town Plantation, Charleston, S.C.

Mr. and Mrs. Walter P. Warren, Bacon's Castle, Smithfield, Va.

Dr. W. W. Wasley, Arizona State Museum, Tucson.

Dr. Eugene P. Watson, Librarian, Northwestern State College, Natchitoches, La.

Justin Weddell, Pensacola, Fla.

W. W. Wells, Assistant Director, State Parks and Recreation Commission, Baton Rouge, La.

Samuel Wilson, Jr., New Orleans, La.

Ted R. Worley, Executive Secretary, Arkansas History Commission, Little Rock.

Index

New York waterfront scene, in 1679. The Dutch *Stadt Huys* (73 Pearl Street) is the dominant building. During the years 1653–1703, it served as New York City Hall. From a mid-19th-century lithograph by G. Hayward. Courtesy, New-York Historical Society.

New York waterfront scene, in 1679. The Dutch *Stadt Huys* (73 Pearl Street) is the dominant building. During the years 1653–1703, it served as New York City Hall. From a mid-19th-century lithograph by G. Hayward. Courtesy, New-York Historical Society.